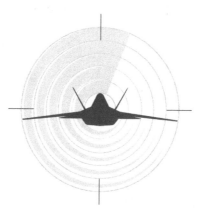

The Prayer War

How to intercede for your missionary on the front line

BIBLICAL MINISTRIES WORLDWIDE

ISBN-10: 1548456136
ISBN-13: 978-1548456139

DEDICATION

At a time when it made more sense to glide to the end of a pastorate and retire, Dick Hester left the comfort and security of a local church ministry to serve a worldwide congregation. As Pastor to Missionaries, Dick and Carol raised their support as missionaries and traveled the planet to serve missionaries. Dick is our "Encourager in Chief." As the consummate pastor, he walks into our lives and leaves us with eyes that can see the sunshine. We know he cares and that is often the catalyst for taking the next step in the challenges of our lives and ministries.

This book is dedicated to this shepherd to shepherds who modeled, motivated and advanced our prayer lives.

ACKNOWLEDGMENTS

These are incredibly challenging days in the world of missions. Political and economic systems are constantly changing. North America is cycling out of a period in Church history in which America was known as "THE" missionary sending country of the world. However, there is still incredible potential for missions from North America, but it must be leveraged by prayer.

During a major vision-casting initiative, BMW's leadership team was overwhelmed with the opportunities and obstacles that faced us. This caused us to go back to the Word to determine what we should do. The obvious answer that emerged was . . . prayer. We should have known that. We readily acknowledge that this is God's work and that there is nothing that we can do to accomplish eternal value by ourselves.

The content of this book is the result of searching the Scriptures to see how people prayed for missionaries in the Bible. David Brown has done a masterful job of compiling these concepts into this book. We are deeply indebted to him for his work. David has put on paper what many of us had in our minds.

David has experience as a school teacher and an attorney. God then moved him and his family to South Africa as church planters. He has also served as an administrator overseeing ministry in Europe and as a professor at a Bible college. He brings all of this ministry background to his computer keyboard in writing this book on prayer. It is our desire that his work will result in radically enhanced prayer for missionaries. Drink deeply at the well of his experience and the principles of Scripture.

Paul Seger
General Director

CONTENTS

WAR PARALLELS: MILITARY & MISSIONS

PRAYER WAR OVER THE SEVEN C'S

MOUNTING A PRAYER CAMPAIGN

WAR PARALLELS:
MILITARY & MISSIONS

Chapter 1

The Grand Spiritual Battle

Comprehending the Air War and the Ground War

*"The key of all missionary success is prayer.
That key is in the hands of the home churches.
The trophies won by our Lord in heathen lands will
be won by praying missionaries, not by
'professional workers in foreign lands.'
More especially, this success will be won by saintly
praying in the churches at home. The home church
on her knees, fasting and praying, is the great base
of spiritual supplies, the sinews of war, and the
pledge of victory in this dire and final conflict."
(E.M. Bounds, The Essentials of Prayer)*

THE EDGE OF LIGHT

Missionaries tend to think globally. Due to travel
and the distance from their relatives, they are very
aware of time zones and the rotation of the earth
from night to day. It is amazing to watch satellite

imagery of the earth rotating and to see the edge of day overtaking the darkness. There are areas on the earth right now that are bathed in warm sunshine but will be engulfed in the dark of night in just a few hours (Genesis 1:4-5).

The Scriptures are very clear that, in the spiritual realm, there is light and darkness (John 3:19-21, Ephesians 5:8, 1 Thessalonians 5:5, 1 Peter 2:9). Spiritual light is seeing, understanding, and receiving God's truth, while spiritual darkness is never seeing God's truth, or worse, rejecting, distorting, or counterfeiting it. As each person has a measure of light and darkness within himself, various regions of the earth also have a light/darkness ratio. Some areas that had been in the light, like Europe, are darker than most Christians suppose. Other areas known for darkness, like China, have a surprising amount of light.

MISSIONARIES ARE ON THE FRONT LINES

Satan, the prince of this world's system, has systematized, organized, and militarized spiritual darkness and keeps humanity confused, deceived, and captive to his disobedient regime (2 Corinthians 4:4, Ephesians 2:2, Colossians 1:12-13). Therefore, light-bearers do not simply walk about unopposed. Like it or not, we are in a war. The name "Satan" actually means the adversary, or one who resists. The Apostle Peter referred to him as "your adversary" (1 Peter 5:8).

Missionaries are light-bearers on the leading edge of the light as it moves into dark places. They are the front lines of the Church, the Body of Christ, as it expands around the world. They purposefully target and move into areas of darkness, and attempt to bolster the light where it may be fading. For this reason, they bear the brunt of attacks from the prince of this world's system of darkness who sees them as subversive intruders who are inciting his people to become traitors and defectors.

Christians often view sharing their faith as a warm-glow, upbeat, win-win situation. But sharing the gospel with a nonbeliever is to incite him to rebel against his prince, to challenge Satan's dictatorship, to resist his mind-grip, to scrap his ideas, to become a defector and a traitor, and worst of all, having been set free and trained, to walk back among Satan's soldiers seeking more defectors. When you start sharing the gospel, you'd better ask God to watch your back. We are in a war.

PARALLELS IN STRATEGY

Mankind is all too familiar with war. In the past 3400 years, only 268 years have been without war. Recent American wars in the Middle East have again reminded us that such conflicts are complicated, expensive, and often unrelenting.

In the old days, wars were open and obvious: one nation declared war on another for some perceived injustice and their armies faced each other on a battlefield. In modern times, with the War on Terror, the enemy is an ideology that lurks in many different countries, including one's own, and battles can spring up almost anywhere without notice.

While skirmishes can happen suddenly, wars must be planned out (Luke 14:31-32). There must be strategy and structure to an advancing army and a firm notion of what the eventual outcomes should be when the objectives are completed. At the risk of over-simplifying military missions, there are parallels between a military combat operation and a missionary operation.

MILITARY PLAN	MISSIONS PLAN
1. "Softening up" the enemy through bombing/missile strikes	1. "Softening up" the enemy through prayer
2. Ground troops advancing and penetrating defenses	2. Missionaries getting through the visa process and cultural barriers
3. Ground troops, with air support, engaging forces as necessary	3. Missionaries sharing the gospel with those suffering in the enemy's kingdom
4. Defeating the enemy's regime	4. Defeating the enemy's regime
5. Freeing oppressed people, providing them with food, water, and medical care	5. Freeing the oppressed people, and even soldiers, providing them with spiritual food, water, and medical care
6. Training nationals to lead their country differently	6. Training nationals to lead their country as part of a new kingdom
7. Minimizing casualties throughout the operation	7. Minimizing casualties throughout the operation

PARALLELS IN PERSONNEL

To implement a military combat operation, and again using very basic terms and divisions, there are three levels to an army: combat troops, combat support troops, and combat service support forces. Each level has different functions, and all levels must work together for the operation to be successful. These also have parallels in the personnel needed to carry out the mission of the Church.

Combat troops are infantry and combat vehicles on the front lines engaged directly in the conflict. Combat support troops are farther back from the lines and out of immediate conflict. They provide fire support using combat aircraft and long-range weaponry, and operational support such as engineering, communications, and intelligence. Combat service support forces, remotely located, provide logistical support, such as food and fuel supply, maintenance, administration, and health services, that is required by combat troops to carry out their mission.

As missionaries look at these three levels, we can see fairly clear parallels in our missions. Missionaries, cross-cultural gospel workers, are the combat troops on the front lines. Believers back home who can quickly pray and respond to requests from the field are the equivalent of combat support troops. And the sending churches and mission agencies (organizations that train, send out, support the troops, and oversee mission work on a broad scale) are combat service support forces.

MILITARY PERSONNEL	MISSIONS PERSONNEL
Combat Troops	Missionaries
Combat Support Troops	Christian Individuals, Families, and Businesses
Combat Service Support Forces	Churches and Mission Agencies

In your church, do you have an organized network of "combat support troops" that are linked with each missionary via email or social media? It seems that in the current structure of missions this middle realm of quick and ready firepower is missing.

THE AIR WAR IS THE PRAYER WAR

Missionaries are involved in the ground war. They are invading enemy territory: places that have been Satan's strongholds for centuries, communities that are known for socially legitimized occult practices, villages that overtly or covertly persecute those who follow Jesus, and nations where the evil one's advocates are government officials who reject visa applications or expel missionaries.

Missionaries also battle on the inside with doubts, anxieties, fears, loneliness, frustration, envy, anger, stubbornness, and physical ailments due to illness, injuries, or physical challenges. (1 Corinthians 4:10-13, 2 Corinthians 4:7-11, 7:5).

To commence the ground war with infantry when there has been no preparatory air war is to invite disaster. In the spiritual realm, the air war is the prayer war. It is the offensive that thousands of remote believers scattered all over the earth make on their knees asking a globally present and powerful God to protect, encourage, enable, and bless the efforts of heaven's ground forces mobilizing in lands still captive in darkness. Obviously, the more precise the coordinates, the better combat support will function. Specific prayer is much preferred over general requests for blessings.

PRAYER WARS OF THE PAST

Calls rise from centuries past – from David Brainerd and William Carey, from Hudson Taylor and Adoniram Judson – that prayer is both the bodyguard and the handmaid of missions. These, who advanced the Kingdom of God on their knees, would tell us that we must mobilize a new and fresh movement of prayer to sustain the works and workers of God.

Moravian Prayer for Missions
(1727-1827)

Count Ludwig von Zinzendorf and the band of refugees he protected, known as the Moravians, began to pray for God to begin a great mission movement. Some 24 men and 24 women decided that prayer should undergird their mission outreaches 24 hours a day, and so they began to pray around the clock . . . and maintained this schedule for 100 years! From their ranks, more than 3,000 people went into missions all over the world.

Haystack Prayer Meetings
(1806+)

A band of five students began to pray for missions near a haystack at Williams College in Massachusetts. They were impressed to send themselves. A mission board was formed and sent the youth to India. As word spread of their prayer and radical commitment, it sparked the modern American missionary movement.

Student Volunteer Movement
(1886+)

Luther Wishard organized the Mt. Hermon Mission Conference in 1886, at which one hundred students volunteered their lives for missionary service beginning a movement. Over the next generation, students on nearly every campus in the U.S. committed themselves to the "evangelization of the world in this generation." Over 20,000 individuals sailed to the foreign mission field, and over eighty thousand others personally committed themselves to prayer and to financially supporting those being sent out.

Indonesia Church-Planting Movements
(2017)

Missionaries are reporting that hundreds of thousands are coming to saving faith in Jesus Christ in Indonesia each year; Muslim leaders say the number is far greater. When we asked why this was happening in Indonesia, the response of the national leaders was, "We have learned desperate prayer." All of us stood convicted. None of us could describe our level of energy and conviction in prayer for the lost and for new churches to be started as "desperate."

BELIEVING PRAYER WORKS

A movement always begins with a few Christians saying, "It must begin with me. I must learn how to pray and be disciplined in it until inspiration carries me beyond mere responsibility." Such passionate prayer has been behind every great revival of God's people, and the spread of the gospel that naturally flows from such revivals.

Few of us would claim to be successful in prayer. Prayer meetings are the least attended meetings of most churches. Prayer is one of best things we can do, and so it is one of the hardest things to do. We are pleading with a God we cannot see, in front of no one who sees us, to achieve results that may be so long in coming that we never see them. That's not easy!

And yet, every prayerless day that goes by is a declaration of our independence against God, quietly intimating that we can do this business of living and speaking the gospel to a spiritually dead, deaf, blind, and skeptical world on our own, with our own passion, methods, and high tech resources. God is the only One who saves. Salvation of a lost person is a spiritual miracle, because without Him, they will never understand (Romans 3:10-12, 2 Corinthians 4:3-6).

At the very least, our prayerlessness indicates a quiet hope that the work of missions will be fueled by the prayers of those involved with it. Financial support requires little effort, and with today's banking no effort at all. Prayer for missionaries is different. It calls us day and night to commune with the Father and to pray His thoughts back to Him on behalf of those in different cultures and time zones. For what should we ask? We will look at that in the pages that follow.

POINTS TO PONDER

Has your church ever sent out missionaries from your own congregation? Might there be a connection between informed and desperate prayer for missions and actually going? What could be done to increase this possibility at your church?

Chapter 2

The Role of Combat Support
*The Many Ways Families Back Home
Can Make a Difference*

*"Prayer gives us the significance of front-line
forces, and gives God the glory of a limitless
Provider. The one who gives the power
gets the glory."
(John Piper, Let the Nations Be Glad)*

WHAT MISSIONARIES NEED FROM HOME

In chapter 1, we noted a couple of parallels
between the military and missions: the plan for
carrying out a combat mission and a church
planting mission can be similar, and the three-tiered
structure of the military has its parallel in the
Church. We said that missionaries are like combat
troops, and the Christians back home like combat
support troops.

When combat troops are in the field, what do they need from combat support forces?

- Frequent communication
- A strong air war to weaken resistance
- Targeted supply of equipment
- Reinforcement and assistance
- Debriefing at the end of a mission

What we are strongly suggesting in this book is that the greatest number of believers who can pray for, and meaningfully interact with, missionaries are in the combat support forces, yet in most cases are the least informed and mobilized to help. A missional church organization will change this.

Mission-minded church leaders will inform the church body that they have a vital role of their own to play in missions on a daily basis, inspire the church body to get involved in glorifying God in all the nations by doing battle in prayer, educate the church body about the unique warfare that missionaries face, and empower their people to begin providing these five basic needs.

FREQUENT COMMUNICATION

While he didn't have our modern forms of communication, the Apostle Paul was constantly sending and receiving envoys with news. Paul referred to them twice in his letter to the Philippians:

> *But I trust in the Lord Jesus to send Timothy to you shortly, that I also may be*

> *encouraged when I know your state . . . .*
> *Yet I considered it necessary to send to you*
> *Epaphroditus, my brother, fellow worker,*
> *and fellow soldier, but your messenger and*
> *the one who ministered to my need.*
> *(Philippians 2:19, 25)*

Communication is the fuel of healthy mission-focused churches. The frequency of interaction largely determines 1) the quality of the relationship between a missionary and his sending/supporting church and 2) the quality of that church's prayer ministry for the missionary. Through brief and frequent exchanges with individuals and families in the church, a congregation can discern real-time needs for prayer (where to aim field artillery), and greatly encourage the missionary.

We are in the information age, and except for those serving in remote settings, most missionaries can communicate fairly quickly with anyone having a computer, tablet, or smart phone. It's no longer desirable to run all communications through the mission office or the church office. "Prayer letters" seldom get to people in time to specifically pray for the items they mention; they are better for reporting on past events or general progress.

What are some effective forms of communication that church families can use to get fresh information from their missionaries? Here are a few ideas you might consider:

- When communicating with missionaries, remember that it is more encouraging to hear from people than institutions. Birthday cards from a Sunday school class are far exceeded by a brief call from someone in the class, and the cost is about the same.

- Have a small group adopt a missionary to communicate more frequently, pray more precisely, and serve as an advocacy group for the missionary.

- Start a Facebook group or a private chat group for a missionary or group of missionaries to communicate with a prayer group in your church on a frequent basis.

Be careful not to republish missionary news on the church website without a missionary's prior permission! Electronic communication may be intercepted and used against a missionary, particularly in limited or creative access nations. Even in "open countries," visa offices search the Internet to review an applicant's connections and communications.

A STRONG AIR WAR TO WEAKEN RESISTANCE

Those serving on the front lines in the New Testament era repeatedly asked for prayer support as they did their work (Luke 10:2, Romans 15:30, 2 Corinthians 1:11, Philippians 1:19, Colossians 4:3, 1 Thessalonians 5:25, 2 Thessalonians 3:1, Hebrews 13:18). The greatest tool believers have back at home is prayer. Prayer is their greatest weapon – the air war is the prayer war! Spurgeon said, "Prayer is the slender nerve that moves the muscle of Omnipotence." A. B. Simpson wrote,

"Prayer is the mighty engine that is to move the missionary work."

In chapters 3-9, we will look at seven specific ways to pray for your missionaries when you have no fresh prayer requests. Instead of an "air war over the seven seas," we call it "The Prayer War Over the Seven C's."

But in a nutshell, believers should call for the Lord's help in the following three areas:

1. <u>For the missionary specifically</u>
    Their spiritual vitality and Christlikeness, their language learning, their cultural adaptation, their encouragement, their marriage, their parenting, their finances, and their health.

2. <u>For the world in which the missionary lives</u>
    Their government's favor, their community's favor, prevention of Satanic opposition, the challenges of their living conditions, climate, diseases, local crime, and the economic and political stability of their country.

3. <u>For the fruitfulness of the missionary's work</u>
    Their creativity in engaging their community, their interpersonal skills with everyone they meet, their courage to build relationships on purpose, their ability to understand and communicate the whole gospel with clarity, their multiplication of disciples, leaders and churches, their unity with teammates, and their need for additional co-workers.

TARGETED SUPPLY OF EQUIPMENT

The famous "I can do all things through Christ who strengthens me" passage from Philippians 4 was in the context of Paul having a financial need and learning to live without it. But the Philippian believers sent him a gift at the perfect time, and he responded,

> *You shared in my distress . . . for you sent aid once and again for my necessities. Not that I seek the gift, but I seek the fruit that abounds to your account . . . . And my God shall supply all your need according to His riches in glory by Christ Jesus. (Philippians 4:14-19)*

Combat support forces can also assist infantry with specific needs. In this case, individual supporters or believers within a church are often quicker to respond than churches, which have slower procedures for allocating funds.

At times believers or small groups can help with computer and car needs, with a missionary kid's college fund or summer job needs, with transition expenses if the missionary family has to move again, with tablets for national pastors, or with thoughtful gifts for children. Some believers also ship equipment, books, teaching materials, and other supplies, which prove to be a huge help.

REINFORCEMENT AND ASSISTANCE

The Apostle Paul, who wasn't always strong, wrote that he got a huge boost from Titus's visit:

> *When we came to Macedonia, our bodies had no rest, but we were troubled on every side. Outside were conflicts, inside were fears. Nevertheless God, who comforts the downcast, comforted us by the coming of Titus, and not only by his coming, but also by the consolation with which he was comforted in you, when he told us of your earnest desire, your mourning, your zeal for me, so that I rejoiced even more. (2 Corinthians 7:5-7)*

After a missionary family has successfully navigated the rigors of culture shock and language learning, it is a huge blessing to have a pastor and his wife enter into their world, eat their kind of food, see where the kids attend school, and struggle with the exchange rate. The missionary will often chatter on and on with stories about their adjustment, about the crime, about the rules of the road, and about the healthcare system. They'll laugh together and cry together.

But field visits from non-pastors can be equally beneficial. In recent years, American churches have spent more than $2 billion annually to send short-term teams to the field. While the stewardship of such trips can be debated, the increased connection between the home church and its missionaries is very beneficial; in many cases, these visitors view the missionary they visited as extended family. They work hard to help them in any way they can, stay in regular contact, and become lifelong friends with them.

But be forewarned! Short-term trips can be truly life-changing, particularly for adults. God often uses meaningful exposure to a field to give a believer the burden and call to join the ranks on the front line. Combat support forces who visit the front lines are at times inspired to join the combat forces.

BMW is experiencing what many others have observed as a trend in recent years – most new missionaries (and new pastors) are in their upper thirties and have one or two marketplace careers in their background. Most have gone to the field on a short-term trip and had their souls stirred, pondering whether God might call them to leave their career to serve Him as a vocational missionary, or whether God might use their career skills as an overseas marketplace minister or tentmaker.

DEBRIEFING AT THE END OF A MISSION

Following biblical precedent, most missionaries return from their mission to gather with their home church and supporters, to report on what God has done, and to remain there for a while:

> *Now when they had come and gathered the church together, they reported all that God had done with them, and that He had opened the door of faith to the Gentiles. So they stayed there a long time with the disciples. (Acts 14:27-28)*

Missionaries need to be surrounded by believers who know them and understand the effect that foreign mission work, particularly third-world work, and most especially work in war-torn or disease-ravaged areas, can have on a couple or a family. A church family needs to understand terms like "reverse culture shock," "third culture kids," and "post-traumatic stress disorder" to properly interact with returning families.

Firstly, be understanding. To a missionary, the foreign place feels like home, and home feels like a foreign place. People say "welcome home," but a missionary family's home orientation has shifted to their new location, and they're struggling with reverse culture shock coming back to their sending culture. The kids may have forgotten English and the names of people they once cherished. The family is now oriented to neither their home nor host culture; they have created their own "third culture."

Secondly, be concerned. Missionaries need to be debriefed by leaders and people who care and who have been keeping up with what has been happening in their lives. That could be a church leader or the missions committee, but what if each missionary had a core team of families in the church focused on them? They would know what to ask: "What was the best and worst thing about your term? What couldn't you tell us in your updates that we need to know? How is your marriage holding up under the stress? How are your kids truly doing? What is your support situation? Do you have any project needs? What teamwork issues have you been facing? What are your hopes and plans for the next mission?" And the list goes on.

Thirdly, be protective. The rigors of stateside ministry are anything but a "furlough." Schooling requirements in many countries allow missionaries only a brief visit to the States. When they hit the ground, they are back on the road, staying in dozens of beds over thousands of miles, touching base with as many as they can. Churches need to do what they can to shield the family from burnout.

Some churches provide private housing for the missionaries rather than staying with church families, which might only increase stress if they have little ones running around an old folk's museum. Might your church help them with the use of a vehicle or a cell phone? Can you provide the family with a getaway in the midst of their travels?

These are just a few of the ways that individual believers and families can care for the missionary families their churches have sent and supported. Church leaders must inform, inspire, educate, and empower their people to do so. Next, we return to our focus on praying for those on the front lines.

THE PRAYER WAR
OVER THE SEVEN C'S

Chapter 3

#1 Praying for CARE

"The prayer giants in our lives are not ourselves, but the prayer supporters, family members and close friends who care for us and stand behind us. These people are our heroes, and our giants."
(Dan Stott, Evangelical Missions Quarterly, January 2005)

PRAYER REQUESTS FOR EVERY MISSIONARY

The prayer "God bless the missionaries" simply isn't good enough. While we all want to be blessed, missionaries are in a war and have urgent and specific needs that a believer can take to the Father that will make a huge difference in how the war progresses. In Piper's celebrated book, *Let the Nations Be Glad*, he wrote, "Until you know that life is war, you cannot know what prayer is for. Prayer is for the accomplishment of a wartime mission."

There are seven specific prayer requests for missionaries that flow from Scripture. The next seven chapters will take a look at these seven requests, each beginning with a "C". They cover some of the most critical things we want to see on any mission field. While we appreciate prayers for finances and our happiness, the real reason we are missionaries is exemplified in these seven requests: Care, Contacts, Courage, Clarity, Conversions, Christlikeness, and Co-workers. Prayer in these seven areas is engaging in what we call "The Prayer War Over the Seven C's."

REAL LIFE OUT THERE

The main highway was congested, and she was late. So she took the exit ramp ending up in the worst section of the city, a section where her car would fetch a good price and the color of her skin was a sign of oppression. At the traffic light, people noticed her and began pointing at her, shouting, and then banging the car. She lurched the car forward, running the red light but trying not to hit anyone. She glanced in the rear view mirror to see men chasing her with pipes, sticks, and machetes.

When she arrived home 20 minutes later, she was still shaking, and the phone rang. "Hi Cindy, how are you guys doing over there? We had a burden to pray and wondered if everything was alright?"

PRAYING FOR GOD'S CARE

Right now! Amy Carmichael, missionary in India from 1867-1951, once wrote, "If you are ever inclined to pray for a missionary, do it at once, wherever you are. Perhaps he may be in great peril at that moment."

Praying for God's care and protection of your missionaries is of critical importance, especially as the world continues to destabilize. The missionary, whom we refer to as the Apostle Paul, wrote,

> *Finally, brethren, pray for us . . . that we may be delivered from unreasonable and wicked men; for not all have faith. (2 Thessalonians 3:1-2)*

Can you remember the number of times Paul was imperiled because of 1) the message of the gospel or 2) his presence in unsafe areas for the sake of the gospel? If you need a reading list, check out Acts 9:19-25, 13:45-50, 14:5-6, 14:19, 16:19-24, 17:5-9, 17:13, 18:6-10, 18:12-17, 19:23-41, 20:3, 21:27-28:30, as well as 1 Corinthians 4:10-13, 4:5-11, 6:4-10, 11:22-33.

> *Indeed, we felt that we had received the sentence of death. But that was to make us rely not on ourselves but on God who raises the dead. He delivered us from such a deadly peril, and he will deliver us. On him we have set our hope that he will deliver us again. You also must help us by prayer, so that many will give thanks on our behalf for the blessing granted us through the prayers of many. (2 Corinthians 1:9-11 ESV)*

Paul asked others to pray for him and his team to be delivered from unreasonable and wicked men. Most of the time, he had difficulties with those who opposed the Christian faith. Some lost business profits due to conversions, and government leaders didn't like the riots he caused. Paul asked others to pray 1) that he would be safe, but if not, 2) that he would have grace to handle the trial and 3) that his suffering or death would bring profit to the gospel and the Kingdom of Christ.

PLAN A: PROTECTION, SAFETY, & SECURITY

These are dangerous days, even in places traditionally thought to be safe. BMW missionaries work in Johannesburg, South Africa, a city which at times has had more than 1000 car hijackings per month at gunpoint. Several have been held at gunpoint, including this writer's wife, but no one has been murdered thus far, by God's grace.

In several countries, missionaries or their wives are abducted, raped, killed, robbed, physically attacked, hijacked, unlawfully arrested, threatened, and sued each year; and the list goes on. Many missionaries live near war zones, in places of civil unrest, or in high crime areas. Some pay the ultimate price.

In an increasing number of cases since 2010, visas have been revoked and missionaries hustled out of the country – this is not just in the Middle East or the 10/40 Window, but in European countries! Religious leaders with government connections stall permits for church buildings. Atheistic government employees tie up the process for getting visas or identity documents. Police give missionaries a hard time through fines or detention, or accuse them of heinous crimes.

Remember that secular leaders and politicians are not the enemy. It is the evil one who hates Christ, rules the world system, and is carrying out his plan behind the scenes to destroy humanity. God's people need to mobilize air support, praying for God to:

- Soften and change the "hearts of kings" and government officials (Proverbs 21:1)
- Keep the missionary from reacting poorly to evildoers or doing things against his conscience (Hebrews 13:18)
- Allow the missionary to elude difficult or dangerous people (1 Thessalonians 3:1-2)
- Show the missionary that he/she is walking under divine protection (2 Corinthians 1:10)

PLAN B: GRACE & PROFIT FROM ADVERSITY

Contrary to what many Christians say, God's will is not the safest place to be. But it is the best place to be. Sometimes, a strong and quiet Christian testimony amid horrid persecution is what the Spirit uses to save thousands. Sometimes, a missionary's death inspires thousands to take his or her place. But sometimes a missionary dies alone and for no overtly apparent reason.

Dan Stott, in an article entitled "Missionary Giants or Just a Giant Need for Prayer?" wrote,

Missionaries don't escape trials, misfortune, or injustice. They may lose children, be stricken with cancer, and the list goes on. I am inclined to believe that missionaries are one of the enemy's favorite targets because front-line ministry puts us in the crosshairs of evil minions. (EMQ, January 2005)

We need to pray that if the situation goes adversely, the missionary will download the sustaining grace available to him or her and capitalize on the situation to spread the gospel to captors, criminals, officers, medical personnel, etc. Think of all that Paul accomplished while imprisoned for years; he said that his hard times had served to advance the gospel (Philippians 1:12, Acts 26:22-23), and the Church has long benefitted from his prison epistles.

POINTS TO PONDER

Based on what you've heard recently from missionaries you know of, what are specific ways in which you can pray for God's care? Name the missionary, the country/region, and the situation they have faced or are facing. Would you quickly lift them up to the Lord right now?

Chapter 4

#2 Praying for CONTACTS

*"God's goal to be glorified will not succeed without
the powerful proclamation of the gospel.
And that gospel will not be proclaimed in power to
all nations without the prevailing, earnest,
faith-filled prayers of God's people."
(Christopher Agenbag, "Is God's House a House of
Prayer for All Nations?")*

CHANGING CHURCH CULTURE

It is not easy for churches to develop a culture of
prayer. If we pray poorly, we often see no clear
answers and are further discouraged from praying.
But once a culture of regular, fervent, informed, and
specific prayer has germinated, the answers often
become clear, even to the point where it seems that
the Lord is showing off by answering so quickly and
so obviously (Acts 12:12-17).

Rather than seeing God's glory as a long-term eventual outcome that we are praying toward, we should encourage God's people to see each step of the process as bringing glory to our God. This is where staying in contact with the missionary becomes so important.

Prayer fuels the evangelistic process where success in each step brings glory to God! God is glorified when the missionary makes a new contact, glorified when he has courage to transition conversations to spiritual things, glorified when he shares the gospel, glorified when he leads someone to saving faith in Christ, and glorified when the new believer grows and begins to serve.

REAL LIFE OUT THERE

A Christian businessman, who was a prayer supporter, visited a mission field and just stood there in the church weeping. When asked why, he responded by pointing at the pastor and saying that he had begun praying for the pastor when a missionary had first met him as a nonbeliever. Then he prayed for him as a new believer, then as a working believer, then as a theology student, and then as a new pastor – and now there was the pastor, right in front of him, doing a fabulous job.

The prayer warrior was overcome with emotion and gave glory to God for all of the steps in this pastor's spiritual journey because he had been well informed throughout the process. And it all began with a missionary making a new "contact" – getting to know a nonbeliever and then praying for him.

PRAYING FOR CONTACTS

Praying for God to open doors and provide opportunities for your missionaries to build redemptive relationships and begin sharing the gospel are of critical importance. The missionary, whom we refer to as the Apostle Paul, wrote,

> *Praying at the same time for us as well, that God will open up to us a door for the word, so that we may speak forth the mystery of Christ. (Colossians 4:3 NASV)*

Paul wrote this in prison! What would you ask prayer for if you were in prison? To be released, to get better food, warmer clothes, and healing? But Paul's focus was on sharing the gospel of Christ, and he asked his supporters to pray specifically for open doors. God's grace in Paul's life enabled him to turn almost every situation into a platform for sharing God's truth.

In Acts 17, Paul was looking for open doors as he walked through the marketplace in Athens and saw that the city was given over to idols. But he probably wasn't expecting an invitation to the elite Areopagus to address the philosophers gathered there. At times, God opens doors that are "beyond us" to show His sufficiency.

ASKING GOD TO GIVE THEM OPEN DOORS

Finding open doors is the first job of a missionary. Paul mentioned it several times (1 Corinthians 16:9, 2 Corinthians 2:12). Missionaries arrive in a new place without knowing a single person. Somehow, they have to bridge into people's lives. You can live out the gospel in your community, but it is impossible to speak God's truth if you don't have a person or group that will listen. Most often, truth moves at the speed of relationships.

The first challenge we missionaries have in sharing Christ is making a "contact" – having a good chat with someone, learning the person's name, and making a plan to see him again. God can open those doors, but the missionary may have to knock and push on a lot of doors. If it is God who opens doors and makes divine appointments, then a remotely located believer can ask Him to do that for a missionary.

What if someone in a robe and a turban with a Koran under his arm knocked on your door in the U.S.? You would think them strange and scary, and probably not open your door to that individual immediately. Around the world, this is how many view the American Christian. There is a built-in resistance to a foreigner, especially if they know you are from another faith. God is the One who can overcome these fears, trigger curiosity, open hearts, and create opportunities.

WHERE MISSIONARIES MAKE CONTACTS

God's people can pray for their missionaries to make contacts, just like you can in your hometown, through several avenues:

- <u>Their Location</u>
  Missionaries must live near people. Developing relationships with neighbors is basic, but it can be a challenge in smaller villages. In Ireland missionaries found that it was easier to make contacts by walking through town with their children in the evenings because people were more open who would not have been so if there were no children.

- <u>Their Vocation</u>
  Missionaries may have part-time work in town. In many countries they make contacts by teaching English as a second language. In Honduras and Niger some missionaries run medical and dental clinics, in part, to make contacts.

- <u>Their Education</u>
  Some missionaries take classes in sign language or floral arrangement, or teach classes in baking or craft-making to make contacts. Their children in local schools often make an abundance of contacts.

- <u>Their Acquisitions (Shopping)</u>
  Missionaries go to shops several times a week and can have dozens of conversations with waiters, managers, owners, and other customers.

- <u>Their Avocation</u>
  In Argentina missionaries join archery clubs, in Scotland photography clubs, and in the Netherlands biking clubs to make contacts.

- <u>Their Recreation</u>
  In the Philippines missionaries meet people by playing basketball, in South Africa by playing cricket, in Austria while skiing, and in Palau by going fishing.

- <u>Their Situation</u>
  Like you, missionaries have health issues and car issues and suffer damage to their homes in a storm. These hardships will often enable a missionary to make fresh contacts with people they would not have met otherwise.

All of these areas of life can be used by God, who loves to create divine appointments. Pray for your missionaries in these specific areas of life, especially for those new to the field or those who have recently relocated to a new area; then get in touch with them to see how it's going.

But having listed these ways to make contacts, the truth is that a missionary whose heart is dull or fearful will let the opportunities pass. We will cover that in the next chapter.

POINTS TO PONDER

Based on what you've heard from missionaries recently, in what ways did they ask you to pray for contacts? Have you prayed for the Lord to open your eyes to contacts all around you? What relationships with nonbelievers do you have now that you could begin to move in a redemptive direction? What's stopping you?

Chapter 5

#3 Praying for COURAGE

"A mission-minded church today must be a praying church. We must pray for workers, for God's provision, for the effectiveness of the missionary, for unsaved contacts, and the national Christians and churches."
(C. Gordon Olson,
What in the World Is God Doing?)

PRAYING FOR WHAT GOD WANTS

It often seems that God's people don't pray because they don't believe that prayer works. After all, they have prayed for this and that, and they never seem to get what they asked for.

It is critical to understand that prayer is not to line up God's will with ours, but to line up our will with His. God often gives believers who walk closely with Him exactly what they want, but that is because He first fixes their "wanters." Their hearts are synchronized with His, and they are bold to call on God to manifest His power in specific and amazing ways because they know from Scripture how He is disposed to act. John Piper wrote,

> *Prayer is primarily a wartime 'walkie-talkie' for the mission of the church as it advances against the powers of darkness and unbelief. It is not surprising that prayer malfunctions when we make it a domestic intercom to call upstairs for more comforts in the den. God has given us prayer as a wartime walkie-talkie so that we can call headquarters for everything we need as the kingdom of Christ advances in the world. (Let the Nations Be Glad)*

There are a number of things that we need that God always wants to give us. He wants us to be filled with His Spirit and to display the moral virtues, one of which is courage. Mark Twain said that "courage is not the absence of fear, but the ability to master or overcome it." Winston Churchill reminds us that "courage is rightly esteemed the first of human qualities . . . because it is the quality which guarantees all others." C. S. Lewis agreed, adding that courage is "every virtue at its testing point."

REAL LIFE OUT THERE

A missionary's wife in southern France kept checking through the blinds to see if they were still being watched. Her husband was used by the Lord recently to lead three Muslim students to saving faith in Christ, and he was confronted by an imam and several others who threatened his life while wearing a smile. She was worried for her husband's safety. His cheerful shrugs about the matter might soon leave her a widow and their children fatherless.

PRAYING FOR COURAGE

If there was ever a person who seemed to be fearless, it was the Apostle Paul. Right? It seemed that he was never intimidated by mobs, by religious leaders, or even storms.

But, in fact, there were times when Paul's confidence was "rattled." When Paul came to Corinth, the opposition of the Jews caused him to shrink back in fear and discouragement. The red letter editions of our Bibles don't have much red in the book of Acts, but Paul needed such help that Jesus Himself appeared to him:

> Do not be afraid, but speak, and do not keep silent; for I am with you, and no one will attack you to hurt you; for I have many people in this city. (Acts 18:9-10, also 23:11)

To "encourage" literally means "to pour courage into." Praying for God to give grace for your missionaries to take courage is of critical importance. The missionary, whom we refer to as the Apostle Paul, wrote,

Praying always with all prayer and supplication in the Spirit . . . that utterance may be given to me, that I may open my mouth boldly to make known the mystery of the gospel . . . that in it I may speak boldly, as I ought to speak. (Ephesians 6:18-20)

Paul confessed that he wrote boldly but that his presence and ability to speak weren't all that remarkable (1 Corinthians 2:1-4, 2 Corinthians 10:10). He asked the Philippian believers to pray that he would be bold enough to live or die for Christ (Philippians 1:18-20).

ASKING GOD TO GIVE THEM BOLDNESS

Although it takes a good amount of courage to get to the field, missionaries are people just like you. They can be fearful. They feel apprehensive about moving into new situations. They can easily be intimidated by others. They can be rattled, especially after difficult incidents, and be afraid to venture out again. No one invites the emotional suffering called "fear;" we tend to flee from it. Therefore missionaries need God's people to pray that they will be courageous.

In Luke 10:2, Jesus said to pray for the Lord of the harvest to send out laborers into the harvest. Have you ever considered that the main thing preventing laborers from entering foreign work is fear? So many people tell visiting missionaries, "Oh, I could never do that!" So, perhaps the first missionaries to whom we should ask God to give courage are the future missionaries in our congregations.

It takes courage to leave your career, to raise finances and prayer support, to prune down and ship your earthly belongings to a foreign place, to leave the security of your homeland, to learn a new language and feel like a pre-school kid for years until you can speak it well, to live in high-risk areas due to crime or disease, to walk up to strangers and begin chatting, and to suffer ridicule, humiliation, or even open persecution.

THE MEANS OF GAINING COURAGE

In chapter 3, we encouraged you to pray for God's care and protection for missionaries. In this chapter, we are asking God's people to pray for the internal aspects of care: for God to protect their hearts and minds from destabilizing and dysfunctional fears.

1. <u>Pray for the filling of the Spirit</u>
Before Pentecost, the disciples were hiding behind locked doors; after the Spirit came, they boldly proclaimed the gospel in the streets. The common denominator for courage throughout the book of Acts was the filling of the Holy Spirit (Acts 4:13, 29-31, 20:24). The same is true today. Whereas the fleshly fear of man brings a snare, the Spirit gives a freedom, a holy boldness, and a reckless abandon to the will and work of God that overcomes fear. To an observer, the situation in front of the missionary is still the same, but it no longer matters because his/her heart is on fire from God and for God.

41

2. <u>Pray for affirmation</u>
Pray that God would move a co-worker or a national believer to affirm what the missionary is doing, to say thanks, or to somehow celebrate a job well done, like Barnabas did (Acts 4:36, 11:23).

3. <u>Pray for fruit</u>
Simply put, no fruit is discouraging. Fruit tells you that you're not a failure, that lives are changing, that you are where God wants you, and that your methods aren't flawed; you feel the courage to go on (1 Thessalonians 3:7-9). Paul prayed for the Colossian believers to "bear fruit in every good work" (Colossians 1:10).

4. <u>Pray for an inspiration</u>
Sometimes seeing another missionary being bold and daring gives you the courage to imitate them and do the same thing (1 Thessalonians 1:6-7). This is something the missionary's leaders try to do, but even a peer can inspire courage.

Once they have the courage, missionaries need to speak God's truth with clarity. That's up next.

POINTS TO PONDER

In what ways could you and your friends "pour courage" into missionaries you know of? Given their line of work, what fruit would encourage them? What motivates you or gives you courage to move a conversation toward the gospel?

Chapter 6

#4 Praying for CLARITY

"One great and imperative need of foreign mission work today is the almost forgotten secret of prevailing prayer. Missions have progressed so slowly abroad because piety and prayer have been so shallow at home."
(Andrew Murray, Key to the Missionary Problem)

NO FUEL AND THE SLEEPING ARMY

When we get to heaven, how will we feel if we learn that prayer was the fuel of revival and mission work? How energized and informed are your church's prayer meetings? And how about your missions program? Most churches report that the energy level of these two is roughly the same.

The lack of energy is due to a lack of meaning and urgency. Some pastors believe that persecution is needed to bring a revival. Why is that? Because if you want to kill the Christian faith, you don't attack it; you give it wealth and comforts and lull it to sleep. Persecution would wake up the Church, with believers calling out to God to manifest His power. But can we stir up the Church short of persecution? John Piper wrote,

> *The crying need of the hour is to put the churches on a wartime footing. Mission leaders are crying out, 'Where is the church's concept of militancy, of a mighty army willing to suffer, moving ahead with exultant determination to take the world by storm? Where is the risk-taking, the launching out on God alone?' The answer is that it has been swallowed up by a peacetime mentality. (Let the Nations Be Glad)*

REAL LIFE OUT THERE

An African pastor asked missionaries visiting his village, "How would you give our people the gospel? What would you say?" The missionary answered, "Well, I would try to create a picture. I would tell them about a great chasm that separates us from God, but that Jesus died for us, as though the cross spans the chasm and allows us to cross."

"No, that is very incorrect," answered the pastor. "Our people are concrete thinkers. You tell them that, and they will go out into the distant fields looking for the chasm and the cross-bridge. You must simply tell them the stories about Old Testament sacrifices and of Jesus' life and death and resurrection and return. Then ask them if they will believe."

PRAYING FOR CLARITY

A missionary who is new to a language or culture can really struggle to communicate scriptural truth and the gospel with clarity. Therefore, praying for God to enable your missionaries to really grasp the language and culture quickly and to communicate with clarity is of critical importance. The Apostle Paul wrote,

> *At the same time, pray also for us, that God may open to us a door for the word, to declare the mystery of Christ . . . that I may make it clear, which is how I ought to speak. (Colossians 4:3-4 ESV)*

To make the mystery of Christ clear is to make it plain, to unpack and unfold its components carefully and lay things open to full view. In the context, Paul was exhorting the Colossian believers to stay watchful and alert in prayer (war imagery) on his behalf.

He follows verse 4, as though giving himself and them a pep talk, by noting that believers should 1) walk in wisdom toward outsiders, 2) buy up every opportunity to speak with them, and 3) make their talks 90% helpful (grace) and 10% with God's truth (salt), which will sting a little, or a lot, depending on the culture and religion. This is a classic formula for missionaries beginning a church planting project!

LEARNING THE LANGUAGE

Paul was speaking in his own languages and was still concerned about making the mystery of Christ clear! You know how hard it is for believers in your church to explain the gospel in English in their own culture. Imagine trying to communicate God's truth in a language you are just learning!

Missionaries can share a host of humorous and horrific stories of their first years trying to evangelize, teach, and preach in a new language. For instance, after completing his language learning, one missionary related that he had given his first sermon in German about Paul and Silas being in jail. He thundered from the pulpit that great strawberries (erdbeeren) had destroyed the jail where Paul and Silas were held . . . instead of a great earthquake (erdbeben)!

SPEAKING TO THE HEART

Some missionaries have to learn two languages – a national language, like Indonesian, and a tribal language, like Saluan, spoken in one small region on the Indonesian island of Sulawesi. In those cases, the language learning process is even longer.

But patience is essential so that missionaries don't take shortcuts when it comes to language. They need to speak the gospel in the "heart language" of the people, the language in which they fall in love and argue. The beauty, richness, and power of the gospel must be given free course by missionaries going the "extra mile" in language learning.

LEARNING CULTURAL CUES

Add to basic language the theological and philosophical terms in the language, the idioms and cultural secondary meanings, and you have a very long learning curve, some say ten years or more, to understand a language well. Language is one thing, but clear cross-cultural communication is a huge step further and requires continual practice and refining.[1]

Some missionaries or short-term visitors use translators, but that only further complicates the communication process. Some churches in the Far East require the translator to be ordained as well as proficient in both languages so that, even if mistakes are made in translation, there will be no doctrinal error.

PRAYING FOR CREATIVITY AND ILLUMINATION

Question: Where do you start when presenting the gospel to someone? Answer: Wherever that person is. It depends upon the person's worldview, beliefs, values, awareness of gospel elements, and heart's readiness to receive truth.

Further, while the gospel never changes, it is multi-faceted and a missionary may choose to emphasize the relational elements over the judicial elements, or vice versa. When Paul spoke to the

---

[1] For further reading, see Duane Elmer, "Cross-Cultural Connections: Stepping Out and Fitting In Around the World," IVP, 2002, and David Hesselgrave, "Communicating Christ Cross-Culturally," 2nd Ed., Zondervan, 1991.

Jews, he began with the Hebrew Scriptures. When he spoke on Mars Hill, he began with their poets and ideas – same gospel, different starting points.

God's people must pray for missionaries to faithfully and creatively communicate God's Word on the one hand, and also pray for the Lord to open minds and hearts that would naturally never receive His truth. The illuminating work of the Spirit is critical; when the lights come on, the conversion of the soul is normally soon to follow.

POINTS TO PONDER

Have you ever met a missionary who came back to America struggling with English? Or their kids didn't speak English at all? Might communicating the gospel clearly in their host culture still be a problem for them? Do you know of any missionaries that will go to language school soon for whom you could ask God's help? Do you know of missionaries struggling with a "second language learning disability" for whom you could ask God's help?

Chapter 7

#5 Praying for CONVERSIONS

*"The key of all missionary success is prayer.
That key is in the hands of the home churches.
The trophies won by our Lord in heathen lands will
be won by praying missionaries,
not by professional workers in foreign lands."
(E.M. Bounds, The Essentials of Prayer)*

INCITING TRAITORS AND REBELS

If we understand that we are in a war, then a "conversion" is not merely a change in someone's thinking. It is a change of armies – giving rise to angelic praises in the Kingdom of Light and to the angry retaliation of the evil one. Jesus mentioned in His model prayer for His disciples that we should ask the Father to "deliver us from the evil one" (Matthew 6:13 NIV). Pray for conversions, but also pray for protection of the disciple-makers:

We must simply seek for ourselves and for our people a wartime mentality. Otherwise the Biblical teaching about the urgency of prayer, and the vigilance of prayer, and the watching in prayer, and the perseverance of prayer, and the danger of abandoning prayer will make no sense and find no resonance in our hearts. Until we feel the desperation of a bombing raid, or the thrill of a new strategic offensive for the gospel, we will not pray in the spirit of Jesus. (John Piper, Let the Nations Be Glad)

REAL LIFE OUT THERE

She was a teen rebel who came to church with her mom and sisters every Sunday. She came to youth group on Friday nights "dressed to kill" in a tight skirt, reflecting the code of the rave dance clubs she was going to attend right afterward. Her relationships with guys and girls were in shambles, her mouth was caustic and foul, and her regard of teachers and parents was small.

But she assumed that she was a Christian. That was until she learned one night that those in Christ are new creatures, that the old man had died, and the new was raised with Christ. She was shaken to the core, saw her lostness, and experienced true conversion. Her heart and mind changed. Her old friends fell away. She began serving and was equipped. Today she is a leader among godly women.

PRAYING FOR CONVERSIONS

The end of the Great Commission is the planting of new churches that are made up of those who have responded to the power of the gospel and become Christ followers. The mission of every disciple is to be one and to make many. Every disciple is instantly called to be a disciple-maker; to reproduce is the nature of all living things. Missionaries are both personal and professional disciple-makers.

We have argued from the Scriptures that believers should pray for Care, Contacts, Courage, and Clarity for their missionaries; those requests are to seek for God to connect His gospel with the lives of those who have never heard. But we can also pray for fruit, for souls to come to saving faith, for Conversions (Acts 3:19). The Apostle Paul wrote,

> *Finally, brethren, pray for us, that the word of the Lord may run swiftly and be glorified, just as it is with you. (2 Thessalonians 3:1)*

Paul asked them to pray that the gospel might "run swiftly," which is a metaphor used in the sports arena. We might say "to spread like wildfire" or "to fly like an eagle." Acts 17:1-4 shows us that many people, both lowly and prominent, in Thessalonica came to saving faith after three weeks of hearing the gospel. Their reputation for a dynamic faith spread around Greece (1 Thessalonians 1:7-10, 2 Thessalonians 1:4), and this became one of the most missionary-minded of the early churches.

ASKING FOR THE GOSPEL TO COVER THE LAND

Some mission fields are "sowing fields." Missionaries work for years to cultivate the soil of hard hearts and build relationships with people resistant to friendship with outsiders and Christians. Paul moved through cities where there was no mention of fruit (Acts 14:24-25). Sowing fields, in particular, need a prayer barrage of God's people seeking God's mercy to soften hearts, to destroy Satan's spiritual shields, and to light the gospel fires in those countries.

Other fields are "reaping fields." People listen with enthusiasm to what the missionaries have to say, some even seek them out to learn about this Jesus that they've heard about (Acts 13:42-44), and people seem to fall as ripe fruit from a tree. To "convert" is derived from a Greek word meaning to turn around or return. Peter called on the Jews to repent and be converted (Acts 3:19). On such reaping fields, God's people should pray for missionaries to get additional co-workers (cf. ch. 9).

Believers in churches can pray for a single soul to be saved, but they should also pray for the "word to run swiftly" and for the gospel to cover the land, praying for multiplication rather than mere addition of believers. They can pray for a new church to be planted, but they should also pray for church-planting movements to begin such as those that have ignited in Indonesia and China in recent years, where discipleships and teacher training simply cannot keep up with the conversion growth.

KEY PEOPLE, PLACES, AND CHURCHES

Although we should join the Lord in desiring that all people come to repentance, it is helpful when key people in key places come to Christ. If a crowd of twenty people is walking and one person says "woe" and turns around, then the crowd often follows that lead. The Scriptures mention that leading women (Acts 17:4, 12), officials of Asia (Acts 19:31), those of Caesar's household (Philippians 4:22), and other people of influence were converted to Christ.

Although there is no such thing as a "group salvation" and not many who are wise, famous, or impressive are called (1 Corinthians 1:26), God saves and energizes an "Apollos" every now and then and energizes believers like those who planted the Antioch church. Many everyday people examine the claims of Christ and believe in Him when they see an educated, sensible, trustworthy person jeopardize his or her position and popularity by converting to the Christian faith. This is a huge blessing to missionaries.

WARFARE PRAYING

Combat soldiers are not nearly as successful when there is no air support. In missions, the air war is the prayer war. Four elderly women gathered for prayer are heaven's equivalent of four F-16s cruising over a spiritual battlefield. They may not hear hell's air raid sirens blaring, but they are certainly engaged in the targeting of God's power and help all over the world.

In sports, this is similar to what we call "an assist" – maybe you didn't shoot the winning shot, but you enabled the person who did. You can ask God to remove Satan's blinders from nonbelieving contacts that a specific missionary has been meeting with, to open up conversations, and to open up their hearts to the gospel.

This war is not fought on our feet, in a gunner's seat, or a pilot's seat; both combat troops and combat support troops fight on their knees because it is God alone who makes the difference. Prayer gives believers far away the same significance as frontline troops.

POINTS TO PONDER

Have you ever prayed that a missionary would see fruit and that people would respond to the gospel under their ministry?

Maybe our air strikes could be more specific. Have you ever called for an "air strike," asking for the salvation of individuals by name? Have you launched a laser-guided missile by specifically asking God to dispel Satan's blinding work and bring conviction and understanding to a lost person's mind and heart?

Chapter 8
#6 Praying for CHRISTLIKENESS

"The person venturing onto the international stage for the purpose of serving as a missionary quickly comes face to face with their weak humanity. They face a new culture and a new and difficult language. Stress levels can become extremely elevated."
(William D. Bowyer, "The Effects of Teaching an International-Focused Prayer Manual," D. Min. Thesis, 2006)

FOLLOWING THE GREATEST COMMANDER

In the military, the drill instructors and commanders who have seen active combat duty are always held in high regard. They are not speaking from an ivory tower or repeating information out of a textbook; they can tell you how it really is.

Missionaries are combat troops in Jesus' kingdom, and they find great consolation in knowing that 1) He has been here and knows what it's like, and that 2) He is still here through His Spirit and knows what the needs are even before they arise. Bob Wenz wrote,

> *Prayer in the midst of ongoing spiritual warfare for the advance of the kingdom has been given the highest priority at the throne of heaven. We have been given Jesus' name to invoke for prayer from the battlefield. Battlefield prayer is tactical . . . . The quartermaster knows from experience what supplies the troops need even before they send in their requisitions in triplicate on the proper form. But the tactical situation on the front lines is fluid and requires communication that reaches HQ directly. It is stamped with the name of the field commander who promised he will never leave nor forsake his troops. (Navigating Your Perfect Storm)*

REAL LIFE OUT THERE

A missionary served in the poor regions of northern China, teaching in a school as well as in the nearby church. When war destabilized the region, his pregnant wife and two daughters returned home, and he moved to an internment camp. While fellow missionaries formed cliques, grumbled, and acted selfishly, he stayed busy helping the elderly, teaching Bible classes, mediating disputes, and arranging games and activities with the children. Others noted how selfless he was, weary but always interested in others.

One day, he collapsed from a brain tumor; and before he passed away, he whispered to a friend, "It's complete surrender. That's what life's about." And those were the last words of Eric Liddell, the Scottish athlete and Olympian of "Chariots of Fire" fame, who died as a missionary in occupied China in early 1945, Christlike until his last breath.

PRAYING FOR CHRISTLIKENESS

Josiah Bancroft once wrote, "Going into missions is like pouring Miracle-Gro on all your sins" (World Harvest Mission, Lesson 10, "Living in Light of the Cross"). In the Christian life, "being" is most important, and then "doing." Good and fruitful action follows the one whose heart is fully yielded to the love and lordship of Christ. Therefore, praying for missionaries to be Christlike is foundational and critical to the gospel's success.

While in prison, the Apostle Paul wrote to the Philippians asking them to pray that, through the power of the Spirit, he would not fail the test he was in but would glorify God, no matter what:

> For I know that this will turn out for my deliverance through your prayer and the supply of the Spirit of Jesus Christ, according to my earnest expectation and hope that in nothing I shall be ashamed, but with all boldness, as always, so now also Christ will be magnified in my body, whether by life or by death. (Philippians 1:19-20)

The writer of Hebrews also asked prayer for him and his team to stay spotless, inwardly before his conscience and outwardly before the community:

> *Pray for us; for we are confident that we have a good conscience, in all things desiring to live honorably. (Hebrews 13:18)*

ENOUGH TO BE LIKE JESUS

Despite our love of theological training, it is character that is the chief quality and qualifier of those in ministry. Being a good person is helpful, but being Christlike involves a much broader set of attributes. To pray for Christlikeness is to:

- Pray that missionaries will love the Father supremely and seek to do His will

- Pray that they will be like the greatest Soldier ever, since Jesus was a missionary sent by the Father and never failed even once in carrying out the Father's will

- Pray that they will love sinners and the poor, and give false religious leaders a hard time

- Pray that they will live out the example of a gospel-initiated, transformed life, filled with the Spirit of Christ who governs their actions and reactions

- Pray that they won't become a spiritual casualty in the fight and that they won't cave in to the enticements of the opposing army

- Pray that they will embrace their identity as citizens of heaven, be true pilgrims on the earth, be able to let go of their earthly home culture and the desire to put down roots, and advocate only heaven's culture

- Pray that they will die daily to the impulses of the flesh and selfish ambition so that the life of Christ can be manifested in them

- Pray that they will meet the 1 Timothy 3 qualities of "blamelessness" and carefully guard a squeaky-clean testimony with believers and those in the community.

THE BATTLE IS WHERE THE BULLETS FLY

Perhaps you never stop to pray for missionaries to be godly. Perhaps you presume that they already have that quality. But missionaries wrestle with the same "sin in the flesh" that all Christians deal with. There are even some added "sin-promoters" that seem endemic to living in foreign lands, such as the stress of living long-term in a foreign place; frustration with corrupt government officials; exasperation with unhelpful and difficult fellow missionaries; annoyance with everything moving unbelievably slow; suffering strange flus, viruses, diseases, and bacterial infections that last for months; coping with higher levels of dust, mold, bugs, rodents, and reptiles; hearing thumping music that never ends; and beholding the inhumane treatment of the young, the sick, and the dying.

Christlikeness is most accurately measured by how a believer responds to negative stimuli. These things can push even the best of Christian leaders into a spin, where the flesh rises up in the guise of spiritual indignation, and where we call our cultural preferences the "right" way. In addition to the flesh, there are the attacks of Satan through temptations such as ambition, jealousy, lust, bitterness, self-orientation, lying, discontentment, stealing, and the list goes on. Missionaries could use your prayers.

WHEN IT DOESN'T GO WELL

Believers must prayerfully do battle for the souls of their missionaries. Missionaries have many bosses to whom they answer and are in the people business, engaging people all of the time. So, when a missionary falls, there is a wide swath of destruction:

- Nonbelievers are repelled from the gospel
- Community scorners are given ammunition
- Young believers become disillusioned and fall away
- The local church may have to invoke discipline or it may collapse
- The mission agency will begin disciplinary steps
- A move back from the field may be necessary
- The supporting and sending churches will be notified
- The sending church may invoke discipline and revoke the missionary's ordination

The chance of such a fall is greatly diminished by continual prayer by everyone involved in the war on both sides of the ocean for a missionary's brokenness, discipline, carefulness, and courage.

POINTS TO PONDER

Have you ever been disappointed by a moment of unspiritual behavior by a spiritual leader? How did you feel?

Have you ever visited a very different cultural setting and felt pushed way out of your comfort zone? What critters (like spiders, snakes, or lizards), do you despise? How spiritual would you be if you and your children lived among them? Would you ask people to pray?

Chapter 9

#7 Praying for CO-WORKERS

*"Without prayer, even though there may be
increased interest in missions, more work for them,
better success in organization and greater finances,
the real growth of the spiritual life and of the love of
Christ in the people may be very small."
(Andrew Murray, Key to the Missionary Problem)*

INTERFERENCE WITH MISSION CONTROL

Americans tend to have a "can do" and "let's fix it"
mentality that is fueled by having money to make
things happen. Would our missionaries have
accomplished nearly as much in the 20th century
with only 30% of the funding they had? What if they
had 70% more funding? Our tendency is to equate
missional capability with money. E.M. Bounds,
famous for his writings about prayer, wrote that it is
prayer that makes the difference, not money:

Foreign missions today need more the power of prayer than the power of money. Prayer can make even poverty in the missionary cause move on amidst difficulties and hindrances. Much money without prayer is helpless and powerless in the face of the utter darkness on the foreign field . . . . The common idea among church leaders is that if we get the money, prayer will come as a matter of course. The very reverse is the truth. If we get the church at the business of praying . . . money will more than likely come as a matter of course. (The Essentials of Prayer)

Being on a mission should be "faith-walking" because it demands continual connection with mission control for guidance and supply. "Sight-walking" is when you don't need faith because you have the money to do what you want to do; it tempts you to do good things without seeking guidance or supply from mission control. How much have we done in missions fueled by presumption because we have the money instead of fueled by prayer because God has a will for even the details?

REAL LIFE OUT THERE

Jim and Maya entered a mission field when it was in a time of great social upheaval. Although there were dangers, people were open to new ideas and dozens came to Christ. With little discipleship, these new believers began leading their friends to Christ. In six months, Jim could count six new spiritual generations. He was asked to speak to business gatherings and in the schools.

Jim and Maya began to feel strain. Five churches of new believers were meeting and looking to them for help. There were discipleships, counseling needs, men's meetings, home Bible studies, youth events, and the list went on. The pace led to strain in their marriage and family life and finally to their mental and emotional breakdown. At the height of "blessing," they had to return to the States for counseling and rest.

PRAYING FOR CO-WORKERS

What happens if God answers prayers beyond your hopes and dreams? Some missionaries labor under the "stress of blessing" and battle with burnout. The Apostle Paul, who admonished others to "be anxious for nothing," admitted to the Corinthian church, "besides the other things, what comes upon me daily is my deep concern for all the churches" (2 Corinthians 11:28 – the Greek word he used for "concern" is a form of the word "anxious").

Jesus began His ministry alone, then engaged the twelve in ministry, and eventually sent out a much larger group two-by-two, evidently to go even beyond Jewish villages to Samaria and into Gentile areas. As He did so, Jesus mentioned a key element of prayer in missions: we are to specifically ask God to send more laborers into the harvest.

> And he said to them, "The harvest is plentiful, but the laborers are few. Therefore pray earnestly to the Lord of the harvest to send out laborers into his harvest." (Luke 10:2 ESV)

JUST HOW STRESSED OUT ARE THEY?

The Holmes-Rahe Scale is used by health professionals to measure stress in people's lives. Basically stated, life events such as a death in the family, a child leaving home, trouble with the boss, etc., can build up stress levels until it gets dangerous. For normal people, reaching levels of 200-300 on the scale would impact their mental or physical health within two years.

In 1999, a team of doctors studied stress levels on the mission field using the Holmes-Rahe Scale. The typical missionary they tested had sustained levels over 300 year after year, with many reaching 600 on the scale, and first-termers getting close to 900![2]

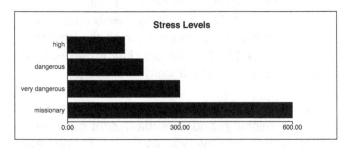

One of the main things recommended was not allowing missionaries to serve alone or isolated. This is one of the reasons our mission family stresses teamwork on the field. The other biblically-based reason is that Paul, the church planter, never travelled alone but worked in teams.

---

[2] Jim Nailing at http://cottrillcompass.com/blog/2012/just-how-stressed-are-missionaries-and-what-can-we-do-about-it.html

PRAYING FOR CO-WORKER BENEFITS

Not meaning to presume upon the Lord, most missionaries will ask you to pray, not just for any laborer, but for good, godly, and suitable servant-leaders. Missionaries get to the field, in part, due to being strong people. Put strong people together and sparks can fly; and due to having some bad experiences with teammates, many missionaries would rather work alone.

Here are some ways you can pray for missionaries to benefit from the new co-workers that God sends:

- Recruiting Zeal
  Missionaries are the best recruiters for their fields, but often they travel about in the States tired, discouraged, and longing to get back home to the field. Pray that God would inspire and animate them to identify and motivate servant-leaders to join them.

- Easing the Shock
  Pray that missionaries would develop clever ways to connect with and appeal to this new generation, structuring meaningful short-term trips, creating internships for on-field training, being a sounding board, offering themselves as mentors, and staying in touch on social media.

- Humility and Unity
  Pray for God to help the older missionaries receive, validate, and graciously mentor new ones. Pray for new ones to bring their

strength under control as they dispel their romantic notions of missions and see the culture, the ministry, and their teammates for what they really are.

- Gift-Mixes
  Pray for God to bring co-workers who would mesh well with the existing team and have spiritual gifts that would help the team where they truly have a need.

- Time Out
  Workaholism is often worse in ministry than in the marketplace. Missionaries need vacations and sabbaticals (since furloughs are often anything but what the name implies). Co-workers can help only if the missionary will take time out, let others run things, and discover he is not indispensable.

- Vulnerability
  Pray for the mission team to build consensus and to move wisely together. Pray for your missionaries to be open to having their ideas shaped or stopped by others and to accept exhortations for better attitudes and people-skills.

POINTS TO PONDER

When you're stressed out, would you rather be with people or be alone? If your hand has an aching laceration, should it just be left alone or should the rest of your body help? What does Ecclesiastes 4:12 say about the benefit of helpers?

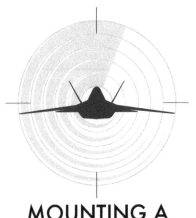

MOUNTING A
PRAYER CAMPAIGN

Chapter 10

Developing a Culture of Prayer
for Missions

*"[The prayer closet] is the battlefield of the Church;
its citadel; the scene of heroic and unearthly
conflicts. The closet is the base of supplies for the
Christian and the Church. Cut off from it, there is
nothing left but retreat and disaster. The energy for
work, the mastery over self, the deliverance from
fear, all spiritual results and graces,
are much advanced by prayer."*
(E.M. Bounds, Purpose in Prayer)

FIVE-MINUTE REVIEW

We have portrayed the work of missions as a war.
Missionaries are light-bearers on the leading edge
of the light as it moves into dark places. They are
on the front lines of the Church as it expands
around the world. Light-bearers do not simply walk
around unopposed. Like it or not, they are in a war.

We have suggested the parallel that 1) missionaries are combat troops, 2) that believers and Christian families back home are combat support troops, and 3) that churches and mission agencies are combat service support forces. While church organizations send out and support missionaries and coordinate the big picture of mission outreach, they are not typically the hub of day-by-day communication and support that missionaries need; they are more like the Pentagon.

With today's technology, it is the individuals, families, and smaller groups within a church (combat support) that are the greatest prayer force. Effective church leaders will mobilize them to do so. These believers can provide frequent communication, a strong prayer war to weaken resistance, targeted supply of equipment, reinforcements, and assistance where necessary, and debriefing at the end of a mission. Most importantly, however, is their role in the prayer war.

In the prayer war, believers can ask the Lord to target His power and grace at certain places and times to accomplish several things: to sustain and protect troops, soften the hearts of nonbelievers, weaken government opposition, soften cultural barriers, and dispel spiritual opposition.

From requests for prayer made by missionaries in the Scripture, we've suggested seven ways to pray for modern missionaries, even when you have no specific prayer requests. As believers pray for these areas, they are engaging in "The Prayer War Over the Seven C's." Missionaries need prayer for:

1. Care
   God's protection from harm, or for grace and profit during adversity

2. Contacts
   God's provision of open doors to develop redemptive relationships

3. Courage
   God's giving boldness to overcome fear of danger, rejection, failure, or opposition

4. Clarity
   God's giving understanding to clearly communicate His gospel to nonbelievers in a different culture

5. Conversions
   God's grace in softening hearts and bringing in the harvest from the seed sown

6. Christlikeness
   God's grace to help them be more like Jesus in actions, reactions, priorities, and love

7. Co-workers
   God's sending of harvesters to assist with the pace and stresses of ministry

THE ROLE OF THE CORPORATE CHURCH

Your church, as an organization, though it would have difficulty coordinating prayer on a daily or momentary basis, can still do hugely important things to highlight the importance of missions, inform believers of missionaries and their needs, create enthusiasm and positive peer pressure, and build a culture of prayer support for them. Here are some ideas:

1. <u>Mission Control Centers</u>
    An old map board in the church lobby or hallway that is not well maintained, lighted, and professional-looking communicates the existence, but not the priority, of a missions program. In some new church buildings, high-tech mission maps are making a comeback. A number of churches keep missionary information on flat-panel TVs or use projectors on the lobby wall – cycling through missionary pictures, maps, and contact information. May we suggest a well-lighted, media-savvy alcove in the lobby called the "mission control center"? The prayer room at BMW's home office is called "The War Room." Maps should be newer and creative. The missionaries' names, towns, and countries should be spelled correctly. Their pictures and prayer letters or email updates should be current. Ways to contact them via social media should be displayed. Some churches have a hall of fame, wall of fame, or other non-map display of their missionaries where a more lengthy profile can be included summarizing the names and birthdates of family members, and the location, nature, and duration of their service.

2. Spotlight Moments

A recent missionary challenge can be highlighted in the church bulletin. In some churches, a different missionary family is mentioned each week in the pastor's prayer, or there is a "missionary moment" before the offering. Some churches, once a month, have a ten-minute segment where a recent email the missionary has written to the church is read and pictures are displayed in a PowerPoint. Some missionaries can send a church a brief video report.

3. Video Calls

Churches can arrange a monthly or quarterly video call to missionaries during a church service to chat for a few minutes, and it should include time with the wife and children. Many missionaries have noted that church missions programs run by just men are usually low functioning. Getting women involved, connected, and concerned is a huge key to having meaningful interaction with missionary families.

4. Reporting

Churches can allow missionaries to give reports and prayer requests when they return for stateside ministry. Sometimes, a Q&A session is helpful. Mission conferences are getting shorter and even disappearing in some churches, sometimes because they are poorly attended, and other times because mission opportunities are pushed year round. If you do have a conference, don't mimic the 1970s; be creative and innovative.

5. <u>Missionary Advocates</u>
Some churches appoint a spokesperson or liaison between the missionary and the church body. These tech-savvy people keep in touch with missionaries by calling, texting, and using email and social media, and then relay that information to the congregation by 1) sending out a "prayer spots" email, 2) posting to the church's members-only website or social media page, 3) sharing requests at prayer meetings, and 4) handling the spotlight moments mentioned above.

6. <u>Budget Talks</u>
Jesus said that where your treasure is your heart is also. This might not seem true of a church that sends many thousands of dollars into missions but doesn't care much about its missionaries. The issue might be information. A pastor or other leader can periodically talk to the congregation about 1) the investments made by the church in missions, 2) the need to learn how the investment is doing, and 3) what they can do in prayer to make sure there is a good return on their missional investments.

7. <u>Preaching on Prayer</u>
Material from this book can be freely used to provide inspiration and information for the development of a preaching series on wartime praying for missionaries.

8. Small Groups

There is a bridge in many churches between the church organization and individual believers, and that is smaller groups that meet during the week. Many churches have used these groups to "adopt a missionary" and communicate with them, check on their needs, ask for prayer requests, send them gifts and cards, and pray for them. Home Bible studies, cell groups, growth groups, small groups, Sunday school classes, and men's and women's fellowships can all fulfill this function. Just remember: everything rises or falls on leadership. If the leader gets apathetic, then the meaningful prayer function will fall away.

9. Monthly Missions Prayer Meeting

A church can designate an entire prayer meeting each month to their missionaries. It is best if someone has just gotten prayer requests from the missionary instead of relying on an older prayer letter or email update.

10. Short-term Trips

American churches now spend more than $2.4 billion each year on short-term trips. Many churches take their teens on these trips, but missionaries have noted that adults older than age 25 take the experience far more seriously, have their gospel-orientation impacted in more lasting ways, strongly consider whether God might want them to stay someday, and are energized to pray and work more knowledgeably for that missionary team.

GETTING INFO TO BELIEVERS AND FAMILIES

Praying for missionaries is primarily the function of the church dispersed, not the church gathered. Making a critical turn around in missional effectiveness through prayer will only happen when our prayer habits change during the week.

As stated in chapter 2, the greatest number of believers who can pray for, and meaningfully interact with, missionaries are Christians and their families in our churches. Unfortunately in most cases, these believers are the least informed and mobilized to help. They need to be mobilized and linked up. Effective communication with God about a missionary begins with effective communication to and from the missionary.

The old days of the quarterly or monthly prayer letter rehearsing things that have already happened are passing away. Using church staff to get information to believers is also fading away and is used only by an aging generation. Using the wartime theme, the old methods are like combat troops writing and mailing periodic letters through the Pentagon. There needs to be an army of believers in between missionaries and their church organizations that can respond and pray immediately.

The Minutemen in America's colonial era were committed to ride and disseminate information on a minute's notice. We can do the same today using social media. Current technology and social networking allows information to flow quickly. This enables the Body of Christ to engage in specific, punctual, wartime, intercessory prayer.

As part of its vision for 2015 and beyond, missionaries with Biblical Ministries Worldwide have each been trying to enroll 300 prayer partners who will pray for them every day. In most cases, missionaries can get information to these prayer partners via social media on a momentary, daily, or weekly basis. Many use email, blogging, and texting, or they begin a group on Facebook only for praises and prayer requests. Some even start a channel on YouTube to upload videos calling for prayer.

GENERAL INTERCESSION

Many young adults continually hop to the latest and greatest media app, maybe check email once a week, and don't look at printed paper at all.

But not everyone is into social media; many adults prefer email and traditional folks still like paper prayer letters. What can those believers or families do to regularly pray for missionaries? Many families try 1) keeping a calendar or 2) having a reminder in a place they come to daily.

We all have appointments to keep. Most of us write them down on a calendar, especially if we take them seriously. Make an appointment with "a missionary a day." Believers can create a prayer calendar to hang on the wall or by placing pictures on a Rolodex that will remind them to pray each day, perhaps in conjunction with a meal or family prayer time.[3] Prayer cards on the fridge still prompt regular prayer from some people. Remember, spiritual activities usually start with inspiration, are carried forward by discipline, and in time become a rhythm of life.

Technologically savvy people can set up a prayer reminder system in their computer's calendar program, on their tablet, or on their smartphone. There's an app for that. People who use a Bible study program each day can set it up to keep a prayer list – like Logos (under File/Prayer List).

A SEVEN-DAY PRAYER GUIDE

We have suggested seven ways to pray for missionaries, and there are seven days in a week. You can create a sheet in your Bible reminding you what to pray for each day. One church created a slick bookmark that their members could keep in their Bibles for their prayer times, with the Seven C's on one side and their missionaries on the other side.

DAILY PRAYER GUIDE FOR MISSIONARIES

1. Sunday is for CARE
   The missionary's protection and safety and

---

[3] Paul Miller, A Praying Life, Colorado Spring: Navpress, pp 221-233.

health in his country of service; for stability, freedom, governmental leaders, passports, visas, and work permits

2. Monday is for CONTACTS
    The missionary's nonbelieving acquaintances and friends, opportunities to make new contacts, the ability to transition conversations to spiritual things and to scriptural ideas and eventually the gospel, open doors through which they may pass to share Christ

3. Tuesday is for COURAGE
    The missionary's boldness through the Spirit, good results in ministry for encouragement, encouragers for him, teammates doing things well

4. Wednesday is for CLARITY
    The missionary as a communicator of God's truth, ability with the foreign language, cultural adaptation, and communicating the truth clearly by the example they set and through the spoken word

5. Thursday is for CONVERSIONS
    The missionary's fruitfulness and satisfaction in their work, seeing key people come to faith in Christ

6. Friday is for CHRISTLIKENESS
    The missionary's own spiritual walk and Christlikeness, growth in grace through the

use of the means of grace (the Word, prayer, fellowship, worship, etc.), death to fleshly desires, humility and cooperation in relationships with fellow workers, nationals, and family

7. Saturday is for CO-WORKERS
The missionary can keep his sanity and avoid burnout by being assisted by new harvesters arriving on the field, working harmoniously with the team, and helping lighten the workload

COACHING MISSIONARIES

As was mentioned earlier, ramping up your church's prayer capabilities regarding missions might be as much of a challenge for your missionaries as for your church. You need to help them to help you. Older missionaries are used to communication that is longer in length and has longer periods of time in between (e.g. quarterly "prayer letters"). Today's believers look at a long paragraph with no pictures, and their brains glaze over – they simply won't read it. If they do read it, there may be things for which to praise the Lord, but no current or urgent prayer requests.

Missionaries need to be coached! Tell them to "keep it short, punchy, and frequent!" Prayer warriors need current and concise information from the missionary, not too long. It should be like calling in coordinates for an airstrike. Combat troops need to stay in frequent contact with combat support. Believers will often pray on the spot and then want follow-up to see how things went. For this reason, prayer warriors shouldn't have too many missionaries – just 1-3. They need to get to know the details, and then pray intelligently and deeply for a few.

FIRST WE PRAY

Our God will unleash great blessings and assistance from heaven for the ingathering of the greatest harvest, and perhaps the last harvest if we will ask Him, if we will come to Him in persistent and desperate prayer.

The church gathered needs to join the Prayer War for missions; but even more so, the church scattered needs to engage in the daily and hourly Prayer War, fueled with fresh communication from the front lines. Change the world from your knees by calling on an omnipotent and omnipresent God to meet the needs of your missionaries in these seven critical areas.

Making plans is just the start!

POINTS TO PONDER

How might God want you to appeal to your church's leadership or otherwise take concrete steps to develop a culture of prayer for missions in your church? What concrete steps would you take?

© Kelly Campbell

ELIZABETH WARREN, one of the nation's most influential progressives and a longtime champion of working families and the middle class, is the senior senator from Massachusetts. A former Harvard Law School professor, she is the author of ten previous books, including *A Fighting Chance*, a national bestseller that received widespread critical acclaim. The mother of two and a grandmother of three, she lives in Cambridge, Massachusetts, with her husband, Bruce Mann.

THIS FIGHT IS OUR FIGHT

THIS FIGHT
IS OUR FIGHT

THE BATTLE TO SAVE AMERICA'S MIDDLE CLASS

ELIZABETH WARREN

PICADOR

METROPOLITAN BOOKS

HENRY HOLT AND COMPANY   NEW YORK

picadorusa.com • instagram.com/picador
twitter.com/picadorusa • facebook.com/picadorusa

Picador® is a U.S. registered trademark and is used by Macmillan Publishing Group, LLC, under license from Pan Books Limited.

For book club information, please visit facebook.com/picadorbookclub or email marketing@picadorusa.com.

Designed by Kelly S. Too

The Library of Congress has cataloged the Metropolitan Books edition as follows:

Names: Warren, Elizabeth, author.
Title: This fight is our fight : the battle to save America's middle class / Elizabeth Warren.
Description: First edition. | New York : Metropolitan Books/Henry Holt and Company, 2017. | Includes bibliographical references and index.
Identifiers: LCCN 2017007458 | ISBN 9781250120618 (hardcover) | ISBN 9781250120625 (ebook)
Subjects: LCSH: Middle class—United States. | United States—Economic policy—2009– | United States—Economic conditions—2009– | United States—Social conditions—1980– | United States—Politics and government—2009–2017.
Classification: LCC HC106.84 .W365 2017 | DDC 305.5'50973—dc23
LC record available at https://lccn.loc.gov/2017007458

Picador Paperback ISBN 978-1-250-15503-0

Our books may be purchased in bulk for promotional, educational, or business use. Please contact your local bookseller or the Macmillan Corporate and Premium Sales Department at 1-800-221-7945, extension 5442, or by email at MacmillanSpecialMarkets@macmillan.com.

First published by Metropolitan Books, and imprint of Henry Holt and Company, LLC

First Picador Edition: June 2018

10 9 8 7 6 5 4 3 2 1

To the people of Massachusetts,
who sent me into this fight

CONTENTS

THIS FIGHT IS OUR FIGHT

Prologue

"I'll get the popcorn."

I yelled up the stairs to let Bruce know I was coming. I also had the beer and my laptop.

He had the television on, with the second season of *Ballers* lined up. Our son had hooked us on it the year before, and we'd been saving the shows until tonight—Election Night.

It was November 8, 2016. The polls were about to close in Massachusetts, and we were about to start our Election Night ritual: clicking back and forth between news reports and binge-watching something really fun on television. I had my laptop so I could check on the local races, and my phone so, assuming the night went well, I could make some congratulatory calls.

Yeah, until I won my Senate race in 2012 I'd have guessed that a senator would watch election returns like a pro: a big group of people in a war room somewhere, multiple television screens on the walls, phones ringing, people rushing in with last-minute information. Lots of coffee cups and pizza boxes strewn over desks. Someone making pithy remarks about what it means that with 2 percent of Illinois reporting, Duckworth has a four-point lead, and turnout in the Seventh Precinct is high, and so on. In fact, I think I've seen that scene in the movies.

But not Bruce and me, not tonight. I wasn't on the ballot this year, so I wouldn't be huddling with a campaign team. Besides, by this point, there wasn't anything else I could do to affect the election's outcome. And with so much on the line, I knew that watching the numbers drift in over the next few hours would be agony.

For so many of these races, I'd been out there with the candidates—cheered them on, given speeches standing next to them, frozen and sweated and stepped in muck right along with them. Hillary Clinton's race, of course, was the night's biggest, but I would be chewing my fingernails watching the Senate races as well. There was Catherine Cortez Masto, a former attorney general in Nevada whom I'd worked with while fighting the banks during the housing crisis eight years ago. Katie McGinty, a former environmental policy official in Pennsylvania who was trying to unseat a Republican who seemed to be funded by an endless supply of Wall Street money. Russ Feingold, the former senator from Wisconsin who had been in the trenches with me as we'd fought to save families from predatory lenders fifteen years earlier and was making a strong push to get his old seat back. Maggie Hassan, the governor from just across the border in New Hampshire, where I had gone time after time to help out. Jason Kander, a progressive Democrat in Missouri who was running uphill hard. Tammy Duckworth, a vet in Illinois who had lost both legs in Iraq and, no surprise, turned out to be a fierce campaigner. Kamala Harris, the California AG I'd gone into battle with shoulder to shoulder many times. And so many more. For months, these candidates had put it all on the line. Faces, names, stories—they all crowded in that night, and I was anxious and hopeful and fearful for every one of them.

No, I didn't want to watch the numbers trickle in with a big group. I just wanted to be at home with Bruce. That night we did what we always did—toggled back and forth between a television show and the election results. Sitting on the couch eating popcorn, drinking beer, and hoping for the best.

Ballers was terrific. The 2016 election, not so much.

The first sign of trouble was how quickly several Senate races were called for Republicans. Indiana. Florida. Suddenly candidates we thought would win were struggling—Russ in Wisconsin and Katie in Pennsylvania. And then it looked like Hillary was in trouble, too.

It was like watching a train wreck in slow motion. One car hurtled off the tracks, then another crumpled, then fires and explosions and bodies flying everywhere.

As I watched the White House slip away and the Democratic losses mount, I knew that a lot of people would spend weeks analyzing what had gone wrong, how this moment had come to pass. There would be lots of pundits. ("I always knew . . .") Lots of partisans. ("Of course this loss happened because they . . .") Lots of political types certain that they could have done it all much, much better.

Sure, there would be endless autopsies of the 2016 campaigns, but as that long night wore on, I found myself thinking less about the political winds and more about how the fallout from this election would deliver one more body blow to so many working families. The television showed crowds of candidates and supporters celebrating or grieving, but what haunted me was the thought that for tens of millions of Americans, life was about to get a whole lot tougher.

LONG BEFORE I ever came within a hundred miles of politics, I had been a teacher and a researcher. I had spent years tracking what was happening to America's middle class, what was happening to working families and families that wanted to be working families. It was a great and terrible story.

The tale of America coming out of the Great Depression and not only surviving but actually transforming itself into an economic giant is the stuff of legend. But the part that gives me goose bumps is what we did with all that wealth: over several generations, our country built the greatest middle class the world had ever known.

We built it ourselves, using our own hard work and the tools of government to open up more opportunities for millions of people. We used it all—tax policy, investments in public education, new infrastructure, support for research, rules that protected consumers and investors, antitrust laws—to promote and expand our middle class. The spectacular, shoot-off-the-fireworks fact is that we succeeded. Income growth was widespread, and the people who did most of the work—the 90 percent of America—also got most of the gains. In the 1960s and 1970s, I was one of the lucky beneficiaries of everything America was building, and to this day, I am grateful to the bottom of my soul.

But now, in a new century and a different time, that great middle class is on the ropes. All across the country, people are worried—worried and angry.

They are angry because they bust their tails and their income barely budges. Angry because their budget is stretched to the breaking point by housing and health care. Angry because the cost of sending their kid to day care or college is out of sight.

People are angry because trade deals seem to be building jobs and opportunities for workers in other parts of the world, while leaving abandoned factories here at home. Angry because young people are getting destroyed by student loans, working people are deep in debt, and seniors can't make their Social Security checks cover their basic living expenses. Angry because we can't even count on the fundamentals— roads, bridges, safe water, reliable power—from our government. Angry because we're afraid that our children's chances for a better life won't be as good as our own.

People are angry, and they are *right* to be angry. Because this hard-won, ruggedly built, infinitely precious democracy of ours has been hijacked.

Today this country works great for those at the top. It works great for every corporation rich enough to hire an army of lobbyists and lawyers. It works great for every billionaire who pays taxes at lower rates than the hired help. It works great for everyone with the money to buy favors in

Washington. Government works great for them, but for everyone else, this country is no longer working very well.

This is the most dangerous kind of corruption. No, it's not old-school bribery with envelopes full of cash. This much smoother, slicker, and better-dressed form of corruption is perverting our government and making sure that day after day, decision after decision, the rich and powerful are always taken care of. This corruption is turning government into a tool of those who have already gathered wealth and influence. This corruption is hollowing out America's middle class and tearing down our democracy.

In 2016, into this tangle of worry and anger, came a showman who made big promises. A man who swore he would drain the swamp, then surrounded himself with the lobbyists and billionaires who run the swamp and feed off government favors. A man who talked the talk of populism but offered the very worst of trickle-down economics. A man who said he knew how the corrupt system worked because he had worked it for himself many times. A man who vowed to make America great again and followed up with attacks on immigrants, minorities, and women. A man who was always on the hunt for his next big con.

In the months ahead, it would become clear that this man was even more divisive and dishonest than his presidential campaign revealed. But on election night, I stared at the television as it sank in that this man was about to become the next president of the United States.

The election results kept rolling in, and I knew that plenty of people would be eager to describe the special appeal of Donald Trump and explain all the reasons why he won. But we need more than an explanation of just one election; we also need to understand how and why our country has gone so thoroughly wrong. We need a plan to put us back on track—and then we need to get to work and make it happen.

We need to live our values, to be the kind of nation that invests in opportunity, not just for some of us, but for all of us. We need to take our democracy back from those who would pervert it for their own benefit. We need to build the America of our best dreams.

Sitting on the couch with Bruce, I watched Donald Trump say that his presidency would be "a beautiful thing." No, I thought, it won't be anything like beautiful. Worse, the man who would soon move into the White House had the capacity to bear down on a middle class that was already on the ropes and deliver the knockout punch.

If ever there was a time to fight, this was it.

1

The Disappearing Middle Class

I was ready to go.

It was a Thursday morning in March 2013. I'd been in the Senate for two and a half months, and this was our first hearing on the minimum wage. For close to four years, the federal minimum wage had been frozen at $7.25 an hour. The rate was already low by historic standards, and a lot of workers were sinking. Minimum wage is just that—the minimum.

When I am home in Massachusetts, I make a point of speaking with as many Bay Staters as I can. This includes the people who do the service work in big buildings. These are the workers who stock the office kitchens, keep the buildings clean, provide security. I've been struck by how many of them hold down two or three jobs just to stay afloat. Women who take the T into Boston, work a full shift cleaning buildings, then stay to work a morning shift at one of the counters at South Station. Men who push wheelchairs and haul bags at Logan Airport all day, then drive cabs or work security in the evening. And I meet them outside Boston too. Mothers and fathers in New Bedford and Fall River, in Worcester and Spring-field, who work at fast-food places in town or on the highway, piecing together a living from whatever jobs they can find. A woman up on the

North Shore told me she sleeps in her car in the parking lot in the hours between when one job ends and the other begins. She said she's so tired that when she drives to her mother's house to pick up her baby daughter, she falls asleep on the couch the minute she gets there. Low-wage workers—in Massachusetts and in all the other states too—are among the hardest working people in America.

I'm pretty hard-core about this issue. The way I see it, no one in this country should work full-time and still live in poverty—period. But at $7.25 an hour, a mom working a forty-hour-a-week minimum-wage job cannot keep herself and her baby above the poverty line. This is wrong—and this was something the U.S. Congress could make better if we'd just raise the minimum wage. We could fix this *now*.

Ten weeks on the job, and it still gave me a thrill to walk into the Senate hearing rooms, notebook tucked under my arm. This room was like a stage set: high ceilings, heavy paneling, and dark blue carpets. The lights were mounted on the walls, giant art deco torches that looked like they were illuminating an ancient temple. The room was so vast that everyone had to use microphones just to hear each other.

Senators were seated on a raised platform, assigned places around a giant, wood-paneled horseshoe-shaped dais. Our chairs were huge, high-backed leather affairs, sort of ancient king meets modern CEO. Witnesses sat at a low table in the open part of the U, with the audience behind them. The room's design is intended to evoke the grandeur and solemnity of the Senate, a not-very-subtle reminder of the power of this body.

In keeping with the Senate's rigid deference to seniority and my junior status, my chair was the farthest from center stage, out on one end of the horseshoe. I didn't care. I was aware that this was pretty routine stuff for most senators. And okay, I understood that this committee wasn't going to do a movie moment and suddenly jump up and demand in the name of working people everywhere that Congress increase the minimum wage.

I knew that, but I also knew that the move to raise the minimum wage was gaining traction around the country. And I knew that this hearing was a pretty good platform to move that fight forward. After all,

Committee hearing on the minimum wage.
That's me at the far right end of the horseshoe.

this committee really did have the power to recommend a raise for thirty million Americans, and even if we weren't going to do it today, I wanted to make sure we made some progress. If you don't fight, you can't win.

I also understood that for more than forty years, workers' pay hadn't kept pace with inflation. Productivity had gone up. Profits had gone up. Executives had gotten raises. Couldn't we at last come together to make sure that the people who did some of the hardest, dirtiest work in the nation got at least a chance to build a little security?

And couldn't we also give this whole "bipartisan" thing another try? Since the 1930s, Republicans had joined Democrats to support periodic increases to the minimum wage, and now, after four years of holding steady, I thought we might come together for some kind of increase. Okay, it probably wouldn't be as much as I wanted, but couldn't we at least do *something*?

No. The Republicans were locked in: they would block any efforts to increase the minimum wage by even a few nickels.

The hearing produced some sharp back-and-forth about the impact that raising the minimum wage might have on jobs. The data are clear: study after study shows that there are no large adverse effects on jobs when the minimum wage goes up—and one of the country's leading experts was sitting right in front of us testifying to exactly that point. I battled a couple of the other witnesses, and I got in my licks about how far the real minimum wage had fallen, but after about an hour and a half, the hearing began winding down.

I gathered up my papers, ready to leave as soon as the gavel fell. Lamar Alexander, the senator from Tennessee and the most senior Republican on the committee, was asking his last questions when a witness interrupted him to point out that Congress was responsible for setting the right level for the minimum wage.

Senator Alexander replied that if he could decide, there would be no minimum.

No minimum wage at all. Not $15.00. Not $10.00. Not $7.25. Not $5.00. Not $1.00.

The comment was delivered quite casually. It wasn't a grand pronouncement shouted by a crazy, hair-on-fire ideologue. Instead, a longtime U.S. senator stated with calm confidence that if an employer could find someone desperate enough to take a job for fifty cents an hour, then that employer should have the right to pay that wage and not a penny more. He might as well have said that employers could eat cake and the workers could scramble for whatever crumbs fall off the table.

For just a blink, I wasn't in a heavily paneled Senate hearing room. I wasn't sitting at an elevated dais. I didn't have an aide seated behind me and cameras pointed my way.

FOR JUST A blink, I was a skinny sixteen-year-old girl, back in Oklahoma City. It was early in the fall, and I had just started my senior year of high school.

By then we were a small family: all that was left of us was Mother, Daddy, and me. My three older brothers had each in turn left for the military, gotten married, and were starting families of their own.

Like every family, we'd had our ups and downs, but from my teenage perspective, life felt a little steadier again. Mother answered phones at Sears, and Daddy sold lawn mowers and fences. Two paychecks. It had been a couple of years since the bill collectors had called or people had threatened to take away our home. Late at night, I no longer heard the muffled sounds of my mother crying.

But it was still tough. There was no extra money, no breathing room. I waited tables and babysat. I picked up a few dollars sewing and ironing, although nothing regular. I was sixteen—sixteen and watching the world slip away. This was my last year of high school, and it looked like everyone at Northwest Classen had a future, everyone except me. All my friends were talking about college. They went on nonstop as they compared schools and sororities and possible majors. No one seemed to worry about what it would cost. Me? I didn't have the money for a college application, much less tuition and books. Some days it seemed like college might as well have been on the moon.

It was a miserable time in my life.

One night my mother and I had another fight about what I should do after high school. I look back now and realize that she was trying her best. She worked long hours, and she sometimes seemed stretched to the breaking point.

On this one night, it all spun out of control. She had been yelling at me. Why was I so special that I had to go to college? Did I think I was better than everyone else in the family? Where would the money come from? I did the usual: I stared at the floor in silence, and when I'd had enough, I retreated to my bedroom. But this time, retreat wasn't enough. She followed me into my room and kept yelling. I finally jumped up from my desk and screamed at her to leave me alone.

Quick as lightning, she hit me hard in the face.

I think we were both stunned. She backed out of my room. I stuffed a handful of clothes into a canvas bag and raced out the front door.

Hours later, Daddy found me downtown, sitting on a bench at the bus station. My face was red, and I was still shaking. I was hurt—hurt and discouraged.

Everything in my life seemed wrong.

Daddy sat down beside me on the bench, and for a long time he said nothing. Both of us stared ahead. After a while, he asked if I was hungry. He walked over to a vending machine and brought back some cracker sandwiches. Then he asked me if I remembered the time after his heart attack, those hard months when he and Mother were sure they were about to lose the house.

I remembered.

It had been nearly four years earlier. After his heart attack, Daddy had been in the hospital for a long time, and when he came home he was gray and even quieter than usual. He spent hours sitting alone, smoking cigarettes and looking off into space. He moved into the tiny bedroom that had been left empty when my brother David joined the army.

For months, my mother carried around Kleenex or the cheap off-brand she usually bought. She worked the tissues into shreds, leaving them balled up in ashtrays and on her dresser. But she always had one ready in case she started to cry. And she cried a lot.

Daddy said it was the worst time in his life. Worse than when the doctors thought the lumps on his neck were cancer. Worse than when his best friend, Claude, died. Worse than when he was in a terrible car crash and smashed through the windshield and tore his shoulder open.

"Your mother was at home when they took the station wagon," he said, his voice low. "And then they said they were going to take the house. She cried every night."

He paused for a long time. "I just couldn't face it."

Sitting there on the bench in the bus station, he told me that he had failed and that the shame had nearly killed him. He wanted to die. He wanted to disappear from our lives and from the earth and from everything that had gone wrong. He would think about how bad things were and ask whether this was the night to leave my mother and me.

What happened? I asked.

Daddy sat silently for a long time, caught somewhere in his memories of those awful days. He still didn't look at me. Finally, he took my hand in both of his and held it tightly.

It got better, he said. Your mother found work. We made some payments. After a while, I went back to work. We had less money, but it was enough to get by. We got caught up on the mortgage. You seemed to do okay.

Finally he turned and looked at me. "Life gets better, punkin."

My daddy said, "Life gets better, punkin."

And that's how I'd always remembered this moment: my daddy telling me to hang on, that no matter how bad it feels, life gets better. I had carried that story in my pocket for decades. It was how I made it through the painful parts. Divorce. Disappointments. Deaths. Whenever things got really tough, I would pull out that story and hold it in my mind. I'd hear my daddy's voice, and I'd always feel better. By now, his line was a part of me.

Life gets better, punkin.

IT WAS JUST a blink before I was back in that fancy hearing room again. But that's all it takes—just a blink—to change someone's life. My daddy's life. My mother's life. My life.

As I walked back to my office, I thought about how close my family had come to disaster. After my daddy's heart attack, we were tumbling down a hill toward a cliff, and we had been just about to go over the edge when my mother grabbed a branch—a job at Sears. She was fifty years old, and for the first time in her life she had a job with a paycheck. She answered phones and took catalog orders. In a cramped room with no windows, eight women, mostly hard-pressed mothers like her, sat all day long, ready to help customers who called. She wore high heels and hose, and every day she and her coworkers took forty minutes for lunch and two breaks that lasted exactly ten minutes each.

And she was paid minimum wage.

So when Senator Alexander said there would be no minimum wage if it were up to him, I thought about how much that job had meant to Mother and Daddy and me. My mother's minimum-wage job not only saved our house—it saved our family. No, it didn't make our lives perfect. It took years to work off the medical bills from my father's heart attack. My mother worked and reworked her grocery list to squeeze out every last nickel. The carpet in the living room got worn through to the bare floor. And there were times when my mother's anxieties took over and she lashed out, and times when my daddy got scary quiet. But we hung together. We made it—shaken, but still standing.

What if Mother hadn't earned enough money to keep us going after Daddy got sick? We'd already lost the family station wagon. What if we'd lost the house? What would the shame have done to my daddy? And if he *had* left us forever? What would the loss have done to Mother and me? Would I have ever made it to college? Or would she and I have clung to each other, both so fatally wounded that neither of us could ever have recovered?

I don't know what would have happened if Mother hadn't been able to break our fall with a minimum-wage job at Sears. But I do know that policy decisions about important issues like the minimum wage matter. Those decisions—made in far-off Washington, reached in elegant rooms by confident, well-fed men and women—really matter.

Back in the 1960s, when my mother worked at Sears, a minimum-wage job could keep a family of three afloat. Mother had a high school education and no work experience, but when Sears needed someone to answer the phones, the law required the company to pay her an hourly rate that was enough to keep our family of three up and on our feet.

And that's where the sick-in-the-back-of-the-throat unfairness of it nearly chokes me. In the years since my mother went to work at Sears, America has gotten *richer*. In fact, the country's total wealth is at an all-time high.

My mother wasn't much into politics, but I'm sure she would have assumed that fifty years later, the minimum wage would be a lot higher. If it could feed a family of three and pay a mortgage in 1965, surely by now a minimum wage would let a family afford, say, a home and a car—and maybe even a little money for college applications for a skinny daughter. Right?

Wrong. Way wrong.

Adjusted for inflation, the minimum wage today is *lower* than it was in 1965—about 24 percent lower. That job at Sears allowed my mother to eke out a living for a family of three; today, a mother working full-time and getting paid the minimum wage cannot afford the rent on the average two-bedroom apartment anywhere in America. In Oklahoma, where I grew up, that mother wouldn't even come close to providing a *poverty-level income* for her family. Paying rent, keeping groceries on the table, having a little money left over for school shoes or lunch money—those are all out of reach. Today a mother who tries to break her family's fall simply can't grab the same branch that was there for my family.

Today, Washington has decided to turn away as more families than ever tumble over a financial cliff and crash on the rocks below. I'm in my fifth year in the United States Senate, and during my time in office I've learned a bitter lesson: a Republican-led Congress just doesn't care.

Where people end up in life is about more than hard work and good fortune. The rules matter, too. It matters whether the government blows tens of billions of dollars on tax loopholes for billionaires or whether that same money is used to lower costs for students who have to borrow money to go to college. It matters whether Wall Street can pocket billions of dollars by cheating people on mortgages and tricking them on credit cards or if there's a cop on the beat to keep them honest. It matters whether the minimum wage is set so low that a full-time worker still lives in poverty or if minimum wage also means a livable wage.

When I sit in meetings or conferences and listen to people who have investment portfolios and second homes worry about the impact of raising the minimum wage on giant businesses like McDonald's and Best Buy without a single thought about how the fry cooks or checkout clerks support themselves and their families from week to week, I grind my teeth until my head hurts. When I hear senators make oh-so-clever theoretical economic arguments while ignoring rock-solid data, I want to scream. When President Trump nominates a labor secretary who opposes a living wage and who made his own fortune by squeezing fast-food workers, I get the urge to bang my head on the table. And when I hear my colleagues in Congress express their deep concern for those who have already made it even as they cheerfully dismiss everyone who is busting their rear just to get by, the fury rises in me like a physical force.

The America of opportunity is under assault. We once ran this country to benefit hardworking people who didn't have much, to grow a middle class, to create opportunities for our kids. We once held up the ideal that poor kids would get the same chances in life as everyone else.

We once believed that opportunity was not a zero-sum game; more for me didn't have to mean less for you.

We once believed that the greatest country on earth could bend our future toward more opportunity for more of our people. But today every decision in Washington has a tilt. Politicians think about how they will fund their next campaigns, lobbyists press for every advantage, and armies of fancy corporate lawyers encircle government agencies. Big-deal executives earn millions on Wall Street, then spin through a revolving door that puts them in charge of government policy for a few years before they go back to the corporate side to make even more money. Think tanks support so-called experts who will offer an opinion on anything—if the price is right. The result is that the rich and powerful flourish, while everyone else is left further and further behind. The cumulative impact of decades of these decisions has been to hollow out America's middle class and to leave us, as a nation, weakened.

The game is rigged. It is deliberately, persistently, and aggressively rigged to help the rich and powerful get richer and more powerful. Whether mild-mannered men or crazy demagogues are pushing policy decisions, it matters what those decisions are and who they are designed to help.

MIDDLE-CLASS AND BROKE

A lot of people say the game isn't rigged. Some very smart people who are fully committed to making this a better country sing the praises of the American economic system. And they have a lot of numbers to back them up. Yes, there was a dip around the time of the 2008 crash, but the big picture looks great. As a country, America keeps getting richer and richer and richer.

There are so many *happy* stories to tell:

- The stock market is up up up.
- Corporate profits are breaking new records.
- Inflation has remained low for years.
- The amount of wealth we produce every year is double what it was a generation ago.
- Unemployment is down, and a lot of people thrown out of work after the financial crash now have jobs.

It's gotten so good that even lavish Wall Street parties have ratcheted up. Citadel, a major hedge fund, had a good 2015. It celebrated with a party featuring Katy Perry (for a rumored $500,000) and another party starring Maroon 5 (also $500,000 or so) along with—my favorite touch—violinists suspended from the ceiling by cables. Maroon 5 and Katy Perry are hugely talented, and both have fought hard for progressive causes. If a billionaire wants to pay them and an army of violinists a fortune, they should all take the money. But good grief, a party where just the entertainment costs as much as it would take to feed a family of four for half a century? The next year, according to news reports, Citadel's CEO was buying a new condo spanning three floors of a high-rise overlooking Central Park, a pad priced at a cool $200 million. This condo in the sky has about the same square footage as twelve typical American homes. And why shouldn't he go for it? He had already set the records for the most expensive home purchases in Chicago and Miami, so obviously it was time to upgrade his New York digs.

Pop the champagne corks!

But before we clink our glasses and exchange air kisses, let's slide past all those cheery headlines and swanky celebrations and take a close look at the reality that is lived by millions of American families. Even a quick glance is enough to cause whiplash. What we see are people who get up when it's still dark outside, work all day, go on to a second job in the evening, and then fold a pile of laundry late at night so they can accomplish that one last thing before they fall into bed. We see men and women who work as hard as they possibly can and still fall behind a little more every month. We see lives that look nothing like those lived by billionaires in eighteen-thousand-square-foot condos, because these people don't live in some fairy tale—they live in today's reality.

NOT LONG AFTER I started writing this book, I talked with a woman I'll call Gina. She is fifty—the same age my mother was when she headed off to Sears. Gina wanted to tell her story, but she asked for her name and some details about her life to be changed in the book so her neighbors and her employer wouldn't recognize her, and I promised to do that.

Gina is full of nervous energy—quick bursts of laughter, quick flashes of anger. Short, compact, and sandy-haired, she's the kind of woman who talks to people around her in the grocery store line and who knows every clerk by name. She's a loyal friend and a proud American.

Gina grew up with four sisters. Her dad died when she was a teenager, and from then on her mom ran the family business, a local bar. Gina gives a throaty laugh as she claims that "her mother knew every single dirty joke" ever told.

Her story starts out well. Gina went to college and got a business degree. She met Darren and fell in love. They had both lived all over the country, and they decided to settle in a small town in North Carolina because it seemed like such a nice place to raise a family. Soon they had two boys, but for Gina and Darren, the grown-up, we-have-found-our-place-in-the-middle-class moment arrived when they bought their home.

It was a tidy, almost-new mobile home, permanently set on a large lot with a long gravel driveway.

Gina speaks in a rush, wanting to make very clear the importance of this house—what it says about who she is and what she has accomplished. "I love the house," Gina says. "We keep it immaculate. We live on the corner here. The whole world sees us."

Gina had a good education, but when their two boys were small she decided to stay home with them. She volunteered at the boys' school and took up scrapbooking, making little treasures out of bits of nothing. It was a good time for their family.

One of Gina's artistic handiworks, a Christmas decoration.

Once both boys were in school, Gina headed off to work. She got a job as a sales rep for a big national company, making calls on retailers across a three-county area. Darren was doing well as a roofer. He owned a truck, Gina had a car, and by the late 2000s, they were bringing in about $70,000 a year.

Their income put Gina and Darren smack in the middle; they earned more than about half of all four-person families in America and less than about half—which is about as solidly middle-class as it gets. But even with a good, solid income, Gina and Darren were mostly stay-at-home people. They shopped at discount stores. An occasional meal out usually meant Denny's or Chili's. Most of all, Gina and Darren were *careful* people. They contributed to their 401(k), bought a few stocks, made extra payments on their mortgage, and put away some cash savings. They were a perfect picture of what it meant to be a member of a huge tribe: solid, middle-class America.

Today, Gina is still married to Darren, still living in the same house, still gluing buttons and bits of lace into her scrapbooks. Is she still middle-class? Her answer is short and bitter:

"I don't think there is a middle class anymore. If there was a middle class, we wouldn't need to go to a food pantry."

Darren's work as a roofer has been spotty, and he's had trouble with his back and knees. Gina works at Walmart now, and that's what keeps them going.

Their stocks and their savings are gone, used to fill in during the stretches when one or both of them were out of work. The small 401(k) has nearly disappeared. There was no money to help either of the boys pay for college, and now their sons are nearly grown men. Both work odd hours and live at home because neither one can afford a place of his own.

Gina's car is now seventeen years old. She and Darren have talked about selling their home, but she says their mortgage is less than they'd pay in rent, and a mobile home like theirs—even though it's on a big lot—doesn't appreciate much. They have a stack of bills that, in her quietest moments, Gina admits to herself they will never pay off. Why? Because today Gina and Darren's combined income is less than $36,000.

What happened? What's the tale of shocking personal tragedy and extraordinary misfortune that landed a solidly middle-class woman like Gina at the doorstep of the food pantry?

Nothing.

No crisis. No accident. No tale of woe. Just the grinding wear and tear of an economy that doesn't work anymore for families like Gina's.

And that's the part of this story that makes me want to pound the table in frustration. What happened to Gina and Darren is the modern economy—the one that produces all those bubbly stock market records and corporate profits and private concerts with Katy Perry. What happened is an economic boa constrictor that is squeezing working families so hard they can't breathe.

Gina's basic story could be repeated in millions of households across America with only small variations. Could be? Shoot, it *is* repeated, again and again and again.

But the part of her story that bothers me the most is that Gina did everything just the way she was supposed to. She worked hard—no, she worked herself into the ground for years, getting up for a two-and-a-half-hour commute to work and stretching her food budget so they could pay a little extra on the mortgage. She played by every rule: savings, insurance, retirement. And now she's fifty years old and on a long slide down. The family that used to eat out occasionally now needs to visit the food pantry to make it to the end of the month.

Fortune smiles on some more than others, and no one is guaranteed smooth sailing. I get that. But Gina is not alone. Instead, she's part of the collateral damage of a mostly invisible dismantling of America's middle class. She and millions of other once-middle-class families may keep up appearances, they may keep their lawns mowed and smile and wave to their neighbors, but their economic lives have become a new kind of hell.

When Gina talks, her voice says as much as her words. The pride in her home. The worry over her sons. The bravado, the gravelly I-can-take-whatever-life-dishes-out attitude. And the small tremor of desperation.

What comes next for Gina? What happens when Darren can't work anymore? When they can't hold it together? What will they do when the doctor thinks it's time to start on a medication for high blood pressure that has a $50 copay or when the transmission finally falls out of the car? No wonder Gina talks fast and sometimes sounds like she can barely breathe.

Consider a few other facts—the not-so-smiley-face facts—about the American economy:

- Nearly one in four Americans can't pay their bills on time.
- Nearly half of Americans would not be able to cover an unexpected expense of $400.
- A lower proportion of Americans own their homes than at any time in the past half century—63.5 percent.
- The typical man working full-time earns less today than his counterpart did in 1972.
- Nearly one-third of the country's adult population—76 million Americans—describe themselves as either "struggling to get by" or "just getting by."

The overall economic statistics—the GDP, the stock market, corporate profitability, unemployment—are powerfully important, but the rosy picture they paint has huge blind spots, and those blind spots hide much of America's lived experience. As America's middle class is hollowed out, these numbers become even less accurate in describing what is happening to Gina or millions of other people like her. Growth in GDP said something far more revealing about America back when that growth was widely shared. Stock prices better reflected the growing security of the middle class when more people saved and when their companies invested in pensions for them. Corporate profitability meant a lot more when it wasn't a function of massive layoffs and moving operations overseas. Unemployment statistics were more useful indicators when people were offered full-time jobs with benefits, rather than twenty random hours at Walmart. Unemployment figures also mattered more when the minimum wage kept people out of poverty.

I'm happy that the GDP is up and unemployment is down. Yay! But I'm not drinking champagne. In fact, I'm hitting alarm buttons everywhere I can. Our once-solid middle class is in mortal danger—in danger and running out of time. Every one of those happy numbers is used by nearly every economic reporter and pundit and politician, but those numbers paper over the fact that America's middle class is literally disappearing.

NO MONEY, NO TIME

Gina says she feels lucky to have a job, but she is pretty blunt about what it is like to work at Walmart: she hates it. She's worked at the local Walmart for nine years now, spending long hours on her feet waiting on customers and wrestling heavy merchandise around the store. But that's not the part that galls her.

Last year, management told the employees that they would get a significant raise. While driving to work or sorting laundry, Gina thought about how she could spend that extra money. Do some repairs around the house. Or set aside a few dollars in case of an emergency. Or help her sons, because "that's what moms do." And just before drifting off to sleep, she'd think about how she hadn't had any new clothes in years. Maybe, just maybe.

For weeks, she smiled at the notion. She thought about how Walmart was finally going to show some sign of respect for the work she and her coworkers did. She rolled the phrase over in her mind: "significant raise." She imagined what that might mean. Maybe $2.00 more an hour? Or $2.50? That could add up to $80 a week, even $100. The thought was delicious.

Then the day arrived when she received the letter informing her of the raise: 21 cents an hour. A whopping 21 cents. For a grand total of $1.68 a day, $8.40 a week.

Gina described holding the letter and looking at it and feeling like it was "a spit in the face." As she talked about the minuscule raise, her voice filled with anger. Anger, tinged with fear. Walmart could dump all over her, but she knew she would take it. She still *needed* this job. They could treat her like dirt, and she would still have to show up. And that's exactly what they did.

In 2015, Walmart made *$14.69 billion in profits*, and Walmart's investors pocketed $10.4 billion from dividends and share repurchases—and Gina got 21 cents an hour more. This isn't a story of shared sacrifice. It's not a story about a company that is struggling to keep its doors open in tough times. This isn't a small business that can't afford generous raises. Just the opposite: this is a fabulously wealthy company making big bucks off the Ginas of the world.

There are seven members of the Walton family, Walmart's major shareholders, on the Forbes list of the country's four hundred richest people, and together these seven Waltons have as much wealth as about 130 million other Americans. Seven people—not enough to fill the lineup of a softball team—and they have more money than 40 percent of our nation's population put together. Walmart routinely squeezes its workers, not because it has to, but because it can. The idea that when the company does well, the employees do well, too, clearly doesn't apply to giants like this one.

Walmart is the largest employer in the country. More than a million and a half Americans are working to make this corporation among the most profitable in the world. Meanwhile, Gina points out that at her store, "almost all the young people are on food stamps." And it's not just her store. Across the country, Walmart pays such low wages that many of its employees rely on food stamps, rent assistance, Medicaid, and a mix of other government benefits, just to stay out of poverty.

The next time you drive into a Walmart parking lot, pause for a second to note that this Walmart—like the more than five thousand other Walmarts across the country—costs taxpayers about $1 million in direct subsidies to the employees who don't earn enough money to pay for an apartment, buy food, or get even the most basic health care for their children. In total, Walmart benefits from more than $7 billion in subsidies each year from taxpayers like you. Those "low, low prices" are made possible by low, low wages—and by the taxes you pay to keep those workers alive on their low, low pay.

As I said earlier, I don't think that anyone who works full-time should live in poverty. I also don't think that bazillion-dollar companies like Walmart ought to funnel profits to shareholders while paying such low wages that taxpayers must pick up the ticket for their employees' food, shelter, and medical care. I listen to right-wing loudmouths sound off about what an outrage welfare is and I think, "Yeah, it stinks that Walmart has been sucking up so much government assistance for so long." But somehow I suspect that these guys aren't talking about Walmart the Welfare Queen.

Walmart isn't alone. Every year, employers like retailers and fast-food outlets pay wages that are so low that the rest of America ponies up a collective $153 billion to subsidize their workers. That's $153 billion *every year*. Anyone want to guess what we could do with that mountain of money? We could make every public college tuition-free *and* pay for preschool for every child—and still have tens of billions left over. We could almost double the amount we spend on services for veterans, such as disability, long-term care, and ending homelessness. We could double all federal research and development—*everything*: medical, scientific, engineering, climate science, behavioral health, chemistry, brain mapping, drug addiction, even defense research. Or we could more than double federal spending on transportation and water infrastructure—roads, bridges, airports, mass transit, dams and levees, water treatment plants, safe new water pipes.

Yeah, the point I'm making is blindingly obvious. America could do a lot with the money taxpayers spend to keep afloat people who are working full-time but whose employers don't pay a living wage.

Of course, giant corporations know they have a sweet deal—and they plan to keep it, thank you very much. They have deployed armies of lobbyists and lawyers to fight off any efforts to give workers a chance to organize or fight for a higher wage. Giant corporations have used their mouthpiece, the national Chamber of Commerce, to oppose any increase in the minimum wage, calling it a "distraction" and a "cynical effort" to increase union membership. Lobbyists grow rich making sure that people like Gina don't get paid more.

The result is that for decades, the policies and rules that once served to build a robust middle class no longer offer the same kind of foundation.

EARLIER I MENTIONED that when I was a kid, my mother's minimum-wage job paid enough to let us cover our mortgage and keep food on the table. We didn't need welfare or food stamps because the minimum wage set a floor that would support us without taxpayer help. But there was something else different about my mother's job. When she got hired by Sears two generations ago, she worked for a predictable forty hours

My mother is the tall one in the plaid dress.
Her minimum-wage job at Sears covered our mortgage and put food on the table.

a week. If Sears was busy, she got a paycheck. If Sears wasn't busy, she still got a paycheck.

Gina describes life at Walmart as a constant fight to get enough hours to support her family. Walmart deliberately overhires, which then puts workers in competition for shifts. Even though she's worked at the store for nearly a decade, Gina doesn't get her work schedule far enough in advance to plan a trip to the dentist. And she doesn't know how many hours she will get each week or whether her paycheck will be enough to cover the basics.

Gina thinks the crazy Walmart system of scheduling work isn't just about keeping the store open. She believes it's about raw power. She talks about her friend named Nicole, who is trying to support herself and her little boy on a Walmart paycheck. "She needs more hours. She was trying to do better, so she was taking classes at the local community college at night," Gina says. Nicole was available every day and five evenings every week, but "she needed Tuesdays and Thursdays off at night" so she could go to class. "They wouldn't give them to her."

Why? Gina says that management wanted to show Nicole that she wasn't any better than anyone else. "They use [the schedule] as punishment," Gina says. "They were going to teach her a lesson."

Once Gina starts talking about her coworkers, the examples tumble out one after the other. There are stories about workers whose schedules are changed without notice. Stories about workers who have anxiety attacks. Stories about workers who burst into tears in the break room because of bullying from higher up the food chain.

Gina has become a sort of anxious den mother. She started a food collection for the coworker living in his car. She sweet-talked one of the store managers into changing the work assignment for an elderly coworker who couldn't do much heavy lifting after his bout of pneumonia. Gina tries to help her coworkers every chance she gets, but it's never enough.

Even though she's worked at Walmart for years now, her position at the company always feels unsteady. Talking to me didn't help things. I repeatedly promised I wouldn't use her name or tell anyone how to find her. She was always willing to talk—in fact, she would say, in a near shout,

"We need to tell this story!" Then, in a much smaller voice, she would add, "But I really need this job."

Employers in other industries have invented new models that are every bit as effective as Walmart's efforts to eliminate guaranteed hours, fixed schedules, minimum wages, and benefits. They classify workers as subcontractors, independent contractors, or gig workers. Today, millions of hardworking people live in a world in which their incomes go up and down, their schedules shift from day to day, and they take whatever work is available. The much-touted virtues of independence and the creativity of the "flexible workforce" are undoubtedly true for some workers under some conditions. But for millions more, the new work economy adds up to little more than another setback in a losing effort to build some economic security in a world that is tilted against working families.

To get a sufficient number of hours, workers need to be available. But that availability comes at a cost. If she can't go to community college, how will Nicole ever build up her skills and get a better job to support herself and her baby? How will she ever make enough to let go of her rent subsidy or food stamps? How will she ever move to a better neighborhood, one with nice parks and good schools?

It's not just Nicole. How does the guy in the stockroom sign up for auto-repair classes at a nearby vo-tech school if McDonald's won't give him his schedule more than a week in advance? How does the woman working the front office set up a time to take her elderly mother in for checkups and physical therapy if her hours change every three days?

What about the food-service people and office cleaners I speak with in Massachusetts? Working two or three jobs is an economic necessity for them as they try to support their families, but with shifting hours in most places, it's hard for them to piece together schedules that will let them show up when called. Some say they look for all-night cleaning jobs so they can have their days free to take second and third jobs. Childcare is a nightmare. No wonder that woman I met falls asleep the minute she gets to her mother's house.

It's a vicious double crunch: low wages and unpredictable schedules combine to make life an unending struggle for millions of Americans. It all works great for Walmart or the food-service company, but for people like Gina and her friend Nicole, it means they can barely scratch by. And it also means they are likely to keep on scratching by for the rest of their lives.

ANOTHER ONE-TWO PUNCH

I think a lot about the risks families face. Maybe anyone would do the same if she had watched her family go from driving around town in an almost-new station wagon to hearing her mother cry for days at a time as she faced the possibility that the family would be put out on the street. But what strikes me now is how much risk has changed. Long before I was born, people lost jobs and got sick and made bad decisions. My family lived through a very tough time when my daddy had a heart attack, but we recovered. The difference is that today's families live much closer to the edge of a financial cliff—so close that millions of people can feel the bits of rock slipping under their feet long before big trouble strikes.

I've described this change before. I've written more than one book about it. I've talked about it. Sometimes I've even shouted about it. But the problem keeps getting worse.

Families today have been hit by a one-two punch. First, income. The best available apples-to-apples comparison of inflation-adjusted earnings shows what the typical fully employed man earned back in the 1970s and what that same fully employed man earns today. The picture isn't pretty. As the GDP has doubled and almost doubled again, as corporations have piled up record profits, as the country has gotten wealthier, and as the number of billionaires has exploded, the average man working full-time today earns about what the average man earned back in 1970. Nearly half a century has gone by, and the guy right in the middle of the pack is making about what his granddad did.

The second punch that's landed on families is expenses. If costs had stayed the same over the past few decades, families would be okay—or, at least, they would be in about the same position as they were thirty-five years ago. Not advancing but not falling behind, either. But that didn't happen. Total costs are up, way up. True, families have cut back on some kinds of expenses. Today, the average family spends less on food (including eating out), less on clothing, less on appliances, and less on furniture than a comparable family did back in 1971. In other words, families have been pretty careful about their day-to-day spending, but it hasn't saved them.

The problem is that the other expenses—the big, fixed expenses—have shot through the roof and blown apart the family budget. Adjusted for inflation, families today spend more on transportation, more on housing, and more on health insurance. And for all those families with small children and no one at home during the day, the cost of childcare has doubled, doubled again, and doubled once more. Families have pinched pennies on groceries and clothing, but these big, recurring expenses have blown them right over a financial cliff.

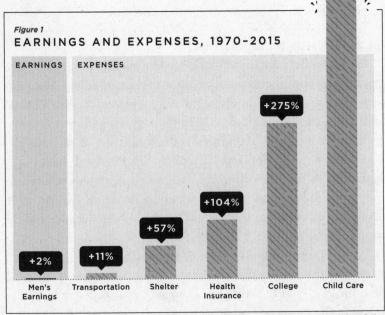

Figure 1
EARNINGS AND EXPENSES, 1970–2015

EARNINGS   EXPENSES

+953%

+275%

+104%

+57%

+11%

+2%

| Men's Earnings | Transportation | Shelter | Health Insurance | College | Child Care |

All figures are adjusted for inflation

From 1970 to 2015, families cut some expenses and income went up a little, but big, fixed expenses skyrocketed.

This one-two punch—flat incomes and rising expenses—has hit the middle class squarely in the gut.

Beginning in the 1970s, many families responded to the growing financial pressure by sending everyone to work. Before then, it was usually just Dad. But as his paycheck flattened, everyone looked for ways to earn—Dad, Mom, and sometimes even the kids. And it helped. As more women took jobs, family incomes went up, and the family-income curve kept rising from the 1970s until the early 2000s. More family members drawing paychecks meant the family made more money overall.

But this new solution came with its own problems. First, many families don't have two people who can go to work. A lot of couples can pull in two incomes, but plenty of them can't. And America has lots of singles—single moms, single dads, singles on their own—and they are flat out of luck. Nicole would love to have someone else in her life who could help pay the rent and raise her baby, but that someone took off a long time ago—and she's got to build some security *right now*.

And that's one more double bind: Nicole and every other single person trying to make it face the same rising expenses that couples face. They struggle with more expensive health care, more expensive housing, more expensive education—the same costs that led other households to send both Dad and Mom to work—but they *can't* send more than one person to work. Instead, they have only one paycheck to keep them afloat.

Even two-income families began to struggle. There were new costs for childcare, transportation, and work clothes. There was more eating out and less mending. That second paycheck wasn't all gravy. On average, full-time care for kids under four now costs more than in-state college tuition.

With everyone in the workforce, new risks began creeping in at the edges. My stay-at-home mom hadn't planned it that way, but when trouble hit, she was our family's safety net. After Daddy had a heart attack, she went to work and brought home a paycheck. No, it wasn't a big paycheck, but it was a *new* paycheck. Today all those single parents flying solo and couples with both partners already working don't have someone new to send to work if there's a crisis. So if the baby gets sick or Grandma falls and breaks her hip, someone has to stay home—and that will cost the family money. And if one of the wage earners becomes seriously ill or is laid off, there's no additional partner to earn a new paycheck. The risks are high, and the safety net has disappeared.

Back in the early 1970s, when the typical family was earning just one income, they were able to put away about 11 percent of their take-home pay in savings. They also had only a sliver of credit card debt—less than 1 percent of their disposable income. But the income/expenses squeeze today means that families have cut their savings by two-thirds while their debt has multiplied a shocking fifteen times.

Now when something goes wrong, they have no savings to fall back on and they are already loaded with debt. (This was the story I told in *The Two-Income Trap*, a book I wrote in 2003 with my daughter, Amelia Tyagi.) Suddenly, when anything goes wrong, all those good, hardworking, solidly middle-class families are tumbling over a cliff.

Gina and Darren fell off that cliff. When both of them had good jobs, they bought a home and then poured every nickel, including their savings and retirement accounts, into keeping it. When Darren couldn't get work or when Gina got sick, it hit their budget like a grenade. And they never had a way to pick up the slack—when they needed extra cash, there was no one else to send out into the workplace. For years they've been working harder and harder, but sometimes she lets out a deep sigh. "The longer I work here," she says, "the farther behind in the bills we are getting."

Gina is the modern-day version of my mother: years ago, she stayed home to raise the kids, but now she's a breadwinner who works long hours for a major retailer. In fact, Gina is better educated and has more work experience than my mom did. Truth be told, she's also a lot feistier. But unlike my mother, Gina can't earn enough to put dinner on the table without help from a food pantry. My mom found a way to save us, but the odds are stacked much higher against Gina and her family.

EVEN HARDER

When America's middle class is under assault, there's pain everywhere, but much of that pain rains down harder on black and Latino families.

The evidence of this assault is especially clear when it comes to homes. Homes are good indicators of stability: when a family has its own home, the kids can go to the neighborhood school and the parents will usually take time to meet the neighbors and maybe even work together to spruce up the playground. Tiny condos and center-hall colonials, triple-deckers and Cape Cod farmhouses—homes are the tangible sign that a family is living the American dream.

Michael had the dream.

He was ready to tell me his story. Unlike Gina, he said, Sure, use my name—Michael J. Smith. Use my picture, too. I'm out there.

Michael is African American, married, and in his fifties. He's a big guy, solidly built, with large hands. His smile is soft and almost sweet, and his voice is deep and reassuring; the gentle rhythms of his speech evoke his early years growing up in the South. For decades, Michael has been very involved in his church. More than once, he said to me, "It truly is our faith that keeps us going."

When Michael's family moved from Atlanta to the Woodlawn neighborhood of Chicago in the 1960s, his family and church held him close. There were gangs in his neighborhood, but Michael stayed on the path he believed in—God and family—and he never made a big decision without praying on it first.

As Michael tells his story, he warms up to all the good memories. In his twenties, he got a good job, married his high school sweetheart, and had three kids. They divorced, but he remarried soon after, and he and his wife, Janet, have a daughter named Ashley. From the first paycheck he ever took home, Michael started saving to make a down payment on a home. He and Janet bought their first home in Richton Park, a suburb of Chicago. As Michael put it, he always wanted "a neighborhood that was safe, that I could raise my children in, that was fenced in in the front and the back." He particularly wanted his kids to have a yard to play in.

He kept those dreams front and center. Michael had a good job with DHL delivering packages and loading planes. Sometimes he was called on to do a lot of heavy lifting and there was pressure to get things done quickly, but he describes his time at DHL as "the most satisfying work I've ever done." Janet worked at Chase for twenty-seven years, and she was proud that she had never missed a payment on any bill—ever. They kept right on saving, and after a few years Michael moved his family again, first to Hazel Crest, a predominantly African American suburb, and then to Homewood, which was more diverse.

When Michael spoke to me about the move to Homewood, he said, "We thought that we could do a little better." But he and Janet didn't jump right in. "We thought about it, prayed about it, looked at the numbers, and we had more than enough."

Michael talks about the house he and Janet bought like it's a beloved child. He tells about the three arches at the front of the house and about the pine trees in the backyard. He also wants me to know about the hedges out front where robins built a nest every spring. "We never clipped the hedges while the robins were there," he notes. "They like their privacy."

His conclusion: "We had kind of a great American story."

Then the crash of 2008 hit and the bottom fell out. In the space of a few months, DHL eliminated 14,900 jobs—including Michael's.

After sixteen years on the job, he felt like he'd been run over by one of his own trucks. Frantically, he spent the months that followed looking for part-time work wherever he could find it. But no one was hiring, and he quickly understood that he had no chance of getting a full-time job that paid as well as his old one and offered health insurance. By this time, Janet was no longer working at the bank, and Michael's unemployment checks didn't cover even their basic expenses. In the blink of an eye, Michael's whole world had turned upside down.

A lousy mortgage made a bad situation worse. Michael and Janet had started out with a plain-vanilla, fixed-rate thirty-year mortgage. They weren't in the house long when a mortgage broker talked them into refinancing, which meant that they agreed to take on a complex mortgage. Michael now realizes that it was a great deal for the bank, but not so much for his family. Once the mortgage payments ballooned and he lost his job, it was the kind of double blow that almost no family can survive.

Somewhere in his heart, Michael knew that his family was doomed. Even so, he held out for as long as he could.

Ashley was now in high school and deeply engaged in her music, playing both the piano and the viola. Michael told me that when it was time to go to school in the mornings, "We did not need to wake her up, because she was so passionate about her instruments, she'd get up on her own." Ashley was beginning to dream that she could pursue a music career; someday maybe she could play with a major symphony orchestra. Michael and Janet paid for extra music lessons for their daughter. "It was important to us to keep her encouraged and inspired," Michael said. To make ends meet, they sold one of their two cars, as well as some of Janet's jewelry. Michael even sold his wedding ring.

While they cut their expenses to the bone, their financial situation kept sliding downhill. Michael looked everywhere for work, taking anything anyone offered. They kept scrambling, but the numbers just wouldn't add up.

Then the phone rang. Did Michael want to come back to DHL? The company was hiring back twelve people. That was twelve out of nine hundred former employees from his branch. Michael was sorry about the other people, but it felt good—very good—to be one of the chosen twelve.

The offer seemed like a godsend—a good job doing work he loved. And somewhere down deep, it felt like respect as well. It meant that someone like Michael who tried hard and did a great job would be rewarded for the extra energy he put into his work.

But the story turned out a little differently. This time DHL wasn't offering him his old full-time job with benefits. This time he was offered part-time work, no guaranteed hours, no benefits.

Welcome to work—twenty-first century–style.

Yes, the job moved Michael from "unemployed" to "employed" on the government statistics. Yes, he had a paycheck. Yes, he was grateful.

But Michael didn't fool himself. "I knew right away it wasn't enough, because my mortgage was too much for me to pay. It was not enough to sustain myself and my family." He shook his head. "It was just an unbearable situation."

As Michael and Janet spiraled toward foreclosure, they desperately tried to work things out with the bank. With hindsight, Michael reflected on how the broker had persuaded him to take on the new mortgage: "I felt like I had been scammed." At one point, he considered suing, but he backed away from the idea after he thought about how much money it would cost to hire a lawyer and how fast his home was slipping away.

Finally the bank moved in to foreclose on the family's home. Michael described his growing depression: "I can remember myself many, many times looking out the window of the house in despair, praying, 'What am I going to do?'"

And then this big, prayerful man—this strong man who had kept the gangs at bay, this determined man who had saved and scratched and purchased a home for his family—this man just gave up.

When Michael and Janet lost their home in foreclosure, their $17,000 down payment disappeared. Their credit rating was trashed. Their financial lives were destroyed.

Michael repeats the date his life changed like a mantra: 10/10/10. That's the day the family moved out and Michael handed the keys over to the bank.

But for Michael, it still wasn't over. He and Janet rented a place nearby. Their former home sat vacant, and every time Michael went to the grocery store or one of the local shops, he would pass the house. When it snowed, the snow just piled up. Every time he saw the place, he relived the failure. His house—*his* house—sat abandoned. So finally he went back to the house again, this time with a shovel, and removed the snow from the driveway and the front walk.

As winter gave way to spring and then to summer, Michael looked after the house and mowed the lawn. He checked on the robins. After he swept up around the place, he would talk with his old neighbors. Several of them had stored the family's belongings, and when they had garage sales, they included Michael and Janet's things and passed along the cash to the family.

Month after month, Michael kept going by the house, thinking about the life he and his family had once built there. Shaking his head, he told

*Michael still keeps a picture of the door of his foreclosed home,
with Ashley peeking through the window.*

me, "I just got this horrible pain in the pit of my stomach every time I
went past it."

How does Michael describe the 2008 crash? "It broke my heart."

I CAN'T LOOK at photos of smiling mortgage company CEOs or read about
the latest multimillion-dollar bonuses for Goldman Sachs partners
without thinking of Michael and his beloved house with the robins in the

hedges. The executives of the giant financial institutions figured they had invented gold. The formula was simple: first, make a fortune by tricking families into signing on to really lousy mortgages; next, make another fortune by bundling those mortgages together and selling them to unsuspecting pension funds and municipalities; and finally, when it all blows up, go to the government for a gigantic handout.

I guarantee that not one of those corporate executives who crashed the economy lost his home. It's also a pretty safe bet that while Michael was shoveling snow or mowing the grass at a house he no longer owned, they had already moved on to their next big financial deal. And now those big banks and those same insiders are partying hard again. They don't care about the Michaels of the world—they didn't on 10/10/10, and they don't now.

There's another layer to the foreclosure story of black and Latino families around the country: discrimination. Ugly, nasty, vile discrimination.

What did mortgage discrimination against black and Latino families look like? Did mortgage brokers sit around and say, "Here are some really stinky mortgages—let's push these off to black families"? Or did they think, "Here's a Latino family, and they probably won't notice if we just shovel some crazy fees and the highest possible prices on them"? Or did they tell each other, "Here's zip code such-and-such, and we can sell a lot of garbage mortgages there," and zip code such-and-such turned out to be a predominantly black or heavily Hispanic neighborhood?

I don't know what happened in the back office, and the mortgage brokers aren't talking. But I do know that regardless of what they were thinking, the impact was the same. Whether the brokers targeted black and Latino families or whether they just stumbled over them, they destroyed the lives of a lot of people.

As the eventual investigations showed, even when adjusted for credit ratings, African American and Latino families consistently got the worst of the worst in mortgage deals around. Countrywide, now a subsidiary of Bank of America, admitted that in just five years, it discriminated against two hundred thousand black and Latino families, systematically targeting them for higher-priced, more dangerous loans than it offered to white families with the same credit histories. And that was just one lender.

Mortgage discrimination often starts with redlining—avoiding zip codes where African American or Latino borrowers are more likely to live. For instance, people analyzing loan data say that the California-based OneWest Bank has shunned nonwhite mortgage borrowers for years. And in city after city, from Los Angeles and Chicago to Miami and New York, banks have paid millions of dollars in fines over discriminatory lending practices. The list is long and shameful.

Did Michael's lender target him because he was black or because of where he lived or just because he was unlucky enough to get the next crappy loan Chase was pushing out to anyone who answered the phone? However it happened, once his mortgage payments started ratcheting up, there was no way Michael could keep that home. And here's the part that really rubs hard: the banks knew that the chances that he would lose his house were high from the day he signed the mortgage refinancing papers—high, but well hidden in the fine print. Michael had been sold a mortgage that was like a grenade with the pin already pulled out.

As he slid toward foreclosure, Michael suspected that he'd been targeted because he was black. "I really did," he told me. "When they found out who I was, especially when it came time to redoing the loan . . ." His voice trailed off.

For Michael, confirmation came later, when he was struggling to hang on to his home. It was at the height of the financial crisis, and he had gone to the Chicago convention center for an event for people in trouble with their home mortgages. He described the scene: thousands of people were lined up, all facing foreclosures and all hoping to find a way to save their homes. He was there for thirteen hours, and as he waited his turn for advice, he looked around. "Thousands of African Americans were there at that time," he recalled. "The place was just filled with African Americans and Hispanics. That told me who was targeted."

Latinos were crushed by the housing crash as well. In the wake of the Great Recession of 2008, nearly one in three Hispanic households had zero or negative net worth. Over the period from 2005 to 2009, Hispanic household wealth dropped 66 percent. Research showed, as the *Washington*

Post reported, that "blacks and Latinos were more than 70 percent more likely to lose their homes to foreclosure during that period."

Years after the financial crash, signs of housing discrimination persist. After analyzing its extensive 2013 data, Zillow reported that compared to whites, African Americans and Latinos are more than twice as likely to be turned down for a mortgage. Government data from 2015 also shows that the hurdles for homeownership are higher for both blacks and Latinos.

Discrimination in the rental market is also widely documented. In 2016, a Connecticut real estate firm paid thousands of dollars to settle allegations that it had discriminated against minority applicants for apartments, including offering a white applicant an apartment tour while denying a tour to an African American applicant. Also in 2016, the Department of Housing and Urban Development settled with a California apartment complex that discriminated against Mexican applicants by refusing their forms of identification while accepting a Canadian's ID. And this sort of discrimination has been going on for a long time: favoring white renters while turning away black renters, for instance, is pretty much what was happening in some of President Trump's apartment buildings back in the 1960s and 1970s—and which ultimately resulted in a settlement with the Department of Justice.

The housing collapse wiped out trillions of dollars in family wealth nationwide, but the crash hit African Americans and Latinos like a tidal wave. And the hit was doubly hard because these were the families that, generation after generation, had already been aggressively discriminated against in housing. Restrictive deeds, land sales contracts, redlining—American history is littered with examples of housing laws and lending strategies that were designed to deny black and Hispanic families mortgages and that prevented them from building housing wealth.

For most middle-class families in America, purchasing a home is the best way to build financial security. A home isn't just a place to live; it's also a retirement plan: pay off the house and live on Social Security. A home provides financial credibility and reassures a banker that someone is a good risk to start a business. A home provides a way to help the kids make it through college and a safety net if someone gets really sick. And, if all goes well and the grandparents can stay in their home until they die, a home can give the next generation a boost. Selling that home can provide a family with the money needed to move up the ladder, which, in turn, means that the grandchildren will have better chances in life.

That was the big and brilliant idea. Start with homeownership, build a little more security, and then build a little more and a little more. Diversify into retirement savings, maybe get a better job or start a business, help the kids, and then the grandkids—and keep the ball rolling forward. And it worked that way, one generation after another, for much of the twentieth century, at least for white Americans. But for black and Latino Americans, it was like swimming with rocks in your pocket: possible, but a lot harder.

Housing discrimination isn't the only way systemic racism pulls black and Latino families down. Discrimination has been thoroughly documented in criminal justice, in employment, in education, in auto lending, in access to bankruptcy relief, and in health care—even in access to stores that sell fresh produce. The cumulative impact of decade after decade of discrimination becomes painfully obvious in just a handful of economic snapshots:

- Among those who work full-time, African Americans earn 59 cents and Latinos earn 70 cents for every dollar earned by whites.
- For each dollar a college degree adds to the income of a black or Latino graduate, the same degree adds about $11 to $13 for whites.
- Compared to whites, African Americans are 80 percent more likely to be unemployed; for Latinos, that figure is 37 percent.
- Compared to white families, black families are 68 percent more likely, and Latino families twice as likely, to have nothing in retirement savings.

The financial crash pounded all families, regardless of race. The devastation wasn't, however, evenly spread out. Everyone—blacks, Latinos, whites—got cheated on mortgages, but a much higher proportion of blacks and Latinos got cheated. And when they got cheated, everyone—blacks, Latinos, whites—often got wiped out, but a higher proportion of blacks and Latinos had nothing else to fall back on. Blacks and Latinos had lower incomes and less in savings, and they got less help from other family members. The lesson is clear: economic racism makes every other problem worse.

Michael will never get over the 2008 crash. The memory of the day he and his family packed up and moved out will be with him forever. Whatever else happens in his life, he will always recall shoveling the snow and mowing the lawn and checking on the robins long after the bank had taken away his home.

A handful of Wall Street insiders boosted their companies' short-term profits and pumped up their own fat bonuses by selling financial grenades with the pins pulled out, and millions of people like Michael ended up with their lives blown apart. I know life isn't fair, but how did our country get to the point where this much unfairness became business as usual? Surely we are a better people than that.

YOUNG DREAMS

In the spring of 1966, when I was sixteen, I started going home every day for lunch. The house was empty, because Mother was working at Sears and Daddy was out selling fences. But I wasn't there for company; I just wanted to check the mail.

I had found two prospective colleges, one by searching through a book in the high school counselor's office and one through a boy I knew; both schools bragged about their debate scholarships. I was a good debater—on my way to the state championship—and I figured that was my chance. So I'd taken the cash from babysitting and waitressing and bought two money orders from the 7-Eleven to cover the two application fees, then played the waiting game. I was putting all my chips on the hope that one of those places would give me a big enough scholarship to make it possible for me to go to college. And now I was praying that one of them would come through.

By that spring, college was all I could focus on. Ever since I'd been a little girl, I had wanted to be a teacher. And no one gets to be a teacher without a college degree.

For weeks, nothing turned up. Friends were getting their acceptances and starting to talk about which dorms they would live in or what majors they would declare. And I kept going home for lunch.

One day I dashed out of history class the instant the bell rang. As I came around the corner onto our street, I saw the red flag up on the mailbox, signaling that we had mail. Inside lay two fat envelopes, one on top of the other. I stood in our front yard and tore into each one. The first letter was from Northwestern. The university was offering me a scholarship, a work-study job, and a student loan. I quickly did the calculations and saw that I would still need to come up with maybe another $1,000 or so each year—an amount I could just about cover with a summer job. This was it: I could go to college. For sure.

Then I ripped open the second letter, from George Washington University, and—wow!—it was offering a full scholarship and a federal loan. That was all I needed to know: then and there I decided to become a GW Colonial. I had never seen either school, and I didn't know how I'd get to Washington or where I would live, but even so, I was headed to GW!

I sprung it on my parents that night. They already knew about the applications, but no one had said anything for months. We'd all been waiting, just tiptoeing around until the news came in. Now I was dancing around the kitchen big-time, waving the forms and talking about the humongous size of the scholarship (or, at least, that's how it seemed at the time). Daddy grinned. Good on you, punkin.

Mother was more shocked, but she recovered. College—and a way to pay for it—was now possible. Within days, she told every grandparent, aunt, uncle, cousin, neighbor, grocer, dry cleaner, preacher, and person she met on the street that I was going to college. She always noted that she didn't want me to go so far away, then explained, "Betsy figured out how to go to college for free, so what could I say?" I think she invented humblebragging before others perfected it into a fine art.

And just in case I was about to get a swelled head, she usually added, even with the news about the scholarship, "But I don't know if she'll ever get married."

On Labor Day weekend before I headed back for my junior year at GW, my first boyfriend (and the first boy to dump me) dropped back into

Me as a college student,
ready to take on the world.

my life. He was now twenty-two, a college grad with a good job, and evidently he had decided it was time to get married. He proposed, and about a nanosecond later, I said yes. At nineteen, I said hello, housewife; goodbye, college. It was definitely not the smartest move I ever made.

But I was living in a time of second chances, and I got lucky again. Even a girl shortsighted enough to give up a full scholarship could get back in the game. Before long, I was back in school, hitting the books at a commuter college that cost $50 a semester. This was an education I could pay for on a part-time waitressing job. I saw that chance, and this time I was smart enough to grab it with both hands and hold on for dear life.

Two years later, I got my first job teaching special-needs kids.

COLLEGE IS THE way up—at least, that's what we believe. For me, college was a chance to fly.

But for today's college students, flying is a whole lot harder. Every time I talk with a college student today, I'm reminded of how lucky I was and how much has changed since I was stutter-stepping my way toward a college degree all those years ago.

I was introduced to Kai through a friend. In October 2016, we agreed to meet at a restaurant within walking distance from my house in Cambridge, Massachusetts. Kai was in her late twenties. As she stood up from the table to say hello, I was struck by her eyes. She was lively and interested in everything around her. She commented on the restaurant, the menu, the silverware, the dishes, the light in the room, the drawings on the wall—and that was only in the first five minutes. Tall and dark-haired, she was an impressive young woman, the kind who could take on the world and succeed anywhere.

She was more than willing to tell me her story, but she didn't want me to use her real name because she was embarrassed about how things had turned out. We agreed that I'd also change some details of her story to protect her privacy.

Kai grew up in Colorado. Even as a kid, she'd had a plan about her future. Her dad was a firefighter, and they loved spending time together playing computer games. It was their time. She explained that she had been playing video games "since as long as I could walk." She knew she wanted to create those games.

Kai was interested in what she saw on the screen, but as she learned more about the science and art underneath those graphics, her interests expanded. From ATMs to airline check-in kiosks to advanced medical imaging equipment, front-end designers are now walking people through more than just games; they now lead people through events across our economy. Kai knew that if she got the right education, she could land a career in a field she had been training for since her daddy lifted her up for her first game.

Neither of Kai's parents had gone to college, and she didn't get college counseling from anyone in her high school. She was pretty much on her own to figure out what would be the right school. She didn't want to study art theory in a big lecture hall. Instead, she wanted hands-on work and sophisticated training that would prepare her for a real job.

Kai worked hard in school, but that wasn't enough.

When she saw a TV commercial for the Art Institutes, a nationwide system of art schools, she thought, "This is it!" The promotional materials were amazing. "One of the deciding factors for me choosing to attend the Art Institute," she explained, "was its focus on being a 'career college' that didn't deal with the typical four-year-college experience driven by fraternities or social events."

Kai now blasted off full speed ahead. "I wanted to be surrounded by professional artists and designers, all aiming for the common goal of making it into the industry with focus and determination," she told me. Her older sister lived outside Seattle, so Kai worked out a way to move in with her and save on expenses when she enrolled in the Art Institute of Seattle (AIS). She was ready to take on the world.

Kai's first two years in college were a lot tougher than mine. She got up at five o'clock every morning to catch a ferry to Seattle and then ride a bus to the school. She saw two years of sunrises, but she never complained about the early hours or the long commute. She was a little uneasy about whether she was learning the cutting-edge material prominently featured in the promotional materials, but she loved being around computers and working with graphics. To support herself, she worked part-time at Barnes & Noble. Even so, she kept her priorities straight. She attended every class and did every scrap of homework. Kai was proud of her 3.9 GPA, and she was determined to keep it up.

Sometimes on those long commutes, Kai thought about her finances. She knew she could do the classwork at AIS, but by the time she reached the two-year mark, she had already run up $45,000 in student loans. That was a lot of money.

Early in Kai's third year, the whole thing came crashing down. The Art Institute of Seattle wasn't like the state schools back home. It was one of fifty college campuses around the country owned by a multi-billion-dollar corporation. That corporation, Education Management Corporation, and its highly paid executives were looking to haul in big bucks for themselves and their investors by scooping up Kai's federal student loan money.

Kai hadn't known it when she'd started out as a freshman, but the Art Institutes were in trouble. Complaints about fraudulent promises, fake records, and programs that didn't deliver were piling up. The Justice Department opened an investigation, and by Kai's third year, her program began falling apart. Faculty and staff members were laid off. The program's reputation took a nosedive. People said the credential it conferred was useless. Kai heard that AIS was shutting down the program, and she panicked. She was worried that even if AIS survived, her diploma might not be worth anything. Besides, she didn't want to lose a year, so she went into high gear, determined to find another school in a hurry.

Kai was doing work she really loved, and she was more committed than ever to getting her degree in video game art and design. When she discovered the program at Ringling College of Art and Design, in Florida, she decided to pull up stakes and go. She would have to move across the country, and she wouldn't have her sister to provide free housing, but her enthusiasm bubbled over. "There were more resources, more connections and opportunities," she explained. "It was more of an Ivy League, as far as art schools go, and so there were possibilities of putting money into endeavors that supported the students' success."

Kai packed her belongings, kissed her sister good-bye, and headed across country to Sarasota, Florida. New school, new program, new part of the country. She could take it all on. But the one part that made her hands shake was the cost. While Ringling wasn't part of a big for-profit company, it wasn't a public school either. As a private school, its students have to bear all the expenses. Kai took on another $30,500 in debt to pay for one year. That was on top of the nearly $55,000 in debt from AIS.

She loved the classwork, but she couldn't finance a second year. She just couldn't do it. Kai hated to leave Florida, but she refused to give up. Instead, she moved back home and started attending classes at the University of Colorado. That school didn't have the same video-design programs, but it was much less expensive. She figured that she'd spend a year at the University of Colorado, get her degree, and then land the job of her dreams. Okay, she might not get her dream job right at the beginning, but she felt certain that she was born to work in the gaming industry and that once she got in the first door, she could kick open other doors for herself. Over time, she would pay down her student loans and start a real life.

Only there was just one small hitch: she needed yet another student loan to attend her new college. So she added another $13,000 to her debt load, which pushed her total to about $100,000. And because she had hit her maximum under the federal loan program, she now owed money to both the government and Wells Fargo.

During her last semester at the University of Colorado, when she thought she was just a few weeks away from graduation, the registrar's office informed her that most of the credits from her first two years at AIS wouldn't transfer. Students like Kai often find out too late that for-profit schools like AIS don't meet the standards set by accreditors of state colleges and universities. After some back-and-forth, the university's administrators explained that she would have to attend the school full-time for two more years before she could earn her diploma.

Kai hit the wall. After years of sacrifice and hard work, completing college suddenly seemed out of reach. "I couldn't afford it," she told me. "Wells Fargo wouldn't give any more, my parents still couldn't afford it, and honestly, at that point, I was done."

It was also a personally difficult time. Kai's dad was dealing with brain cancer, and the pressure was more than she could bear.

Kai didn't finish the semester at the University of Colorado, and she never got her degree. So where is she now? She is twenty-seven, living with another sister in Connecticut, waiting tables at an Italian restaurant. She puts every penny of her paycheck toward her loans—literally every penny. "If it wasn't for my family," she says, "I would be homeless and poverty-stricken." And even with this level of commitment, and after five and a half years of payments, her loan balance is still over $90,000.

This is the point in the story when all her apparent confidence drains away. Her hands drop to her lap, and she looks down at the table: "I'm the poster child for what not to do."

KAI PLACES ALL the blame on herself, but I don't see it that way. Kai was doing exactly what everyone told her to do: work hard and get a good education. She didn't goof off and party. She kept her grades up. She had good recommendations from her professors. She had chosen a career path that promised a good job. Yes, she would have been better off if she hadn't been taken in by a for-profit college and then set her heart on attending a high-priced private art school. But I don't put all of that on the shoulders of a seventeen-year-old high school senior trying to figure out how to build a future.

Of course, Kai would also have been financially better off if she had been born into a family that could shell out $100,000 for her education— but I don't put that on her, either.

Kai now joins the millions of Americans who have incurred student loans—some of them monstrously big—and have no diploma to show for it. And even when these young people do have a diploma, that alone won't always do the trick. One and a half million people over age twenty-five have college diplomas but no jobs.

Kai's story speaks of everything that's broken with American higher education. She went through a college search process that runs on parallel tracks: rich kids benefit from parents who can work their connections and hire expensive coaches to help them make perfect matches with perfect schools, while middle-class kids like Kai get a hearty "good luck" from an overworked guidance counselor. After graduating from high school, Kai got snared in the trap laid by for-profit schools. These places are pulling in one out of every ten people who go off to college, getting them signed up for huge federal loans, and often leaving them with little to show for it. Even when Kai finally made her way to a terrific state school, she came smack up against the hard reality that the school still cost more than she could afford.

Years ago, I got lucky with my scholarship. Later, when I returned to college and earned my degree, it cost me only $50 a semester. I grew up when America was investing in education and keeping the doors open wide for any kid who had the pluck to come in and do the work. But since the mid-1970s, the cost of an education at a state school, adjusted for inflation, has quadrupled. And it shows. Today, two-thirds of kids in state schools must borrow money to make it to graduation.

Ah, the debt. The bone-crunching, never-ending debt. Kai works every day just to tread water on her student loans. Her $90,000 adds just a tiny bump to the giant ball of outstanding student loan debt nation-wide. She has joined an army of Americans who are struggling to pay back money they borrowed to get an education. The way I see it, every happy-face story about this economy should include a footnote that tags this fact: forty million people are trying to figure out how to pay off a combined $1.4 trillion in student loan debt.

That debt is toxic in more ways than one. It casts a huge shadow on a person's credit report, driving up the cost of everything from insurance to a home mortgage. And unlike a home mortgage, student loans can't be refinanced when interest rates drop. And unlike casino loans or credit card debt, these loans can't be discharged in bankruptcy when the borrower can't pay.

The loans can also chop off big parts of a former student's future. In Kai's case, they kill her opportunity to take out a mortgage to buy a home. They kill her chances to borrow more money to go to school and finish her degree. Without that degree, those loans kill her dream of get-ting an entry-level job in a business that employs people with a degree in visual arts. And she can just plain forget about building up a little savings, buying health insurance, or stashing away some cash for retirement.

Kai still sees visual arts as "her field." But will she ever work there? Her answer is short and defeated: "No."

Kai and her friends were born into a country that told them to work hard in school, get a good education, and the world would be theirs. But a grim new reality is starting to sink in: they can work their butts off and they still won't be able to carve out a place for themselves in the middle class.

Kai and her friends have prepared themselves for the future better than any other generation in history. They are more educated: today a higher proportion of young people graduate from high school, graduate from college, and even pick up postgrad degrees. They have more part-time work experience from their high school and college years. They are computer savvy, and their experience with technology often makes them teachers rather than apprentices to people a generation older.

As young people enter the job market and begin to put shape to their lives, they should be flying high. But they aren't.

- The unemployment rate for people sixteen to twenty-four years old who are actively looking for jobs is 12 percent—almost three times higher than for their older counterparts.
- The $1.4 trillion burden of student loan debt that's being carried by those who went to college is unlike any in history—and the amount keeps climbing, at a rate of about $100 billion a year.
- For the first time in modern American history, more people between eighteen and thirty-five live with their parents than have a place of their own.
- The odds that a young person today will earn more than their parents have gone from a near certainty a generation ago to a coin flip today.
- Despite their better educations, today's millennials earn about 20 percent less than boomers earned at the same point in their lives.

Young people—America's future—have been dealt a terrible hand. Those who don't make it through college have little chance of making it into the middle class. And those who make it through college are often so swamped with debt that they begin their adult lives in a deep financial hole. College is the big divide between those who will have a lottery ticket for the middle class and those who won't, but in the end, even for those who get a diploma, it's still only a lottery ticket. Millions of college graduates today are unemployed or working at temp jobs or part-time jobs or jobs that don't require a college degree, trying to get a foothold in an economy that is no longer providing expanded opportunity for anyone who can flash a diploma.

Today twenty-five-year-olds start their adult lives in an economy where the most sustained job growth is in minimum-wage and near-minimum-wage work. Many have no realistic chance of ever owning the kinds of homes their parents purchased or ever starting the kinds of businesses their parents did. Today's young people may be the first generation in American history to end up worse off than their parents.

Kai's story breaks my heart—and the unfairness of it makes me want to spit. How can the country that once gave a kid like me multiple chances to do something with my life now shut out a talented and hardworking young woman like Kai? How can any country expect to build a future if there's no room for a person like Kai to get an education, start down the road toward a good career, and build the foundation of a good life?

THE SQUEEZE NEVER STOPS

When she was younger, Gina worked hard to build that foundation. As she's aged, however, it has all but crumbled. She is fifty now, and when she thinks about retirement, she seems to be at a loss. "In a perfect world, I can retire to Key Largo," she says, and then she gives her throaty laugh. But in her real world? "You know what? I don't really know." She notes that climbing up and down ladders and carrying loads of shingles is taking a toll on Darren. He is really feeling his arthritis. "He said he'll probably die outside," she tells me, trying not to sound too downbeat. Mostly, she tries not to think about the future too much. "Just hope for the best," she says.

The economic punches that have hit America's middle class have reverberated through their retirement years. Once again, the numbers that lurk just underneath the overall good news about the economy tell a grim story:

- Bankruptcy filings for people sixty-five and over have increased almost fourfold since 1991.
- For fifteen million seniors, Social Security is all that stands between them and poverty.
- Among seniors who live in nursing homes, 62 percent don't have enough money to cover the cost of their care.
- Nearly half of all families don't have a single dollar put away in a retirement account.

Part of the economic problem starts with good news: people are living longer. The fastest-growing age group in America is known as the "old-old," the term coined to describe people eighty-five and up. The next-fastest-growing group includes those aged seventy-five to eighty-four, and the one after that is for those sixty-five to seventy-four. Yes, there's a pattern here.

That's heartening for everyone who is facing old age and for everyone who loves to have a grandma or grandpa around to buy ice cream and admire every crayon drawing the kids produce. But it also means that retirement now costs more than it used to, a whole lot more. People retiring today at sixty-five need enough money to sustain them for an average of twenty more years. That's about four years longer than they needed in 1970.

Retirees also need to worry about the rising expenses of those final years, particularly for health care and nursing homes. Today, the average cost of a semiprivate room in a nursing home is more than $82,000 a year, and the costs just keep going up.

Rising costs: sound familiar? In fact, many of the problems facing those who are approaching their later years are a lot like the problems facing other working families. But for older people, the punches land just as they are ending their working years and heading into retirement.

It starts with savings. Once again, the top-line number looks great: Americans have saved a total of $25 trillion for retirement. Wow! Let's order a double round of desserts from the Denny's senior special!

Not so fast. "Retirement savings" includes a lot of fancy investments that are held by folks at the tippy top of the income scale. A handful of CEOs and superstars have socked away large fortunes, but for most workers, the numbers are still surprisingly grim. The median worker—the person right in the middle of all those who have retirement accounts—has only $18,433 tucked away. And they are the lucky ones. About half of families have nothing saved. Zero. Zip. Hmm: maybe we should change that celebratory dessert to one small dish of ice cream with two spoons?

And what about those employer plans? By the 1960s, about half of all private sector workers had retirement plans that guaranteed benefits for life. Today that number is down to about 13 percent. As corporate executives figured out that they could boost profits (and their own compensation packages) by squeezing rank-and-file workers, generous retirement plans were put on the chopping block. With every passing year, those employer plans look more like an endangered species headed for extinction.

But Social Security can make up the difference, right? Wrong. Social Security has one wonderful feature: no one ever stops receiving money. The monthly check came regularly even for the lady in Worcester, Massachusetts, who, at 113, was the oldest living American. Social Security also has one really lousy feature: it's not much money to live on. On average, recipients get less than $16,200 a year.

It's tough out there for seniors, and since the economy is going gangbusters, why not give them a little raise? After all, cost of living increases for those on Social Security have been tiny—or nonexistent—in recent years. In 2015, CEOs got a 3.9 percent raise—and seniors living on Social Security got bupkis. Hoping to correct that obvious mistake, I recently proposed a bill to stitch up the tax loophole that lets corporations take a tax deduction whenever they give an executive a bonus over a million dollars, with the idea that we could use the same money to give seniors (and veterans and people with disabilities) a one-time 3.9 percent raise. Corporations could still dispense those bonuses; they just wouldn't be getting tax subsidies from everyone else. Made sense to me.

But—no surprise—the Republicans wouldn't let the bill get anywhere. And also no surprise: I was beyond frustrated. I wanted to call every one of those naysayers and yell, "*You* try paying rent, utilities, grocery bills, car expenses, insurance, and health-care copays on $1,348 a month—then come back in here and vote."

Gina tries not to get too anxious about her own future, but she often worries about her coworkers. Once, she talked about Hank, the produce manager at the Walmart where she works. Hank is sixty-five, but he can't even think about retirement. In fact, he worries about losing this job and wonders where he could earn another paycheck. Gina paused. Hank's not alone—his mother works at the Dollar Tree forty-five minutes away. "She's eighty-seven years old," Gina said. "She had her knees replaced so she can keep working. She has to work."

Good grief! I'm glad that Hank's mom is still able to get up and go to work at eighty-seven. But is that America's retirement plan: work until you drop dead? Can we really call this progress?

One in five Americans is still working after age sixty-five, but that's a short-term solution at best. And for people who physically can't perform their jobs anymore—construction workers who have been beat up by the job, nurses who have spent years holding up tottering patients or rolling them over in bed, teachers who have picked up children all day long in preschool, kitchen workers who are on their feet all day and carrying heavy loads—it's often a real struggle to keep working until sixty-five, much less beyond. Darren's arthritis is starting to cripple his hands, and he often needs a boost to get out of a chair—and he's only in his fifties. Even so, he is still out there day after day, bidding for jobs and trying to pull in enough money so the family doesn't have to hit the food pantry early. No wonder Gina can't explain their retirement plan. It's the same as Hank's mom's plan: work till you drop.

For someone who has a home that is fully paid for, Social Security might be enough to cover their other expenses. But an increasing number of Americans are entering their retirement years still shouldering a heavy mortgage. Today nearly one in three homeowners sixty-five or older is still carrying a mortgage—and the amount of mortgage debt has jumped 82 percent in just a decade. Rent is getting higher too, and finding housing that is accessible for older adults is a tough challenge in most communities.

More mortgages and bigger mortgages are weighing down a lot of seniors, but for many of them, selling the family home isn't a good option. An estimated 3.5 million people fifty or older owe more than their homes are worth.

So how are they making it? Even though they are employing lots of strategies to save money, millions of seniors are slipping into debt. They cover basic expenses by using credit cards, and in many cases they won't be able to pay off that debt. For more and more seniors who find themselves in a downward spiral, bankruptcy is the only answer.

The story of today's seniors—the need to work longer, the mounting debts, the slide into bankruptcy—is mostly a bleak continuation of the bigger story of what has happened to America's working families over the last generation. The squeeze caused by flat wages and rising expenses, the relentless chipping away at steady hours and predictable schedules, and the risks of trying to make it in an increasingly uncertain world take their toll. These problems translate into less savings and higher debts that pile up over time. And as challenging as these problems can be during the working years, they land a crushing blow at retirement.

People work hard for most of their lives, and they hope to retire with some dignity. For the majority, this means living independently; they aim to have enough money to cover their expenses without having to rely on their children. But for millions of Americans, that dream of independence is dropping away.

At eighty-seven, Hank's mom doesn't want to make it harder for Hank, so five days a week she gets up, takes her medicines, pulls on her clothes, fills her thermos with coffee, and leaves home in time to punch the clock at Dollar Tree. Her plan is to keep pushing herself out the door at eighty-eight. And eighty-nine. And ninety. And forever.

THE LAST THREADS OF FAITH

My brother David was the kid with the paper route when he was eight, and he was buying and selling cars by the time he was fourteen. He was always up by five a.m., and he always had some deal going. After he got out of the army, he started his own small business, and when that one didn't work out, he started another and then another. His nervous energy and quick smile made him a natural salesman, and he put it all on the line to build a life for his wife and kids. The kids are grown up, and his wife lost a battle with breast cancer. And in the end, he got caught up in the larger economic hurricanes that swept through America. Today he and his dog, Blondie, live on his Social Security and some family help.

We were on the phone a while back, talking about the economy—the rising stock market, record corporate profits, CEOs making tens of millions of dollars. David paused for a moment, then said, "Did you hear about the three guys sitting in a bar, having a few beers, when Bill Gates walks in?"

I'm always the straight man in these exchanges. "No. So what happened?"

"One guy yelled, 'Woo-hoo! On average, everyone in the bar is now a billionaire!'"

And there it is. On average, we're doing great.

It's time to raise this question: Is this the best that capitalism has to offer? A booming stock market and a rich payoff for those with big investment portfolios and fancy corporate jobs, while everyone else is left hanging on by their fingernails?

Like everyone else, I want our economy to be great. But an economy is great only if it produces the things we value most, things like security and a chance for our children to do better than we did.

Those blind spots in our economic headlines are hiding a lot of misery. GDP, corporate profits, and employment stats give us important measures of economic activity, but they don't tell us everything we need to know. Our riches—and our aching pain—can't be measured by lumping all of us together. Instead of boasting about terrific averages, we need to focus on who is benefitting from a growing GDP and who cashes in on those corporate profits and what employment looks like to the tens of millions of people who draw a weekly paycheck.

We should do better. We should be measuring our successes and failures by testing the way we live day to day, person by person and family by family. Those tests should be pretty straightforward:

- Is our economy producing opportunities for pretty much anyone who works hard to get ahead?
- Is our economy producing security, so that people aren't bankrupted by illnesses or accidents and seniors aren't abandoned in poverty?
- Is our economy delivering on the promise that our children will have a good chance of doing better than their parents did?

If our economy isn't producing all three—widely shared opportunity, more security, and a better future—then something is badly broken. And there's a lot of evidence that our country's current economy is failing on all three counts.

But to do something about this, we have to believe that we can act and that our actions will make a difference.

After emerging from the Great Depression and World War II, most Americans believed that together we were stronger. Succeeding generations of Americans have been confident that together we can do anything. Together we eradicated polio. Together we cared for our elderly, raced to the moon, and promised our kids a life that would be brighter than our own. Together we expanded access to voting, declared war on poverty, and dreamed that a world of truly equal opportunity was within reach. Yes, there was racism and sexism and too many forms of bigotry. Yes, we argued with each other, and yes, government was never perfect. But government was our way of working together to build more opportunity for each succeeding generation.

Now the changing economics of America have assaulted our collective security. And this persistent economic insecurity has done more than make life much harder for millions of Americans. It has also undermined our collective confidence in what we can achieve and left millions of people frustrated and angry.

"Everyone should be able to do their job, work hard, come home, and be happy," Gina says. "I don't want to be rolling in the dough. I just want to be happy. I don't want to worry about what I'll do if my husband dies, or if I have to go in the hospital again."

But Gina does worry. She worries about herself and Darren and their two sons. She worries about this country and where it is headed.

Gina's future looks darker than she ever imagined it would, but the numbers tell a discouraging story, too.

- More than half of Americans believe that when today's kids grow up, they will be worse off than their parents.
- More than half of people under sixty-five believe that Social Security will completely disappear before they retire.
- In 2016, 72 percent of voters believed that "the American economy is rigged to advantage the rich and powerful."

People have not only begun to doubt themselves as they look ahead; they have begun to doubt what we can do together to build a future.

And here's the scary part: they are right to doubt. They are right because none of this happened as a result of some immutable law of physics. After generations of work and sacrifice, after building an ever-stronger middle class, millions of families didn't start to stumble because of gravity. No, the forces that aligned against hardworking people are far more deliberate and far more dangerous. And instead of trying to fix the problem, many leaders in government now seem intent on either standing by while our middle class becomes ever less secure, or pushing policies that will make the situation even worse.

I supported President Obama. I spent a year working as an assistant to the president, and I applaud much of what he accomplished during his tenure. He expanded health care and strengthened regulations over Wall Street. He supported the Consumer Financial Protection Bureau (for which I will always be doubly grateful, because I worked so hard to get the agency established). He also made this planet safer, signed a historic climate deal, and negotiated to keep nuclear weapons out of Iran.

But there were times when President Obama and I parted company, and one of them was in the summer of 2016. He gave a commencement speech in which he talked about the influence of the rich and powerful over government. "Big money in politics is a huge problem," he admitted. And then he put a happy face on it: "But the system isn't as rigged as you think."

No, President Obama, the system *is* as rigged as we think.

In fact, it's worse than most Americans realize.

Here's the truth: we can't keep gazing happily at the face of cheery economic reports; we've got to dive into the reality of what's happening underneath the surface. Tens of millions of people across the United States understand that this country no longer works for them, and they are angry about it. And unless our government provides real solutions to their problems, their anger will only increase.

Donald Trump understood their anger. He connected with people when he channeled that anger during his campaign, but his plans will make the problems faced by working families worse. I am absolutely certain that even his most die-hard supporters will be deeply unhappy with a lot of what President Trump actually does. He likes to talk about forgotten working people, but he opposes raising the minimum wage, plans to propose the largest tax cut in history for the rich, and promises to get rid of the rules that hold Wall Street accountable. That is not populism. That is trickle-down economics on steroids. After vowing to "drain the swamp" and fight for the little guy, Trump turned the keys to our government over to a group of Wall Street insiders, billionaires, and CEOs who have a long history of looking out only for themselves and others just like them. This isn't the way to strengthen opportunity in America—it's the way to help the rich to get richer and shove everyone else out of the way.

We Americans cling fiercely to our optimistic belief that hard work wins out, but the facts tell a different story. Today an American child has a smaller chance of climbing the economic ladder than a child does in Canada or most of Europe. The chances that young children will do better than their parents have been cut nearly in half over the last generation. More than ever before, millions of kids aren't getting a fighting chance to move ahead; poor kids stay poor while rich kids get even richer. That's the ultimate rigged game.

"There's no middle class anymore—there are the haves and the have-nots," Gina says with a heavy voice. "This is the world we're leaving to our kids. What's going to happen after I die? What's going to happen to my kids?"

Stagnant wages, rising student loan debt, seniors who can't retire: the warning signs everywhere show us that distress is wide and deep in

America. And the new reality of uncertain hours and insecure income that underlies those numbers should sound an even louder alarm. These are the signposts of a redefined America, an America in which the country generates more and more wealth while an ever-growing majority has no chance to share in the bounty they work to produce.

The time for happy talk is over, and simply promising to "Make America Great Again" won't do the trick. It's time to get serious about understanding what has gone wrong and working out a plan to fix it. It's time for a hard look into how we once built a strong and vibrant middle class, how we lost our way, and how we will fight our way forward.

Most of all, it's time for some deep-down optimism, the kind that says, Yeah, our middle class is on the ropes, but we have the strength and the determination to build an America that works—not just for some of us, but for all of us.

2

A Safer Economy

The story of rigging the American economic system doesn't start with "What went wrong?" It starts with "What went right?"

America—like much of the world—had a boom-and-bust economy from the very beginning. George Washington was in his second term as president when, in 1796, a real estate bubble and resulting collapse shook the young country and hurtled it into a major financial crisis. Then, one after another, the booms and busts moved in cycles of about twenty years each. Land speculation, currency speculation, railroad speculation, and even speculation about war—all these triggered panics at one time or another. The specific details varied, but the overall pattern was clear. The economy would grow a bit, people would do a little better, and then speculation would start to bubble up. The promise of greater riches was like a song that started softly but soon got louder and more insistent—right up until the moment the music stopped and everyone ran for the exits.

Crashes came hard. They brought down many of the speculators, and millionaires sometimes watched their fortunes disappear with the delivery of a single letter or the loss of one ship. The busts bankrupted farmers as well as small business owners, who were caught short

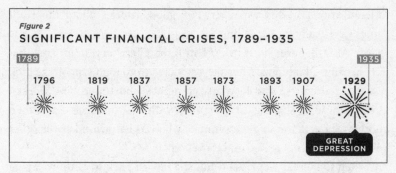

From the 1790s to the 1930s, America had a boom-and-bust economy.

when prices dropped without warning or banks collapsed. The crashes hit factory workers and shop clerks, carpenters and ranch hands, leaving millions without work and struggling to feed themselves and their children.

From the 1790s to the 1930s, America's boom-and-bust economy was like a natural rhythm of the universe, sweeping in good fortune like a benevolent tide, then sucking it back out again with terrible ferocity.

ROCK BOTTOM

Then the really big one hit. This bust was so big and so thorough, and walloped so many people across this country, that it got its own name: the Great Depression. Thousands of banks failed. One out of every four Americans was out of work. A million and a half people were homeless, and hundreds of thousands of people took refuge in ramshackle camps around the country. Children went hungry, and crowds of people fought over scraps of food in the garbage. Today it is hard to appreciate how much this economic downturn tore through people's lives.

In my family's story, the Great Depression was a constant presence, not unlike a powerful but unseen character in a play. Babies' births and the moves from one town to another were dated before, during, or after the disaster. (My brothers Don Reed and John were born "during," and my brother David and I were born "after.") Whenever relatives gathered or when someone was about to throw away an old pair of pants or a tattered armchair that was "perfectly good," stories about the Hard Times were ready for the telling.

My Aunt Bee was born in 1901 in Indian Territory, in an area that later became Oklahoma. After she graduated from high school, she took a secretarial course and learned typing and shorthand. She worked at different jobs, sharing an apartment with first one friend and then another. She was the single roommate who was left behind as the other young women got married and moved on.

When the Great Depression hit, she moved back in with my aging grandparents, bringing home her pay envelope every week to keep them all going. When her salary was cut in half, she cried—not from the loss of money but from relief that she hadn't been laid off. Nearly everyone else in the office had been sent home.

Years later, when I was a little girl, Aunt Bee would talk about the exact day the local bank failed. She told stories about people dropping packages and letting go of their children's hands as they ran to find out the news; she described the crowd gathered outside the bank and the locked doors. My grandfather used to say that after the bank closed, all he had left from a lifetime of working construction were "my tools and the house I built with my own hands." Aunt Bee's half pay was their lifeline.

All across America, men who had no jobs and no prospects hitched rides in freight cars, dropping off to hustle up a meal and maybe a little work before moving on. My family lived in one of the hundreds of small towns where the train tracks cut across the prairie.

Aunt Bee said that a handful of strangers showed up nearly every morning at my grandparents' back door. The men were always polite. They took off their caps, asking respectfully if there was anything they could do around the yard for a little food. She said they were gaunt, with dark circles etched under their eyes and clothes that hung loose: "All skin and bones."

And that's when the fights started in our family. "Mama would feed them," Aunt Bee told me. "Day after day, she would dish up plates of stew or grits or whatever we had."

Aunt Bee asked my grandmother to stop. She pleaded with her to stop. Finally, she yelled at her: "Stop feeding these bums! We don't have enough for ourselves, and you're giving away food."

Bread lines formed in the cities, and in smaller towns,
hungry men went door to door.

My grandmother would say nothing. She would just keep stirring pots on the stove and putting another round of biscuits in the oven. When Aunt Bee went off to work, my grandmother shared whatever they had. And every night Aunt Bee would cross-examine her: What happened to the potatoes she bought yesterday? Why were they running out of lard? Had Mama been giving away food again?

In 1969, my ninety-four-year-old grandmother had a massive stroke. As she lay dying, Aunt Bee sat by her bed for days at a time, holding the old lady's frail hand. More than once, Aunt Bee told her how sorry she was that she had yelled at her for helping people so long ago. She bowed her head, and the tears fell into her lap.

I was born in 1949, years after the Depression had ended. Even so, I watched up close what Hard Times had done to people. Aunt Bee was the gentlest and most generous soul I knew—much kinder than anyone else in our family. Not only did Aunt Bee keep my grandparents afloat during the Depression, she quietly gave small bits of cash to pretty much

That's Aunt Bee on the right, with three of her former roommates.

everyone else in the family. She always set aside 10 percent of her small Social Security check for the Baptist church, then dug deeper to make contributions for missions and revivals. She dropped coins into every collection box in every grocery store or dry cleaners, and she was there to help every relative or neighbor who got into trouble.

Aunt Bee saved me, too. When I was struggling to hold down a job and take care of two small children and my life was pretty much a mess, Aunt Bee dropped everything in her world and came to rescue me. She lived with us for years, helping out with those two lively (and sometimes obnoxious) children, and I never once heard her raise her voice or even get a little stern. Frankly, she was a pushover, and we all knew it. Even Bonnie, her little long-eared cocker spaniel, would crowd Aunt Bee off the couch while we watched television.

And yet she had yelled at her mother for feeding hungry people, and yelling at my grandmother had cut her so deeply that nearly forty years later, Aunt Bee still cried over it. It told me something about what it means to be afraid that you can't provide for those you love. It told me about how worry gnaws at a person's soul. It told me that economic crashes bite hard and the memories don't fade.

PROTECTING THE BANKS FROM SPECULATORS

The Great Depression began in 1929. Gripping the country like a vise, it wore on and on, one year following the next. In 1933, just when it felt like the Hard Times would last forever, the newly sworn-in president, Franklin Delano Roosevelt, made an audacious claim: We can do better.

Roosevelt was an unlikely leader for the millions of men and women who were out of work, out of food, and nearly out of hope. He was a pampered only child, born into great wealth and all that came with his secure social position: private schools, servants, balls, and annual trips to Europe. He had been an active young man who learned to shoot, ride, hunt, and sail, and he'd filled his time with tennis, polo, and golf.

But Roosevelt was not interested in building up the family fortune. Early on, he felt the call to public service, running for the New York State legislature before he was thirty. When he was crippled by polio eleven years later, his political career seemed to be over. At the time, no one imagined that a man who was unable to stand on his own could become a leader. But Roosevelt did not give up. He pressed forward, first as governor of New York, then as the calm and unflappable president leading the nation during some of our darkest and most frightening days.

Roosevelt was deeply beloved. My grandmother never followed politics much, but later, when I was a little girl and Roosevelt had been dead for years, his name always prompted the same response. Her voice would drop a notch and she would say, "He made us safe."

In a time of great danger, Roosevelt embraced experimentation, trying whatever he could to get this country out of the ditch of the Great Depression. He believed in action, believed in the idea that government does not stand passively by, believed that government has an active and critical role to play in making the lives of our citizens better.

The first order of business was to get the financial system back on track. Wild speculation, a stock market crash, and the failure of thousands of banks had nearly destroyed the U.S. economy. FDR didn't suggest permanently shutting down Wall Street or nationalizing the banks. He proposed something far more audacious: capitalism that works for all Americans.

Roosevelt rejected the idea that economic booms and busts were inevitable—that they were part of the natural order, much like floods and forest fires. Instead, he proposed that we pass laws to make the economy safer. Keep capitalism, but make it work better for all Americans. Although there were some twists and turns, ultimately the plan for the economy, passed in 1933 and 1934, had three main parts:

- Make it safe to put money in banks by establishing the Federal Deposit Insurance Corporation, or FDIC.
- Separate ordinary checking and savings banking from Wall Street speculation with the measure known as Glass-Steagall.
- Put a cop on the beat on Wall Street by creating the SEC.

Three ideas, born of desperation and experimentation in the early 1930s, helped put our financial system right. All three strengthened the hand of government to help make the economy safer for everyone.

With 20/20 hindsight, these ideas look, well, pretty obvious. But their simplicity was part of their power. My aunt Bee was in no position to evaluate the strength—or weaknesses—of a bank, and neither were most of the other customers. They just wanted to know that if they put their hard-earned money in the bank, they could be confident that the bank would still have cash when they wanted to take it out.

By guaranteeing that depositors' money would be there *no matter what*, FDIC insurance eliminated the kind of panic that had triggered devastating bank runs. No customer needed to worry that if trouble hit and they didn't get to the bank right away and grab all their cash, they would be left with nothing. In exchange for this extraordinary benefit of a federal government guarantee, the banks agreed to submit to careful regulation. They agreed to be constantly scrutinized to ensure that they were safe and sound and that they would not need to call on federal insurance to bail them out.

Before giving a bank its blessing, the FDIC checked out the bank's assets and management talent. Banking quickly shifted from a speculative undertaking to a far more stable business that produced regular profits year in and year out. Banking became boring—and boring worked.

The thousands of small banks across the country became institutions where customers could reliably deposit their earnings and carefully tuck away some savings, as well as places where people could borrow the money they needed to buy homes or start their own businesses. Bank regulation steadied the financial system. It was a good deal for the banks, a good deal for the depositors, and a good deal for the U.S. economy.

Glass-Steagall, named after the two members of Congress who sponsored the legislation, Senator Carter Glass and Representative Henry Steagall, was a corollary to FDIC insurance: any financial institution that took taxpayer-guaranteed deposits was barred from engaging in other, higher-risk activities. This meant that Aunt Bee's little bits of savings couldn't be scooped up by the bank to be used for gambling on Wall Street or in some crazy deal that some bank manager wanted to run on the side. Her money was safe, in part because taxpayers would never have to bail out the bank because its management had ended up on the losing end of a highly speculative deal. One happy side effect of this new rule was that the money deposited in a local bank was more likely to stay in the community in the form of small business loans and home mortgages. It was a pretty straightforward deal: bankers had to make a choice between low-risk, boring banking and high-risk, Wall Street–style investing. One or the other—but not both.

The third tool for making the financial system safer involved policing the giant corporations so that they couldn't cheat investors. Once again, the idea was pretty simple: put a cop on Wall Street. A cop would force the companies to keep honest books and would also be on the lookout for scams and frauds. Thus, the Securities and Exchange Commission was born. The SEC helped level the playing field so that investors—not just Wall Street insiders—could figure out the difference between good deals and bad ones.

The new laws addressed a number of other issues, but Roosevelt started where the need was most urgent: get the financial institutions under control. He understood that if depositors couldn't count on money being available in their banks, the whole economy would be crippled because people and businesses wouldn't be able to move around the cash needed for buying, selling, and investing. He also knew that if people

Roosevelt looked pretty cheerful about breaking up the big banks.
As he signed Glass-Steagall into law, Senator Glass (hands in pockets on the left)
and Congressman Steagall (hands in front of him on the right) looked on.

thought that Wall Street was the financial equivalent of a lawless jungle, then crazy speculators and scam artists would be attracted to the market, while good, steady investors would stay home. That mattered a lot, because if the prudent investors stayed home, growing businesses wouldn't be able to get the money they needed to expand.

All three of these moves—providing FDIC insurance, breaking up the big banks, and putting a cop on Wall Street—triggered huge battles with the CEOs and millionaires who liked things just the way they were. Sure, the crashes had been hard on them, too, but they didn't like having the government look over their shoulders, and they saw any limits on what they could do as an attack on capitalism.

Despite the resistance of some very powerful people, the three new laws passed. Better yet, they worked together to stabilize the financial industry, which proved to be good for everyone, rich and not so rich. And they were all built on one crucial idea: banking is special, and only if it is carefully governed can the rest of the economy flourish.

BREAK 'EM UP: ROUND TWO

Stabilizing the banking industry was just the start of Roosevelt's effort to build a stronger, more stable economy. He also used the tools of antitrust law to roll back the concentration of corporate power in other industries. He was determined to block giant companies that were smothering their smaller competitors—not by offering better products or lower costs, but by using shady practices that stopped competition before it started.

After he got the banking laws in place and operational, Roosevelt brought in Thurman Arnold, a man often described as a maverick lawyer, to head the Justice Department's Antitrust Division. Fiercely independent, Arnold was widely respected for the power of his intellect and the force of his character. The turnaround was immediate. In short order, the division grew from eighteen lawyers to five hundred, and investigations—and lawsuits—ramped up. In just five years under new leadership, those attorneys filed almost as many cases as there had been in the previous quarter century. Arnold said his approach was "to hit hard, hit everyone and hit them all at once." From fertilizer to newspapers to motion pictures, from shoes to tobacco to petroleum, monopolies and collusive dealings had taken root in one industry after another—and now the government was breaking up these huge corporations and shutting down their predatory practices.

Industry CEOs were shocked—shocked—that a previously complacent government would call them out, and they responded with fury and fulmination when some mere government official tried to apply laws already on the books to halt aggressive and dangerous business practices. In fact, some of these CEOs were so outraged that they fought all the way to the Supreme Court of the United States, confident that those troublesome government officials would be slapped back.

This shift in approach—from markets where the rule of the day was pretty much "anything goes" to markets that had tough cops enforcing strict laws—reflected a tectonic shift in American law and the American economy. By the 1930s, the idea began to take root that without basic rules, markets won't work. Government—the people working together—could pass strong laws and enforce those laws to level the playing field; this, in turn, would give consumers, investors, shopkeepers, and small farmers a fighting chance to build their own economic futures.

TAKING THE FIGHT DIRECTLY TO THE POWERFUL

This history may seem like a dusty tale about a time long past, but the economic battles of the 1930s were as intense as any attack launched during the over-the-top 2016 political season. And these early economic battles had a transformative effect on our country. They set the stage for the development of our economy and our financial laws—and for nearly half a century of stunning prosperity.

Even as the economy slowly began improving, the corporate big shots whose powers were being challenged did not like the direction in which the country was headed. Newspaper titan William Randolph Hearst referred to FDR as "Stalin Delano Roosevelt" and insisted that his reporters substitute "Raw Deal" for "New Deal" in news articles that were published throughout the country. Millionaires warned about Roosevelt's "socialist government." *Time* magazine reported that, "with few exceptions, members of the so-called Upper Class frankly hate Franklin Roosevelt." One member of that class said ominously, "What that fellow Roosevelt needs is a thirty-eight-caliber revolver right at the back of his head."

My grandmother might have believed that Roosevelt made the country safe, but among the rich and powerful, deep resentment was growing over the changes Roosevelt had brought about. Battle lines were forming.

In June 1936, Roosevelt went to Philadelphia to accept the Democratic nomination for his second term. One hundred thousand people crowded into the University of Pennsylvania's sports stadium, Franklin Field. The cheers were deafening as the president entered the arena in a limousine and rode a long loop around the field.

It must have been a gratifying moment for Roosevelt, but it's also likely that he was thinking about an immediate challenge: he needed to get out of his car and onto the stage. In the fifteen years since he had been stricken with polio, Roosevelt found walking—and even standing—a painful and precarious business, and he always went to great pains to hide his paralysis from public view. Now the task would be more hazardous: it had been raining, and the stadium's grass was slick.

As the president slowly made his way to the speaking podium while leaning on the arm of his son, people jostled for a better view and to shout their good wishes. The president was bumped. When his metal leg brace sprang open, he fell heavily. As he went down, the papers of his speech flew out into the crowd. On the ground, Roosevelt was pale and shaken, his clothes smudged with dirt.

After a shocked moment, his aides quickly pulled him to his feet. Most people in the stadium couldn't see what had happened, but his aides were panicked. Roosevelt immediately pushed ahead.

"Clean me up," he ordered.

Within minutes he was standing on the platform, enduring grinding pain and staring into the bright stadium lights at a crowd of a hundred thousand people. As the cheering built to a roar, he waved and smiled. And then he went on the attack. Roosevelt called out the "privileged princes" and "economic royalty" running corporate America. The crowd went wild as FDR declared war—not just "war against want and destitution and economic demoralization," but "a war for the survival of democracy."

Four months later, as his campaign moved into its final week, Roosevelt was still on the attack. On the Saturday before Election Day, he kept his sights trained on those moneyed interests, declaring, "They are unanimous in their hate for me—and I welcome their hatred."

Three days after that, he was reelected, winning a majority in every state in the union except Maine and Vermont.

*In Philadelphia, one hundred thousand people heard Roosevelt
declare war on the country's "economic royalty."*

REGULATION WORKED

World War II demanded massive mobilization. The war effort put millions of people to work fighting for our country, while millions more
worked to manufacture the equipment and supplies those soldiers and
sailors needed. The war, for all its terrible carnage and destruction,
pumped new spending into the economy.

But it was Roosevelt's new vision of the role of government that fundamentally changed America's economic system for decades to come.
Coming out of the Great Depression, an American president decided
that we could do better—and we did. For nearly half a century, Roosevelt's ideas influenced his successors, both Democratic and Republican.
Leaders used government more deliberately to level the playing field in
markets and to create more stability. In the 1970s, a Republican president
added the Environmental Protection Agency and the Consumer Product Safety Commission so that companies couldn't cut costs by dumping their wastes in our rivers or by selling dangerous products with

hidden defects. Antitrust law was enforced, and small businesses got a chance to take root and grow. America kept that cop on Wall Street and continued reining in the biggest corporations.

And here's the thing: regulation worked.

By the postwar era, the boom-and-bust economy was gone. There were some ups and downs, but nothing like the crash of 1929. Instead, once the new financial regulations were in place, from the mid-1930s forward, America experienced decade after decade of economic peace. No crashes. No bread lines. No need to shutter the banks.

But we didn't just hold steady: year over year, decade over decade, our country got richer. From the late 1930s forward, our gross domestic product (GDP) also maintained a pretty steady upward march.

Best of all, as our country got richer, our families got richer. Not everyone, but almost everyone, did better. Incomes rose. In 1947, after the war created labor shortages and wages were allowed to rise, life looked good for the middle class. But the good times had only just begun. Adjusted for inflation, a man working full-time and making the median income would see his earnings grow 65 percent between 1947 and 1980. His family was spending that money, too, meaning that businesses prospered and corporations' profits swelled. Small businesses flourished. Our country was rich beyond the wildest dreams of earlier generations.

By 1960, only two decades after the end of the Great Depression, it was clear that America had produced the equivalent of an economic miracle: we had built the greatest middle class on earth. The skies were sunny, and our future looked bright.

THE FORGOTTEN RICH MAN

But resentments run deep—often really, really deep. Corporate executives and millionaires had gotten richer and richer, but for some of them, Roosevelt's work to rein in the big banks and break up giant corporations still rankled. It seems that the divine right of kings had translated in the New World into a Divine Right of CEOs. The idea that a democratically elected government could and would curtail their corporate rights was perceived as a threat—and they didn't like threats. Sure, they were already rich, but that's the mouth-watering, heart-pumping thing about being rich—it's better to be even *richer*. There's no limit to how rich the rich can be. Besides, any kind of government regulation signaled interference with their deeply held notions of right, wrong, and the undeniable privileges that belonged to them as masters of powerful corporations.

In 1971, the U.S. Chamber of Commerce enlisted a corporate lawyer named Lewis Powell to write a secret memo. As soon as Powell finished his thirty-three-page paper, the chamber, a national organization representing the interests of many of America's largest corporations, quietly began passing it from one power broker to another. For the CEO crowd, the memo was electrifying. Powell had held nothing back. He forcefully argued that the entire free-enterprise system was under attack—and he called on the super rich to counterattack with all their might.

Powell was an unlikely firebrand. He was mild-mannered, gentlemanly, and unfailingly polite. Many people remarked on his deeply ingrained civility. He was intensely proud of his Virginia roots, which were noticeable in his soft drawl, and he idolized Robert E. Lee. Tall and thin, Powell wore thick glasses and old-fashioned suits. Yet despite all his courtly manners, when it came to defending his corporate clients, he was a take-no-prisoners, shoot-them-all kind of guy.

Powell served on the board of directors for more than a dozen of America's biggest corporations, and his dedication to advancing the interests of corporate America was legendary. His work for tobacco company Philip Morris included signing off on the company's annual reports touting the health benefits of cigarettes, and he railed against the press for failing to give adequate credence to the industry's claims about tobacco safety. He was close personal friends with the top lawyer for General Motors, and when newspaper articles about cars with dangerous designs and product defects began appearing, Powell viewed those stories—and the reporters who wrote them—with alarm. He fervently believed that such challenges undermined people's confidence in corporate America and put our country right on the slippery slope to socialism.

Many of those who received Powell's memo shared his view that America's system of free enterprise was at risk, but it was his call to action that really galvanized his CEO readership. His advice was visionary:

Fight back! Reshape Americans' views about business, government, politics, and law. Fund conservative think tanks. Influence young people by reasserting business interests on college campuses. Pay professors to publish pro-business work. Using example after example, Powell made it clear that he wanted to return America to the pro-corporate, largely

51/167 4cc 8/23/71

CONFIDENTIAL MEMORANDUM

ATTACK ON AMERICAN FREE ENTERPRISE SYSTEM

TO: Mr. Eugene B. Sydnor, Jr.   DATE: August 23, 1971
         Chairman
         Education Committee
         U.S. Chamber of Commerce

FROM: Lewis F. Powell, Jr.

This memorandum is submitted at your request as a basis for the discussion on August 24 with Mr. Booth and others at the U.S. Chamber of Commerce. The purpose is to identify the problem, and suggest possible avenues of action for further consideration.

Dimensions of the Attack

No thoughtful person can question that the American economic system is under broad attack.* This varies in scope, intensity, in the techniques employed, and in the level of visibility.

There always have been some who opposed the American system, and preferred socialism or some form of statism

*Variously called: the "free enterprise system", "capitalism", and the "Profit system". The American political system of democracy under the rule of law is also under attack, often by the same individuals and organizations who seek to undermine the enterprise system.

The beginning of the typewritten Powell Memo, which changed how giant corporations wage political war.

unregulated government that, in his view, had served this country so well before the Great Depression.

In the darkest days of the Depression, Roosevelt had offered hope to "the forgotten man at the bottom of the economic pyramid." Without a hint of irony, Powell now spoke tenderly to America's millionaires: "One does not exaggerate to say that, in terms of political influence with respect to the course of legislation and government action, the American business executive is truly the 'forgotten man.'"

Rich guys just can't catch a break.

THE PLAN: TAKE OVER GOVERNMENT

Two months after Powell sent his memo to the Chamber of Commerce, President Nixon nominated him for the Supreme Court. The paper remained secret until after Powell was confirmed. But his idea had already spurred the millionaires and CEOs who'd read the memo to stop complaining and start acting. The rich and powerful enthusiastically took up his call to arms and began to use their considerable wealth to alter America's political landscape.

Their efforts began to pay off almost immediately. Just over nine years after Powell's memo began to circulate, and with considerable support from a "Business Advisory Panel" of corporate CEOs, Ronald Reagan was elected president.

Reagan swept into office under the banner of free-market economics, and he was cheered on with many boisterous calls for "liberty" and "freedom." Reagan's approach was unmistakably aimed at helping giant businesses and their top executives, but its advocates promised working people that all those benefits going to big corporations would "trickle down" to them as well. The economic plan was as simple—and as sweeping—as the plan Franklin Roosevelt had put in place nearly half a century earlier during the Great Depression. But Reagan's plan turned Roosevelt's on its head.

Step one was to fire the cops—not the cops on Main Street, but the cops on Wall Street. An increasingly subservient Congress had already

A smiling President Richard Nixon shakes hands with new Supreme Court Justice Lewis Powell, while Supreme Court Justice William Rehnquist looks on.

begun doing more of the bidding of big financial institutions, but following Reagan's election, those banks were given far more leeway. Antitrust enforcement that had kept some corporate goliaths in check now slowed way down.

The Reagan administration proudly embraced the idea of "deregulation," as if financial and corporate regulations were the biggest problems faced by Americans—rather than the wrongs those regulations were designed to prevent. From Reagan's perspective, it was far more important to protect a corporate giant from the government than it was to protect a customer, investor, or small competitor from the actions of a corporate giant. Regulation became the new enemy. Forget exploding gas tanks, cancer-causing chemicals in the water supply, or drugs that caused birth defects—regulation was proclaimed to be the real danger in America. From the 1980s onward, "deregulation" became a sacred tenet of all conservatives, a mantra that can be translated to mean: let corporate America do more of whatever corporate America wants to do.

Trickle-down economics ushered in a new approach to the economy. Instead of using the tools of government to help level the playing field for all Americans, government should let those at the top call the shots and, in the words of Ronald Reagan, rely on the "magic of the market-place" to create "spectacular broad-based economic progress."

Ooh, magic marketplaces. No need for rules or regulators—just put your faith in giant corporations.

Even now, President Trump serves up the same tired old recipe. He promises to "unleash" corporations to create more jobs by, among other things, reducing regulations. True to his word, he picked an Environmental Protection Agency director who fights against rules that protect our air and water, and a Secretary of Labor opposed to rules that protect our workforce.

Oh yes, it is very clear from Donald Trump's cabinet that he thinks the virtues of deregulation know no limits. Indeed, Trump delivered this across-the-board approach to making America great again: "We're getting rid of regulations which goes hand in hand with the lowering of the taxes."

Let the big corporations do whatever they want. What could possibly go wrong?

The enthusiastic corporate sponsorship of conservative economics should have been the tip-off. The embrace of trickle-down economics was nothing more than a brazen ploy to ensure that this country would be run so that the rich and powerful can get richer and more powerful.

The concept of trickle-down economics was bad enough. But it also had an evil twin: the idea that government was the enemy. After Roosevelt harnessed the federal government to work for millions of Americans, powerful corporations pushed back with the idea that government—not corporations—was the enemy. Many helping hands heaped ridicule on government, and America's poor corporations were cast as its victims.

As with any movement, the idea couldn't have taken hold if there hadn't been some truth to back it up. Let's face it: some of the government's rules are stupid, and some rules are stupidly enforced. Anyone who has ever tried to erect a new building or open a new business and along the way run into a series of codes and inspections and petty bureaucrats may be ready to sign on with a politician who promises "smaller government."

But chanting "deregulation" at the federal level didn't actually fix many problems for small businesses. Mostly, it created huge giveaways that only giant companies could take advantage of. Repealing Glass-Steagall in 1999 helped a handful of gigantic banks get even more gigantic, but it didn't do much for the community banks trying to compete with them. The same can be said about the decision not to regulate risky new financial instruments. Government's hands-off approach to this new danger fattened profits for giant banks while it bankrupted families. Regulatory rollback and tax breaks for large corporations help large corporations, but they don't help anyone else.

For decades now, Republicans have been feeding small businesses the same lines about how the GOP is the party of small government. But after promising the moon, they sure haven't delivered much. Maybe that's because most of the benefit they deliver is scooped up by the big guys.

Despite pretty promises, Republicans have delivered a rigged system that lets giant companies and multimillionaires treat the American economy like a candy store that's open only for them. What does the couple running a great little restaurant in Somerville, Massachusetts, get from federal rollbacks? Nothing—which is about what most families and small businesses get.

WHEN THE COPS WORK FOR THE CROOKS

Trickle-down ideology started with raw power: the powerful devised ways to exercise even more power. With fewer regulators to say no, big corporations began venturing into territory that had long been closed to them. Wall Street firms showed the way. For years they had chafed under the restrictions put in place in the 1930s, and they had fought back from the beginning. But now, one battle at a time, they began to win. Big banks were turned loose to load up on risks. Those risks boosted both revenues and profitability, and—no surprise—the executives cashed their paychecks, pocketed their bonuses, and didn't ask too many questions.

The jump in profitability was like a cocaine high—it felt amazing while it lasted, but it was potentially deadly. Risks always come back to bite someone. The CEOs knew that, but they expected they could grab their money and get out, and the drug would keep working. And if it all came crashing down, everyone else, including investors, customers, and taxpayers, would be left holding the bag.

A banking scandal that erupted in the late 1980s should have sounded a warning. The country's savings and loans associations, once sleepy little consumer banks that specialized in mortgage lending, were largely deregulated in 1982. They immediately started growing, offering bigger and bigger loans and many more new products. In just three years, the S&Ls jumped 50 percent in size, and speculators began buying them up as if each one was a goose that could lay golden eggs. But no bubble lasts forever, and soon many of the high-flying, poorly regulated S&Ls became insolvent. When the bubble popped, more than a thousand of the nation's 3,200 S&Ls were shut down. And, in a show of real accountability, government regulators criminally prosecuted more than a thousand bank executives.

Because the S&Ls were relatively small and because the problems rolled from region to region over time, they didn't crash the entire economy. But to keep the system functioning and keep depositors from losing any money, U.S. taxpayers laid out about $132 billion. Yes, $132 billion. Stop for a minute and think about that pile of money: in 1995, when the last S&L was shuttered, the federal government had funneled more to these financial institutions than it had spent on education, job training, veterans' benefits, social services, and transportation *combined*.

At this point, alarms should have been sounding everywhere— shrieking sirens and clanging bells. The pattern was unmistakable: (1) bank deregulates; (2) bank loads up on risk; (3) crisis occurs; (4) bailout follows.

The S&L scandal should have screamed at regulators and Congress to pay attention and tighten up bank regulations. If they had, the next round of problems with banks crashing the economy would have been stopped before it started. But the politicians didn't want to hear it. (I guess it's hard to hear when your ears are stuffed with money.) The banks—particularly the giant banks—kept pushing for less and less oversight, and the politicians followed right along.

Instead of sobering up in the aftermath of the crisis, the big banks charged ahead. Their target: Glass-Steagall. Licking their chops over the chance to combine boring banking (and all the money in those checking and savings accounts) with high-risk financial speculation, the banks lobbied to pull down one of the pillars of our financial system. And they didn't worry about the fallout. They figured that if anything went wrong, the government would step in and make sure that all those little depositors were protected—and in the process, the government would protect the big banks as well. Throughout the 1980s and into the 1990s, high-paid lobbyists aggressively attacked a wide array of financial regulations. Over time, they targeted one brick after another in the wall that separated banks from Wall Street trading, and, over time, the bank regulators caved in again and again. In 1999, the few remaining provisions of Glass-Steagall were repealed.

The results were immediate. Big banks grew into giant banks, and giant banks grew into monsters. In 1980, the ten biggest banks in America controlled less than one-third of the market; by 2000, they had captured more than half the market, and by 2005, their share had risen to almost 60 percent. By 2008, just five uber-banks controlled 40 percent of the market. Through it all, bank CEOs displayed a boldness that would have put a medieval royal prince to shame.

Take a look at just one example. In 1998, when Citicorp decided that it wanted to merge with a giant insurance company, the two corporations faced a teeny-tiny problem: the merger would be illegal. Such a bank-nonbank merger would violate the existing provisions of Glass-Steagall and other banking laws that had been in place since the 1930s. But why should these princes of finance let mere federal law slow them down? Laws were for the little guys, and these CEOs were bound for greatness. If the two companies joined together, it would be the biggest merger in history. The two finance giants reflected a bit, and then very deliberately, very publicly, and very illegally, they merged their companies, confident that a compliant Congress would change the law after the fact.

And, wow, did they get it right: a subservient Congress did just what it was told to do. In 1999, after the repeal of Glass-Steagall, the big-time financial world got even riskier and—for a while—even more profitable.

In the same way that some Republicans had signed on for greater regulations in earlier decades, some Democrats now got on the deregulation bandwagon big-time. As he signed the repeal of Glass-Steagall, President Bill Clinton cracked a few jokes, then praised the move for "making a fundamental and historic change in the way we operate our financial institutions." He had fought for the repeal, and now he claimed victory: "It is true that the Glass-Steagall law is no longer appropriate to the economy in which we live." As he presciently explained, it will help "expand the powers of banks."

AROUND THE TIME Congress and the bank regulators were rolling over and playing dead for the big banks, I was in Massachusetts, teaching at Harvard and studying another sign of danger in the American economy: during the 1990s, American families had been loading up on debt. Credit card companies were making their products more and more complex. Credit card agreements that back in 1981 had been about a page and a half long had morphed into contracts that ran to thirty pages of tiny type by the early 2000s. Increasingly, the agreements were larded with obscure legal terms, hidden tricks, and bizarre accounting practices. Ultimately, some members of Congress became concerned. During one hearing, laughter broke out as credit card executives were called on to explain certain incomprehensible terms.

But there was nothing funny about the effects of this rising spiral of debt on working people. Banks and credit card companies encouraged families to get in way over their heads, and predatory contracts trapped people into years of staggering fees and astronomical interest rates. Credit cards were handed out like candy, and they soon began producing tens of billions of dollars in profits for their issuers. Newspapers and radios regularly reported lighthearted stories about a baby, a dog, or a cat that had been issued its own preapproved card.

The numbers I was coming up with in my research were so alarming that I started looking for more ways to get the word out—speeches, articles, op-eds, interviews, and pretty much anything else I could think of. One day in 2005, I got a phone call and was asked a surprising question: Would I please come to Washington to meet with the regulators at the Office of the Comptroller of the Currency?

Woo-hoo! This was the big-dog bank regulator, the cop that had authority to tell many of the biggest credit card issuers in the country to *cut it out*. Really. This was an agency that could eliminate tricks and traps from millions of credit cards. Oooh, this could be fun.

I flew to Washington on a cloudy February day. I'd never been to the OCC offices, which were sleek and modern. The acting comptroller, Julie Williams, welcomed me in the lobby and waved me through security. Upstairs, we visited for a few minutes in her office, which was outfitted with elegant modern furniture. No standard-government-issue, banged-up stuff here. Everything had a cool, well-designed look.

Acting comptroller Williams—"call me Julie"—was tall and thin, with a fashionably short haircut and an elegant cashmere jacket. She had ramrod-straight posture and an intense stare. She always kept her voice at a low volume, but every word was carefully weighed and measured for maximum impact. Here was a woman who would never disrupt markets with so much as a misplaced syllable.

Julie led me to an elevator and then to a large conference room, where she introduced me to a big group of OCC economists and bank supervisors. In these pre-PowerPoint days, I had assembled a presentation that relied on transparencies and an overhead projector. For over an hour, I carefully went through my data. First I demonstrated the increasingly precarious position of millions of American families; next I provided abundant evidence that the banks were boosting their profits by tricking many of the people who were borrowing money from them. Even when giving an academic presentation, I could get pretty wound up—and even in a room full of sober government officials, I didn't hold back. Cheaters are cheaters.

The economists and supervisors had lots of questions. They were engaged and thoughtful, and I stayed until the last person had asked the last question. Finally I picked up my slides. I was exhausted, and I needed some water.

Julie and I headed back to her office to pick up my backpack. As we stepped into the elevator, she said that I had made a "compelling case" that credit card debt was creating serious problems.

For a moment I closed my eyes: yesssss! My fatigue evaporated. This was exactly what I wanted: the regulator in chief had recognized that there was a problem! I couldn't wait to hear her confirm that she would put some of the OCC's thousands of employees to work investigating these shady practices and reining in some of the predators. I had worked so hard on these data, and now they were going to have an impact. I was ready to break out my dancing shoes.

Then Julie gave a small, sad smile. She said it was just too bad.

I waited several seconds, and when she didn't say anything more, I said, "Uh, yeah, it's too bad. But you can stop it."

"Stop it?" She jerked back as if the thought had never occurred to her. "Why would we do that?"

Well, because it's wrong? And because millions of people are getting hurt? And because it's dangerous for banks to build their profits by cheating people? And, finally, because this is the sort of financial adventure that usually ends very badly for both the banks and the economy?

Again I pointed out that the OCC—her agency—had both the power and the responsibility to shut down these dangerous practices.

"Oh, we can't do that," she said evenly.

As we headed to the lobby, I started to press her. I figured this might be my last chance. "Of course you can do it," I said. "You have the authority, you are responsible, you can make a huge difference in people's lives." As I made my case, my voice started to rise.

She smiled. "No, we just can't do that. The banks wouldn't like it."
The banks wouldn't like it.

What? Are you *kidding* me? I almost didn't believe what was happening. I knew this was the Bush administration, but gimme a break. Who cares if the banks don't like it? You don't work for them. You work for the American people—for the people who are getting cheated. I was so furious my hands were shaking.

Julie never raised her voice or broke her smile. Instead, she walked me through the lobby and said good-bye. So far as I know, neither she nor anyone at that entire agency ever followed up on anything I said that day.

And I know for sure they never invited me back.

But it wasn't just the bank regulators who fell down on the job. Other government agencies also competed for their place in a book that could have been titled *Profiles in Cowardice*. In the 1980s, the SEC began the shift from sending out aggressive regulators to letting the big financial players police themselves. By the time I was making my presentation to the OCC in 2005, the SEC had effectively neutered itself. As investment banks gobbled up more and more risk, the SEC put in place voluntary regulations, and then the SEC chair said that the banks were free to comply with these regulations—or ignore them.

Voluntary regulations? Jeez, can you imagine Tony Soprano in a world of voluntary regulations? All these years later, I want to scream at the SEC, "What was wrong with you guys? You were supposed to be on the side of the people!" But that, of course, was the very root of the problem. The SEC had absorbed the message of deregulation that the agency's job was to serve the investment industry.

And, boy, did they serve the industry. The SEC's ineffectiveness became legendary. A former SEC chair described the commission's enforcement division as "handcuffed." Its agents couldn't even detect a plain old-fashioned Ponzi scheme—the kind that had been around since the 1920s and that even the dullest cop on the Wall Street beat was supposed to be able to sniff out from a mile away. Despite repeated warnings, the SEC completely missed the Bernie Madoff scandal, the largest financial fraud in U.S. history. Waking up only after the scheme—which lasted years, maybe even decades—had collapsed and people who had trusted him and given him their savings had lost more than $17 billion, the SEC was widely seen as willfully blind. Or, as journalist Matt Taibbi put it, the SEC appeared "somehow worse than corrupt—it's hard to find the right language, but 'aggressively clueless' comes pretty close."

During the same period, antitrust enforcement also began to fade, dropping sharply in the Reagan and Bush Sr. years. It ticked up during

Democratic administrations, but not nearly enough to keep up with the growing numbers of mergers and dominant corporations in many markets. The government policemen formerly known as trustbusters seemed as eager as everyone else to embrace the new motto in Washington: Let the big guys do whatever they want.

Industry consolidation took off. In one market after another, a handful of competitors dominated.

- By the 2000s, the number of major U.S. airlines dropped from nine to four. The four left standing—American, Delta, United, and Southwest—now have over 80 percent of all domestic airline seats in the country.
- Two beer companies sell more than 70 percent of all the beer in the United States.
- Five giant health insurance companies now own more than 83 percent of the country's health insurance market.
- Three drugstore chains—CVS, Walgreens, and Rite Aid—now manage 99 percent of all pharmacies in America.
- Monsanto holds the patents for about 93 percent of all the soybeans and 80 percent of all the corn planted in the United States each year.
- Four large companies now run nearly 85 percent of the U.S. beef market.
- Three big companies now produce almost half of all chickens.

The list goes on and on and on.

Giant corporations now dominate much of our lives. Why does this matter? Because when a handful of giants dominate, markets don't work very well. The whole free-enterprise system is built on the idea that when markets are competitive, we'll get lower prices, better services, cool new innovations, and many other benefits as companies vie for our business. Antitrust laws help keep markets strong.

The impact of consolidation is everywhere. Prices go up: as Monsanto has dominated seed production, corn seed prices have risen 135 percent since 2001. Small competitors face an uphill battle: craft brewers are having a tough time challenging the giant beer companies. Same with drugstores. The meat monopoly has hit in all directions: consumers are paying more, farmers are earning less, and profit margins for Tyson Foods, the nation's biggest meat producer, are breaking all records.

Or think about the cable industry. Giant cable companies prefer to control most of their markets, which gives them the chance to boost their profits by raising prices, delivering inferior products, and providing lousy services—all at the same time. In Massachusetts, nearly two out of three towns have only one cable provider, and most of the rest have only two. That's why I fought the merger of Comcast and Time Warner—number one and number three cable companies. (That's a fight we won!) If you're one of a handful of big corporations, why compete with one another when you can divvy up the markets, charge customers until they beg for mercy, and make much higher profits?

I'll sing the song again: Markets without rules don't provide value to customers and don't work for small businesses, but they make the big guys as happy as pigs in mud.

WITHOUT COPS, ANOTHER CRASH

As more and more politicians preached the gospel of markets with few rules and even fewer cops, the role of government quickly changed. Starting in the 1980s, the federal cops—the ones who were supposed to keep the markets honest and competitive—began backpedaling, especially in banking. Timid regulators, timid investigators, timid prosecutors, and timid legislators made it clear that government would do little to help level the playing field or to guard against the kinds of booms and busts that had once wiped out our economy. While these officials looked sideways and shuffled their feet, billions of dollars traded hands as companies sold deceptive mortgages, smashed their smaller competitors, moved operations overseas, devised new tax scams, and rejiggered their own books to make their bottom lines look even rosier. Meanwhile, Republican leaders endlessly repeated the claim that government—not giant corporations—posed a dire threat to our economy.

One by one, the regulatory threads that had been woven together in the 1930s and the decades after were pulled out. What remained was a tattered fabric of laws and regulations that did little to protect people.

And here's the thing: deregulation worked exactly as we should have expected.

For nearly half a century before Reagan swept into office, the mantra for both banks and bank regulators was "lend money only to people who can show pretty clearly how they will be able to repay." This was part of what made banking so boring—and what made the economy so stable.

But as regulators started looking sideways in the 1980s, big banks began building high-risk, high-profit portfolios loaded with credit cards. They boosted profits by burying dozens of tricks and traps in the fine print, so that fees were tacked on and interest rates were jacked up long after a purchase was made. Families were losing everything in bankruptcy, while bank profits shot through the roof. Meanwhile, bank regulators looked off somewhere in the middle distance, wearing the same expression as a dog owner who's pretending that his pooch isn't pooping on your lawn.

After a decade or so of big profits on credit cards, the banks got an even more delicious idea. Credit cards had become kid stuff; why not target the real money and go after home mortgages? New, much bigger bottles, but it was the same wine. In the 2000s, the banks loaded up mortgages with variable-payment schedules, triggers, high fees, and lots of surprising gotchas buried in the fine print and sold them to unsuspecting buyers. When some buyers couldn't pay, the banks refinanced the loans, added on new fees and more tricky terms, and started the game all over again. Again, bank profits exploded and regulators looked sideways.

Wall Street wanted in on the deal. This time, financial firms packaged these mortgages into bundles and sold the bundles to pension plans and municipal governments and other naïve customers. Those who purchased the bundles thought they were buying safe, steady investments; they didn't have a clue about the dangers buried in the risky mortgages. And the bank regulators? Cue the foot shuffling.

There were a zillion variations on how the big banks pulled it off, but the bottom line is this: they made a fortune by cheating people. The bank regulators knew about the swindle and could have shut it down, but they did nothing.

When the housing bubble burst and no one could refinance anymore, the whole scheme came crashing down. And just like the busts leading up to the Great Depression, this crash blasted through the economy. During the financial crisis of 2008, more than twenty-six million people couldn't find a full-time job. More than nine million families lost their homes. Hundreds of thousands of businesses were shuttered. Entrepreneurship plummeted as fewer Americans started new businesses. College students hit graduation with limited or no job prospects, and those who didn't go to college faced an even bleaker future. Retirement savings took a nosedive. Thousands of suicides were linked to the crisis.

Overall, the 2008 crash cost the U.S. economy an estimated $22 trillion and more human pain than anyone could ever count.

And yet and yet: even after the crash nearly blew our economy back into the Stone Age, Republicans continued to sing the song of deregulation. In 2010, one bank-friendly congressman declared, "In Washington, the view is that the banks are to be regulated, and my view is that Washington and the regulators are there to serve the banks." Yeah, the bank regulators served the banks, all right—and they nearly destroyed the American economy in the process.

FINANCIAL REGULATIONS MATTER

And that's really my point here: regulations matter. From the 1790s to the 1930s, there weren't many financial regulations, and the economy swung back and forth from boom to bust every twenty years or so. Banks boomed and banks crashed. The busts were long and hard; with no cop on the beat, uneasy investors held tight to money that might have funded good business ideas on Wall Street. With no antitrust laws, corporations began to grow much bigger, and many ran roughshod over both customers and smaller competitors.

When Franklin Roosevelt said we could do better, he reined in the big banks and giant corporations in ways that had never been done before. Government became a more active participant in keeping

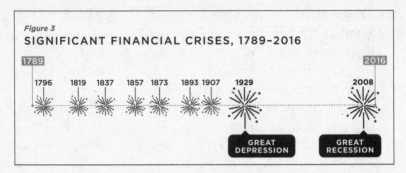

Figure 3
SIGNIFICANT FINANCIAL CRISES, 1789–2016

1789   2016

1796   1819   1837   1857   1873   1893 1907   1929   2008

GREAT DEPRESSION   **GREAT RECESSION**

After the Great Depression, regulations helped stop crashes.
When the regulations were undone, a bust followed.

markets honest. Together, over time, we built economic stability and growth. In the 1980s, Ronald Reagan turned that around. He declared that government was the enemy and began unraveling the regulatory net, and he led the country down a path that ultimately resulted in the greatest economic crash since the Great Depression.

The timeline above says it all: basic rules of the road bought us decades of financial stability, and weakening those rules put us back on the path to a giant boom and an even bigger bust.

Sure, there are lots of other pieces to the puzzle, and I'll talk about some of them later. But it's time to face facts: we have already paid dearly for the deadly mistakes of Reagan-era economics, and if we ignore the big lesson here, our country will ultimately pay an even higher price. Despite the evidence, a significant portion of the political elite seems determined to stay on the same path. The Republican president, the Republican leadership, and the Republicans in Congress continue to sing the same song: To propel this economy forward, put the regulators on a tight leash and then let giant corporations do whatever they like.

I've been in the U.S. Senate for four years, and I've listened to these guys until I can deliver most of their speeches in my sleep—after all, most of them are reciting the same mind-numbing nonsense they've chanted since Ronald Reagan first smiled and waved his way into the White House. It's as if the deregulation of the last thirty-five years never happened and the crash of 2008 was just a bad dream that can be whisked away with an elegant silk hankie.

When Donald Trump says he wants to repeal the financial regulations that President Obama put in place, he's just signing up for the same old deregulation strategy that Republicans have embraced for decades. He even said Dodd-Frank "made it impossible for bankers to function." Well, it definitely made it harder for bankers to function in the reckless way they used to—that was the whole point! Republicans like Newt Gingrich say Trump's presidency is one more "great effort to break out of the Franklin Delano Roosevelt model" of government. I wonder if Newt is planning to bail out the banks himself next time around.

I don't love all regulations—no one does—but some problems can be solved only when our government writes and enforces a set of rules. How else are we going to take on fraud, antitrust issues, and a banking industry that has the power to wreck our economy? Look at it this way: if corporations *can* cheat people or crush their competitors or load up on risks—and if their top executives *can* stuff their own pockets by leading their corporations in those directions—then sooner or later, one of them *will* do it. And once one of them cheats, everyone else is caught in a bind—follow the cheater or get left behind? Not every CEO of a giant bank may have wanted to get into the scam-your-customer mortgage business, but once the competitors were raking in hundreds of millions of dollars from it, the practice got really hard to resist.

This big, dynamic, very complicated economy of ours needs some basic regulations in place to make sure markets work, and it's not hard to come up with some straightforward rules that can make an enormous difference.

For starters, we should put in place a modern version of Glass-Steagall and separate plain-vanilla banking like checking accounts and savings accounts from crazy risk-taking on Wall Street. This doesn't have to be partisan. My first cosponsor for a twenty-first-century Glass-Steagall bill was the Republicans' 2008 presidential nominee, Senator John McCain. In 2016, Donald Trump campaigned on this idea, and, at his insistence, adopting Glass-Steagall was added to the Republican platform. But the

Republican leadership in the House and the Senate has refused to move any such legislation, and now President Trump has put in place an economic team that is headed in the opposite direction. No one ever offers to explain exactly why giant banks should be able to benefit from government insurance and gamble on Wall Street at the same time, but the bank lobbyists have managed to block this bill from going forward.

Here's another idea: the SEC should hire a leader who doesn't work for Wall Street—and it should get a much bigger budget so that the agency can actually go out and enforce the law. There have been some good SEC commissioners who have shown some real courage, and this shouldn't be partisan either, but the latest nominee to head up the SEC built his entire career by aggressively protecting Wall Street from government regulators. Anyone who thinks he's suddenly going to get tough on the same people who fed him so well for so many years doesn't know the chummy Wall Street fraternity.

Oh, and here's a good one: when CEOs break the law, they ought to go to jail, just like anyone else. The words chiseled in stone above the Supreme Court are EQUAL JUSTICE UNDER LAW. This is not followed by EXCEPT FOR CORPORATE EXECUTIVES.

Let's also put some steel in the spines of our prosecutors and start enforcing antitrust laws again. Small drugstores and start-up airlines and even innovative new approaches to health insurance should get a chance to try out their ideas. I believe in a government that works for the people—not for the giants in the industry—and that government should promote competition every chance it gets. Concentration is bad for consumers and bad for innovators; worst of all, it puts everyone at risk when things really go south.

I understand that not everyone will agree with me on each of these proposals. But let's be clear: America has been warned, first with the S&L crisis in the 1980s and then with the crash of 2008. We survived, but that last financial bomb was nearly fatal for our economy—and for tens of millions of American families. We can't afford another hit.

And the risk is *still there*. As one top economic commentator pointed out recently, "Since 2010, there have been major scandals at banks on nearly every continent for every reason: malfeasance, incompetence, complacency." In 2016 alone—*eight years* after the financial crash and even after tougher regulations were put in place—three major banks got into serious trouble. Deutsche Bank hid so much risk on its books that the International Monetary Fund said it posed a substantial threat to the global financial system. Wells Fargo was caught pumping up its stock price by cheating more than two million customers. And Citigroup agreed to pay hundreds of millions of dollars in fines for manipulative practices that gave it an illegal advantage in trades.

Meanwhile, banks are *still* Too Big to Fail. Actually, some are bigger than ever, or So Big We Can't Let Them Stub Their Little Toesies. The Federal Reserve Bank and the FDIC recently announced that Wells Fargo was so large and so badly managed that if that bank alone started to stumble, it could drag the whole economy down with it—unless, of course, it got a bailout. In a long academic paper, a former Treasury secretary and an economist analyzed volumes of financial data about banks. Their conclusion: in 2016, the big banks are not significantly safer than they were just before the crash in 2008—in fact, they may be even riskier. The financial crisis is long past, yet the banking sector is still loaded with corporations that could blow up the economy? Good grief. We need stronger rules, not weaker ones.

This stuff is serious—serious as a heart attack. The big banks put *all* of us at risk, and it's the kind of risk familiar to my grandparents: it's lose-your-house, lose-your-job, lose-all-your-savings risk. Giant corporations that jack up their prices or run over their competitors may not cause our economy to explode, but they squeeze us in so many ways that they're capable of causing a long, slow decline, one that could become irreversible.

Every problem is made worse by the fact that the world in which these giant banks and corporations operate is getting faster and more complex every day. A debt crisis in Greece or Hong Kong can have ripple effects that influence lives in small towns in Ohio or Alaska. Republicans may want to look the other way, they may continue to make their mindless demand for smaller government, and they may pretend that helping giant corporations will always help America's working families. But this is a fiction we can no longer afford.

Roosevelt was right: we can do better. We need some clear-eyed people in the room, people who recognize that we are heading straight into disaster. We need fearless public servants who will pick up the tools of government, put the interests of the people ahead of those of the banks, and do everything possible to reduce the risk of catastrophe.

Aunt Bee and I were on the phone in late 1999, not too long before she died. At ninety-eight, her health was beginning to slip a little, but she still loved to talk. We often spent these calls remembering the people who were gone—her brothers and sisters, my grandparents, little Jimmy, who died of leukemia when he was twelve. The other character in our family play—the Great Depression—was still there, too. "Those were hard times, Betsy," she said during that call. "But we made it."

Yes, the Great Depression was a bone cruncher, but it was also our chance to build a stronger America—and that's what we did. We built a better country then, and we can build a better country now. We have to be smart: as conditions change and as corporations figure out new ways to cheat people or crush their smaller competitors, we must adapt our regulatory tools so we can fight back. But we've got to start by picking up those tools and using them.

Government is not our enemy; government *for the people* is our ally. Government—not corporate America—provides a way to enforce some basic rules so that all kinds of markets work. And as Roosevelt showed us, the markets must not be allowed to work only for the rich and powerful. They've got to work for all of us.

3

Making—and Breaking—the Middle Class

When the kids were little, I took them to church most Sunday mornings. The Methodist church near our house out in the far-flung suburbs was not a big place—it looked a lot like a child's drawing of a church and steeple. As a sign of keeping his priorities straight, the preacher started every sermon in the fall with an important reassurance: "Good morning. Kickoff today will be at twelve-oh-five. Relax. We'll be out by eleven fifty-five."

I helped out in little ways at the church from time to time, like corralling the shepherds for the Christmas pageant, but mostly we drove to church, stayed for the service, and went home. When the preacher pulled me aside one Sunday morning to ask a favor, I was surprised to learn that he wanted me to teach fifth-grade Sunday school. My children were still very young, I was just getting started as a law professor, and I had no experience with fifth graders. Besides, between work and children, I was barely keeping it all together.

I politely said no.

The preacher urged me, then finally pretty much begged me. *Please*, he said. Everyone else has turned me down. It's an emergency. We've gone through four teachers in three months. The kids are *very active*. Please do this. You don't actually have to teach them anything. Just make sure no one gets hurt.

I went in with low aspirations, and the first couple of weeks I didn't even clear that bar. Boys climbed out the windows. An art project ended up with one girl's braids cut off and a gaping hole torn in a boy's shirt. One Sunday, several children left the class with parts of their hands, arms, and faces dyed blue (it's a long story).

I finally realized that forty minutes of running art projects was going to result in more chaos—and possible permanent injury. So I decided to try the one thing I thought I could do: teach.

I figured that if I knew how to teach law students, I could surely teach something to these kids—right? When teaching the law, my approach was to use the Socratic method, which means that everyone reads the assigned materials, and the professor, instead of lecturing, asks questions. If it works right, the questions prompt the students to examine the materials more closely and develop tools to understand more difficult materials.

The next Sunday, I handed out a Bible story and told everyone they had ten minutes to read it before I was going to ask them some really hard questions. A few kids wiggled around and kicked their legs, but everyone made it through the story. Then I started.

"So what do you think Noah felt when he first heard God's voice?"

It took a little pushing and a few very silly answers: "He thought he was going crazy!" "He thought Martians were talking to him!" "He thought he had a talking worm in his ear!" But the kids began to engage, just a little. And by the time the class was over, no one had escaped or been seriously injured.

Sunday after Sunday, we fell into a rhythm: a story and a lot of questions. We dropped the art projects, started passing out cookies, and talked about floods and lions and loaves and fishes. We also talked about fear and courage and mercy and revenge.

One day we talked about charity and giving. The particular story from the Bible mattered less than the fact that the fifth graders had their own stories to tell. They liked talking about why we give.

And then I reversed the question: What do we *owe* to each other? Not just what do we decide to give or not give, but what are the basic things everyone should promise to do?

Kids jumped in. At the top of their list was not to hurt each other.

They started piling on examples—no pushing, no hitting, no calling names, no putting boogers in your little brother's food. (That was a rule I'd never thought of.) But was that all? Did we owe anything more to other human beings?

One of the kids, Jesse, was bigger than most of the others. A sturdy boy already nearly as tall as I was, he was often a ringleader for trouble. Jesse had hung back for most the discussions, so when he raised his hand, I went straight to him.

Jesse said, "Everybody gets a turn."

THE AMERICAN DEAL

Jesse might have had playground rules in mind—including some he had chafed under—but I liked his answer. A chance. An opportunity. An opening. Everybody gets a turn.

Almost from the beginning, America defined itself as the land of opportunity. Opportunity had originally meant a chance to come to a new country to exploit its riches or to build a community of like-minded worshippers or to move west and homestead new land. By the twentieth century, education had created new opportunities. Our public school system helped integrate immigrant families and opened up new possibilities for poor children. Public universities were founded throughout the nation to give anyone who worked hard a chance to get an education and build a future. Our country wasn't perfect, but we were opening up opportunity for more and more people, and growing a stronger, more innovative economy.

During the Depression, Roosevelt doubled down on what we owed each other. He pressed for assistance to our fellow citizens: unemployment insurance, Social Security for the elderly, aid for widows and orphans, and help for the blind. While many described these moves as acts of charity, they weren't. Charity is freely given or withheld. Maybe help will be there, and maybe it won't.

In the 1930s, when America created Social Security, unemployment insurance, and aid for those in trouble, we laid down a new social contract. Through our government, we worked together to form a giant insurance program, with each of us contributing through taxes. When we needed a hand, we could turn to each other, through our government, to help us make it through. It was a forceful statement that we were all in one big American boat together—rich and poor, working and nonworking, young and old.

The idea behind this statement may have begun with the desire to help those hit by misfortune, but it encompassed much more. It was also about helping people have access to more opportunity. Or, as a fifth grader like Jesse might put it, everybody gets a turn.

After World War II, a grateful nation offered soldiers returning from World War II the GI Bill to help them go to college or technical school. In the 1950s and 1960s, the federal government funneled even more money into our colleges and universities, both by supporting on-campus research and by making student loans and grants available to people who couldn't afford tuition. The federal government also started pouring billions of dollars into building new elementary and high schools across the country. The impact was immediate: the number of Americans in elementary school, in secondary school, and in colleges and universities skyrocketed.

Government—all of us together—made other investments during the twentieth century that helped foster opportunities. We put a lot of money into infrastructure—roads, bridges, dams, power. That spending was also about building opportunity. By advancing giant projects all around the country, Roosevelt gave jobs to people stuck in bread lines. But long after the Great Depression had eased and World War II had created a labor shortage, the federal government continued to invest heavily in infrastructure, embarking on huge projects like an Interstate Highway System and magnificent dams, along with smaller projects like footbridges and new post office buildings.

Infrastructure spending was like education spending: an investment in future possibilities. No one knew who would dream up the next great business idea or where a new invention might come from, but we were pretty sure that to turn it into a successful enterprise, the innovator would need infrastructure—electricity to power their operations, roads and bridges to bring their goods to market, and public transportation so workers could get to work every day. It was an unspoken agreement with benefits for all: everyone would contribute to help build the roads and power plants, and then, when the businesses grew, there would be profits for the investors and better jobs for the workers. Not every business undertaking succeeded, not by a long shot. But every investment in infrastructure helped expand opportunities for all of us.

And one more form of public spending shot up during the postwar period: investments in research. Research of every kind—medical, scientific, engineering, psychology, social science—was honored and supported. Government agencies and universities brought together teams of researchers who worked on hugely ambitious projects. We were like explorers, and the unknown territories included destinations as near as our own DNA and as far as the moon.

This commitment to invest in research was an innovation in its own right. We had long invested in education and roads and bridges, but now we were even bolder: America was investing in ideas. The results were transformative; they included some of the greatest technological achievements the planet has ever seen. We took chance after chance, funding basic research that eventually led to the Internet, GPS, and a map of the human genome.

Most of the time, we couldn't point to a specific outcome or benefit that we knew would result from our investment in research. But at the core of our American optimism was the belief that if we helped smart people study hard problems, our scientists and engineers and inventors would build a pipeline of ideas that would permit our children and grandchildren to do truly remarkable things. And for a nation of adventurers, that was the very definition of opportunity.

For me, this is the basic American contract, one that's as simple as a handshake agreement. We all pay taxes, and in return we all benefit— sometimes immediately, sometimes down the road—and we also help build opportunity for the generations to come. I first tried to put this into words in 2011 when I was thinking about running for the Senate: "There is nobody in this country who got rich on his own—nobody." My point was that everyone who succeeds gets some help from the investments we've all made. And we keep on making those investments so the next kid will get a chance, too.

Education, infrastructure, research—investing in all three during the twentieth century built a bright future for our country. And we forged that future together.

UNIONS HELPED BUILD AMERICA'S MIDDLE CLASS

The onset of the Great Depression forced millions of unemployed people to compete for jobs, and a lot of them would take just about any work. Aunt Bee watched as most of the women she worked with were sent home. People lined up by the dozens—and even the hundreds—for a single job opening. Most observers at the time thought the high rates of unemployment would be the death knell for American unions. For a while, it seemed they were right. By 1933, union membership had been cut almost in half from its high point in the 1920s.

But Roosevelt thought that stronger unions could help get America's families back on their feet. During his first term, he pushed through laws that guaranteed unions the right to organize and that required companies to bargain in good faith with any union the workers chose. He protected workers who wanted to unionize; no longer could an employer intimidate or fire workers who tried to organize. And he used his bully pulpit, famously saying, "If I were a factory worker, I would join a union." The laws weren't perfect, but they set the groundwork and signaled that the president was committed, and the unions swung into action. They aggressively recruited members and then called strikes for better working conditions, higher wages, and more job security—right in the middle of a severe depression.

Amazingly, it worked.

Unions slowly began to gain strength, and the numbers of union workers started rising. The impact was felt by millions of union families; surprisingly, it was also felt by millions of *non*-union families, as unions changed the economics of the workforce and used their growing clout on behalf of all workers.

Over time, unions joined other groups to pass child labor laws, a federal minimum wage, the forty-hour workweek, workplace safety rules, and workers' compensation. The unions lobbied aggressively for unemployment insurance—not just for union members, but for every worker. Together, the unions helped rewrite the social contract between American workers and American corporations.

Union membership rose dramatically in the late 1930s, and during the postwar years it continued to climb. By the mid-1950s, more than a third of all workers carried union cards. When she was in her fifties, Aunt Bee finally married. Her husband was a widower who had a tidy little house and a nice pension—courtesy of thirty years with the meatpackers' union. Uncle Stanley's hands were scarred from years of working long shifts around heavy cleavers and sharp knives, and his back and knees were pretty much shot. But I never heard him complain. When the cold weather made his hands ache, he would rub them together and tell me, "It was good to have a job, Betsy—a good *union* job."

The rise of union membership in the depths of the Great Depression reflected—and influenced—a changing vision of how our country would build success. Union membership was as much a moral commitment as an economic strategy. Unions thrived on solidarity, a notion that people have greater power when they work together and that shared prosperity helps insulate everyone from the consequences of individual misfortune.

As unions gained strength, workers built more leverage, and they used it to bargain for a greater share of the wealth created by an expanding

Uncle Travis and Aunt Lucy
with Aunt Bee and Uncle Stanley (on the right)
in front of the tidy little house that a good union job bought.

economy. The share of new income going to union workers increased, but the share going to non-union workers increased as well.

Listen to that again: as more people joined unions, all workers did better. How much better? According to detailed studies by labor economists, unions raise the wages and benefits of non-union workers by about 28 percent. I should say that all workers did a *lot* better.

Decades after union membership began surging, I got a small taste of what union power meant—and how hard some corporations fought to keep it at bay. My first husband, Jim, was the full-package 1970s math geek: pocket protector, sci-fi addict, computer obsessive. IBM had hired him straight out of college, and he worked on the Apollo space missions. A couple of years later, he was assigned to work on the antiballistic missile defense system. He spent his days poring over spreadsheets and hunting down bugs. I confess that I was a little surprised when he breezed in one evening and announced, "I'm going to be a manager." He wasn't really a people person. But he'd be managing other math-geek programmers, so maybe it would work out fine.

IBM quickly packed him off to its own special management school. He came back loaded with notebooks and stories. Top among the instructions drilled into all new managers was the "one-breath rule."

Okay, I was hooked. What's the one-breath rule? I asked.

Jim explained that whenever any employee uttered the word "union"—at lunch, in the men's room, while drinking a beer after work—a manager was allowed "one breath" before he passed the information up the line to his own manager. In other words, *report this person immediately*!

I didn't get it. Why was this so important?

Jim sighed as if I'd missed a very obvious point and then spelled it out for me: Because our division of IBM isn't a union shop, because we don't want to have anything to do with unions, and because management needs to know whether there's any union talk, so they can stop it immediately.

I must have looked a little shocked, because he rushed on. This is a good thing, he explained, because we don't *need* unions. And here's how we lock them out: we keep tabs on exactly how much union guys are getting paid for the same kind of work and then pay 2 or 3 percent more. Everybody wins.

I shot back, with maybe just a touch of acid in my voice: But wait, somebody else's union did all the work to negotiate the best possible pay, and then you guys made sure no one at IBM joined up. How exactly does this mean that everybody wins?

The way I saw it, whether or not unions collected dues from workers at IBM or any other company, those unions helped push up wages and improve benefits for everyone who earned a paycheck.

GOVERNMENT WORKED FOR MOST AMERICANS

From the 1930s through the 1970s, America deliberately invested in opportunity. The government worked hard to expand chances for millions of people: the chance for children to get a good education, the chance for workers to build economic security, and the chance for seniors to retire with dignity.

And here's the best part: this dynamic investment in the future worked. We made it work for *all* of us, not just those at the top.

It wasn't perfect, but for almost half a century, incomes in our country grew across the board. The median worker was doing better and better. Wages picked up rapidly from the end of the Depression through World War II, and then they kept right on climbing for decades. As I noted earlier, even after adjusting for inflation and even after the low wages of the Depression and the impact of World War II—even after all that, from 1947 to 1980, the man smack in the middle increased his earnings by about 65 percent.

The GDP kept growing, and as the country got richer, it was regular, hardworking America who accrued most of the benefits. From 1935 to 1980, 90 percent of America—everyone outside the top 10 percent—got 70 percent of all income growth. Sure, that's not ideal, but when 90 percent of the country enjoys real growth in earnings—not including government transfers like housing subsidies or Social Security—it's pretty great. For nearly five decades, when we built wealth in this country, just about everyone got a piece of it.

Let me underline that point: this isn't a story about the very top and the very bottom—about the 1 percent or the 0.01 percent. It isn't a story

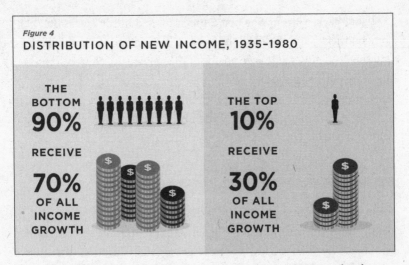

Figure 4
DISTRIBUTION OF NEW INCOME, 1935–1980

THE BOTTOM **90%** RECEIVE **70%** OF ALL INCOME GROWTH

THE TOP **10%** RECEIVE **30%** OF ALL INCOME GROWTH

From 1935 to 1980, most of America shared in the new income produced.

about billionaires. This is a story about widely shared prosperity. About people buying homes and washing machines. About people putting aside a little savings and helping the kids through college. About a paid-off mortgage and a secure retirement. About the understanding that Mom and Dad worked hard so the kids would do even better. Our extraordinary achievement as a country was the very ordinariness of what we built: millions and millions and millions of families had solid, secure lives, and millions more weren't there yet but could see a path to their own home and their own security. We shaped federal policies to build a middle class, and then that middle class became the very identity of this country.

From 1935 to 1980, people at *every* income level—poor people, working families, middle-class families, upper-middle-class families, rich people—were doing better and better. In fact, incomes were growing faster for families across the bottom and the middle than at the very top. We designed our policies to make this country work for most of America, and that's exactly what it did. It was truly amazing.

This is what makes me hopeful. We don't need to sit around and say, "Gee, I wonder how we could get some serious income growth for most of America." We don't have to invent an anti-gravity machine or some other sci-fi wonder. It's not necessary to debate whether such a thing is even possible. We know how to do it because we've *already done it*.

THE SHADOW OF RACE

The story of how America built a great middle class—and how we were on track to expand that middle class to wider and wider circles of Americans—is not nearly so neat and tidy as I have told it. There were lots of potholes and backward steps along the way.

One of the harshest failures was that our country didn't provide equal opportunity for everyone. Growth was widely shared, but the New Deal loaded its gains toward white families and building a white middle class. For example, two occupations held by most black workers—farm laborer and household worker—were initially excluded from Social Security. Dragged down by more than a century of systemic racism, African Americans struggled to catch up with white families economically. The black-white wealth gap, which has been present for as long as we've been counting—with whites consistently earning more than blacks at the top of the economic ladder, at the bottom, and at every place in between—remained far too wide. Meanwhile, women and Jews were often deliberately and aggressively shut out of certain jobs and certain schools, while gays and lesbians were locked firmly in the closet.

But opportunity is a stubborn idea, and America kept expanding the dream. As the civil rights movement gained steam in the 1960s and 1970s, the belief that everyone deserved a chance at a good life began to grow in new directions. Laws prohibiting discrimination in employment, housing, and transportation were passed, and the Supreme Court banned the deliberate segregation of schools. Enforcement was tentative at best, but when African Americans trying to take advantage of their new freedoms met resistance, the federal government got more and more actively involved in protecting the equal rights of all people. Voting rights increased the political clout of African Americans as well.

The impact was measurable. Over time, the financial disparity between black and white families began to shrink. From the mid-1960s through the 1970s, the black-white wealth gap shrank by 30 percent.

This was no more than a start, but it signified real and meaningful progress.

The period from 1935 to 1980 was both turbulent and exciting. Change didn't come easy; it never does. But change did come, and as a country we slowly expanded the idea of greater opportunity to encompass more and more of those who had once been excluded. And as opportunity for everyone became a more essential part of our national identity, we strengthened economic security for ever-wider circles of Americans. For decades, government—the decisions we made together—was central to forging those changes.

AN AMERICAN STORY

Growing up, I was the direct beneficiary of investments in America's middle class.

I was the family baby—the child born long after the baby crib and high chair had been given away, the surprise that came along after my mother thought (as I often heard her say) that she was "through with such things."

I was a cheerful, high-energy kid. I careened through much of my early life covered in Band-Aids and a bright red antiseptic called Mercurochrome. I broke my nose for the first time when I was seven, and again in an accident with Uncle Stanley, before I hit my theoretically more ladylike teens.

We lived in Norman, Oklahoma, in one of those little houses thrown up in the years right after World War II. One living room, two bedrooms, and a single bathroom, which was in high demand by our family of six. My three older brothers slept in the converted garage, with a slab floor that was cool in the summer and icy enough to freeze your toes off in the winter. Years later, when I was preparing a university lecture about housing finance, Daddy told me that he and Mother had gotten a federally guaranteed loan to buy that little house.

It was twelve blocks to Wilson Elementary, an old, red brick building that had recently been expanded, with a new wing out back. I loved that school. Even today, I can describe countless details of my second-grade classroom: the arrangement of the chairs for the reading groups, the big charts on the wall where we recorded the books we'd read, the too-sweet flavor of the orange drink that cost a dime. Our classroom was sunny and cheerful, organized and calm, and Mrs. Lee presided over all of it—a woman with sturdy shoes, an ample bosom, and a surprisingly gravelly voice. I lived for her soft, smoky hugs.

Back in the 1950s, not many women worked, especially after they were married. But teaching was different, or so Mrs. Lee said. In the fall of my second-grade year, she took me aside to say that, if I wanted to, I could *do something*. Sometime around the middle of the year, I went up to Mrs. Lee and delivered the announcement that I would be a teacher—a schoolteacher just like her! She smiled her small but satisfied smile and said to me, "Yes, Miss Betsy, you can."

After that, she put me in charge of the Yellow Birds reading group, the kids who couldn't read as well as the Blue Birds or the Red Birds. I settled in on the teacher's chair while eight or nine kids sitting in a horseshoe around me read out loud, and I patiently (I hope) filled in the words they didn't know. When the kid with thick glasses finally recognized the word "together" after three or four tries, a blast of pure delight shot through me. Sure, I knew how to read it, but now, so did he!

I was a goner. I harassed the neighborhood children to read out loud so I could play teacher, and when I couldn't get any takers, I lined up my dolls and propped books in their laps.

My mother thought the whole idea of my being a teacher was ridiculous. No one in our family had graduated from college; besides, Mother was suspicious of women who had families and worked. Working was for women who weren't lucky enough to have a husband and children. I think she assumed that I'd give up on the idea as I got older, but I didn't. She fretted that I didn't do "normal girl things" like trying on makeup or curling my hair, and she used to remind me not to wear my reading glasses. "Men never make passes at girls who wear glasses," she would say.

By the time I was a teenager, whenever she heard me talking about my dreams of teaching, my mother would break into the conversation and explain to whomever I was talking to, "But she doesn't want to be an old-maid schoolteacher." (You could almost hear the fright music playing

Scattered through this picture are the kids from my reading group.
I hope I was nice. (I'm in the middle of the back row with the tall kids.)

in the background.) Then she would turn to me, pause, and narrow her eyes. "Right, Betsy?"

At seventeen, I headed off to college on a scholarship, listing my intended major as "education." Two years later, Jim Warren, the same math geek I mentioned earlier, took me out for a cheeseburger and proposed. We were married less than eight weeks later.

I know it sounds nuts. How could I have said yes? I was in college on a full scholarship, halfway to graduation and my teaching certificate. But I didn't hesitate to drop out of college and marry Jim.

For nineteen years I had absorbed the lesson that the best and most important thing any girl could do was "marry well," which roughly translated into "find a decent man" and "get some financial security." And for nineteen years I had also absorbed the message that I was a pretty iffy case—not very pretty, not very flirty, and definitely not very good at making boys feel like they were smarter than I was. Somewhere deep in my heart, I believed that no man would ever ask me to marry him. When Jim popped the question, I was so shocked that it took me about a nanosecond to say yes.

I was going to get to be a wife after all, and probably a mother, too. I was walking on air. And that whole plan to go to college and teach? My mother had predicted that it would go away, and now I supposed she was right.

A week after Jim and I were married, I started doing temp work at an office, mostly answering the phones and substituting for people who were sick or on vacation. I still thought about teaching. I mentioned it, but with the kind of I-wish tone that meant I knew it wasn't going to happen. Then one day, my supervisor asked me if I knew that there was a commuter college about forty minutes away. I'd never even seen the University of Houston, but I got on the phone and started asking questions.

That night, I pounced on Jim as he came in the door: "I could go back to school. I could get my degree."

We were already on a tight budget, and Jim immediately threw up the most obvious objection: "We can't afford it."

But I was ready with my counterargument: "Tuition is only fifty dollars a semester. Even with books and gas, I can cover the cost with a part-time job."

And that's what I did. Along with the thousands of other people who filled up the University of Houston's parking lots, raced to classes, and then returned to their families and jobs just as quickly, I worked my way toward a college degree. This was my chance, and I was desperate to make the most of it.

A year and a half later, Jim was transferred from Houston to New Jersey, and we moved to the Northeast. This time I didn't let anything throw me off: I finished up my degree with two correspondence courses. With my college diploma at last in hand, I found my first teaching job, working mostly with special-needs kids.

And that was how it went. One door opened, and behind it was another door. After Amelia was born, Jim didn't want me to work full-time, but after a couple of years, he was okay with my going back to school. I loved my work as a teacher, only now I headed in another direction. What I knew about law I'd learned from television; still, working as a lawyer and defending those who needed help sounded good.

A little research led me to Rutgers, a public law school that cost $460 a semester. The tough part would be getting there: a long drive through back-to-back towns, dotted with stoplights and school zones and tangled traffic. Then, just a couple of months before the fall term began, a new section of the interstate highway opened, a spur that made it possible for me to zip from our house in Rockaway, New Jersey, to the law school in Newark in just twenty-five minutes. If it is possible to love a highway, I loved that highway.

Every weekday morning, I packed up little Amelia and dropped her off at day care, then aimed my old Volkswagen Beetle toward the interstate and drove to Rutgers. The students proudly called the place the "The People's Electric Law School." The people's school—that sounded about right to me.

I graduated nine months pregnant and 100 percent unemployable. I practiced law out of my living room for a while. When clients came by, I kicked the toys under the couch and tried to look calm and lawyerly. And then I got another chance to do the thing I loved most: teach. The call came, and this time I was teaching law students in their twenties instead of little kids, but I loved it all the same. The prospect of bringing some-

Big kids or little kids, I loved teaching.

one right to the edge of a new discovery—and then watching them make the leap—was as thrilling as ever. Even now, I still have dreams about teaching.

I worked hard, really hard. But I never forgot that a big part of my opportunity to become a law professor came from the fact that America invested in kids like me. Together, America built decent housing, good public schools, a state-of-the-art transportation system, and affordable state colleges. Our economy provided plenty of good jobs for people with all sorts of backgrounds. And woven throughout was the strong belief that even if you fell off the track, you could pull yourself up and get another chance. To this day, I remain deeply grateful.

TAX CUTS FOR THE RICH

After future Supreme Court justice Lewis Powell wrote his secret memo in 1971 urging conservatives and the leaders of giant companies to fight for a more pro-business agenda, Republicans seized on the notion that deregulation could do wonders for corporate and individual wealth. But limiting regulations was only half of the loaf, and businesses wanted the whole loaf. If the taxes they paid could be cut, these corporations would have more money—more money to distribute to shareholders, more money to pay executives, more money to buy other businesses, more money to expand. So the essence of what became known as trickle-down economics was a two-pronged approach: fire the cops *and* cut taxes for big companies and those at the top.

Tax cuts were a key ingredient in the magic, trickle-down formula. And in 1981, President Ronald Reagan was sworn into office and became the chief wizard. Picture Reagan and a bunch of other old guys waving magic wands as glitter dust sprinkles across the land. With each wave of the wand, corporations (and millionaires and billionaires) could keep more of their money, and then—here comes the magic part—everyone else would be richer, too! Even the national debt would shrink, because when rich people have more money, the government will also have more money. In fact, these apparently benevolent wizards promised us that incomes and government revenues would grow so fast that all those tax cuts would just pay for themselves. The future was all rainbows and pots of gold—really, just like magic!

True, there were a few Debbie Downers raining on the magical parade. Reagan's own vice president, George H. W. Bush, once labeled it "voodoo economics." Others worried that those tax cuts wouldn't make anyone richer except the rich people who pocketed more money. Eventually, study after careful study—government studies and academic studies—showed that Reagan's tax cuts did exactly what a lot of people had expected they would: they reduced government revenues and increased the national debt.

Sure, the whole idea was nuts. It was a little as if Marie Antoinette told the starving French peasants that they were better off every time she got another piece of cake.

In France, the starving peasants wouldn't buy it, but Reagan and all his economic advisers kept selling their wacky idea, and eventually tax cuts became the new religion. First there was one tax cut, and then another and another. While he was president, Reagan slashed rates across the board, but especially at the top, resulting in small breaks for working families and giant breaks for giant corporations and millionaires.

Over time, this bad idea got worse. Instead of demanding across-the-board tax cuts (the kind that would show up on charts like the one on the next page), corporations began to press for more targeted—and more secretive—cuts. Lobbyists devised highly specific loopholes in the laws, then sold them to pliable friends in Congress. As the tax code got more and more complex, special breaks often applied only to a specific industry or even a particular company. Best of all, at least from the corporate perspective, the complexity of these tax loopholes kept them hidden from the public. And without public oversight, it got easier and easier to make changes to the tax code. Inevitably, the corporations and their lobbyists got greedier and greedier.

Some of these loopholes rewarded big corporations for doing exactly what they were already doing. So, for example, guys who owned golf courses got a loophole that had been intended for environmental conservation. (Donald Trump, for one, used this deduction more than once.)

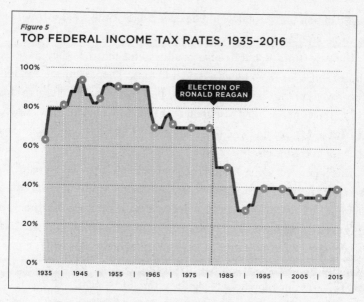

Figure 5
TOP FEDERAL INCOME TAX RATES, 1935–2016

*Once Reagan became president, the wealthiest Americans
got to keep more of their money.*

I'm all for protecting the environment, but giving developers a special tax break for their fancy private golf courses is crazy.

Some loopholes gave corporations breaks for investing overseas instead of here at home. One loophole even gives corporations a tax deduction for paying punitive damages when they break the law. In 2015, the *New York Times* reported that "at least 80 percent of the more than $42 billion that BP has paid out because of the 2010 Deepwater Horizon rig explosion that killed 11 people and spewed oil into the Gulf of Mexico qualifies for a tax deduction." Think about that: BP got fined for killing people and nearly destroying the Gulf of Mexico—and its fine was tax deductible, sort of like a charitable contribution or a regular business expense. And BP wasn't the only corporation rewarded this way. In the same article, the paper reported that "the same day in 2013 that JPMorgan Chase announced a $13 billion deal [to escape prosecution] from the Justice Department, the bank's chief financial officer emphasized that $7 billion of the total would be deductible." Golly, that sort of takes the sting out of being fined for nearly destroying the U.S. economy.

The next time Republicans proudly point out that they have not raised a single tax by so much as one thin dime, I hope someone holds up a picture of smiling executives at BP and JPMorgan Chase. Refusal to close tax loopholes has worked just great for a company that nearly destroyed the Gulf of Mexico and one that helped wreck the economy—but not so much for everyone else.

This high-level game of Find the Loophole had another consequence. These new tax cuts were effectively out of reach for anyone who couldn't devise all kinds of sophisticated accounting techniques and complex business arrangements and who couldn't hire the most expensive tax lawyers and lobbyists in the country. Local businesses, smaller companies, and industries that didn't invest in lobbying were just plain left out. This was one more way to rig the economic system.

The lopsided system is on full display in our international tax rules. Most small businesses keep their money in a local bank or credit union. Not so for a handful of giant U.S. corporations that today hold a collective $2.3 trillion overseas. (Just to provide a little context: that's more money than *all* reported corporate profits in the United States in 2013.) How much do those companies save? Well, for the corporations that stash their money in tax havens, their average federal income taxes run about 3 percent.

For years, numerous high-powered business commentators and CEOs, usually with well-coiffed hair and hand-tailored suits, have appeared on business news shows to whine that the 39 percent corporate tax rate in the United States is one of the highest in the world. Hold on just one little minute here. What all those executives and corporate suck-ups fail to mention is that, after all the deductions, exceptions, and credits, the *average* corporation's tax rate is about 20 percent.

And where does our corporate tax rate rank us compared to other countries? Not compared to the tax havens, but to the rest of the developed world? In the bottom 25 percent. Yup, about three-quarters of all developed nations, including Japan, Canada, and the United Kingdom, charge higher corporate tax rates than we do. So when the CEO of Chase,

Jamie Dimon, gives an interview about the advice he's offering to Donald Trump, and he explains, "The problem is that our tax rate is so much higher than the rest of the world," either he's badly misinformed or he's just doing a little old-fashioned, hands-on, slick-move lobbying by telling the president to give corporate America another tax cut.

But what the give-us-lower-business-taxes crowd really doesn't want to talk about is plain old tax evasion. In fact, the tax code is now so knotted with exceptions and credits that, for some of the biggest companies, their effective federal income tax rate is zero. You heard that right: not 39 percent, not 20 percent. Zero percent.

Want some examples? For five years, Verizon, Boeing, and General Electric paid *nothing* in net federal income taxes. These three Fortune 500 companies hauled in nearly $80 billion in combined profits and actually got tax *rebates* from the federal government. How clever is that? They dodged all federal income taxes—and the government essentially paid them a bonus to do it.

Who actually pays to keep the lights on at the Social Security Administration? Who pays the heating bill at the Pentagon? Who pays to pave our interstate highways and keep our research labs open? Who pays to make sure our military has equipment and our veterans have medical care? That burden increasingly falls to families and small businesses. In the early 1950s, corporations paid about one out of every three dollars it took to run the government. Today, that share has dropped, and now corporations pay about one out of every ten dollars.

No question: the crazy "cut taxes for those at the top" mantra never made any sense. But it worked magic for the giant corporations, for their highly paid lobbyists, and for Marie Antoinette. It helped the rich get richer.

MORE BOMBS AND FEWER TEXTBOOKS

More cake for the rich and privileged may sound harmless enough, but there was a far more sinister game at work here. One of the central players was Grover Norquist, the former chief economist for the U.S. Chamber of Commerce. It was his strong-arm strategy that gave away the darkest secret of the tax-cut game.

Starting in 1986, with a strong push from Ronald Reagan, Republicans made a big show of demanding that loyalists sign a "no new taxes" pledge. Norquist became the movement's lord high executioner. As the enforcer who had the power to banish any Republican who didn't sign the oath, he didn't pledge that tax cuts would somehow grow the economy and put caviar on every table. His pledge didn't pay lip service to trickle-down nonsense or say that somehow America would still find the money to build roads and fund medical research. Nope, not good old Grover. He just put on his brass knuckles and explained that the goal of his tax cuts was to shrink government so much that he would be able to "drown it in the bathtub."

And that's what began to happen—well, sort of. No, the military didn't shrink. In fact, defense spending rose by 34 percent during Reagan's presidency. And spending that was already guaranteed by law, like Social Security and Medicare, remained out of the Republicans' reach. But all other spending that Congress had to approve year after year was now on the chopping block. All the spending on education, on infrastructure, and on research. All the spending that had once helped build opportunity for America's families.

For decades, the surest sign that America was committed to opportunity was the government's consistent effort to provide ever-expanding access to education. From Head Start for children barely out of diapers to a growing public university system available to nearly everyone, we had been a country that lived by the rock-solid belief that a good education opened doors.

But the trickle-down policies of the Reagan years shifted America's priorities. At the same time that military spending expanded significantly, school funding was slashed by 15 percent. More bombs and fewer textbooks. And when the politicians figured out there was no price to pay politically, the cuts just kept on coming. Even during the Obama years, federal funding for education took a hard hit. In 2011, Republicans bargained for another 15 percent cut in return for increasing the debt ceiling and thus preventing the complete disruption of financial markets around the world. (Thanks for being such good-hearted patriots, guys!) Meanwhile, the states played their own trickle-down tunes. By 2014, thirty-one states had cut their K–12 funding to the point that it was below the 2008 prerecession levels.

It wasn't just the little kids whose opportunities took a beating. College kids' prospects also got pounded. Over the past thirty-plus years, the modern economy has crashed headlong into trickle-down economics, with disastrous results for students. Three things happened at the same time:

- A post–high school education was increasingly necessary for anyone who wanted a shot at the middle class.
- States cut their per-student support for public colleges, shifting more costs to students.
- Instead of reducing the burden on student borrowers, the federal government insisted on making a profit off lending to kids.

A $50-a-semester tuition changed my life. Today those kinds of options have simply disappeared. The commuter college I went to in 1970 now charges tuition of $10,312 a year for in-state students—and that's cheaper than most state schools. (Just so we're all on the same page: my $50 tuition from 1970 works out to about $300 in 2016 dollars.) The tuition for the University of Massachusetts Lowell, for example, now tops $14,000 a year for in-state students, and of course that doesn't include books, a dorm room, or any living expenses. Tuition for out-of-state students is more than double that amount. So it shouldn't be a big surprise that by 2015, more than 70 percent of college graduates had to borrow money from the federal government to make it through school. No wonder students have amassed a loan burden of $1.4 trillion.

And good luck to anyone who wants advanced technical training. A lot of companies desperately need highly trained workers: in manufacturing alone, there are an estimated six hundred thousand unfilled jobs, good jobs that could go to people with advanced technical training. But federal funding for career, technical, and adult education is minuscule; less than 3 percent of the Department of Education's budget goes to these sorts of programs. In many cases, there's too much demand for too few slots in community and technical colleges that offer vocational–technical training.

The quality of that training varies widely as well. Some community colleges offer first-rate vo-tech programs. Too often, however, these schools treat technical training as less important than their other programs, and they often measure their success by how many of their students go on to four-year colleges rather than by how many go on to good jobs. Making a bad situation worse, when there are budget cuts—and there have been plenty of them across the country—the vo-tech programs are frequently the first to be slashed, denying even more students a chance to enroll.

Recently the federal government has taken a stab at supporting apprenticeships, but the amounts available are far smaller than for other educational paths. Federal funding for certain kinds of apprenticeships currently ranges from $100 to $4,000 per student, versus $11,400 per student for those enrolled at two-year public colleges. And although some community colleges have expanded their training programs, no one believes that the supply of openings in good programs matches the need.

Some for-profit colleges have also discovered there is money to be made from students looking for technical training. A number of these schools boost their bottom line by making big promises and not delivering any real education, leaving their students saddled with high debts but little improvement in their job prospects. Remember Kai and her high-promise, low-performance art school in Seattle? These students are the losers in a cruel Darwinian game. Today, about 10 percent of all students are enrolled in for-profit colleges. Those students have signed on to about 20 percent of all student loan debt. And those same students, who heard great promises on the front end but often didn't get the training they needed, are responsible for more than 40 percent of all the student loan defaults.

The failure to invest in education is trickle-down economics at its ugliest. Cut taxes for those at the top and then pay for part of the resulting gap in federal revenues by forcing kids who need student loans for college to borrow more and more? That sure sounds like a plan to make America proud: crush the dreams and opportunities of millions of young people so that rich people and big corporations can pile up even more wealth.

What kind of country does something like that?

POLITICIANS SIDE WITH THE BILLIONAIRES

This is what really burns my behind: the trickle-down Republicans paid no price politically for helping the rich get richer and leaving everyone else behind. Okay, they could get away with it, but this still raises a serious question: Why would any elected official in this country want to push tax cuts for billion-dollar corporations while jacking up costs for kids just starting out?

Partly the answer is money—campaign contributions and subtler forms of financial grease, along with the lobbyists and the partisan marketing campaigns that play like background music in our democracy. (More coming up about that in the next chapter.)

But there's a deeper, uglier explanation for this disaster: a lot of people with real power simply don't care about these students.

People who hire lobbyists and wield a lot of political clout are often the same people who can pay for the finest private preschools and the most exclusive prep schools for their own children. Some of them don't get terribly alarmed when there are forty-two kids in a sixth-grade class and tiles are falling off the walls in the kids' bathrooms, because those things don't happen at the schools their children attend. And even if millions of kids have fewer and fewer opportunities, they know their kids will be guaranteed plenty of opportunities—all the opportunities money can buy. For some people, the problems faced by everyone else's children seem very far away.

So when I joined the U.S. Senate in 2013, I decided to plant a flag: whenever and however I could, I would take on some of the enormous challenges we face as we try to improve educational opportunities in our country. As it turned out, my first target would be the obscene amounts of money the federal government was making on student loans.

Not long after I was sworn in, my top education staffer was digging around in a federal budget document. Buried deep in the document was some complex language that, when carefully parsed, seemed to say that student loans were turning a profit for the U.S. government. We dug deeper still and then began asking a bunch of questions. Soon we learned that the Congressional Budget Office had estimated that overall, the federal government was on track to make about $174 billion in profits on its student loan port-folio. That's *$174 billion*. Off the backs of a bunch of young people who had to borrow money to make it through school. Oh, Lord.

The way I looked at it, that $174 billion was basically an extra tax on kids who go to college but whose parents can't afford to write a check for it. It's not a tax that Grover Norquist focuses on—he's devoting all his attention to long-suffering global corporations and rich people—but it's a real tax all the same.

Back in the 1960s, the government set up the student loan program to give middle-class kids and working-class kids the same shot at college as their wealthier counterparts. The students wouldn't get a free ride— the terms of their loans required that they pay a modest amount of interest—but at least they could borrow enough money to cover their basic expenses. Back then, the interest received by the government didn't cover all the costs, but because the American people believed in expand-ing educational opportunities, the loans were subsidized by the taxpay-ers. Imagine that: once upon a time, the government deliberately *lost* money on student loans.

Once again, I had been touched personally by this policy. When I'd first set off for college, at seventeen, my scholarship had come with a loan package. I would have to pay a small amount of interest, but the rest of the cost of that package would be picked up by U.S. taxpayers. That's how I got started. And now, here I was, a United States senator, and the gov-ernment budget that I would soon vote on would include profits made off students. The world had turned upside down.

During my first few weeks in the Senate, a parade of corporate exec-utives had trooped through my office. One of these executives, Jamie Dimon, the CEO of JPMorgan Chase, had deigned to offer me his advice on everything from public education to trade policy.

Mr. Dimon was not alone. The president and CEO of the Mortgage Bankers Association, the head of the American Bankers Association, and several representatives from big hedge funds all came knocking on my door—and the doors of most of the other new senators. Bankers and their highly paid lobbyists swarmed Congress like bees scouting out new flowers.

These were the guys who had made it through the crash, and now they were riding high again. In many cases, the government had lent a generous helping hand: JPMorgan Chase had picked up $25 billion in the bank bailout, and Bank of America had gotten $45 billion, unmistakable signs of how close to oblivion these giants had come. But the part of the story that had never gotten much attention involved the backdoor hand-outs that JPMorgan Chase, Bank of America, and the other big banks had received. During the crash, when sensible investors were fleeing for their lives and no one knew if the banks would survive until tomorrow, much less pay back anything they borrowed, the Federal Reserve Bank stepped up and very quietly lent them a truly astronomical sum: $1.1 trillion. Just to put that amount in perspective, the entire U.S. GDP in 2009 was a little over $14 trillion. To keep the giant banks solvent, we were giving them 8 percent of our *entire* economy. And better yet—at least from the banks' point of view—the government charged interest rates that were laughably low.

At the same moment that the taxpayers were shoveling money into the hungry mouths of the big banks, those same banks were pulling the plug on small business loans across the country. That didn't seem to matter to the people opening the federal government's wallet: they were too intent on playing sugar daddy for the likes of JPMorgan Chase and Bank of America to ask hard questions about what those giant banks were doing with the money.

As we know, the big banks recovered. Boy, did they recover. In fact, by 2013, they were making money hand over fist. They were slathered in money. They rolled around in money. They skinny-dipped in money. And yet, rich as they were, these giant banks could *still* borrow as much of the taxpayers' hard-earned money as they wanted—and pay less than 1 percent interest for the privilege.

While banks were paying a fraction of 1 percent, students were paying 6 percent, 8 percent, or higher on their student loans. I wanted to climb to the top of the Capitol, hang off its side like King Kong, and shout at the top of my lungs, *Unfair! Wrong! Stop this craziness RIGHT NOW!*

Okay, I didn't do that. But when I discovered this bizarre disparity, I instantly decided that it was time to find a way to reduce the interest rate on student loans. And then I thought: "In fact, let's wrap it all up in a neat package. Why don't we charge students the same amount the big banks pay?"

I was a freshman senator. I had an office (well, a trailer posing as an office), a few pieces of furniture, and about half the staff I would eventually hire. By then I had given my first speech, though it wasn't the one I'd expected to give. Instead, it was a speech delivered shortly after the Boston Marathon bombing, during which I did my best to honor the dead and injured and the heroes who helped get the city through that awful day.

I was past the "maiden speech," but I was still a newbie, and lots of people were offering plenty of advice, including tips about when and what to propose as my first bill in the Senate. "If you go for boring," said one of these wise counselors, "you'll never get embarrassed." Or: "Wait—no rush to do this." Also: "Don't make anyone mad." And my personal favorite: "Read the bill first, because someone might ask you a question about it." Gee, what a good point!

But I didn't want to wait. I had an idea, and I wanted to go after it now—right now. This was the first thing I wanted to use my Senate seat for: cutting the cost of college. My staffers and I wrote up the bill, I took it to the floor of the Senate, and then I stood up and gave a heartfelt but not very exciting speech about it.

I wasn't sure what would happen next, but the bill caught fire. Television reports, newspaper articles, online editorials. Petitions started making the rounds; combined, they gathered nearly a million signatures. Groups started organizing. Twenty-five colleges in Massachusetts alone endorsed it. Suddenly, lots of people wanted to know why the banks paid so little and why students paid so much.

Legislation like this was sure to irritate a lot of rich and powerful bankers. They and their well-paid lobbyists could cite chapter and verse on why they—and not some grubby mob of student hooligans—should get such favorable loan rates. Their excuses came thick and fast: Banks were sure to pay back the loans, and students might not. (So charge a fee to cover bad debts. And anyway, the U.S. government was making a profit *after* all those bad debts were accounted for.) Bank lending helps the economy. (And student lending doesn't?) Students could afford to

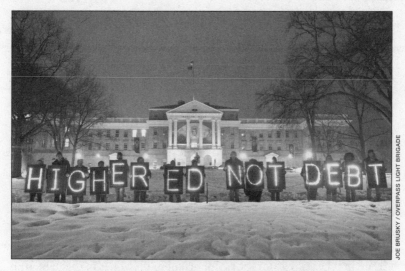

Demonstrators hold a lighted message on the University of Wisconsin–Madison campus protesting the high cost of student loans.

pay more. (*Really?* More than JPMorgan Chase?) But the excuse machine couldn't keep up with the growing demand for an answer: Why did the banks get a subsidy while the students paid a penalty?

Students began to latch onto the idea and make noise about it. As word spread, the bill picked up some momentum. I started getting inquiries from other senators. Harry Reid, our party's majority leader, asked me to attend a leadership meeting for the Democratic caucus so I could explain what I was up to.

But it didn't take long to realize that my bill faced a serious problem. No matter how much attention the bill got or how many Democrats were interested, it would go nowhere for a very simple reason: if the bill required the federal government to give up the profits on student loans, a bunch of people in Congress—both Republicans and Democrats—would insist that Congress had to find enough money somewhere else to fill the new hole in the budget. That would mean stitching up a tax loophole or two, and Grover Norquist and his acolytes would call that a tax increase. For Republicans (and many Democrats), anything that smacked of a tax increase was a bill killer.

So my staffers and I wrote other versions of the bill. We finally settled on an interest rate for anyone who wanted to refinance old student loans (3.9 percent) that would cover all the bad-debt losses, the administrative costs, and the capital costs; most important, it would still lower the interest rate for most students. We also realized that we could offset the profits the government would lose by proposing that Congress close up exactly one tax loophole: the bill would require that anyone who earned more than a million dollars per year had to pay a tax rate of at least 30 percent. According to the scorekeepers at the Congressional Budget Office, that one small change in the tax laws would more than compensate for all the profits lost from refinancing student loans.

It galled me that I couldn't find a way to write the bill so that students would pay an interest rate of less than 1 percent, the rate the government was giving the banks. But it was important to find allies in the fight, so I picked a rate that other senators liked. I also picked a way to pay for it that President Obama had proposed in 2011, a sensible idea that had been endorsed by Warren Buffett. By the time I was done, I figured that it would be pretty hard for reasonable people to object to the bill.

Of course, Washington isn't exactly full of "reasonable people." Democrats introduced the final version of the bill in June 2014, and the Republicans immediately launched an all-out filibuster to block it.

But now the battle lines were drawn, and battle lines can be valuable. People are forced to confront an issue. And now, with a bill on the table, the Senate's Democrats got on board—100 percent of them. We got both independent senators as well. We even picked up three Republican votes. And we persuaded Congress to reduce the interest rates a little bit on all new student loans. By this point, we were almost there: if we could find just a few more votes, we could refinance all those ridiculously expensive student loans. But on June 11, the Republican filibuster held and the bill died.

In 2015, the Republicans took over the Senate, and they made absolutely sure there were no more votes on the student loan bill. I'm a long way from accepting the idea that this fight is lost, but for now I must acknowledge the bitter truth that we'll have to bide our time before we get enough votes on our side.

How can this be so hard? The government should not be making a profit on student loans—period. We should cut the interest rate on new loans and refinance the old ones. And we could do so much more: Invest in colleges so the next kid has a chance to go to school without taking on any debt. Step up our oversight of nasty for-profit colleges like the one that trapped Kai. Fund more technical training to help people keep their skills right at the cutting edge. Add extra support for colleges that demonstrate real results in helping disadvantaged kids make it into—and through—school. There is so much we can do to open up opportunities for more people, but the Republicans have consistently blocked even the smallest step in that direction.

The effort to lower the interest rate on student loans is a sober reminder that although spending money is about math, it is also about values. Which matters most to us: Money for loopholes that favor giant corporations and the ultrarich—or money for education? Money for those who have already made it—or money to give the next kid a chance to make it big?

The night of the vote on student loans I lay in bed in the dark thinking, *What has happened to this country?* What has gone so horribly wrong that democratically elected officials can offer a big wet kiss to rich people and giant corporations while they spit on students? And why isn't every one of these elected officials who voted to keep raking in profits by overcharging on student loans facing an angry mob back home? "Government for the people" still looks great printed on all those souvenirs for sale in Washington, D.C., but it doesn't seem to be working so well anymore.

Where do we go from here? In 2014 and 2016, a lot of Democrats who ran for office argued for debt-free college, and that issue may have helped Democrats win a couple of new seats in the Senate. We also got debt-free college included as a core plank of the Democratic Party platform. But is the new president of the United States going to give our country's college students a break? Here's a good indicator of Donald Trump's approach to education: a few weeks before he was sworn in, he settled one of the lawsuits against his own for-profit university for $25 million. Sorry, but even an optimist like me finds it hard to be hopeful when the man who now sits in the White House built a business by cheating people who were looking for an education.

CHOKING OFF GROWTH

Once Ronald Reagan moved into the White House, Republican orthodoxy grew stronger and stronger. Education wasn't the only investment in our future that got squeezed. The country's infrastructure—our roads, bridges, railroads, power grids, water supply, and all the other stuff we don't pay a lot of attention to but we need to carry on our lives— also took one hit after another. Year after year, decade after decade, both new construction and plain old maintenance of existing structures were short-changed. One economist calculates that, adjusted for depreciation, America currently spends nothing—zero—on infrastructure. It's little wonder that the American Society of Civil Engineers now gives the United States' infrastructure a grade of D+.

The failure to maintain infrastructure can be seen in nearly every city and town in America—pipes leaching lead into the drinking water in Flint, Michigan; bridges collapsing in Minnesota; and a once-proud mass transit system in Boston that is so ancient that it simply shuts down during heavy snows.

Recognize the picture on the next page? That's a photo of the bridge on a stretch of highway in Minnesota that fell down in 2007. I sometimes think about that bridge when I'm zipping along other parts of the Interstate. How did we arrive at a point where we've starved our government so badly that we can't even keep our roads and bridges safe, up-to-date, and in working order?

Not investing in infrastructure inflicts damage everywhere. That aging bridge in Minnesota was carrying about 140,000 cars every day. When it collapsed, 13 people were killed and 145 were injured. With the bridge shut down, drivers were rerouted for more than a year. Small businesses took a hit, people lost jobs, and the county applied for disaster relief. The economic impact of the collapse rattled through the region for years—and that was just one bridge.

When this bridge in Minnesota fell down, 13 people were killed and another 145 were injured.

Infrastructure matters. Shortchanging our commitment to building and maintaining it causes more than spectacular calamities like a falling bridge or everyday irritations like bone-jarring potholes. The failure to invest in clean energy has left us with a dirty supply system that pumps poison into the air and an aging power grid that is vulnerable to storms and rising sea levels. The failure to invest in new communications means that many small towns and rural areas have been delayed in their chance to participate in much of the high-tech boom. The failure to invest in the upkeep of our eighty-four thousand dams and levees means that catastrophic floods threaten cities like Sacramento and great masses of stinking algae occasionally close South Florida beaches. The failure to invest in planned drainage and canal projects played a key role in the devastating floods that swamped tens of thousands of homes and claimed thirteen lives around Baton Rouge in 2016. And we all remember Katrina.

It's not like we're actually saving any money. Look at communications, even something as simple as basic Internet access. It's pretty hard for any business to operate or any family to get by without a cheap, reliable Internet connection. Lacking sufficient tax revenues, most cities and towns have left it to the private sector to lay the fiber optic cables and deliver services. And how's that working out for us? Internet speeds in U.S. cities tend to be slower than those around the world—but we pay more. Those tax cuts that starve government so that it hands over basic services to private companies are really paying off for a few people, but not so much for everybody else.

Worst of all, the country's failure to build and maintain infrastructure has robbed us of our vitality. In the short run, infrastructure spending works. Real infrastructure spending—not phony tax breaks for projects that were going to get built anyway or giveaways to campaign contributors—creates good, well-paying jobs that give workers money to spend in their local economies. Over the long run, infrastructure dollars buy workers something even more important. Infrastructure spending is a collective investment in our country that makes it easier for businesses to flourish right here in America. Roads and bridges, cheap and dependable energy, rapid communication, educated workers—all these investments create a more favorable business climate.

Much is uncertain about the economy of the future. We know that we are already competing on a global scale, that information is exploding, and that technical innovations will continue to appear at breathtaking speed. Inevitably, we're all uncertain about who the winners of the future will be—and scared about who the losers might be. But if we're going to have a prayer of competing, we *must* invest in the building blocks of our economy.

Consider just one of our competitors: China is spending 8.6 percent of its GDP on infrastructure. Why? Because the Chinese are working hard to build a country where their businesses and their people will have a better chance to be winners in the global economy. And here in the United States? Our infrastructure spending is stuck at 2.5 percent of the GDP—and it has been for years and years. By that measurement, America now lags behind India, most of Asia, the Middle East, and Eastern Europe. In fact, the only region of the world spending less on infrastructure than the United States is South America, which comes in just a smidge lower, at about 2.4 percent of GDP.

America ramped up its infrastructure long before many other parts of the world, but our refusal to maintain and upgrade it is catching up with us. The overall quality of infrastructure in the United States is now rated just slightly ahead of Taiwan's and far behind the quality of that in Germany, Spain, and, of course, Japan.

This failure to invest in our future is incredibly shortsighted. It means that we're planning to compete for jobs and resources and markets in the coming decades wearing a blindfold, handcuffed, and with our shoelaces tied together. This plan isn't pro-business. This plan is pro-stupid.

More investment in basic infrastructure would transform much of our daily living, along with our long-term prospects. What would those investments buy us? Clean, cost-effective, renewable energy (with the added bonus that America's economy would no longer be dependent on a handful of oil giants in the Middle East, but that's a story for another day). Top-of-the-line Internet and communications infrastructure. A state-of-the-art transportation system, so employees can get to work, customers can get to markets, and goods can get everywhere. This means investment in roads and bridges, but it also means airports and train tracks, subways and bike lanes, cable lines and fiber optics. Because let's face it: we're not going to build the economy of the future sitting on our couches or stuck in traffic all the time. And we're not going to attain success by suffering through rolling power brownouts, unable to connect to the Internet.

Farmers plow their fields. They fertilize the soil and dig drainage ditches. They pry out rocks and uproot tree stumps. Why? So they can do better in the future. For a big, diverse country, infrastructure is the same thing—it is how we get ourselves ready for a more productive future. First-rate infrastructure would give America a crucial advantage in the competition for twenty-first-century jobs. Instead, a crumbling infrastructure is a drag on new investment by forward-looking companies and an obstacle to the successful launch of new companies.

When we fail to invest in infrastructure, it's as if everyone in America is joining hands and saying, "Let's get poor together!"

HAVE WE STOPPED INVESTING IN DISCOVERY?

Tax cuts also put the squeeze on federal research spending. Think of the irony: as science is opening new frontiers everywhere—from altering the human genome to probing black holes in outer space—America is cutting back on investments in all kinds of science. As a proportion of the federal budget, more than half of our federal investment in research has been lopped off since the 1960s.

I'll admit it: I love research. I enjoy reading research papers, and I get a kick out of those video clips about weird things scientists have found, like the rare sea turtles that glow green and red. I know that not everyone shares my enthusiasm for science, but even a confirmed stick-in-the-mud should be glad to see government invest in research, if only because it's a smart financial investment. All that work on new tests for cancer or targeted therapies pays off big-time. Here's just one example: for every dollar spent on medical research, the American economy gets back $2.20 *immediately*. Long-term, new research translates into new industries, new approaches, new cures, and new businesses.

And then there's this: just like with infrastructure spending, if we don't invest in research right here in America, other countries are champing at the bit to take over. They want to move these discoveries—and all the ancillary business activities and patents and copyrights and start-up companies that come with them—from the United States to their home countries.

A while back, I spent part of an afternoon talking with the head of a Massachusetts medical school. This is a fellow I really like. He's passionate about medicine in all its aspects. His face lights up when he talks about how changes in medical science have made it possible for tiny babies who wouldn't have survived just a few years ago to live long and full lives. He loves talking about how delicate new eye surgeries and cutting-edge treatments for balance problems allow seniors to care for themselves and their spouses and reengage with the world. He's a happy warrior for his medical students, his medical researchers, and the future of medicine. But on this day, he wasn't any kind of cheerful.

Worry lines etched his face, and frustration tinged his voice. He was in the middle of a bidding war to keep one of his top young researchers, and he was afraid that he was on the verge of losing this woman to a competitor. After he described his researcher's new approach to dealing with an intractable problem affecting millions of people around the globe,

I asked where she was about to go. A fancier medical school? A big-time drug company? A hot new med-tech start-up?

Nope. To a foreign country.

And here was the part that really stung: his researcher had no family ties to that country and did not speak the language, and she really didn't want to leave. But her research was very promising, and the government officials who were wooing her understood that if their investment in her paid off, a new industry might be born in their country. So they were bidding hard and fast, offering every kind of support for her research: lab space, assistants, equipment, materials—whatever she needed.

The dean finished telling me this story, then added flatly, "I can't compete."

Today, only two out of every eleven research proposals that are finalists for research grants at the National Institutes of Health get funding. The NIH is leaving good science on the table because it is chronically short of money. One in five biochemistry research scientists admit that they are considering leaving the United States so they can continue their work. It's not an exaggeration to say that an entire generation of young researchers is threatened with extinction—or exile.

Some of the work may migrate to another country, but much of the research that is desperately needed simply doesn't get done. Shortly after I settled in as a new senator, the Senate's Health, Education, Labor, and Pensions Committee (HELP) held a hearing with the director of the National Institute of Mental Health. I asked him what he could do with more funding, and he described how we are "on the cusp of a revolution." He and other scientists believe that researchers are right on the edge of unraveling the most important puzzles about the brain. They believe that we are inches away from opening exciting new lines of treatment for mental illnesses, Alzheimer's, autism, Parkinson's disease, Huntington's disease, psychosis, and schizophrenia. But there's a catch: without government funding, those discoveries will be delayed by years, maybe decades.

And then there's the personal impact of these untreated conditions.

People often drop by our office in Washington. We get visits from folks who are in town from Massachusetts for a convention or business trip or vacation. School groups and families on spring break come by. Some people come to talk about a particular issue they care deeply about—the oceans, human trafficking, music education. Some people just want to say hello and stick a pin on the Massachusetts map next to their hometown.

When I can, I have an open house. Visitors form a rough line. We shake hands, they tell me a little about their issues or themselves, and we usually take a picture together. (We've done some killer selfies.)

At one of these gatherings, a nice couple stood first in line, holding hands. The guy was sturdy and about my height, with close-cropped salt-and-pepper hair. As I stretched out my hand, his face lit up with a broad smile. He wore a dark suit and a nice purple shirt and tie, but what caught me were his eyes—bright and engaged and completely locked on mine.

"Hi, Senator," he began. "I'm Mike, from Douglas, Massachusetts, and I have Alzheimer's. Early-onset—I'm fifty-five. Soon, I will have forgotten this conversation. I will have forgotten everything. You. My children. My wife."

His wife stood quietly as he paused, searching for words.

Finally he said, "Everything I know will be taken from me."

That was all it took. My eyes filled with tears, and I held my breath. How does anyone deal with that future? For an instant, the faces of those I loved flitted across my mind. My grandchildren. My husband, Bruce. My brothers. All those who had already died. Daddy. Mother. Aunt Bee. Our beloved dog Otis. Who would I be if I forgot them?

Before I could recover enough to speak, Mike bounded on: "I will have forgotten, so I'm here today, while I can remember. I'm here to ask you to fight for more funding for research on Alzheimer's. Please. I'm going to forget, so I need you to remember."

I'd walked into that room with my mind on some annoying paper-work, thinking ahead to my next meeting, and Mike had stopped me cold. His story was like a spear thrust between my ribs, reminding me that everything we do in Washington matters to real people—people who never planned to ask for help but who needed it right now.

Alzheimer's disease offers the perfect example of how foolish it is to shortchange investments in research. In 2016 alone, Americans spent $236 billion caring for people with Alzheimer's. That's $236 billion *just for care*: all that money didn't delay the advance of the illness by a single

Mike and Cheryl Belleville, near their new home in Bellingham, Massachusetts

day. And we will keep on spending these astronomical sums year after year; in fact, the amount will continue to grow, so much so that by 2050, Alzheimer's could bankrupt Medicare.

We know that this financial tsunami is coming, and we've still got time to do something about it. So how much does the NIH allocate to Alzheimer's research? In 2016, the amount spent on research was less than one half of 1 percent of the money spent on care. The NIH isn't heartless or stupid—it just doesn't have enough funding. Even as the population ages and the number of diagnoses increases, Congress continues to cut research dollars. Medical research at the NIH now receives 20 percent less funding than just ten years ago.

And Alzheimer's isn't the only pressing medical concern. Think about other diseases on the cusp of scientific breakthroughs, like diabetes, heart disease, breast cancer, and HIV. Think about kids with life-threatening allergies or autism. Think about people with ALS, trapped in a nonresponsive body until they suffocate. Think about people addicted to opioids and people in chronic pain. Think about how a single medical breakthrough could give new life to hundreds of thousands of people.

I get worked up over this. But the way I figure it, we should *all* be worked up. It isn't just medical research. If our government had spent the same proportion of its 2016 budget on research that we spent back in the mid-1960s, we would have devoted an additional $162 billion to basic research in just one year. That would more than quintuple the budget for the National Institutes of Health and the National Science Foundation combined. Five times the funding. Think of the additional scientists and laboratories that would have been working hard to solve problems. Can you imagine how much further along we'd be on clean energy development or disease-resistant crops or cheap ways to turn seawater into fresh drinking water? And if we made progress on those three fronts alone, just think how much money we could save and how much better off our people and our planet would be.

A large majority of Americans agree that we should increase the money we spend on research. If we can't come together as a country and make this happen—if we can't, at the very least, double the tiny fraction of our federal budget that we invest in basic research—then what kind of future *do* we believe in?

A COUPLE OF years ago, I got an up-close look at what the Republicans and their determination to hold tight to trickle-down economics has done to research funding. The 2014 midterm elections had been a bloodbath for the Democrats, so the Republicans were now firmly in charge of both the Senate and the House. This meant that the Republicans would chair the committees and, therefore, decide which legislation moved forward and which died without a vote. By early 2015, I knew my student loan bill was going nowhere, but I was still on edge, waiting to see what other ideas the Republicans would offer and what we might do with them.

When the Senate Republicans started outlining their legislative initiatives, "medical innovation" was high on the list. When I saw that, I wanted to break out my infamous rendition of "Yankee Doodle Boy." "Now they're talking my language," I thought. Surely their bill would provide a chance to get more resources for scientists. It would fund new labs, which, in turn, would deliver exciting new inventions. Or maybe the bill would go for something really ambitious, like funding the BRAIN Initiative to map the brain, or fully supporting President Obama's precision medicine initiative announced that year. Whatever the details, "medical innovation" had to mean more money for research. Right?

Wrong. Turns out, medical innovation Republican-style meant something entirely different. No new money for scientists or labs or doctors. Nope, to the Republicans, "innovation" evidently meant "weaken the FDA" and "help out giant drug companies." It was called the 21st Century Cures Act—or Cures, for short—because, after all, who could be opposed to twenty-first-century cures? But when push came to shove, they just wanted to deregulate.

The effort to get a bill like this one passed doesn't start on the floor of the Senate. Instead, a lot of the work is done through committees, and in this case I was on the right committee—HELP. Now I'd have the opportunity to force the Republicans to talk about what they were up to. I decided I would show up for every single hearing or meeting and raise this issue every single time. I might not be the most popular girl on the block, but I also might get something done.

I also looked for allies, starting with the senior Democrat on the committee, Senator Patty Murray of Washington State. I asked Patty if we could make getting more research money on the Cures bill a priority. She has been a longtime supporter of medical research, and her answer was immediate: "Go for it!"

Over the next few weeks, I talked with every other Democrat on the committee, and I quickly learned that there was a real enthusiasm for more NIH funding. And not just more—a *lot* more. Senator Al Franken of Minnesota, one of my favorite partners in the Senate, was also on the committee. He kept needling me. Every time I would name a number, he'd say, "Hey, this is a big deal. Couldn't we ask for more?" Al is my kind of guy!

For months, I kept banging on the issue in both public hearings and private conversations. To anyone who would listen, I would say: We need more money for medical research. I said it over and over and over.

I worked it every way I could. I had good conversations with several Republicans, and every one of them agreed: the NIH needs more money. When the *New York Times* ran an op-ed from Newt Gingrich, former Republican Speaker of the House, in April 2015, I immediately called him. He had argued that America should double its NIH funding, and I said "Hurrah!" about ten different ways. In the course of our conversation, I asked if he would be willing to work with me on getting more funding.

I put together an informational hearing, and I invited Speaker Gingrich to make a presentation. He was terrific. His best line: "To allow research funding to languish at a time of historic opportunity when you could be saving lives and saving money takes a special kind of stupidity that is reserved for this city."

In October 2015, I asked for an appointment to see the HELP Committee's chairman, Senator Lamar Alexander.

On the appointed day, I walked over to the chairman's office with my top health-care staffer. I had not been there before, and I confess that I was surprised. It was an amazing office. The walls were adorned with lots of memorabilia and all sorts of things I'd never seen before. A sign explained that all of it was from Tennessee, the chairman's home state. There was a violin made of matchsticks, a display of old tools, and the original sheet music from "Tennessee Waltz." Beside the chairman's desk was his prized possession: Sam Houston's walking stick.

Chairman Alexander greeted me cordially, and we observed all the rituals. He offered me a seat on one of his heavy, upholstered chairs. He opened the conversation with a few pleasantries. He showed me his walking stick, and I expressed my admiration.

After a few minutes, I introduced my senior health-care expert, and he introduced his senior health-care expert—sort of like our seconds at an old-fashioned duel.

I thanked the chairman for considering some provisions that I had written for the Cures bill. He thanked me for "engaging so thoroughly in the process." I wondered if that was Senate code for being a pain in the neck, but I thought it was better if I didn't ask.

By now we were on a first-name basis. "Thank you, Lamar," said I. "Thank *you*, Elizabeth," said he.

From there, the conversation got a little bumpier. We each had a bottom line: I believed that real medical innovation would come only from increasing funding for medical research, and now was the time. Chairman Alexander feared that any requirement for new money would kill the bill.

Chairman Alexander was gracious and courteous, but his job was to protect his bill. I had made it my job to fight for more funding for research. In fact, I had already proposed a bill to add funding to NIH. I thought that whenever the biggest drug companies in America broke the law, they ought to pay an extra fine that would be used to help fund NIH. How much money would that deliver? If this bill had been in place over the preceding five years, NIH would have had nearly $6 billion more every year to fund thousands of grants to scientists and universities and research centers around the country.

Chairman Alexander and I went nowhere.

But he really wanted to pass the Cures bill. So he tried to find another way to move it along—without adding more funding for the NIH. In the spring of 2016, he broke the bill into lots of small parts; he included modest proposals supported by various Democrats, on the theory that, one by one, these givebacks might pick up support from just enough Democratic senators to allow him to get the bill through the committee without adding funding for medical research.

To be fair, I was happy about some of the things he added. He included a provision on genetic privacy I'd written and another section on targeted therapies that would help kids with rare diseases. He also inserted a section I'd helped develop about using more women and minorities in clinical trials and squeezing more information out of the research we already funded.

I loved every one of those provisions, but I wasn't giving up my fight for more research money. So I made a countermove: I rallied Democrats behind an amendment to create a Biomedical Innovation Fund that would add $5 billion a year to the NIH's budget for the next ten years.

The Republicans didn't support it, but at $5 billion, every single Democrat signed on—and Senator Al Franken promised he'd throw in a few bucks of his own. And in the end, the Democrats held together: without more money for the NIH, the bill wouldn't go forward.

Before long, Chairman Alexander realized that he had been blocked—there weren't any more Democrats to pull over to his side. In the final markup of the Cures bill, he conceded this, noting that he understood that the only way his bill would move in the Senate was if it included new funding for medical research.

The Senate Republicans, however, still refused to agree to more money. Instead, they looked for another way to get the bill moving. On June 22, my birthday, I received a not-so-friendly present: one of the Capitol Hill newspapers ran a story with the headline "Republicans Blame Warren for 'Cures' Delay." One Republican senator talked about the "significant contributions to improving health care" that the Cures bill would provide—and he made it clear that I was holding up these significant contributions. Another accused me of being "desperate to find a partisan issue to ruin a bipartisan committee."

I guess they figured that a little heat might soften me up and get things moving. It didn't.

The Democrats held firm right through the 2016 election. When Trump was elected, and the Republicans held on to control of both the House and the Senate, suddenly the Cures bill moved with lightning speed—at least as measured in congressional terms. Over Thanksgiving, while most people were off eating turkey, the House revised the Cures bill and loaded it up with giveaways. Drug companies would be allowed to hide kickbacks to doctors; a Mitch McConnell donor got a provision to facilitate FDA approvals of some regenerative medical products he wanted to bring to market; and Big Tobacco would get a lot of smoking prevention defunded. I was stunned. Kickbacks? Donor deals? Big Tobacco? I wondered if the House had provided free gift wrapping as well.

Even the good parts came with hidden traps. There were a lot of "future money" promises that might or might not be kept, but the guaranteed money coming in was pretty limited. For example, there were promises of—sometime, maybe down the line—$400 million for opioid-addiction treatment. The money was desperately needed; in fact, ten times that much was desperately needed. I had met families all across Massachusetts that had been devastated, mothers who had lost children to addiction and children who had lost mothers. I'd talked with people who spoke of loved ones who seemed to disappear in front of their eyes, only to be replaced by a stranger. I'd held hands with those who had kicked their addictions and who fought every day to stay clean and to help others do the same. And all of them, the grandmas and the teen-agers, explained how there weren't enough treatment centers, not enough beds, not enough help.

The opioid crisis knew no limits. Old and young, rich and poor—all sorts of people had been hit hard. The need for money was urgent. When I heard that the bill had actual funding, and not just promises, I was hopeful about its impact on the families I knew across the Common-wealth. But, as I was quickly learning, it paid to read the fine print. The Cures bill would let the incoming Trump administration play poli-tics: they would get to decide which states would receive the funding—and which states would be shut out completely. They would have full authority to decide on whatever distribution they wanted.

I couldn't believe my eyes. I read the revised bill and thought: good luck to Massachusetts and every other state that voted for Hillary Clinton. How deeply unfair could these guys be? We all needed help for people suffering from deadly addiction, people who were dying, people whose families were being torn apart—and these guys wanted to poi-son it with politics.

There was also $100 million for Vice President Joe Biden's cancer moon shot. I was glad for every extra penny for cancer research, but $100 million is only about 2 percent of what the NIH already spends in a single year on cancer research. This work is very expensive, and even $100 million doesn't shoot very far.

Worse yet, under this bill, Republicans could also just cut the under-lying budget and there would actually be less money next year.

This kind of smoke-and-mirrors funding was deeply disheartening, but what made me downright angry was the revised bill's kick in the face to general medical research. After supporting billions of dollars of new money in earlier drafts of the Cures bill, the Republicans slashed the funding portion and put in a grand total of $300 million for new NIH money. That's about half a penny for every dollar the Democrats had asked for in our amendments. Half a penny to fund more work on Alzheimer's, ALS, autism—the list breaks my heart.

The bill did have some good parts, and lots of Democrats signed on, including President Obama. Several of my friends said, in effect: Take this, because it will only get worse once Donald Trump is sworn in as president. But I didn't. I couldn't. I objected—very loudly. I gave a speech, made calls, talked to the press—whatever I could do. There was a lot of back and forth, but the Republicans finally caved and the doctor-kickback provision came out. Yes! I couldn't believe it had been in there in the first place, but I was very glad to see it removed. Score one for the good guys!

There was also another change that had a positive impact much closer to home. Again, after much pushing and shoving, the opioid money would now be distributed by a set formula, giving a fairer distribution to every state, including Massachusetts. This meant that some of the families struggling with this crisis would get help. I thought the funding was still too little, especially when spread among fifty states, but at least I knew I could face people at home and say we would get a part of it.

This was a lesson for me: sometimes it pays to fight back, even when everyone says it would be better to give up. I still couldn't stomach voting for the bill, but at least the fight made it better. We would get some help in battling the opioid epidemic that was sweeping through our state. In December, the Cures bill was passed into law.

Although we didn't get the money we desperately need for research, I will keep fighting for it. I'll fight for money for the National Institutes of Health and money for the National Science Foundation. Money for the Centers for Disease Control, the Food and Drug Administration, NASA, and Department of Defense research.

For me, this fight is about building a future. This fight is also about remembering Mike from Douglas, Massachusetts, because Mike is starting to have trouble remembering his wife and children.

LESS POWER FOR WORKERS

During all this trickle-down time, during all the tax cuts and all the cuts to education and infrastructure and basic research, what was happening to workers? Where were the unions?

Back in the 1970s, when Lewis Powell urged corporations to "fight back," unions had real power—both in the economy and in politics. But that was about to change.

Eight months after he was sworn into office, Ronald Reagan delivered big-time for corporate America. The air traffic controllers called a strike. Because they were public employees, the strike was illegal, but brief, illegal strikes had occurred with some frequency for decades. Besides, as a candidate, Reagan had sought (and won) the endorsement of the air traffic controllers' union, with the promise that he would improve their terrible working conditions. Now that he was president, Reagan changed his loyalties: he threw a lightning-quick punch at the union. No negotiations or discussions of the problems they faced. Instead, he told the workers they had forty-eight hours to return to their jobs, and when most of them did not, he fired them on the spot and banned them from government service for life. The blow was devastating. The union went bankrupt, and many of the air traffic controllers were personally broken as well.

After that union was smashed to pieces, nothing was ever the same for American workers, whether union or non-union. In the same way that Roosevelt had sent a strong message to workers to join unions, Reagan sent his own unmistakable message to corporate America: It's now open season on unions. They heard him loud and clear.

Over the next few years, unions came under powerful pressures. As automation increased and jobs migrated overseas, membership steadily declined. When my uncle Stanley carried a union card, unions represented about a third of the workforce. Today, they represent about 11 percent of workers.

It is no surprise that the political party that advances trickle-down economics has relentlessly attacked labor unions for decades. As union membership has declined, Republicans have redoubled their attacks. For example, they delayed confirmation of President Obama's second secretary of labor for months, and they stalled filling vacancies on the National Labor Relations Board, all in the hopes of grinding government protection of workers to a halt. And now President Trump has named a secretary of labor who made his fortune squeezing low-wage workers and who railed against unions—the kind of unions that would have given his fast-food workers a chance to bargain for a raise or maybe even some sick time. Republicans continue to use every possible tool to break the backs of unions.

The battle lines on this issue are drawn and unlikely to change, but what's at stake in this fight should be front and center: when the Republicans attack unions, they attack *everyone* who works for wages. It's like an undertow: it may take people a while to feel it, but over time the effect of these attacks will pull them under. And that is without a doubt the Republican plan: sink more and more workers, union and non-union alike.

I saw it again at a birthday party last fall. After the candles were blown out and the presents were opened, the conversation turned to local politics. A terrific young teacher at a charter school said she was hoping the teachers' union would fight to boost wages—maybe even strike for more money. I was puzzled. Is your charter school unionized? I asked.

She laughed. No, she said—in fact, the charter schools in her city were known for union busting. "But my school pays exactly what union teachers get in the school district—plus ten thousand dollars. That's how they can pick off good teachers and not have a union."

Pass the cake.

The teachers' unions are under attack; some people want to weaken the unions, and some people want to get rid of them altogether. I wondered if this cheerful young woman understood that the day the teachers' union dies is the day her $10,000 bonus disappears—along with a lot of other benefits that she takes for granted.

The diminishing power of unions has caused a subtle shift in our economy. As union membership declines, all workers end up losing. That

28 percent boost in wages and benefits that unions add for non-union workers is real, and the decline in union membership has tracked the decline in middle-class wealth.

America's unions helped build America's middle class. Now the Republicans are working to destroy both.

DESTROYING AMERICA'S MIDDLE CLASS

From the 1930s through the 1970s, government took an aggressive role in leveling the playing field and reining in corporate giants and gargantuan banks. In 1980, Ronald Reagan shifted the political dynamic, declaring instead that government was the enemy to be most feared.

Across the two time periods, the country headed in two very different political directions, but the economy kept right on growing. And our nation kept getting richer—richer through the stronger regulations of the first four decades and through the deregulation of the next three and a half decades. Through higher taxes and lower taxes. Through world wars and a cold war, through inflation and stagnation, through growing international competition and a tech revolution. Through race riots and a feminist revolution and fierce debates over marriage equality. Through the crash of 2008 and the subsequent recovery. Through it all, the GDP has maintained a relatively steady upward climb. In other words, despite all the debates and differences, the economy has continued to work.

The economy kept working. What changed is who the economy worked *for*.

From 1935 to 1980, as the economy grew, prosperity was widely shared. Remember when I pointed out earlier that 90 percent of America—everyone outside the top 10 percent—got 70 percent of all income growth? Take another look at the graphic on page 106. Look at all those coins for 90 percent of America. For nearly half a century, when we built wealth in this country, pretty much everyone got a piece of it.

Trickle-down economics fundamentally changed that division. Instead of taxing giant corporations and millionaires and using some of that money to build opportunities for our kids, the rich and powerful got to keep more money. And, over time, opportunities for everyone else began to shrink.

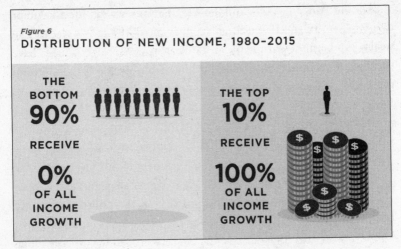

*Since 1980, nearly all the new income produced in
America has gone to those at the top.*

From 1980 to 2015, 90 percent of America—everyone outside the top
10 percent—got almost nothing. Not even 1 percent. Yup, since 1980,
nearly 100 percent of the growth in market income—the income individuals earn before taxes and government transfers like Social Security—
has been gobbled up by the top 10 percent. Or, to put it more simply, the
10 percent got just about everything and the 90 percent got essentially
nothing.

True, government aid softened the blow a little, as more Americans
qualified for—and received—food stamps. And as the population continued to age, more seniors got Social Security. But the basic point still
stands: 90 percent of America didn't receive even a measly 1 percent of
the new income produced in the past thirty-five years!

Let's be clear on this point. Someone like Gina isn't looking for a
handout from the government. For his part, Michael has worked double
shifts and extra hours and jumped on every job he can find in order to
take care of his family. And Kai just wants a chance to get started. All
three of them are part of the 90 percent who have gotten nothing from a
generation of Republican-led trickle-down policies. Nothing, that is,
except pain.

And for African American families, trickle-down has been a double disaster. Remember how, during the 1960s and 1970s, the black-white wealth gap began to shrink? Since the Reagan years, black families have been falling behind again—waaaaay behind. From 1984 to 2013, the wealth gap between black and white families tripled. Adjusted for inflation, in 1984, the median white family had amassed about $83,400 more in net worth than the median black family, but by 2013, that gap had grown to $245,000. So much for bending the arc of history toward equality.

THE TRICKLE-DOWN LIE

Trickle-down economics promised that if the rich got richer and Marie Antoinette got more cake, everyone else would benefit. But study after study showed that tax cuts did not boost the economy. Careful, sober studies by the International Monetary Fund, the Roosevelt Institute, and the nonpartisan Tax Policy Center came to the same conclusion. Trickle-down did not produce more jobs. Tax cuts did not build opportunities for our children. This wasn't just a broken promise—it was a shattered, pulverized, ground-to-dust promise.

Trickle-down is a lie. But thirty-seven years after Ronald Reagan's election, it's the lie that won't die. Donald Trump has clearly embraced Reagan's voodoo economics. Cutting corporate taxes, he declared in September 2016, is "going to be a job creator like we haven't seen since Ronald Reagan." Trump clearly believes that he can ignore all the data and analysis that showed that trickle-down economics was pure fiction. Why? Because in Trump World, facts don't matter: he knows in his golden gut that once the tax cuts kick in, the economy will grow so fast that the new tax revenues will more than make up for the money lost from tax cuts. There it is, the same old trickle-down lie.

Trump isn't alone in his stubborn belief in trickle-down economics. Senate Majority Leader Mitch McConnell has said pretty much the same thing, and Speaker of the House Paul Ryan has also chimed in, calling tax cuts for rich people the "secret sauce" that will help poor and middle class families. Evidently, all the current Republican leaders were issued the same songbook.

In other words, nearly forty years after Ronald Reagan launched his presidential campaign and unveiled an economic approach that is at best dangerous fiction, trickle-down is still the best the Republican leadership has to offer. Even now, they are still waving their magic wands and spreading glitter dust across America.

I'd laugh, except this is deadly serious. If we don't put a stop to this nonsense, trickle-down economics will eventually wipe out our middle class. It will complete the job of turning America into a country that works for a narrow slice of economic royalty at the top while the peasants live on the crumbs carelessly tossed off the banquet table.

Does that mean we should go back to everything Roosevelt did during the Depression? Do we invest in the Interstate Highway System of the 1950s? The moon landings of the 1960s? The computer technologies of the 1970s?

No and yes.

No, not the same projects. Times have changed, and needs have changed. We need to invest in digital highways as well as concrete highways. The brain—rather than the moon—is likely to be the new frontier. Global warming and the threat of worldwide extinction should change every calculation we make when deciding which investments make sense and which don't. And there are lots of problems that don't fit neatly on a list of potential investments, problems like how to negotiate trade deals that produce jobs and how to rethink the employer-employee bargain in a gig economy.

So no: let's not do the same old same old.

But yes, we should go back to the idea of taxing those who have already made it, so that everyone else will get a chance, too. Yes, it is time to bury the idea that tax cuts for the rich will pave the way to a bright future for everyone. And when we bury that lie, we must also bury the poisonous idea that our children will have a good future if they get only a second-rate education. Bury the foolish notion that businesses will flourish here in America with decaying infrastructure. Bury the staggeringly shortsighted idea that innovation will continue to drive our economy as we choke off investments in basic research. We must bury trickle-down economic theory deep and call out every last person who tries once again to sell this dead-end idea.

Government gives us a way to come together to create opportunity, and opportunity is and always will be about education, infrastructure, and research. We need to seize that principle with both hands and hang on for dear life, because it's going to take some really hard work and really smart ideas to start rebuilding America's middle class. The future is coming fast, and we can't afford more policies that undercut working people.

Republicans and their corporate buddies and billionaire donors say they believe in free markets. They get their sheep to bleat about "liberty" and "freedom." I don't know if they're deeply cynical or if they've just drunk too much of their own Kool-Aid, but markets without a cop on the beat are not the free markets of our dreams. The cops make sure that everyone follows the rules—and those rules are critical to the functioning of a free market.

This truth applies everywhere, but I've watched it up close and personal in financial markets. When giant banks weren't held to some basic rules and accountability, people got ripped off, risk-taking exploded, and markets blew up. And hard-working people got hurt, badly. That's just a fact, one that was obvious in 1929 and obvious again in 2008.

I'm a deeply pro-market person. I believe that competition delivers great value for American consumers. That's why I also believe in enough regulation to keep those markets honest. When I buy aspirin, I don't want to wonder whether the company is boosting profits by substituting baking soda for a key ingredient. I don't want to wonder if managers cut costs by failing to steam-clean their equipment or mop their floors. And I don't want to wonder if the firm's executives jacked up the price by figuring out back-alley ways to wipe out any competition. I believe in competitive markets, but I know that following a few basic rules is key to keeping those markets competitive.

The same is true for building our future. If we create honest markets, invest in education, infrastructure, and research, and take in enough tax revenue from those who have made it big, then we will have the schools and roads and bridges that will give the next kid a chance to make it big, too.

This isn't about magic wands and glitter dust and economic theories that make no sense. This is about living our values, about making our laws and our rules line up with what we believe in. All those years ago, my Sunday school student Jesse had it right: everybody gets a turn. It's up to the rest of us to make sure that happens.

4

The Rich and Powerful Tighten Their Grip

On Tuesdays and Thursdays at one o'clock, senators gather for lunch. The doors are flung open to two large rooms, each across wide hallways leading from the Senate chamber. Both rooms are ornate: gold-trimmed plaster curls, giant paintings of men who once led the Senate, carpets patterned in deep shades of red and blue, high ceilings. Both are outfitted with round tables and heavy white tablecloths. A lectern with a microphone is placed up front. In one room, Democrats meet with Democrats; in the other, Republicans meet with Republicans.

These lunchtime gatherings provide a chance for the leadership to explain the current bills or the latest procedural strategies. They also give the rest of the members a chance to complain—loudly about the other party, but also in softer voices about one another.

Lunch is served buffet-style. The dishes are unremarkable, though one stands out, at least on the Democratic side: there's always a big pile of red Jell-O cubes. It always gives me the vague feeling that I'm stuck in a fancy elementary school, with white-haired children play-acting their parts.

Throughout the fall of 2014, each Democratic caucus lunch included a report about the current status of negotiations over federal spending for the coming year. This giant bill had taken the name "cromnibus," a made-up word that described a cross between extending the current funding (Continuing Resolution) and the sprawling reach of a full budget rewrite (Omnibus). The Democrats' negotiating team was led by Senator Barbara Mikulski, the longest-serving woman in Congress and, at four foot eleven, as tough a broad as any who has ever walked the halls of the Capitol. Men a foot taller and a hundred pounds heavier openly feared her.

Negotiations over federal spending took place behind closed doors, and the details of the cromnibus—now running to more than sixteen hundred pages—were kept quiet. Trying to settle on the spending numbers created huge friction between the two parties: our side thought there should be more money available for background checks on gun purchasers and food safety inspections, while the other side wanted more cuts in the operating budgets for the IRS and the Environmental Protection Agency. The battle went on and on. It didn't help that the Republicans used the appropriations process to attempt to block administrative actions they despised but didn't have the votes to overturn. For example, they used this process to try to defund anything related to the president's administrative orders on immigration. Other bills that had nothing to do with federal spending, such as an attempt to undermine Washington D.C.'s move to legalize marijuana, were also rolled into the negotiations.

On Tuesday, December 9, 2014, with time running out, Senator Mikulski stood up to deliver the news we all wanted to hear: We have a deal, and it's a pretty good one. She explained that we'd need to pass a short-term resolution to keep the government funded while the final papers were inked, but the negotiators had reached the finish line. The House would pass the new spending bill, send it to the Senate for a vote, and then it would go on to President Obama to be signed. Important priorities had been protected. The government would stay open. All was good in the world.

To much applause, the then-Democratic leader, Senator Harry Reid of Nevada, praised Senator Mikulski and her negotiating team. Several other senators stood up and appreciatively mentioned their collaboration with her on their own legislative priorities, such as the ongoing work to support the health exchanges for the Affordable Care Act and the work to deal with the drought in the West. As the speakers began to repeat one another, the audience's attention flagged and small conversations broke out around the tables. A few people wandered back over to the buffet table for more Jell-O.

With the speeches winding down, Sherrod Brown, a strongly progressive senator from Ohio, raised his hand. Sherrod usually doesn't speak unless he has something interesting to say, so when he talks, people listen. He started by delivering the same praise that several others had offered, but he quickly pivoted. "This all sounds great," he said, "but what did we have to give up?" The room grew quiet. Sherrod ticked off several Republican priorities and asked what had happened to those. Then he added, "And what about Dodd-Frank? Any changes?"

My head snapped up. Dodd-Frank? The banking regulation that had passed after the 2008 crash? The law that had established the Consumer Financial Protection Bureau, a.k.a. the CFPB? My staff and I had been watching the appropriations process like hawks, and we thought we'd been able to beat back any attacks on the financial regulations laws. If Sherrod was worried, I was worried.

Senator Mikulski said that, as usual, we had had to accept some things we didn't like, but she had cleared the details with others in our caucus, mostly the committee chairs, and they had signed off on each one. My heart skipped a beat or two as she spoke, and then it started to pound. I was pretty sure that no one would have cut a deal on the consumer agency without consulting me, but there were a lot of complex pieces in Dodd-Frank and other opportunities to do serious damage to the law—and Republicans and their banker friends were always swarming around them.

Now on high alert, I left the lunch before it was over. I was too impatient to wait for the little underground train that ferries senators and staffers between the Capitol building and the Senate offices, so I took off on foot. I generally walk fast, but now I was really hustling. Dodd-Frank had been passed in 2010 to put more cops on the beat and, thus, keep the big banks from wrecking the economy again. Getting the bill through Congress had required a brutal fight. The financial services industry had spent more than a million dollars a day lobbying against it. Back then, I was still in teaching and also working for Congress to try to force some account-ability in the bank bailouts, but I had joined many good people and we'd built a grassroots coalition and, near the end, shed blood (at least meta-phorically) to get the legislation passed. The final bill had some good parts—particularly the provisions setting up the consumer agency—but it was not nearly as tough as it should have been. Cutting back the protec-tions provided by the bill would be not only infuriating but dangerous.

Since arriving in Congress in 2013, I had been on the Senate Banking Committee and I knew that lobbyists were always on the prowl for opportunities to roll back some or all of Dodd-Frank. But in the nearly two years I'd been in office, Senate Democrats had drawn a protective line around it. The Republicans had fulminated, but we'd held strong, and there were no Senate bills advancing that would water down financial regulations. So what had the Republicans slipped into the bill? Fearing that something really bad was up, I nearly broke into a run.

As I banged through the door of my office, my legislative director, Jon Donenberg, was waiting for me. Jon is young, smart, and totally plugged in. He also has another advantage: the staffer grapevine is much better than the senator grapevine. Jon had already gotten hold of a copy of the bill and was deep into an analysis of it.

Jon had news for me, and it wasn't good. Buried in the more than six-teen hundred pages of that budget deal were a few lines that would knock a big hole in Dodd-Frank. They wouldn't mandate an across-the-board rollback. Instead, they would deliver a precision-aimed rifle shot to take out one rule, and when that rule was gone, four of the biggest banks in the country—and pretty much no one else—would benefit handsomely.

Then Jon hit me again: "Guess who wrote the Dodd-Frank amend-ment."

"Who?"

"Citigroup lobbyists."

I clenched my jaw.

The provision under assault was not only about the safety of the bank-ing system, it was about the safety of our whole economy. The provision was called "Prohibition Against Federal Government Bailouts of Swaps

Entities." In other words, this section of Dodd-Frank stopped FDIC-insured banks from engaging in risky swaps trading, a type of transaction that could once again blow up the financial system and force the government to bail them out. As the *New York Times* explained, this kind of trading had been "a main culprit in the 2008 financial crisis."

And now the Citigroup lobbyists had persuaded the congressional negotiators to knock out this basic protection and convinced the rest of Congress to fall in line.

Hello? Did anyone remember the financial crash? Millions of jobs lost? Millions of homes lost? A whopping $22 trillion flushed down the toilet?

The banks didn't remember because they didn't *want* to remember. This was about profits. Swaps trades are complex, but the basics are pretty simple: partly because they are very risky, they are also potentially very profitable. As long as they guessed right, the giant banks could make big bucks off these trades, but Dodd-Frank prevented them from doing so.

Because they didn't engage in these risky forms of swaps trading, community banks, credit unions, and even billion-dollar regional banks weren't affected by the rule. Besides, community banks and credit unions weren't ever going to be Too Big to Fail. The giant banks, however, wanted exactly what they'd had before the crash: both the profits from high-risk trading and government guarantees for their regular boring banking. For more than a year, we had fought off their relentless efforts to undo the prohibition on swaps trading, and the banks hadn't come within a mile of succeeding. But now Citigroup, along with JPMorgan Chase, Goldman Sachs, and Bank of America, had slipped in a provision that would eventually let them add about $10 *trillion* of risky swaps to their books—all backed up by the U.S. taxpayer.

These four banks believed that their fervor to make bigger profits should override the interests of millions of taxpayers, thousands of smaller traders, and hundreds of smaller banks. They wanted Congress to once again ignore the regulators and economists who had warned of the risks posed by these huge banks. And they wanted the American people to forget that just six years earlier, this country had suffered the worst crash since the Great Depression. Yup, these four ravenous banks wanted more—and at the moment, it looked like they had figured out a way to get it.

The swaps provision would never have passed Congress if it had come through the Senate Banking Committee. Once it was public, there would have been too much public outrage, and the cromnibus would have been stopped in its tracks. Heck, for two years I'd watched as the House passed one bill after another in an attempt to gut Dodd-Frank, but the bills rarely even made it onto the Senate's agenda because a lot of my colleagues figured they would be radioactive. So the lobbyists devised the perfect play: bury the swaps provision in a giant funding bill and hope no one understood or even saw the language until after all the votes were counted.

I was too angry to sit down. I stood behind my desk, throwing questions at Jon like poison darts. My rational brain kept reminding me that my frustration was misplaced—Jon was on my team. But the battles we'd suffered through during the fight over Dodd-Frank were still too fresh.

Finally, I calmed down enough to take a few deep breaths. Then I asked what we could do. Jon said we could launch an attack and try to get the provision removed, but he wasn't very optimistic about our chances. The leadership of both parties had already signed off on the deal, and it would be a Hail Mary pass to get *anything* changed, much less something that had this much lobbying muscle behind it. And since the first vote on the bill would be in the House, not the Senate, it would be very tricky to lead the opposition from our side. But the only alternative was to play dead, and I didn't feel like playing dead for anyone.

So Jon and I made a list and hit the phones. We called Democrats in the House of Representatives, asking them to oppose the budget deal unless the swaps provision was taken out. I called Nancy Pelosi, the former Speaker of the House and leader of the Democrats, to ask for her help. This was a tough request: the Democrats badly wanted to get a bill passed, so that the government would be funded and remain open, and yet I was asking her to slow down that process. But she was strong, and she quickly agreed to work on getting the provision removed. The next morning, Wednesday, I went to the floor of the Senate and publicly asked the House—especially House Democrats—to remove the provision. I gave interviews and e-mailed supporters and called more people and sounded the alarm on Facebook and Twitter.

This was a really complicated provision, buried in a really complicated bill. And by this point, six years had passed since the financial crash. I think the Citigroup lobbyists figured no one would care. They were wrong—really wrong.

Petitions and YouTube clips flew around the Internet, and as the deadline for a government shutdown drew nearer, dozens of House Democrats announced that they couldn't support the current spending bill. Reporters camped out in the hallways, shoving microphones in people's faces and asking how they would vote. Now that we had most House Democrats on board, I went back to the Senate on Thursday to give another speech, this time calling on House Republicans to take out the provision.

For a few hours, it looked like we might actually turn up the heat enough to persuade the House to change the bill. But the banks had no intention of being denied their prize right at the finish line. Jamie Dimon, the CEO of JPMorgan Chase, got on the phone personally to persuade his friends in Congress to help. Bank lobbyists swarmed Capitol Hill and issued statements to the media, zealously defending the provision. Late Thursday night, the House voted on the cromnibus: 219–206 in favor. The spending package with the Dodd-Frank bullet hole passed.

Then the House Republicans made the next move: they adjourned for the holidays. Very slick. They passed the spending package, closed up shop, and went home—back to their states or off on vacation or whatever.

Slick, because now they'd really stuck it to the Senate. We could either ratify the spending package in exactly the form that came over from the House—warts, bullet holes, and all—and forward it on to the president to sign. Or we could amend it and send the nation spiraling toward a government shutdown.

We knew what a shutdown would mean. A year earlier, Republican Senator Ted Cruz had led a sixteen-day shutdown over Obamacare, and it had halted paychecks to government employees, closed national parks, and shuttered Head Start classes. The impact of the shutdown echoed through mighty defense contractors and small sandwich shops alike. The final cost of the closure was pegged at $24 billion and 250,000 lost jobs.

But maybe we could avoid a shutdown. If the Senate amended the bill, the House might come back into session. If it did, maybe, just maybe, it could be persuaded to pass the Senate version of the cromnibus.

But if the House stayed out of session for even a day, the costs would be enormous. In the end, the Democrats had no stomach for the fight. The math was impossible: it would take forty-one votes in the Senate to stop the cromnibus, and the votes just weren't there. The bill would pass, the swaps trading restriction would be repealed, and the president would sign it.

I went back to the floor to give one more speech. I had already lost— and I knew it. Shoot, anyone who followed the news knew it.

I guess I should have felt humiliated, or maybe depressed. But that's not what was pumping through my veins as I prepared my speech. I was mad, spitting mad. Four big banks had dictated a change in the law, and the United States Congress had obediently bowed down as instructed.

I stood on the floor of the Senate. I took a deep breath, asked to be recognized, and then said:

> Here we are—five years after Dodd-Frank—with Congress on the verge of ramming through a provision that would do nothing for the middle class, do nothing for community banks, do nothing but raise the risk that taxpayers will have to bail out the biggest banks once again.
>
> There's a lot of talk lately about how the Dodd-Frank Act isn't perfect. There's a lot of talk coming from Citigroup about how the Dodd-Frank Act isn't perfect.
>
> So let me say this to anyone who is listening at Citi: I agree with you. Dodd-Frank isn't perfect. *It should have broken you into pieces.*

It's true. In the aftermath of the great crash of 2008, the biggest banks—the ones that got bailed out by the U.S. taxpayers, including Citigroup, JPMorgan Chase, Goldman Sachs, and Bank of America—should have been broken up. They posed so much risk that if even one of them failed again, either they would need another bailout or they would risk bringing down the entire economy. It was wildly reckless to let these banks get even bigger by adding $10 trillion of risk to their balance sheets, especially since taxpayers would be shouldering that risk. But that's exactly what this new provision did.

The bullet hole in Dodd-Frank is devastating, but in the end it's about more than four giant banks. In fact, it's about more than economics or bailouts. This kind of attack on existing law is about power—raw, naked, unapologetic power. Think about it: just a few years after a major crash, bank lobbyists wrote a provision that blasted a hole in a crucial financial regulation. Then the banks muscled it through Congress.

A handful of giant banks called the tune, and America's lawmakers danced. Now a provision that protected taxpayers and kept bank risks under control has been blown to bits. The biggest banks have once again found a way to boost their bottom lines, and the American people are once again the losers.

And these few banks aren't the only ones who play this game. Time and again, giant corporations or super-rich individuals have gotten favors, breaks, exceptions, special deals, riders, subsidies, loopholes, and all kinds of handouts from the government. From one industry to another, these companies and people have persuaded the government to tilt the system in their favor. Eventually, all those favors add up. The power to bend a democratic government now threatens our entire country.

Long ago, when the trustbusters first swung into action in America, they focused less on the power of giant corporations to dominate markets and more on the power of giant corporations to dominate government. In the 1930s, Supreme Court Justice Louis Brandeis warned, "We can have democracy in this country, or we can have great wealth concentrated in the hands of a few, but we can't have both." The fights to break up those powerful trusts were ferocious, but democracy eventually prevailed, and the big corporations were finally reined in and denied the power to write their own rules.

In 2014, four giant banks proved once again that they had the loudest voices in Washington. Three years later, it's about to get a whole lot worse. When President Trump assembled his team, he abandoned all pretense of appointing people committed to public service. Instead, he invited billionaires who took special favors on their way to Washington (yes, Rex Tillerson, I'm looking at you) and who refused to resolve their conflicts of interest (Betsy DeVos is the latest poster child). Now they are on the inside, with their hands on the controls. Big corporations call the shots in Washington and rig the system in their favor. These companies now exercise so much political power that we can no longer deny an ugly truth: when they marshal their resources, giant corporations are fully capable of holding our country hostage until the government does whatever they want.

THE MONEY GRAB

Big corporations and rich individuals have more influence in Washington than everyone else because they can offer politicians the ingredient that's essential to any battle for reelection: money. In recent years, campaigns have become really, really expensive. Television ads, radio spots, grassroots organizing, mailings, campaign offices, travel, staff, yard signs, coffee, pizza—it all adds up. In 2016, the average winning Senate campaign raised more than $10 million, and an additional $10 million was spent by outside groups to aid that campaign. In the 2016 presidential election, the Trump campaign was fueled by $932 million in funding, and the Clinton campaign had $1.4 billion behind it. Wealthy donors and corporations help shoulder that burden, and they are now well positioned to use their influence to tilt the playing field in their direction.

This stinks of corruption, an issue Trump tried to sidestep by vowing to self-fund his campaign. But it was just one more empty promise: he held out his hand for cash, raked in huge donations from billionaires, and benefitted from spending by groups that kept their donors secret.

Money slithers through politics like a snake. And, like a snake, it sometimes bites unexpectedly. I watched this up close. When Justice Antonin Scalia died, in February 2016, President Obama nominated a highly respected judge, Merrick Garland, to replace him. Garland looked like a safe choice. Back in 2010, one of the Senate's most senior and most respected Republicans, Orrin Hatch, had declared Garland "a consensus nominee," the kind Republicans and Democrats could support. But six years later, Majority Leader Mitch McConnell quickly declared that no one nominated by this president—regardless of qualifications—would be considered by the Senate because the Republican leadership preferred to keep the seat vacant until the next president took office.

Most people, including a lot of Republican senators, were taken completely by surprise, first by Scalia's death and then by the quick announcement that no nominee would get a hearing. In all of U.S. history, no leader of either party had ever tried to block a president with a year remaining on his term from filling a Supreme Court vacancy, and no one had ever suggested that the Senate, bound by the Constitution to "advise and consent," could issue a blanket refusal to act. It was one of those so-far-over-the-edge moves that a lot of people felt as if the ground beneath their feet had disappeared—shades of Wile E. Coyote and his still-churning legs when he's run off a cliff but hasn't quite realized it.

One of those who needed to find some solid ground was Republican Senator Jerry Moran. At a small gathering back home in Kansas, he was asked about the Republicans' refusal to consider Judge Garland. Moran is no novice, having spent fourteen years in the House before winning his Senate seat by a very wide margin. He had held Republican leadership positions, but he also prized his independence. He is fond of saying, "I will always put Kansans ahead of the pressures in Washington." His campaign website emphasizes his core beliefs, which include "Never backing down from what you believe in."

Since joining the Senate, I had talked with Moran several times about the importance of increasing funding for medical care and other issues, and he always seemed like a straight shooter, a really solid guy. So I wasn't surprised when I read that he'd declared that it was wrong to hold up the Supreme Court nominee, that Judge Garland should get a hearing and a vote.

Senator Moran was no friend of President Obama's, but he believed in fair play. "I can't imagine the president has or will nominate somebody that meets my criteria, but I have my job to do," Moran said in a statement. "I think the process ought to go forward."

Not long after the statement was made public, two billionaire brothers took note. These ultrarich brothers, Charles and David Koch, are also ultraconservative. They aggressively push their political agenda, and money is their primary tool. It works for them because they have plenty of money to spend: their various corporate interests in chemicals, coal, and oil pull in about $100 billion every year.

When the Kochs heard about Moran's statement, they quickly brought down their well-financed fist: if Moran did not change his position instantly, they would find another Republican to run against him in his next primary and launch an all-out offensive from the right. Koch-funded groups then flooded Moran's office with tens of thousands of e-mails and distributed flyers at one of his local town hall meetings.

Moran assessed the threat and realized that even his very safe Kansas seat could be at risk. With head-snapping speed, he reversed his position.

In effect, two men—excuse me, two billionaires—turned a United States senator 180 degrees merely by *threatening* to spend big money. And they did it so brazenly that Senator Moran had to publicly humiliate himself to satisfy the brothers' demand. Maybe they also made him kiss their feet, just to make sure he'd learned his lesson.

David Koch at a meeting of a conservative group he and his brother sponsor

When Chuck Schumer, now our party's leader in the Senate, stood up at the next Democratic caucus lunch and told the whole story, he finished by saying, "I almost feel sorry for the guy."

After a couple of seconds of silence, I shouted from my spot at the back of the room: "I don't!"

And I didn't. My sympathy level for anyone who gives in to this kind of pressure is exactly zero. If my job ever depends on pleasing a couple of billionaires, I'll quit.

POLITICAL MONEY FLOWS through many conduits. Direct giving to campaigns or PACs, the organizations that gather up money and give it to campaigns. Giving to super PACs, the organizations that run parallel efforts to get a candidate elected—or get the other guy defeated. Giving to groups that can receive money without having to disclose who contributed the money. Giving publicly. Giving secretly. Giving personal money. Giving corporate money. Giving money through multiple shell companies. Give. Give. Give. Or, more to the point: Take. Take. Take.

Small contributions can keep campaigns going without the stench of influence purchasing. But the influx of big dollars—particularly the big dollars that come from rich individuals and corporations trying to pull in the same direction—looks a lot like thinly disguised bribery.

For example, assignment to the House Financial Services Committee is regarded as a plum assignment because lots of corporate executives and lobbyists for the banking industry are likely to shower the representatives with lavish campaign contributions. No one is crass enough to say it out loud, of course, but when the financial services industry spends nearly half a billion dollars a year on political contributions, much—not all, but much—of that money comes with an implicit understanding that banking interests will be well protected by the people taking the money. And who is on the front lines to help out the banking industry? Who else but the elected officials on the House Financial Services Committee.

Even when no legislation that might affect the financial services industry is on the committee's agenda, all those dollars represent access. A big contribution from a bank or a financial company buys nothing specific, but it means that the company's lobbyists are much more likely to get a meeting—and maybe two or three or four meetings—whenever they request one. It also means that everyone is all smiles when the company's CEO places a personal call to one of the committee members just to chat about industry concerns. It means building ties—holiday cards, birthday calls, drop-by visits—between those who hold elective office and those who have lots of money.

The Koch brothers may have come by their political views from the cradle. Their wealthy father was a founding member of the ultraconservative John Birch Society, which saw Communist conspiracies throughout the government and railed against the 1960s civil rights movement. The Kochs have also supported a number of issues that are not related to their business interests, including criminal justice reform and marriage equality.

But follow the money. Koch money comes from oil, gas, and coal, and the brothers' business interests have expanded into chemicals, mining, and finance. Think of the Paris climate accord, EPA rules on clean air, mining regulations, worker safety rules, offshore oil exploration—because of their business interests, the Kochs are directly affected by such matters. Meanwhile, their dual mantra of low taxes and small government and their consistent efforts to weaken the regulatory framework of the government are all part of their relentless drive to put more money in their own pockets. At every turn, they provide major financial support to causes that help out billionaires just like themselves.

Raising money requires a huge investment of an elected official's time. The battle to win and keep a seat in Congress is an endless arms race: incumbents are always trying to amass more money than any potential opponent, so it's no surprise that many in Congress spend hours every day dialing for dollars. Estimates vary, but it's probably accurate to say that candidates and members of Congress generally spend 30 to 70 percent of their time raising money. Think about that. If these public servants work a six-day week, then somewhere between two and four days *every week* are spent doing nothing but asking people for money. And who gets all those phone calls and invitations to meet? People who have lots of money to give.

In 2016, Congressman Steve Israel announced that he would not run for reelection. "I don't think I can spend another day in another call room making another call begging for money," the representative from New York explained. Keep in mind that this is the man who sought and won the chairmanship of the organization in charge of raising money for Democratic congressional campaigns. In an interview with comedian John Oliver, Israel said that fund-raising "is, in my view, a form of torture." After Israel described what it's like to dial for dollars—sitting in a featureless call-center room, asking donors for money for hours and hours on end—a stupefied Oliver muttered, "Oh my God, that's depressing." Israel replied, "Not what our founders had in mind." That's for sure. But nowadays, the constant need to raise money is very much on the minds of most members of Congress.

The consequence of spending all those hours and weeks and months talking to people who are rich enough to put thousands (or millions) of dollars into political campaigns goes beyond the question of whether an elected official will cast votes that promote the business interests or personal causes of those who gave money. In fact, I believe that all that time with zillionaires and CEOs actually alters a person's worldview. Think of it this way: Does a candidate for Congress spend more time with people who worry about whether drug companies will be able to continue seventeen straight years of revenue growth or with people who can't afford the $100,000 cure for hepatitis? Does a senator spend more hours talking with Walmart investors or with Walmart employees? Political priorities are shaped by the perception of what problems need to be addressed, and money powerfully shapes perception.

Without money, campaigns sputter and die, but what is the cost of raising all that money? I do my level best to make sure that fund-raising and campaign contributions never interfere with my job and I know many of my colleagues do the same, but this isn't about just the intentions of individual candidates for office. It's about misaligned incentives and enormous structural problems.

Small donations help undercut the influence of big donors. In his 2016 presidential race, Bernie Sanders raised hundreds of millions of dollars with an average contribution level of just over $27. In 2012, in my race to represent Massachusetts in the Senate, I raised millions of dollars in $5 and $10 contributions, and more than 80 percent of the contributions to my campaign were for $50 or less. Fortunately, small-dollar donors still power the heartbeat of at least a few big political campaigns, and I'm grateful to every small donor, regardless of whom they support. They can help keep our campaigns and our political system honest. But in the current system, not everyone can power their campaigns that way.

The more-money, more-money, more-money drumbeat is relentless. Its corrupting influence is felt everywhere, and it is transforming Washington into a place where a cornucopia of favors are for sale. If we don't fight to stop this dangerous trend, our democracy will turn into the political version of a shopping mall.

Many books have already been written about the need to root money out of politics. Many sensible proposals have been made. My small addition to this movement is to say as loudly as I can that this is an emergency: we need to get started *now* with a comprehensive strategy for ending this money madness. We need constitutional amendments, reversal of the *Citizens United* Supreme Court opinion that let money flood into politics, new ways to finance campaigns, better disclosure of political spending, restrictions on giving by government contractors—and that would only begin to clean up the muck. Until then, the politicians who know best how to work the money angles will be among the most powerful in Washington, and the playing field will tilt even further away from the people who voted them into office.

LOBBYIST HORDES

I wish I could start this section with a joke, but the only one I can think of is this: As a presidential candidate, Donald Trump promised that if he was elected, he would "drain the swamp" and get rid of Washington's lobbyists. Once he was elected, he quickly put in place a transition team made up of—you guessed it—lobbyists!

Okay, that's not funny, but there's more to this story.

When I saw who Trump had appointed to his transition team, I sent him a letter that said, in effect, "Hey, what gives? You said no lobbyists!"

Others asked the same question, so he fired all the lobbyists and replaced them with *former* lobbyists—that is, people who had just turned in their official lobbying credentials.

Still not funny? Let me try again.

Right after the election, Trump's former campaign manager, Corey Lewandowski—the guy who led the charge against lobbyists during Trump's campaign—set up his own lobbying outfit precisely one block from the White House. When asked how he squared this move with his campaign rhetoric, he explained that when Trump said "drain the swamp" and railed at all the lobbyists in Washington, he was criticizing "bureaucracy that has run amok," not *actual* lobbyists.

Okay, maybe this story never gets funny. But it gives a little glimpse of what Washington is really like. Corporations and the ultrarich advance their interests by hiring lobbyists—lots and lots and lots of lobbyists.

Lobbying is big business. In a single year, lobbyists make about $2.6 billion while trying to persuade Congress to do their clients' bidding. Corporations now spend more money lobbying House and Senate members every year than taxpayers spend keeping the House and the Senate running. It's almost as if there's a shadow government that's been hired by rich and powerful people to make sure that the elected government doesn't get out of line.

Remember the U.S. Chamber of Commerce? That's the organization that commissioned Lewis Powell's secret memo, the document that rallied the poor, downtrodden corporate executives to demand a bigger share of America's economic pie. Well, decades later, the chamber still follows Powell's advice. In fact, in the world of lobbyists, the chamber holds a special place as leader of the pack. Its name might lead you to assume that it's an organization of small business owners who get together at a local restaurant for a lunch meeting once a month, but don't be fooled. The national Chamber of Commerce is a well-funded giant that swings a heavy stick in Washington and works full-time to further enrich a number of very wealthy corporations.

The chamber is located in a massive temple directly across Lafayette Square from the White House. A tourist might easily mistake it for a government agency. The organization brags that it owns "one of the most historic and valuable pieces of real estate in the nation's capital—if not in the entire country." The building sits on the original site of the home of Daniel Webster, the famous orator and Massachusetts senator who served twice, from 1827 to 1841 and from 1845 to 1850. But in the 1920s, the chamber tore that building down and hired the same architect who had recently designed the very grand United States Supreme Court Building. The chamber wanted a much bigger and more lavish building "to reflect the organization's prestigious mission."

Mission? No. The Chamber of Commerce runs a business—a lobbying business. It gets its revenues from dues and special financial deals with its members. The service they sell is influence over our government.

In April 2011, while I was setting up the Consumer Financial Protection Bureau, I met with the CEO of the chamber. As I walked into the building, I was struck by how much this lobbying business cloaks itself in trappings that suggest that it runs a powerful alternative government:

The Chamber of Commerce's building, located directly across from the White House

the giant Corinthian columns, the grand entrance, and the elevated office that permits the chamber's CEO to look down on the president of the United States sitting in a smaller office directly across the park. The chamber even has a Hall of Flags—seriously, I'm not kidding—which reinforces the impression that it just might be a sovereign nation.

In those days, I was merely a newly appointed government official running an agency out of a rented space in an anonymous office building. I wondered if I was expected to bow. No, I decided, but I did wonder how many other people who visited the chamber's grand offices asked themselves the same question.

The chamber spends its time explaining to the federal government what laws should and should not be passed. Its employees' time costs money—bags and bags of money. In 2013, the chamber and its affiliates raised $260 million to advance the interests of big business. That's a one-year price tag, and to keep its army of lobbyists well fed, the organization raises it over and over again, year after year. As Tom Donohue, the silver-haired head of the chamber, calmly explained, "We have to raise $5 million a week to run this place."

Lobbying at this level is quite profitable for those who do the lobbying. CEO Donohue, for one, is at the top of his class. According to a profile a few years ago, "He zips around town in a chauffeured Lincoln and flies around the globe in leased private jets." His salary was reported as $6 million in 2014, which makes him the highest-paid trade association head. It also means he pulls in fifteen times the amount the president of the United States makes. After all, it's a big responsibility to peddle influence all over Washington.

The chamber collects annual dues from all its members; although many small companies are included on its roster, the big money comes from big businesses. The chamber also offers one very special service to its biggest contributors: secret lobbying. If the price is high enough, the chamber will take a corporation's money and then lobby the government without triggering pesky reporting about how much that company or even that industry is spending to influence a specific piece of legislation.

The tobacco industry uses this dodge to great effect. Now that America has discovered that tobacco kills—and that the tobacco companies knew this fact for years and hid it from the public—tobacco companies have decided that they should keep a low profile. For a price, the chamber steps in and does their dirty work. When foreign countries have tried to pass anti-smoking initiatives, for example, the chamber has actively lobbied overseas to block those actions. And when the FDA was working to develop warning labels that would discourage children here in the United States from starting to smoke, the chamber fought against those restrictions. One internal memo from tobacco giant Philip Morris described how the game is played: the tobacco giant directs the chamber's work while Philip Morris "stays in the background."

Tobacco, health insurance, megabanks—the chamber's list of clients is long, but the overall plan is clear. Not shy about promoting his organization's value, Donohue once told *Washington Monthly* magazine that he wanted to give the chamber's members "all the deniability they need."

Donohue has also been there for the Wall Street big banks. After the 2008 crash, he proudly described how, when the public was furious over the bailout and Congress was under a lot of public pressure to regulate them, the chamber would "build coalitions and go out and help them."

Translation? The chamber's job is to help big companies hook kids on cigarettes and rewrite financial regulations to sell a self-serving story—and do it all as loudly and obnoxiously as it wants, while its corporate clients stay quiet and out of sight. No wonder the chamber pulls in big bucks. Service like that is priceless.

The chamber is the eight-hundred-pound gorilla stomping through the Washington jungle, but there are plenty of somewhat smaller animals that are equally deadly. Many businesses hire their own lobbyists or pitch in together for industry lobbyists—often to great effect. The collective choice by corporations to invest billions of dollars every year on lobbying usually boils down to a simple business decision: if they can persuade the federal government to favor their company, what kind of return will they get on their investment? One study found that $1 spent on lobbying earned a company $220—a return of 22,000 percent. And an investment-research firm created a financial index of the companies that spent the most on lobbying as a percentage of their assets; when the firm ran the numbers, they found that this index outperformed the S&P 500 by 11 percent a year.

But there's no need to rely on the researchers to shine a light on this issue, because the lobbyists aren't at all ashamed of their influence peddling. On the contrary, they make "bang for the buck" their selling point. One of the most notorious lobbyists ever was Jack Abramoff, who raked in tens of millions of dollars in fees from clients. In 2006, his enthusiasm for his job landed him in prison for tax evasion, fraud, and conspiracy to bribe public officials. Twenty others connected with him (including a Republican congressman) were also convicted of crimes. After he was released from prison, Abramoff was asked about that 22,000 percent return-on-investment figure. His response? "Surprised it's so little." He was pretty sure he'd done better.

Not to put too fine a point on it, but lobbying is one of the most profitable investment strategies in the history of the world. No wonder it flourishes.

President Reagan meeting with Jack Abramoff (center) and Grover Norquist before Abramoff was sent to prison for bribery

Lobbyists didn't always own Washington. An award-winning 1963 study by three political scientists described lobbying in the 1950s as "poorly financed, ill-managed, out of contact with Congress, and at best only marginally effective." The study's authors added that lobbying's "opportunities to maneuver are sharply limited, its staff mediocre, and its major problem not the influencing of Congressional votes but the finding of clients and contributors to enable it to survive at all." Many businesses resisted the idea that they should hire people to represent them in Washington.

Over time, attitudes changed. Businesses began to recognize that persuading the government to favor them could be highly profitable, and that lobbyists were the right tool for the job. And they found an ever more willing audience in Washington. Drug companies, for example, had long argued against the notion of providing a prescription benefit for Medicare because they feared that the federal government would use bulk purchasing to drive down the cost of the drugs. But, as lobbying expert Lee Drutman explains, "Sometime around 2000, industry lobbyists dreamed up the bold idea of proposing and supporting what became Medicare Part D," which requires the federal government to pay for prescriptions without any price negotiations. That provision delivers enormous profits to the drug companies—and costs American taxpayers an estimated $25 billion a year.

Bold lobbying indeed! My hunch is that the drug industry's backup plan was to tell the U.S. government to hand over one of the Treasury's printing presses so the industry could simply print its own money.

Although the size of our Congress hasn't changed, the growth in the size of the lobbying business is mind-boggling. Take a look at the chart on the next page, which has been adjusted for inflation.

Lobbying is like a gold rush: after a few prospectors tried influencing Congress and struck gold, more and more showed up to make their fortunes. Now Washington is a boomtown, thick with newly rich lobbyists and people ready to be their new friends.

As businesses discovered the benefits of jawboning the government and ramped up their lobbying efforts, the balance among lobbyists also shifted. In the 1950s and 1960s, most experts agreed that labor unions

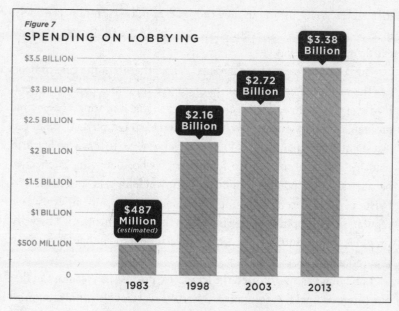

Figure 7
SPENDING ON LOBBYING

The growth in lobbying has been staggering.

and public interest groups had far more influence on Capitol Hill than business groups did. Today, there are still some lobbyists that don't hail from the business world. The Sierra Club has lobbyists, for example, and so do a number of labor unions. But the seismic shift has been in the amount corporations spend on trying to influence the government. One expert calculated the change this way: "For every dollar spent on lobbying by labor unions and public-interest groups together, large corporations and their associations now spend $34. Of the 100 organizations that spend the most on lobbying, 95 consistently represent business." It's as if corporate lobbyists have erected a series of giant flashing billboards by the side of the road, while other groups have put up a handmade poster. Yeah, they're both trying to persuade passing drivers, but one has a much better shot than the other of getting its message across.

What the businesses want is nearly always some variation of tax breaks or deregulation or both. They want a piece of the trickle-down action, in other words, but they want it custom-tailored, built just for themselves. With all the money they can spend—or, more accurately, invest—in making their arguments, these lobbyists tilt the playing field a little more every day.

Think about complex regulations. Who, other than the government, has the resources and the skills to dig into a thousand-page document, read every single line, and tweak a sentence so that it no longer bans some profitable industry practice? Who will find the paragraph that, if changed just slightly, can create a giant loophole? Who? A partner at a big law firm paid by a big corporation to lobby, that's who. Lobbying is effective because a major industry can hire an army of lobbyists, and those lobbyists can dedicate a vast supply of resources to scouring every law, regulation, and opinion letter issued by the government. All this work provides the ammunition to get the government to change the rules in that industry's favor.

Lobbying has so distorted the legislative process in Washington that our congressional representatives now have real trouble connecting with the people who sent them to D.C. A few years ago *The Onion* published a story with this fictional headline: "American People Hire High-Powered Lobbyist to Push Interests in Washington." Beneath that tease was an article about a lobbyist from the high-powered firm Patton Boggs who was hired by the people to represent their interests because they lack "a voice in the legislative process."

But truth overtook comedy. The vice president of the Association of Government Relations Professionals—the lobbying group for lobbyists—asserted that lobbyists don't crowd out ordinary constituents. He declared that "ordinary constituents can have just as much influence 'if they organize' or 'hire a professional to help them make their case'"—in other words, if the people hire a lobbyist.

Just when I thought I'd come across a good joke, a lobbyist snatched it away.

GOVERNMENT/CORPORATE REVOLVING DOOR

It was Thursday, November 13, 2014, and I was rushing through Reagan National Airport to catch the five-thirty plane back to Boston. Jack Lew, the secretary of the Treasury, was on the phone. "I'm calling about Antonio Weiss," he began.

The day before, the White House had nominated Weiss for a top spot at the Treasury Department. I'd told the Obama administration right out of the gate that I thought this was a big problem.

Now Secretary Lew was on the phone in full sales mode. "I think you'll like him," he said cheerfully. I stopped dead at the top of the escalator, causing the person behind me to bump into me. I mumbled an apology to the man I'd blocked and then shuffled off to the side, acutely aware that I was not in a private place.

Antonio Weiss. He had spent his whole career working for Lazard, an investment bank on Wall Street. Oops, let me correct that: Lazard isn't a Wall Street investment bank, because it officially moved to Bermuda a decade ago to avoid paying U.S. taxes. Weiss's most recent claim to fame, in fact, was that he'd played an important role in an $11 billion "tax inversion" deal to help Burger King become a Canadian company so that it could also avoid paying a big chunk of its U.S. taxes. Weiss was a guy who in his twenty-year career had no record of public service, who had been behind job-cutting deals that looked just like the ones Barack Obama slammed Mitt Romney for, and who had much more experience in international mergers than in domestic economic policy. And he was also the guy Secretary Lew thought should be put in charge of domestic economic policy at the U.S. Department of the Treasury—a job that included protecting the Dodd-Frank financial reforms.

Secretary Lew's hail-Senator-well-met approach to our phone conversation suggested that the secretary expected me to thank him for calling, then politely sit down and fold my hands in my lap. I tried as calmly as I could to explain my concerns. But with each back-and-forth, my voice got a little louder. I moved away from the escalator, looking for a place where I might not be overheard.

Secretary Lew continued to press his case. Finally, in a cajoling tone, he said, "C'mon. He's a progressive. He was even the publisher of the *Paris Review*."

What?

You know, he said, the literary magazine.

I laughed out loud. Did Secretary Lew seriously think that I was the kind of idiot who would assume that just because someone liked poetry he shared my concerns about stagnating middle-class incomes or the importance of reining in giant Wall Street banks? This was like some kind of a comedy show, and it was getting crazier by the minute.

By this time, I had worked my way over to a deserted corner of the airport near a rarely used ladies' room. And now I was speaking into the phone at full volume. A woman exiting the bathroom looked over, startled, when she saw me facing a wall and carrying on a heated argument.

I told Secretary Lew that Weiss was an awful choice for a high-ranking policy position at Treasury. As strongly as I knew how, I said the administration needed more voices for Main Street and fewer for Wall Street.

Secretary Lew finally seemed to grasp that I would not support his pick for the job, so he suggested I stay quiet long enough for Weiss to "get to know some people." In other words, Secretary Lew wanted me to let him line up support for his nominee before I raised any red flags.

"No."

"Excuse me?"

Over the years, I had watched person after person go through the revolving door from Wall Street to government and back again. Some were well qualified, and some had shaky qualifications. Many were already in place by the time I'd joined the Senate, and I'd done my best to play nice with them. Then this guy shows up. Was I really supposed to ignore the fact that he had no relevant experience beyond working on Wall Street and making friends on both sides of the revolving door?

Enough was enough.

I said no again.

Secretary Lew wasn't happy. Neither was I.

After Weiss was nominated, Bloomberg.com reported that Lazard had paid him $15.4 million over the previous two years. But that wasn't enough. It also turned out that Lazard had generously agreed to give him an additional $21.2 million in "unvested compensation" on his way out the door. As best as I could determine, that compensation would not be available if he went to work for a competitor. But Lazard would definitely write out a $21.2 million check for a top employee who wanted to spend a little time working in a high-powered government position where he could influence policies that would directly affect Lazard and Lazard's many clients.

I wasn't the only one who understood what was going on. David Schmidt, a specialist in executive compensation, explained to a Bloomberg reporter why Lazard would make a multimillion-dollar gift to a departing employee. Such companies "may want to stay in their former employee's good graces for policy influence," the story noted. Schmidt expanded on that: "If he does come back after his term in government, he's coming back with a pretty interesting resume that could be helpful to the company." Oh, goody.

That's the revolving door in a nutshell: the executive moves to a government job where he can help his former employer, and as soon as the government service is over, the executive comes back to the corporation with government connections that he can use to help that same employer.

The rest of us can wonder: Exactly who does this guy work for? The taxpayers? The corporation? Or some secret-sauce blend of the two?

Secretary Lew had plenty of reasons to be shocked by my response. After all, Weiss was just the latest to join the parade of travelers through the government/Wall Street revolving door. Secretary Lew himself had circled through that revolving door, picking up a sweet bonus along the way. From 2006 to 2008, he worked for Citigroup, the outfit that, when all the checks were added up, received nearly half a trillion dollars in bailout money during the crash—almost $140 billion more than the next bank. Citi was also the bank that had its lobbyists write the amendment that blew a hole in Dodd-Frank.

How did Citigroup get that kind of juice? Let me count the ways: Three of the last four Treasury secretaries under Democratic presidents had close Citigroup ties. The fourth was offered the CEO position at Citigroup but turned it down. Both the vice chair of the Federal Reserve System and the undersecretary for international affairs at Treasury were former Citigroup executives. The U.S. trade representative and the person nominated to be his deputy were Citigroup alums.

Wait, there's more: a recent chairman of the National Economic Council at the White House was a Citigroup exec, and a recent chairman of the Office of Management and Budget went to Citigroup immediately after leaving the White House. And that counts only the guys at the tippy top.

The Republicans have their own in-house banking team. Henry Paulson was the chairman and CEO of Goldman Sachs when he was named as George W. Bush's secretary of the Treasury, and when he joined the government, he brought along a team of Goldman executives. In fact, the team was so big that other bankers gave the firm a new nickname: Government Sachs: ha, ha, ha.

Pretty funny, right? Except that when the economy cratered in 2008, the guys in charge were the same guys who were supposed to have been on guard duty and prevented this crash. They were also the guys who turned right around and told Congress that it had to pony up for a $700 billion bailout, pointing out that the banks had gotten so big that if Congress didn't agree to give them the money, those banks would collapse and bring down the entire economy. Government Sachs, ha, ha.

For some people, the first spin of the revolving door is from Wall Street to Washington, but for others the trip is from Washington straight to Wall Street. Eric Cantor, a Republican from Virginia, spent nine years in the state legislature, followed by almost fourteen years in Congress. Ultimately, he rose to House majority leader, the second-in-command role. When he lost his seat in 2014, the shock must have run deep. But the blow was surely softened by his new job: within weeks of his defeat, he was hired as vice chairman of an investment bank, with pay totaling $3.4 million. Despite Cantor's complete lack of experience in banking, the firm said that he would earn that juicy paycheck because he would play "a leading role in client development and advise clients on strategic matters."

Wow, that's not very subtle. But I guess the negotiations for a $3.4 million newcomer salary included leaving subtlety at the door.

The revolving door also works for ambitious staffers. In 2012, it became clear that Republican Congressman Jeb Hensarling would become chairman of the influential House Financial Services Committee, that plum assignment for anyone eager to raise political contributions. Within weeks, his chief of staff made a beeline for the exit and promptly became a lobbyist working for the American Bankers Association, one of Wall Street's top trade groups. His new employer boasts on its website that the former staffer is Hensarling's "go-to guy." In other words, the congressman with the biggest role in writing the laws that govern the financial sector will continue to lean on his former longtime employee—who is now on Wall Street's payroll.

And that's just two stories out of a zillion. As Congress debated Dodd-Frank, no fewer than 125 former members of Congress or former Hill staffers were working as lobbyists for financial firms. Each and every one of them was trading on those government connections as they helped promote the rules and regulations the banks wanted.

Big banks aren't the only corporations taking full advantage of a well-oiled revolving door, of course. So, for example, Navient, the spin-off from student loan giant Sallie Mae, had fifteen "revolvers" on its payroll in 2015. It seems that Navient hired three former members of Congress, two former agency staffers, and ten former congressional staffers, all offering their employer inside knowledge about the Department of Education's operations and plenty of connections to the people who still work there.

Of course, a big daddy corporation needs big daddy lobbyists. In 2014, ExxonMobil had three former senators—a Democrat and two Republicans—lobbying Congress on behalf of just this one corporation. The oil and gas industry's stable of lobbyists included twenty-six former members of Congress, fifty-four former White House employees, twenty-one former staffers from the Department of Energy, and ten employees of the Department of the Interior. Jeez. That's enough lobbyists to field a baseball team, four hockey teams, eight basketball teams, and three football teams, with a handful of sumo wrestlers left over.

THE REVOLVING DOOR spins faster than ever when a new president comes to town. Sure enough, as soon as the Republicans took back the White House in 2016 and Donald Trump began making appointments, Goldman Sachs was once again riding high. Within days of winning the election, Trump named Stephen Bannon, a former Goldman banker, as his chief strategist. Three top economic positions—secretary of the Treasury, director of the National Economic Council, and senior counselor for economic initiatives—went to Goldman execs.

Make no mistake about what these executives are expected to do for Goldman Sachs and for investment bankers generally once they are supposedly working for the government: soon after the appointments were announced, *Bloomberg Businessweek* ran a story saying that Goldman execs "are poised to preside over a rollback of financial regulations that arguably threatened Goldman more than any other top bank." After Trump's election, Goldman's stock price shot up 31 percent, adding another half billion dollars to its valuation. Move over, Disneyland: as one writer put it, Goldman Sachs is now known as the "Happiest Place on Earth."

At Goldman, the revolving door is so important that the *New York Times* reported, "It is a widely held view within the bank that no matter how much money you pile up, you are not a true Goldman star until you make your mark in the political sphere."

Goldman's Masters of the Universe obviously have stellar résumés, but just how much special expertise do they bring to their new jobs? Take a look: When Henry Paulson needed someone to manage the huge TARP bailout in 2008, where did he turn? Was it to someone with years of experience in housing finance? Was it to someone who understood that the way to rebuild this economy was to focus on how to get families back on their feet and boost consumer demand? Was it to someone who had such a sophisticated understanding of our economic system that they had sounded the alarm and warned us that dangerous mortgage lending would crash our economy? Nope. Here's how the *New York Times* crisply described Secretary Paulson's pick:

> When Mr. Paulson needed someone to oversee the government's proposed $700 billion bailout fund, he again recruited someone with a Goldman pedigree, giving the post to a 35-year-old former investment banker who, before coming to the Treasury Department, had little background in housing finance.

Now, with Trump in the White House, a new Goldman team is taking over our government. Shortly after the election, Trump nominated Steven Mnuchin, a hedge fund manager, to be his Treasury Secretary. Many years ago Mnuchin followed his father into the upper echelons of Goldman Sachs, and he made his money early on by selling the high-risk financial instruments that eventually destroyed the economy in the Great Recession of 2008. Then he ran a $14 billion bank and earned the nickname "the Foreclosure King." Mnuchin was not only a Wall Street insider, he was a hands-on executive who brazenly squeezed a fortune out of other people's misery.

The idea that Wall Street executives and executives in training can waltz in and out of the government, claiming they have special knowledge of how all the machinery works, was unmasked by the financial crisis. Goldman Sachs executives such as Paulson and Mnuchin had worked at the firm while it was peddling mortgage products like the kind that caused the 2008 crash. These executives, once reputed to be savvy managers and detail-oriented experts, later claimed to know nothing—nothing—about any of the wrongdoing. So what exactly was their expertise? Making profits by swindling people? Forcing risks onto the taxpayers? Padding their own bank accounts?

It makes me gag.

Don't get me wrong: experience on Wall Street shouldn't disqualify someone from government service. Shoot, when I set up the Congressional Oversight Panel, which reviewed the Treasury's management of TARP, I brought in people with experience in the financial industry. When I built the Consumer Financial Protection Bureau, I had Wall Street professionals on my team. They were good people, and I appreciated the work they did. But they had other, non–Wall Street experience too, and they were surrounded by coworkers who had never been steeped in Wall Street culture and were highly skeptical of business models that rely on cheating people.

Wall Street experience shouldn't disqualify people, but how does that experience alone qualify someone to serve in government? What has Steve Mnuchin done to demonstrate that he has even a shred of independence from his old buddies on Wall Street? Where is the evidence that he has the backbone to stand up to Wall Street giants? What line on his résumé can reassure us that he has the experience and the judgment necessary to run the U.S. Department of the Treasury in the interests of homeowners and small savers and students and investors all across this country?

With no good answers to these questions, why would we hand over the country's top economic job to him? More to the point, why should we hand over our entire economic system to the same guys who completely wrecked it less than a decade ago? That idea is stupid on its face.

It makes no sense to entrust every one of these crucial jobs to people who have absorbed a culture that focuses almost exclusively on profit making. At least some of our highest-level public officials should be people with experience working on problems like stagnating incomes, market transparency, and trade deals that undermine job growth here in America—the issues, in other words, that government officials should be thinking about. The revolving door puts people in charge who shouldn't be in charge and shuts out people who could help build a stronger economy for the rest of America.

Wall Street executives roll into Washington and start calling the shots in government, while both elected officials and young government staffers start thinking about their post-government futures. There's a reason why Congress is known as the "farm team" for lobbying firms and industry. But let's speak plainly: much of the "team" operating in our country's capital has mixed loyalties at best, and somehow an awful lot of people have accepted the idea that it can never be anything better, that it's just "the way things are."

No, and no again. I don't care how many people, Republican or Democrat, tell me that this is reality; I will not look at this filth and call it clean. The American people deserve a government that's better than a training camp for those planning to cash in.

EXECUTIVES RUN IT ALL

Sometimes corporate CEOs get to call the shots in government without leaving the comfort of their corner offices and executive washrooms.

Several months after I arrived in Congress, I met with Michael Froman. He had already taken several turns through the government/Wall Street revolving door. Back during the 2008 crisis, at the same time that he was a high-level Citigroup executive and Citigroup was getting a ginormous government bailout from TARP, Froman was personally helping pick the Obama economic team—straight from his desk at his Citigroup office. Now, in June 2013, he had left Citi again, and was back in government as a senior White House official. He was about to take over as the U.S. trade representative, which meant he would lead the U.S. negotiations involving any trade deal. He would be helped by teams of "advisers," who would whisper in the ears of the official negotiators, counseling them about how to shape the details of these trade deals.

Trade touches all of America. Sure, multinational corporations are directly affected, but so is every small business that wants to sell supplies or services to bigger companies. Every start-up company that hopes to compete with a multinational will also be affected by our trade deals. Every farmer who competes with a grower in Vietnam or a rancher in Argentina will be touched. If American workers are undercut by child labor or prison labor because of trade deals, then labor is affected. And if a trade deal makes it easier and more profitable to move a company to a country where there are no environmental regulations and expand operations there, then everyone will feel the impact. I could go on, but the point is that trade is hugely important to pretty much everyone in America.

It matters who helps call the shots on America's trade deals, so that was the first question I asked Froman: Who is on the trade advisory teams?

Froman knew about my concerns before he ever walked into my office, and he immediately reassured me: about half represented corporations and half represented labor and other nonprofit groups.

Really? Half and half?

Yes, absolutely, for sure.

When he left, I asked my staff how hard it would be to find out who was actually on the advisory teams and what their affiliations were. The answer: it would take some work, but the names were public. So we dug in, and our math didn't match Froman's—not by a long shot.

In fact, according to an analysis published by the *Washington Post* eight months after Froman was confirmed, corporate executives and industry lobbyists filled 85 percent of advisory roles. Everyone else—workers, environmentalists, human rights activists, small farmers—split up the remaining 15 percent. Of the twenty-eight working groups, more than half didn't have even a single adviser who wasn't working for the corporations that potentially stood to gain from the trade negotiations. Not one.

These trade deals are negotiated behind closed doors. It matters who sits at the table. Here's how I saw it: rigged process, rigged outcome.

Remember Michael Smith, the man from the Chicago suburbs who lost his home? He didn't expect to be affected by our country's trade policy—why should that ever have anything to do with him? After he lost his job at DHL and the bank foreclosed on his house, he kept searching for steady work. He had good references, and he was determined—determined to see his youngest daughter, Ashley, through high school, determined to buy another home, determined to regain his footing in America's middle class.

His break came late in 2011 when he got a good job offer at a Nabisco plant. He was in his fifties by now, but when the company started him out on the eleven-to-seven graveyard shift, working all night putting the creme in the middle of Oreo cookies and packaging belVita biscuits, he thanked the managers and worked as hard as he could.

Eventually he worked his way to a day shift. He really enjoyed the job. He explains, "My wife absolutely loved belVita, and I was proud because I was the one who made it! I actually knew which ones I made." Did he like to sample the wares, too? "Oh man, yes!"

He took every shift he could get and piled on extra work whenever he could. In 2014, with the foreclosure in his rearview mirror and three years on the new job, Michael could finally qualify for a mortgage again. He and his wife, Janet, bought a new home nine miles from his old one. Ashley was in college, Michael had a new driveway to shovel, and once again he felt like his family was part of America's middle class.

The Nabisco plant was profitable, and in 2015 Nabisco's parent company, Mondelez, posted revenues of $30 billion. Michael was happy to

Michael and Janet Smith

know that people everywhere seemed to love their belVita biscuits. And he was proud to help make Oreos, which he calls "part of American culture."

In fact, as demand for Nabisco's products grew, investing in expansion began to make more and more sense. Nabisco and its parent company, seeing a big opportunity, worked all the angles. In the 1990s, the company had been given $90 million in incentives to stay in Chicago. That had boosted its bottom line, and from 2013 through 2015, Mondelez had sucked up tax rebates and loopholes and slashed its average federal taxes. In 2015, the corporation's tax rate was 7.5 percent of earnings—a whole lot lower than the rate Michael paid.

But after taking a close look at all their costs, Nabisco and its parent company estimated that they could save $46 million a year by building a plant in Mexico. Because of America's trade deals, it was far cheaper to make Oreos in Mexico and then ship them back to the U.S. So what was the point of investing in Chicago? In March 2016, the company handed Michael and about six hundred other Chicago workers a pink slip.

An endless parade of government officials, experts, pundits, and oh-so-sophisticated commentators point out that opening up U.S. markets boosts our gross domestic product, which means that sellers are making bigger profits and shareholders are getting richer. Sure, the liberals among them might be willing to throw a few crumbs in job-retraining money to Michael and his laid-off coworkers. But the basic premise is that what's good for giant multinationals is good for the almighty GDP.

A lot of economists who look at our economy from ten thousand feet up will undoubtedly agree. So will executives staring at spreadsheets that turn people into "heads" and plants into "facilities." But Michael can't pay his mortgage with the GDP. He can't buy health insurance with the GDP. He can't eat the GDP. Michael needs a good job, but neither Nabisco nor the U.S. trade team worries about Michael, or his family, or his home.

What really makes this infuriating is that most of the pro-trade guys act like everyone who opposes a trade deal is some medieval troll who thinks we'll survive by crushing our own berries, weaving our own cloth, and eating raw squirrels. But the alternative to a bad trade deal is not to shut down all trade. The alternative to a bad trade deal is a trade deal that works for everyone and not just for a handful of corporate executives and big investors.

No surprise: trade deals are complicated. They are sort of like very long contracts with lots and lots of fine print. They include all kinds of promises about things that countries will and won't do, but—also no surprise—not every country follows up on every one of those promises. Deep in the fine print of our trade deals is a provision saying that if a multinational corporation thinks a country has not done what it promised to do under the terms of the deal, then the corporation can go to an arbitration panel made up of corporate lawyers, get a quick judgment, and, if the corporation wins, it can demand immediate payment from the government. No appeals, no nothing, just pay up. But what if that country violates other terms of the trade agreements, such as those that prohibit companies from using prison labor or dumping toxic waste in the rivers? Can workers or environmental groups go to that same high-speed arbitration panel? No. They have to go to their own government and try to persuade it to bring a lawsuit in an international court. Ask the steelworkers how that's worked out. On just one product, the steelworkers union filed case after case for violations of trade laws and watched our government drag its feet while more than seven thousand workers lost their jobs, capacity was shut down, and local companies teetered on the brink of bankruptcy. Yes, the union was persistent, and yes, they eventually won, but as Steelworkers president Leo Gerard testified, "a substantial portion of the industry will never come back."

This is why it matters who advises the U.S. trade representative. Currently, trade deals favor giant corporations because giant corporations help write them. But what if industry had, say, only 25 percent of the seats at the negotiating table while unions, small business owners, non-union workers' groups, and environmentalists had the other 75 percent? Would our workers still get their legs cut out from under them by the low-wage labor and prison labor and child labor too often used by other countries? No way. If labor representatives had a substantial number of the seats at the table, I guarantee that the trade deals would be written differently and that any promises that were made would have some serious muscle to back them up.

There's so much more we could do if we actually had a trade policy that was about making the economy work better for more of America. If companies that invested in the United States had better access to American markets than companies investing overseas, then those companies would be more likely to invest here and American workers would be in greater demand. If companies that moved jobs overseas paid higher taxes on their foreign profits, and if those tax revenues were reinvested here in the United States, then the benefits of those trade deals could be shared by more of our country's middle class. This isn't just about asking corporations to pay more taxes; it's about using a portion of the profits generated from trade to invest in American industries and to put serious money into things like low-cost renewable energy or state-of-the-art infrastructure or better education. Those are the kind of investments that would build a bigger, more resilient, more highly skilled workforce here in the United States.

There are many ways to make trade work better for all Americans, but as long as 85 percent of the trade rep's advisers care about little more than corporate profits and their own executive bonuses, it won't happen. And as long as companies aren't given incentives to invest in America's workers rather than pay low wages to foreign workers, it won't happen. Trade deals that are great for giant corporations are rarely quite so great for America's middle-class families.

And that brings us back to Nabisco, which had no interest in how to make trade produce benefits for Michael or for any other American worker. As Americans ate more and more Oreos and belVita biscuits and other signature products, Nabisco closed plants in Pittsburgh, Philadelphia, and Houston; it shuttered factories in Niles and St. Elmo, Illinois, and in Buena Park, California. It closed American plants and hired Mexican workers for twelve dollars a day, which no doubt did wonders for its bottom line.

But hey, the GDP kept going up, so who cares?

Michael cares. He feels deeply betrayed. He was part of "the Nabisco family," as he still calls it. He worked hard and did whatever was needed. And now that his job has been shipped to Mexico, he has thrown himself wholeheartedly into the struggle against the Nabisco layoffs.

His union has launched a campaign to boycott Mexican-made Nabisco products. "Check the label" has become the campaign's top message. "If a Nabisco package says 'Made in Mexico,' do not buy" it. Michael has spoken with reporters, appeared in videos, and traveled the country to spread the word about the boycott—just about everything humanly possible to publicize the campaign and fight the corporation's move. Still, Michael never wanted to be an activist. He just wanted to do his job. He keeps hoping that the Nabisco jobs will come back to Chicago. He is once again looking everywhere for work, and he worries about whether he can keep up with his mortgage payments.

Meanwhile, Mondelez's CEO is doing just fine. She has distinguished herself through her focus on cutting costs. For her efforts, she has been raking in about $20 million a year.

Michael and the CEO—on average, they are doing just great.

SECRET SECRETS

The same techniques that can be used to sell soap and cat food can also be used to sell really bad policies. But with soap and cat food, at least we know who is paying—and that reminds us to keep a hand on our wallets. Not so with ads aimed at tilting the political playing field in favor of giant corporations.

Okay, I'll admit it right up front: I've appeared in one of these ads, and it was just plain bizarre. Here's the backstory.

Coming out of the financial crash of 2008, I proposed that the government set up the consumer agency mentioned earlier—the Consumer Financial Protection Bureau—and when Dodd-Frank passed, the agency came into being. Its mission was simple: make sure families don't get cheated on financial contracts like mortgages and credit cards. So far, the agency has handled more than a million complaints and forced big banks to return nearly $12 billion that they had scammed from families. In 2016, when Wells Fargo was caught trying to boost its profits by creating a couple million fake accounts, it was the CFPB that smacked it with a $185 million fine.

For the big banks, that's the problem: the CFPB works. Families are doing a little better—$12 billion better. And financial institutions are doing a little worse—$12 billion worse. In fact, the true impact of the consumer agency is greater than that, because at least a few financial institutions have noticed that there's now a cop on the beat and so decided to dial back on padding the bottom line by cheating people.

Some banks may tolerate the CFPB, but a lot of Wall Street financiers *hate* it, so they spend heavy-duty bucks lobbying against it. Enter: the American Action Network.

AAN is the same group that a few years ago made the bizarre accusation that Democrats want to give Viagra to sex offenders. This time around, it stepped up and spent millions of dollars on a television commercial suggesting that the CFPB is some kind of Commie plot. And here's where I come in. The commercial featured a photo of me imposed on a Chairman Mao–style banner hanging above a hall full of robotic-looking workers. It was my "Mao and me" moment.

*From an ad against the CFPB. If I'm going to get the Chairman Mao treatment,
I really wish they'd use a better picture.*

By the way, the face on the other banner is not the guy from *The
Office*. It's Rich Cordray, who runs the consumer agency—and who, by
the way, is one of the most effective and honest public servants I have
ever met. It nearly broke my heart when I couldn't stay on to run the
CFPB, but every time I think of what a terrific job Rich does, I smile.

So who is this American Action Network? And what exactly *were*
they trying to sell by running commercials that alerted America to this
Commie threat using weirdo pictures of Rich and me?

AAN's board includes a hedge fund executive, a venture capital executive, and two registered lobbyists for a student loan company that was
under investigation by the CFPB during the time the commercial was
running. Naturally, none of that was mentioned in the ad.

If banks and student loan companies hate the CFPB, they certainly
have the right to say so. And if they hate the agency even more when they
are under investigation, they can say that, too. Have at it, boys. But how
about putting that information out in the open, where everyone can see it?

What really makes this whole thing galling is that the American
Action Network is considered tax-exempt as long as it spends its money

on "promoting social welfare"—and anti-CFPB ads seem to count as "social welfare." This means that a corporation that's getting investigated by the CFPB can put a bucket of secret money into a nonprofit group, install its own lobbyists on the board, and then watch as the group runs ads attacking the CFPB. Meanwhile, because of the way the organization is structured, taxpayers will give it a special break.

Think about that. Our tax code is so screwy that consumers who got cheated and who like having a cop on the financial beat are forced to subsidize a group that runs stupid ads attacking the consumer agency. The owners of a community bank and the members of credit unions—people who don't make it their business to cheat other people—are subsidizing those ads. Students who got swindled by a student loan outfit are subsidizing those ads. Shoot, Rich Cordray and I are subsidizing those ads. I know it sounds nuts, but that's how crazy things are in Washington.

But for the people behind outfits like AAN, there's one more cherry on the whipped cream: those corporate donations and backroom conversations are kept secret. I'm all for free speech, but free speech is about the open exchange of ideas. Secretly funded speech is a lot harder to evaluate. And secretly funded speech that is bought and paid for by big corporations doesn't create the marketplace of ideas that the founders envisioned.

Groups like AAN and its board members—some of whom may be working for companies under active investigation by the agency they are attacking—have a legal right to do what they do. But don't try to pretend that it's a level playing field and we're going to hear from everyone, because we're not. All those people who got cheated on mortgages or student loans might like to run their own ads about how important it is to have a strong consumer agency, but most of them don't have the money to get into the political ad game. Inevitably, their stories won't get the same kind of play.

Corporations want you to think their campaigns come from the grassroots, from real people, so they create nonprofit organizations as fronts. The fact is, the corporate nonprofit business is one more scam. A big company sets up a group that sounds like it's pro-consumer or organized by a grassroots movement, but the group pushes the corporation's point of view. Fake grassroots movements are so common they have their own name: AstroTurf movements. Their ads are often expensively produced, and they frequently show actors posing as family farmers or concerned doctors who explain the benefits of sugary drinks, pesticides, or restrictions on malpractice suits. As one reporter noted, "Voters may not readily be able to identify the patrons behind the millions of dollars in ads, but a who's who of corporate America—soda king Coca-Cola, agriculture magnate Monsanto and malpractice insurer The Doctors Company—are among them."

Some corporations take a different approach. When the defense budget was working its way through two committees in Congress, weapons manufacturers were spending tens of millions to advertise all around D.C.—in Capitol Hill newspapers, in the Metro, on local radio. As the *Washington Post* observed, "The ads are seen by many but are intended for just a few. With two of the largest defense contracts ever on the verge of being decided, the targets are the several hundred—and in some cases, several dozen—people who determine how billions of federal defense dollars will be spent." Or consider the American Petroleum Institute spending $85.5 million on advertising in 2012 while the Keystone XL Pipeline was under consideration. With billions on the line—billions of corporate profits—a few tens of millions on advertising to a handful of people who might affect those policies looks like a good investment. Too bad the American public doesn't get equal time.

All those corporate dollars have another impact: big ad purchases can also shape the news coverage of those same corporations. A recent academic paper examined whether the coverage by U.S. newspapers of their advertising clients was affected by advertising dollars. The researchers sampled newspapers published from 1999 to 2012, analyzing both advertising purchases and news coverage. They concluded that the ad dollars often produced better news coverage for the corporations that purchased those ads. Does a corporation want lighter coverage of its illegal conduct or better promotion of its campaign against a new city ordinance? Start by writing a fat check to the local news outlets.

Farm News, an Iowa newspaper with a readership of twenty-four thousand households in thirty-three counties, illustrated the point with

This cartoon got Rick Friday fired.

deadly seriousness in 2016. Rick Friday is a farmer who also sketched editorial cartoons for *Farm News* for over twenty-one years. But his cartoon career abruptly ended when he poked a sharp stick at Big Agriculture. I thought his cartoon was pretty tame, but when a seed company protested by withdrawing its advertisements, *Farm News* fired its cartoonist.

Rick Friday's story hit the news, but it's anyone's guess how many other cartoonists, columnists, reporters, and editors have learned the brutal lesson that they should be tough and fair and honest—except when it might anger paid advertisers.

Money talks. Everyone else whispers.

EXPERTS FOR HIRE

If too many politicians seem bought and paid for and the lobbyists are just guns for hire, is there anyone left in Washington who can be trusted?

Bring on the experts.

I like experts. I like people who do research, who come up with new ideas, who test out theories, and who are willing to push against the conventional wisdom. I like people who live in the world of data, even if they're sometimes a little, um, unusual. I even like most of the conservative experts. Stands to reason, I guess, since I've spent a lot of time in universities.

Academia has long provided a home for experts, but in recent years Washington has become a magnet for them as well. The nation's capital is chock full of think tanks that employ dozens of experts to churn out reports, studies, and testimony designed to shape America's policy agenda.

The oldest and one of the most prestigious of these think tanks is the Brookings Institution. Founded more than a century ago, its stated mission is "to conduct high-quality, independent research and, based on that research, to provide innovative, practical recommendations." Sounds impressive, doesn't it? I certainly thought so, which is why in July 2015 I was glad to see that Robert Litan of the highly prestigious Brookings Institution would be a witness at an upcoming Senate hearing about investment advisers.

The issue was kickbacks. Yes, the people who accepted them called them something else, but here's how the game worked: The investment advising industry is huge, and for many years some (though not all) investment advisers had been receiving "prizes" in return for steering retirees to higher-priced annuities and other investments. These prizes included points toward vacations at fancy resorts, luxury cars, "Super Bowl–style rings," and plain old cash. The Department of Labor eventually figured out that these prizes were costing American consumers about *$17 billion* a year, and for years they had tried to pass rules to shut down the practice, but the industry had beaten them back.

In 2015, the Labor Department developed a tough new set of regulations to clean up the investment advising industry, and once again the advisers and their bosses fought back. Of course, they had a lot of reasons to fight back—about 17 billion reasons, in fact. Unsurprisingly, Republicans in Congress sided with the industry. To put pressure on the Labor Department to back off, they called a hearing about the proposed rule.

When Dr. Robert Litan testified, he was introduced as a nonresident senior fellow at the highly reputable Brookings Institution.

Like most witnesses at congressional hearings, Dr. Litan submitted written testimony in advance. He described a study he had done that came to a pretty shocking conclusion: banning the kickbacks could actually *cost* consumers as much as $80 billion. Holy cow! This well-credentialed expert was basically saying that if investment advisers couldn't steer people to bad products, the customers would lose money.

But wait. Litan's claim ran exactly counter to studies prepared by the Council of Economic Advisors at the White House and by the Department of Labor, as well as independent peer-reviewed academic studies. Besides, his conclusion just didn't make sense. How could kickbacks possibly be good for consumers? Something didn't smell right.

As it turned out, there was indeed some serious stink. While I was reading Litan's prepared testimony, I noticed that it carried the bland notation that "funding for this study was provided by the Capital Group, which provides investment services worldwide." The Capital Group had publicly opposed the new regulations, but Litan had been called to testify as an independent expert. He didn't describe himself as a gun for hire. Instead, he was introduced at the hearing as a Brookings Institution "nonresident senior fellow" and was referred to by that title in the hearing notice.

When the hearing was over, I followed up with some questions and learned that the Capital Group had paid $85,000 for Litan's report. And there was more: corporate executives from this investment company had "helped" Litan prepare the report by providing "feedback" and "editorial comments" before the document was made public.

Here we go, I thought—time to grab the bull**** whistle. I fired off a letter to the president of Brookings, asking about the connection between a reputable think tank and a study that had been bought and paid for by the financial services industry to advance its political agenda. (Okay, I said all those things in much more polite language, but I don't think anyone missed the point.)

The *Washington Post* picked up on my complaint, and others followed. One commentator pointed out that Litan's work was "a spectacularly unpersuasive hack-job" and that his report had not undergone peer review by other experts, a process that is standard for reputable research. Even the Brookings Institute didn't remain utterly silent: without naming Litan specifically, another prominent Brookings researcher described how the investment advising industry was trying to influence Congress, noting that special interest groups had "paid for research to try to discredit the proposed rule."

Litan's research looked pretty shaky, but a lot of daggers came flying my way just for asking about it. I was accused of "McCarthyism," "intimidation," and "silencing any viewpoints different from" my own. Wow—I'd clearly struck a nerve. Simply by asking who'd paid for research that favored the investment advising industry, I had upset a lot of people. Perhaps I was threatening to disrupt a very cozy—and very profitable—relationship between corporate sponsors looking for experts to turn out pre-screened and very favorable reports, testimony, and commentary, and the experts who were willing to sign on to such deals. If so, it wasn't surprising that lots of folks on both sides of that relationship weren't happy about my nosy questions. And why should they be? If senators become a bit more skeptical about some of those "expert reports" passed around

Washington, a lot of experts-for-hire will stand to lose money and a lot of corporations will stand to lose influence.

That dustup about the investment advising industry led to some real nastiness, but in the end, Robert Litan left Brookings and Brookings updated its rules about conflict of interest.

THE STORY OF my row with an expert doesn't qualify as the tip of an iceberg. It isn't even a little ice shaving on a snow cone. I found out about this so-called expert because I stumbled across a small disclosure in his testimony and kept asking questions until I discovered the payments and editorial influence. But there's no general requirement that anyone testifying before Congress reveal who paid for the research that's offered up or what influence they had over its content. None. These guys could be taking wheelbarrows full of money on their way into the hearing rooms and the senators listening to all the sober testimony wouldn't know about it—and some wouldn't mind anyway.

Drummed-up expert opinions and slanted research aren't used just in congressional hearings, though. Corporations use this kind of sleazy work all the time to influence legislation, rulemaking by regulators, and litigation. Robert Litan's study had one goal: get the Department of Labor's fiduciary rule about giving prizes to investment advisers overturned and let the industry continue collecting kickbacks. But it was just one example of a widespread practice.

Often this sort of research-for-hire is salted into press releases. Summaries of the bogus research is handed out by publicists to gullible reporters and then picked up in the news as if it were gospel. It's used in advertisements—remember those actors playing farmers and doctors?—and it shows up in op-eds and "fact" sheets circulated by lobbyists. Over time, the "research" is accepted as truth, and its authors are happy to serve in a standing army that is ready to prove anything for a price.

Some experts-for-hire come from the world of higher education. In the stuffy atmosphere of high-prestige universities, published articles are the mark of great accomplishment. But these articles aren't published in newspapers or popular magazines. The articles that count—really count—appear in academic journals, which are highly specialized publications that few people other than professors, grad students, and other researchers (and, occasionally, the author's mother) actually read. Getting published in these journals is so critical to furthering one's career that academics call it "publish or perish."

The articles in these journals bear all the hallmarks of scientific objectivity—technical language, numerous citations, lots of numbers. The articles themselves might as well be wearing little white lab coats. Some journals require complete disclosure about where research funding came from, but what is hidden from sight in many of them is how businesses use sponsorship dollars to influence both the journals and the research that gets published in them. And once that favorable research is published, the corporations that supported the research peddle it whenever they lobby Congress or the courts.

Here's an example. In 2006, a *New England Journal of Medicine* article compared three diabetes medications. It reported that Avandia, a diabetes drug produced by GlaxoSmithKline, performed best. Yay! GlaxoSmithKline touted the findings everywhere, but it failed to mention that all eleven of the article's authors were on the company's payroll. Worse, it turned out that every one of these well-paid authors missed the evidence of something that became tragically apparent years later: Avandia significantly increased the risk of heart attacks. Before the drug could be pulled off the market, it was estimated to have been associated with eighty-three thousand heart attacks and deaths.

Or how about this nasty little story. Over lunch one day, Senator Sheldon Whitehouse told me about the time he sued the lead paint industry. He was the attorney general of Rhode Island, and he had uncovered evidence that several paint manufacturers had kept selling their product long after they'd learned that the lead dust it produced was poisoning children. The jury agreed with Whitehouse, and the manufacturers were ordered to pay to help remove lead paint from homes.

But the paint companies didn't give up. They appealed to the state supreme court, which reversed the jury's decision, based in part on an article published in a scholarly journal. That's hardly unusual: convictions sometimes get overturned, and courts often cite law review articles when they are dealing with complex issues of law. But Whitehouse later discovered that the "independent expert article" that the supreme court relied on was in fact, as Whitehouse put it, "a piece planted mid-litigation by a paid adviser to the lead paint companies." All in secret—all to bail out corporations that a jury believed had poisoned our children.

Because of the court's ruling, the paint companies didn't have to put up a large sum of money to fix the problem. A little baby can keep breathing the lead dust that's shaken loose every time his mommy raises or lowers a window, and that mother's toddler can eat little bits of brightly colored paint that have chipped off the baseboard trim. And the CEO of a paint manufacturer can sleep snugly, knowing that his next quarter's profits are up another tenth of a percent.

Fake experts put everyone at risk. Consider the climate deniers. Let's be clear: when these experts lie to us, they put all of us in grave danger, because the climate of our planet is changing in ways that could make life as we know it impossible. This issue is hugely complicated, and scientists are grappling every day with the challenges involved in interpreting enormous volumes of data. But the basic evidence is unequivocal: 97 percent of climate scientists agree that climate change is here. Already, the American Academy of Pediatrics has warned that global warming endangers the health of our children, and the American Lung Association has concluded that "millions of people face greater risk to their health because of climate change."

Then comes the second blow: humans are affecting the change in climate. Those dirty power plants and emissions from our cars and the clear-cutting of forests are accelerating changes that are likely to have catastrophic consequences for our planet. There's overwhelming scientific consensus on that, too.

The solutions to this monumental problem—and, happily, there are some—may make a lot of people pretty uncomfortable, and in many cases they will cause severe disruptions. But for giant polluters, the pain is financial, since many of these solutions could cost them real money. So these companies are faced with a difficult task: shift their power sources, change their business models, and make every possible effort to reduce their environmental impact. Or they can take a simpler and much cheaper approach: find some "experts" and pay them to say the problem doesn't exist.

Guess which option the billionaire Koch brothers took? Here's a hint: their vast conglomeration of businesses has been one of the top polluters of our country's air and water, as well as one of the top emitters of greenhouse gases. No surprise, then, that they (among others) bought up a bunch of experts-for-hire and gave them PR training so they could serve as spokespeople. They funded phony op-eds, underwrote fake academic articles, and shoveled big money into friendly think tanks to support even more fake experts.

The Koch brothers and their organizations poured more than $88 million into groups that deny the existence of climate change—that is, $88 million that anyone could count. Starting around 2006, the Kochs mostly stopped making publicly traceable donations to climate-denial organizations. Since then, however, there's been a huge surge in secret donations through opaque nonprofit organizations. One study turned up $558 million in secret donations made between 2003 and 2010 to groups denying climate change. In a perverse way, that makes perfect sense: when someone has dirty hands, why would they hold them up for all the world to see?

At one point, the deniers organized a petition stating that humans aren't causing climate change, and it was supposedly signed by thirty-one thousand scientists. Wow, thirty-one thousand scientists—that's a lot, right? Here's the rub: 99.9 percent of the signers weren't actually *climate* scientists. Instead, the petition was signed by computer scientists, mechanical engineers, medical doctors, you name it—and very, very few actual climate scientists who knew the hard science. You've got to hand it to the climate deniers: these guys take fake experts to a whole new level.

Forget about the fact that 97 percent of climate scientists believe that climate change is happening; the well-funded deniers just keep repeating the fiction that there's no consensus, which inevitably breeds uncertainty. And not just a little uncertainty: only 33 percent of Americans think climate change is a very serious problem.

Why are the Koch brothers and others working so hard to shape public opinion? Because if the public doesn't feel the need to demand action, there won't be any action. Climate change is perhaps the most difficult problem humans have ever faced, and only an enormous effort by our government and other governments can solve it. But as long as the public isn't quite sure that climate change is real, as long as we can't quite accept the idea that it actually threatens our existence, there will be no sense of urgency about the need for the government to take action. The politicians who refuse to act to shut down the worst polluters or reduce tax breaks for oil companies or promote alternative sources of energy can get elected over and over. And the regulators who don't enforce environmental or safety rules—remember the accident that spewed more than 200,000,000 gallons of oil into the Gulf of Mexico?—get a free pass, too.

Here's the point: since the climate is changing, we need to change, too. Solving this problem will require new technologies, new laws, and profound changes to our economy. But the companies that profit from fouling our air and water and land don't want to change. They don't need to get any tough new laws passed; they just need to play defense and hold off efforts to make changes that would damage their business models. The goal of the climate deniers is gridlock and paralysis—three cheers for the status quo! The longer things remain the same, the longer they can keep raking in big bucks for drilling and dumping and spewing, with no thought for tomorrow.

Let's face it: solving this problem will be *hard*. This challenge is going to take the best we've got—the best minds, the hardest work, the most determination. And it will require global action, which means that countries that can barely agree on what time it is will need to work together and make tough choices, a herculean diplomatic challenge in the best of circumstances. As the 2016 Paris Agreement on climate change suggests, we're making some progress, but the problem continues to accelerate, and we will likely need solutions that we haven't even dreamed up yet.

I don't know the answers to the tough questions posed by climate change, but I do know this: we need to work much harder on climate issues *starting right now*. We need to explore all the ways we can tackle this incredibly difficult problem—and singing, "La-la-la, protect corporate profits!" is not one of them. Hiring fake experts is not one of them, either. Calling climate change a "hoax" created by China, as President Trump has said, is not the answer. We need to *learn* from scientists, not prop up bogus scientists on news shows and pretend that their opinions help provide a "more balanced view."

I believe in science. No matter what the issue, we need our best scientists giving us the best evidence and their best opinions about how to resolve the problems we face. But in the case of climate change, when the corrosive influence of money undercuts both our confidence in science and the work of our scientists, we are inflicting a wound on ourselves from which the human race may never recover.

THE NOT-SO-NEUTRAL COURTS

Our judicial system is supposed to be removed from the influence of the rich and powerful. In many courtrooms, judges sit at a distance from the litigants, literally on a raised bench behind a bar. They wear robes to mark the solemnity of their jobs and to set them apart from all who come before them asking for a ruling in their favor. And in most depictions of Lady Justice, she wears a blindfold to show that she is balancing her scales objectively. For Americans, her image is the true soul of justice.

It's no wonder, then, that most of us believe big money has no place our courtrooms. Our judges and courts provide the last holdout of clean government, right?

Well, sort of.

Judges don't run for office—or at least federal judges don't run for office. But some state judges have to run for reelection every few years, and as soon as they start soliciting and accepting campaign contributions, many of them cozy up to big-time corporate contributors. Welcome to the slippery slope. But even when judges don't run for office, the rich and powerful are still sniffing around, looking for a way to influence the outcome of legal disputes.

The reason is pretty simple: even if an industry loses a battle to get a law written exactly the way it wanted—and that sometimes happens, believe it or not—the industry can try to have the new law or regulation overturned in court. For those with plenty of money to spend, the courts can provide a second bite of the apple. Don't like a new rule issued by a regulator who oversees your industry? Bring a lawsuit, and maybe a judge will knock it out. Don't like the outcome of a court case? Fight to overturn it, and maybe a higher court will overrule the first court.

Courts listen to the lawyers who bring or defend cases, but they also listen to outsiders who offer their opinions in amicus curiae briefs—documents that are literally "friends of the court." Once again, the Chamber of Commerce, that longtime friend of big business, plays a starring role. For decades, the chamber has worked to influence court cases that help big companies. The chamber will file an amicus brief in a case and advance a blizzard of arguments that are meant to persuade the court that their corporate client ought to win.

And boy, has the chamber been successful. When filing amicus briefs before the Supreme Court, the chamber's win rate has steadily increased.

And who are the Supreme Court justices who have delivered all these wins for business interests? A conservative federal judge, an economist,

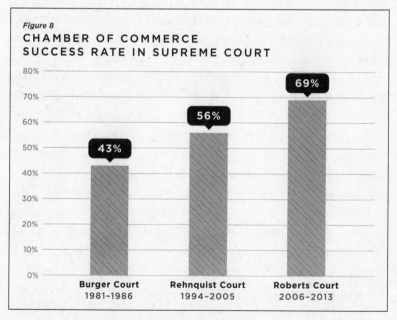

The Chamber of Commerce wins more and more cases in the Supreme Court.

and a political scientist who specializes in data analysis got interested in that question, so they analyzed decades of Supreme Court decisions. They discovered that at the end of 2012, the five conservative justices (Justices Samuel Alito, Anthony Kennedy, John Roberts, Antonin Scalia, and Clarence Thomas) were among the top ten most pro-business justices in half a century. In fact, Justice Alito and Chief Justice Roberts were listed as number one and number two.

Recent decisions made by the Supreme Court didn't help just a few corporations or one or two industries. Those same five justices handed down the *Citizens United* decision, which opened the floodgates for unlimited campaign spending by corporations. Those same five justices limited the ability of workers to sue their employers when they were discriminated against because of race or sex. Those same five justices made it easier for sophisticated, deep-pocketed corporations to prevent people they cheated or hurt from ever bringing a case to court. Those same five justices handed down one decision after another that helped out big corporations as they rolled over start-ups, employees, and consumers. The list is much longer, but the point is pretty clear. The consequences of having the highest court in the country stacked with pro-corporate justices are profound, and ultimately they have the potential to shake the very foundations of our democracy.

And the Chamber of Commerce isn't the only business-friendly organization that works hard to nudge the courts in their direction. Several outfits specialize in scouting out possible cases, contacting potential litigants, and arranging for top-notch, prepaid legal help. The whole point is to get the most winnable cases in front of judges. By advancing such handpicked cases, these groups help win rulings that favor their corporate clients that are secretly footing the very expensive bills.

Corporate America doesn't limit its attempt to influence our judicial system to the courtroom, though. There are many ways to persuade, such as invitations to attend fancy retreats—at no charge to the judges, of course. At some retreats, judges have been wined and dined lavishly, and golf, fishing, massages, and other treats also have been offered gratis. Often their only obligation is to attend a seminar or two that advance certain pro-business points of view. In one four-year period, groups like the Charles G. Koch Charitable Foundation and the Chamber of Commerce, as well as multinational corporations like ExxonMobil and Pfizer, picked up the tab for about 185 federal judges to attend more than one hundred all-expenses-paid trips. Some corporations even sponsored seminars for judges who would later rule on cases affecting their industries.

The Koch brothers have been laying the foundation for this kind of influence for many years. In 2008, they funded a political retreat in Palm Springs for, among others, Supreme Court Justices Scalia and Thomas. Justice Scalia and Justice Thomas later heard the infamous *Citizens United* case, and several groups funded by the Koch brothers contributed hundreds of millions of dollars to help elect senators and Congress members who would support *Citizens United* and oppose transparency. Some advocacy groups have cried foul, saying the justices should have recused themselves on the money-in-politics decision because of their participation in retreats like that one, but their complaints have fallen on deaf ears. Without the favorable votes by Scalia and Thomas, *Citizens United* would have gone the other way—but the justices brushed off the complaints, and *Citizens United* is now binding law.

It's impossible to know how much one free retreat might affect the views of a justice, but the pattern is unmistakable. Justice Scalia, for instance, took an estimated twenty-one trips sponsored by a single group. In 2014 alone, Scalia took at least twenty-three trips, nearly one every other week, to places like Hawaii, Switzerland, and Ireland—all paid for by wealthy people or the organizations they sponsored. Justice Scalia was particularly fond of hunting trips and the challenges he faced while stalking game. As he told one interviewer about his experience with turkeys: "You get one shot. If you miss, the whole day's ruined."

The night he died, in fact, Scalia was a guest at the exclusive Texas ranch of the owner of a billion-dollar company that had had business before the Supreme Court just a year earlier. Earlier in the day, the justice had been out on a quail hunt on the scenic property, where multiple movies have been filmed.

Justice Scalia died early in 2016, and Majority Leader Mitch McConnell immediately announced that the Republican-controlled Senate would refuse to consider any Supreme Court nominee from President Obama. As mentioned earlier, the Koch brothers backed him up by strong-arming Republican Senator Jerry Moran, prompting him to change his position and support McConnell's edict. But the Kochs weren't finished: an organization claiming to represent small businesses—but raking in millions of dollars from the Kochs—jumped in, aggressively attacking President Obama's nominee, Merrick Garland. Another outfit backed by the Kochs spent $2 million airing ads attacking Democratic senators for trying to fill the Supreme Court vacancy. It was an unprecedented and risky maneuver, but to McConnell and the Koch brothers the gamble was worth it. Scalia died during an election year, and they wanted to keep open the possibility that a Republican president could name his replacement.

A few months later, Donald Trump became the GOP's nominee. While campaigning that fall, he promised to fill the Supreme Court vacancy with someone "like Justice Scalia." And then, sure enough, Trump went on to win the election. Big gamble, big payoff!

Will the courts save us from the influence of giant corporations and billionaires? We can always hope so. But let's be dry-eyed about this: hope isn't going to win a high-stakes battle with the rich and powerful, especially when these guys want Lady Justice to take off her blindfold, hike up her robes, and give a sexy wink to their business interests.

BILLIONAIRE WORLD

The influence of money is everywhere in politics. And because it is everywhere, it's almost impossible to see and absorb the scalding truth that money has changed every perception.

One recent example of this blindness really set my teeth on edge. In the spring of 2016, billionaire Michael Bloomberg climbed up to the podium at the University of Michigan to deliver the commencement address to tens of thousands of cheering students and families. The day was sunny, and the stage was bedecked with flowers and flags; meanwhile, the presidential campaign was really heating up. Resplendent in flowing black robes trimmed in black velvet and gold braid, Bloomberg took the opportunity to denounce those who "fan the flames of partisanship," and he accused both Republicans and Democrats of demagoguery.

I wasn't at the ceremony, but when I began reading about his speech the next morning, I thought, "Great! He's right that both sides have misbehaved. Give 'em hell, Bloomberg!"

The examples he went on to cite were quite specific. He scolded Republicans for blaming our problems on "Mexicans who are here illegally and Muslims" and Democrats for blaming our problems on "the wealthy and Wall Street."

Wait, whoa, hold up a minute. Are you kidding me? Did Michael Bloomberg actually propose that these two groups are roughly equivalent? Does he believe that if "Mexicans who are here illegally and Muslims" and "the wealthy and Wall Street" were to decide to push back against the attacks launched at them, the two groups would have about the same access to the media? Does he believe that both groups spend

Michael Bloomberg speaking at the University of Michigan's commencement

anything like the same amount of money attempting to influence politicians through political contributions and by hiring lobbyists to represent them? And does he believe that both groups run about the same number of paid media advertisements—the kind that reporters and editors pay attention to? And does he believe that both groups have pursued a long-term strategy to recruit friendly "experts" who favor their perspective? And does he believe that both groups have about equal chances to put a few of their own in high government positions—and pay them millions of dollars for their time in government service just so they will remember who their friends are? And while we're at it, does he believe that both groups were equally responsible for crashing the economy and costing American families a collective $22 *trillion*? That might all be true in Michael Bloomberg's Alternative Billionaire World—but not so much here on planet Earth.

Bloomberg's speech stirred up some controversy, but only for the things he said about whether college campuses should have safe spaces. ("A terrible idea.") The part of his speech about how it's pretty much the same to blame our country's problems on Mexicans and Muslims as it is to blame them on Wall Street and billionaires got no attention at all. None. Zip. Zilch. In Michael Bloomberg's view, he and his trembling rich buddies are just as vilified as Muslims and undocumented immigrants. He concluded that it's all scapegoating—no difference—and he got away with it. Pass the caviar.

This story may seem harmless enough, but it scares me down to my toes. Not because Michael Bloomberg is a bad guy; in fact, I've never met him, but I assume from what I've read that he's a pretty decent person who has tried to do a lot of good. The story scares me because it reminds me of two fundamental truths: the playing field isn't level, and the people at the top often don't notice that.

Perspective matters. It matters because a multi-millionaire can say to himself, "I give away money to the poor, and I never shove the person in front of me in line"—if really rich people ever actually stand in lines—"so I'm a good guy."

And therein lies the danger. The I'm-a-good-guy standard doesn't work.

Sure there are rich people who use their money for good causes that do nothing to advance their own financial interests, but when people with money use their money to help themselves get more money, they aren't evil—they're just acting rationally. And they're also acting rationally—in the narrowest sense of that word—when they use their money to buy favors from the government. But when they buy favors from the government, they are taking something that belongs to the rest of us. And when enough rich people (or rich corporations) buy enough favors, the whole economic and political system starts to tilt their way. And if the American people allow this to go on long enough, there will come a point when the rich and powerful will be using so much of their money to buy so much influence over our government that they will unwind the whole premise of democracy. Instead of one person, one vote giving each of us an equal say in how this country is run, we will become an oligarchy, a nation in which the powerful few make sure that the government runs to serve their interests.

Revolving doors and campaign contributions, lobbying and hired-gun experts—in these pages, I haven't written a comprehensive exposé, and I haven't listed every example I can think of. In fact, I've barely waved a small flashlight around in a great dark space. But I've done my best to make a case that the rich and powerful have a well-stocked armory for seizing control of our democracy—and that they are already using it very effectively.

Enter the billionaire president.

Donald Trump describes himself as a guy who knows how to work all the angles. He says he knows how to make the government work. In fact, he says he's done it many times.

He's telling the truth. In 2013, Trump made a $25,000 contribution to the reelection campaign of the Florida attorney general. Two days later, despite local complaints, that same attorney general declined to join an investigation of fraud at Trump University. And there's more: Trump didn't even reach into his own pocket or his Trump U pocket or any of his other corporate business pockets to make that $25,000 "contribution" to the attorney general. Nope. He illegally took the money out of his charitable foundation and had it sent along to her.

Work all the angles? C'mon, give the man full credit. He is the master of making everything work better for the guy who has lots of money to spread around. He is the king of figuring out how to make a profit by cheating people, the czar of getting special deals from government officials, and the prince of forcing someone else to pay for his mistakes. And now he is running the federal government.

Trump has built a team of like-minded pals who reflect this same approach, people who know how to work all the angles—or, at least, how to work those angles for themselves. A Treasury secretary from Wall Street who raked in a fortune helping Goldman Sachs build the weapons to blow up the economy, and then pocketed another fortune foreclosing (sometimes illegally) on homeowners who bore the brunt of the crash. A commerce secretary from Wall Street whose legendary history of squeezing his companies for every dollar caught up to him when a dozen coal miners were killed in an explosion at one of his chronically unsafe mines. A labor secretary who as a fast-food CEO made big bucks squeezing minimum-wage workers and paying people for far fewer hours than they actually worked. A secretary of education who contributed millions to privatize public education and who crudely explained that when she and her family contributed money, "We expect a return on our investment." A secretary of state from the sovereign state of Big Oil who improved his corporation's profits (and pumped up his own bonuses) by cozying up to Vladimir Putin.

Trump and his team collectively control billions of dollars of wealth. Now that they are running the government, they have the potential—either while in office or once they pass through the revolving door—to turn those billions into tens of billions, hundreds of billions, or even more.

As for Trump himself, why should he wait to cash in? He has already said that "the president can't have a conflict of interest," so he sees no need to make a distinction between the work he does as a public servant and the work he does to put more money in his pocket. So, for example, after he was elected he again refused to release his taxes. That means the American people will never find out the truth about his financial interests and never know whether he is deep in hock in Russia or making big bucks in the Middle East—things that could profoundly influence the decisions he will make as President. He also refused to give up ownership of his businesses. He said his sons would run them—wink, wink, nod, nod—while Dad was in the White House. No surprise that ethics experts condemned this approach. Make America great again? Absolutely, because what's good for Trump Inc. is good for the USA!

The levers of government—the ability to enforce laws, to make rules, to award contracts, to rattle cages and invade countries and help friends—all those levers are now in the hands of a man who has spent his entire life making the government work for exactly one person: himself. The influence of money on the government—on *our* government, the one *we* own—is about to be tested to the breaking point.

The Moment of Upheaval

October 24, 2016, was one of those glorious days that make New England famous. The college campus in Manchester, New Hampshire, looked postcard-perfect—old brick buildings set on gently sloping hills. The sky was blue, the trees were splashed with reds and golds, and it was just cool enough that I'd pulled on a cheery red jacket.

Standing inside Geisel Library at Saint Anselm College, I was waiting for Secretary Clinton to arrive. Only a handful of people had been allowed into the building: the university president, the Democratic candidate to be the next governor, the two women running for congressional seats, the state Democratic Party chair, and a few of the volunteers who had been working their rear ends off for over a year.

Maggie Hassan—the state's governor, who had taken on the very tough task of challenging the Republican incumbent senator—and I were in a large side room that was furnished like a living room. She was talking on the phone, clearly caught up in some political tussle. I thought about how hard it must be to carry on with all her duties as governor *and* run for the Senate.

I sat down, but a moment later I was up again, pacing around the room. I looked out the window. I could see the crowd gathering in front of an outdoor stage only a short walk away. It looked a little like a football crowd—full of high spirits and optimism and ready to cheer the team on. That was great, but would this crowd and others like it be enough to carry the state for both Hillary and Maggie? How about the other states where the races were very close?

I was operating on nervous energy. Over the past few months, I had lost something like eight pounds—about what I'd lost when I ran for the Senate in 2012. I'd traveled to state after state making the case for Clinton and our Senate candidates. And there were some really memorable events. Bernie had invited me to join him for a rally for Hillary in Denver. (There's no other way to say it: Bernie was amazing. Passionate. Smart. Totally committed. I was reminded why we had been friends for so many years.) I'd stood on basketball courts and back porches and pickup truck tailgates. I'd been hugged and sweated on and kissed and shaken and even lifted straight off the ground. I didn't sleep much, because hitting the campaign trail and staying on top of Senate hearings and votes felt like I was going 24/7. But that was just fine with me: if I could help Democratic candidates make it across the finish line with a big win, I would keep going until we ran through the tape. I knew how much this election meant—and I knew how close many of the races were.

Hillary arrived early. She looked good, calm and serene. With only fifteen days to go before Election Day, her lead in the polls seemed solid. The controversy about her private e-mail server when she was secretary of state seemed to have receded. She was openly pleased about how well she'd performed during the final debate, and her campaign staff had asked me to say something at the rally about Donald Trump calling her "such a nasty woman." I'd promised I would.

She posed for pictures in the library and chatted with the local candidates. Then she and I went to a small room to talk, just the two of us.

Policy, politics. More policy, more politics. She smiled and said the numbers looked good.

Oh Lord, I hoped so. I had dozens of ideas for things we could accomplish together, ways to build public support, ways to pressure Congress, ways to make a difference by working through the government's agencies even if Congress stayed gridlocked.

I had spent a lot of time thinking about those ideas and how we could move them forward. I knew some people on Hillary's team wanted to push in the same direction I did and others didn't, but that wasn't what kept me awake at night. I was anxious, right down to my bones. What if Donald Trump won? What if he became the country's president? I didn't worry because I knew something the pollsters didn't or had super into-the-future X-ray vision. No, I was worried because there was so much on the line.

For decades, the differences between Republicans and Democrats had been big, but not like *this*. The first three Republican presidents who had followed FDR—Eisenhower, Nixon, and Ford—had mostly taken the same basic approach to governing that Democrats like Truman, Kennedy, and Johnson did. In their view, government could be a force to build wide-spread prosperity, and it should regulate industry and advance opportunities for the future. For decades, each president had carried out policies started by a previous president, even when they'd belonged to different parties. Eisenhower, for instance, followed in the footsteps of FDR and Truman by expanding Social Security and supporting New Deal programs.

When Reagan ushered in trickle-down economics in the 1980s, some Democrats resisted, but many others helped push forward his tax cuts and deregulation. Bill Clinton, for example, presided over the repeal of Glass-Steagall, and Obama flirted with a "grand bargain" that would cut Social Security benefits, although in the end the two parties weren't able to strike a deal.

But this election was different. Trump's vision was like the conservative philosophy on steroids: trickle-down economics, a determination to roll back regulations and cut taxes, all of it extreme and all of it mixed with giant buckets of poisonous bigotry. He offered big corporations and billionaires a grab bag of things they asked for—to weaken the Environmental Protection Agency, gut key bank regulations, cut back on workplace safety inspections, repeal the Affordable Care Act, and institute even more big tax cuts for those at the top. And then he wrapped up everything that was relentlessly eating away at our country's middle class into a glittering package of lies that started and ended with a promise to work hard for the little guy.

Sure, Trump broke with some of his party's traditional views: he criticized existing and proposed trade deals, claimed that he wanted to tax Wall Street, and said he would break up the banks with a new version of Glass-Steagall. But there were no details and lots of inconsistencies. As best I could make out, this man wanted to take most of the ideas promoted by Reagan and all the trickle-down priests and make them HUGE.

After thirty-five years of trickle-down hooey, however, America's middle class was already on its knees, and opportunities for millions of people had already dried up. Trump could be the punch that knocked out everyone's lights and changed our country forever.

Once Donald Trump and his ultra-right-wing vice presidential pick became the Republican nominees, I was ready to fight—all in, no holding back. Hillary Clinton had the chance to level the playing field a little more, a chance to rebuild opportunity for more of our kids. Trump seemed determined to crush the last vestiges of hope.

As we headed outside to the rally, I kept thinking, We've got to win this. Please, please, please. Please give us the chance to do the work that needs to be done.

The sun was brilliant. Hillary, Maggie, and I all wore bright colors, dressed in anticipation of a lively rally. The leaves were dancing in the breeze, and their tiny shadows made everything look electric and alive. As we headed over to greet the crowd, we walked past old brick buildings where students crowded one another at the windows, cheering us on.

I fairly bounded up the steps to the temporary stage, waving and shouting. The stage faced a large open green filled with thousands of cheering people. I could see faces, and I recognized a number of people who had volunteered on my Senate campaign and were now here in New Hampshire to help. In some ways, a political rally—particularly in a place like this one—feels like a scene out of the nineteenth century.

But a bank of television cameras, klieg lights (yes, even in the bright sun there were enormous lights turned toward the stage), and sound amplifiers made it clear that this event was firmly grounded in the twenty-first century. Besides, in the nineteenth century, three women—one a candidate for president, one a candidate for the U.S. Senate, and one a senator from a nearby state just trying to help out—would not have

Shortly before the 2016 election, spirits ran high at this New Hampshire rally.

been on that stage. The world was changing, and as the three of us looked out at all the little girls and sisters and aunties and grandmas in the audience, we knew we had a glorious chance to celebrate our progress and cheer each other on.

When I introduced Hillary, I talked about her life's work and made the case for why she should be elected President. And then I tore into her opponent. I spoke about how he cheated college students at Trump University, how he called Latinos rapists and African Americans thugs, and how he vilified Muslims. The crowd got louder; so did I.

And on this bright and sunny day, speaking to thousands of women and girls—and their husbands, fathers, and friends—I did my best to take a stand for every one of them. I leaned into the microphone and here's what I said:

Donald Trump is incapable—physically incapable—of showing an ounce of respect to more than half of the human beings in this country.

He thinks because he has money, that he can call women fat pigs and bimbos.

He thinks because he is a celebrity, he can rate women's bodies from one to ten.

He thinks because he has a mouthful of Tic Tacs that he can force himself on any woman within groping distance.

I heard much hooting and hollering but didn't wait for it to die down. I just kept going:

Well, I've got news for you, Donald Trump: Women have had it with guys like you. And nasty women have really had it with guys like you.

Get this, Donald: Nasty women are tough. Nasty women are smart. And nasty women vote. And on November eighth, we nasty women are going to march our nasty feet to cast our nasty votes to get you out of our lives forever.

The response was like an explosion. Laughter, shouting, applause, whistles. It was a great show of toughness and solidarity. Lots of hands shot up into the air. We could own Trump's insult and then throw it right back at him. We had the power!

The three women on the stage and all the girls and women in the audience owned the day, and we had a chance right here, right now, to talk about America's future. I hit the same points I'd been talking about since long before I'd come to the Senate. I spoke about an America that had given chances to women like Hillary and me—she the granddaughter of a factory worker and me the daughter of a janitor. It was the America of opportunity.

We believe in that America. That is the America we fight for.

We believe, but we are worried—worried that those opportunities are slipping away. In fact, a lot of America is worried—worried and angry. Angry that far too often Washington works for those at the top and leaves everyone else behind.

I laid it out as best I could. This is about our values, I said, about the things we believe in, the reasons we get up every day and work as hard as we can. About debt-free college and expanded Social Security. About science and climate change. About our capacity to invest together to create something better. The biggest cheer came when I reached the end:

> We believe that millionaires and billionaires and giant corporations should not be able to buy our elections and our politicians. Corporations are not people. We will overturn *Citizens United* and bring democracy back to the people!

The speech seemed to connect with everyone listening. And on this beautiful fall day, the message felt absolutely right.

After Hillary spoke and received enormous cheers, we climbed off the stage and down into the crowd. There were lots of pictures and smiles and hugs. More selfies, more people shouting, "We're going to make history!"

Twenty-five minutes later, I was in our bright blue SUV, which we affectionately called the Blue Bomber, heading back across the state border to Lawrence, Massachusetts, to urge people to vote early. A big rally followed by a crowd surf is a little like a sprint—you give it all you've got until you cross the finish line. Although I was tucked up in the car, I was still breathing hard, still feeling the over-the-top enthusiasm of the New Hampshire crowd. And despite all the cheers, I was still anxious that I was failing to sound the alarm loudly enough.

Still worried deep in my bones.

NOT RUNNING

For me, 2016 started back in early 2013, when people began asking if I was planning to run for president.

Huh?

I had been in elected office for only a few weeks. Before that, I'd spent a year setting up a federal agency. The way I saw it, the question deserved a pretty simple answer: anyone who wanted to put themselves forward for president of the United States ought to have more experience than that.

Besides, I liked this new job in the Senate. I was busting my tail every day trying to find opportunities to make a difference—with student loans, funding for medical research, bank regulation, Social Security. I was working out ways to help people day by day in Massachusetts— veterans who were having trouble with their benefits or homeowners still getting the runaround from mortgage companies. I was learning the ropes and beginning to see some daylight here and there; slowly, I was starting to believe that I might have at least a little success. I was working hard to crack down on for-profit colleges that were cheating people. I was pushing for more accountability when giant banks broke the law. I was doing everything I could to protect retirement savings. Okay, I knew these things might sound a little dorky and weren't the stuff of sexy head-lines. But I didn't care: fighting to make progress on these issues could make a difference for people like Gina or Michael or Kai.

That felt like my job, and when I could make even a bit of differ-ence, it was a job I deeply loved. I was happy to have the chance to press Republicans for more money for medical research and better Medicare reimbursement rules to protect rural hospitals. I was eager to work on lowering student loan interest rates and boosting investments in basic infrastructure. I was glad to fight the good fight because I believe in these public investments. And I was grateful that Bay Staters had picked me to go fight for them.

Even so, there had been plenty of speculation in the media that I would run for president. Polls tested me against this person and that. Anonymous people who claimed to "know her thinking" speculated about my future. (Um, seriously?) I received invitations to dinners, fes-tivals, parades, picnics—even a pie eating contest—in other states. They all sounded like fun, but I worried they might be about more than pie.

By January 2015, multiple "draft Warren" efforts had sprung up. They were supported by really good people, and I knew their intentions were the best, but my heart wasn't in it. I wanted to learn my Senate job. I liked this work—from finding money for fire trucks to helping shut down for-profit college scams. In fact, I really, really liked it, and I still do.

Late one night, I asked Bruce if he thought I should run for president. We were upstairs in our house in Cambridge, sitting on the small couch in our bedroom. We'd been watching television, and after he switched it off, we sat for a few minutes in the near dark, a little too tired and a little too comfortable to get up immediately. The room was cool, almost cold. I was covered in a big red fuzzy blanket, leaning up against him.

When I broke the quiet with my question, he shifted and put his arm around me. I knew what he would say first, and he said it: "I want you to do whatever you want to do. I'll be there."

I said, yeah, I know you will. But that's not what I want to know. I want to know if you think I should do it.

Bruce waited a long time. He took a deep breath and held me tighter. "I don't know if you should run. I know there are a lot of things you care deeply about, and I know sometimes you have to fight. That's just who you are. But a race like this one looks pretty terrible. The Senate thing was bad enough, and running for president would be worse—a lot worse."

It's one of those funny things about being in love with someone: their hurt is worse than your own. I had pretty much forgotten about the painful parts of the 2012 Senate race. It was sort of like having a baby: awful at the time, but once it was over and you get to hold the new baby, the memory was packed off to some distant place in the brain. Bruce, however, still remembered the parts that had been difficult for me.

And I hadn't forgotten that the race had been painful for Bruce, too. It was hard for him to see me ridiculed and called names, hard to see our children dragged into political attacks, hard to see both his sister and my brothers worry.

I asked him: Would you be okay if I ran?

Bruce said yes, and I smiled in the dark. I didn't believe him, but it was the right answer.

And I knew what the right answer was for me, too. Talking with Bruce and asking the question out loud had settled it. I wanted to stay buckled down and keep doing my job—my Senate job—as completely and as effectively as I could.

So that's what I did.

THE DANGER

Every Tuesday morning, the Democratic leadership of the Senate meets at nine o'clock. We sit in the same fancy room where lunch will be laid out later in the day, but with only a few senators present, the room always feels hollow. This meeting gives us a chance to talk about upcoming bills, new strategies, and whatever issues happen to be urgent that week. But throughout the election cycle, these sessions always started—and ended—with gossip about the presidential campaign.

During the primary season, I had been a bit on the outside of these conversations; it was no secret that all the rest of the Senate leadership had come down on Hillary's side, but I had remained neutral. In November 2015, when all the Democratic women of the Senate came together for a public event to endorse Clinton over Sanders, I didn't join them. And over the next several months, as one Democrat after another signed on with her campaign, I stayed out. People put some pressure on me— actually, a lot of pressure—to take sides. But I kept to my path and just kept doing my job.

Throughout the primaries, Hillary and Bernie debated important issues—bank regulation, health care, college affordability. It was a thoughtful debate, one that added energy to our party and forced tough questions out into the open about what Democrats wanted to accomplish with four more years of power. It was also a debate between two smart, capable people, each far better than anyone the Republicans were putting forward. I resisted making an endorsement because I didn't want to undermine either of our candidates or to short-circuit any part of that debate.

The Republican primary season, meanwhile, bordered on the surreal. The field of candidates was huge. Whenever I watched the debates, I half-expected to see someone get voted off the island. The conversations were loaded with weird pledges and off-the-wall claims: who would lower taxes the most, who was most like Reagan, who'd be the best buddy in a duck blind. The not-very-subtle appeals to bigotry were layered on, day after day. And day after day, no matter what else happened, no matter the national celebration or the local catastrophe, nearly every news outlet featured one or more stories about Donald Trump.

Trump's unlikely campaign caught fire in one state after another. The coverage of his antics multiplied. The public fights, bawdy jokes, and giant rallies all received unending attention. Even the Republican leadership was openly hostile to Trump, and the press was deeply critical, although reporters sure as heck kept giving him plenty of free media. Watching this spectacle, a lot of Democrats smirked: a three-times-married man who didn't seem to know squat and couldn't hold on to a policy position from one day to the next was delusional enough to believe he was going to be the next president of the United States.

During our leadership breakfasts that winter and spring, senators would wonder aloud whether we Democrats would be lucky enough to have what one called "that unhinged nitwit" as our opponent. We talked about all the Republicans who were struggling to figure out what to say about him, many of them stumbling and stepping on their own tongues. Our side mostly tried not to laugh out loud.

But it wasn't just Democrats. It was all kinds of people. Serious people. Informed people. Smart people. Many of them laughed Trump off: the guy was a joke!

By early 2016, however, there were plenty of reasons to be alarmed. Trump's one-two punch of bigotry and economic lies was catching on. He spoke about people's very real worries and then made wild promises. He called out the anger that people like Gina felt, and he lied about the solutions to their problems. He was Ronald Reagan without the charm. Reagan understood that the middle class wanted more, so he made up a voodoo cover story for his giveaways to the rich. Trump didn't even bother with that—he just waved his hands and said, "I'll make it great!" And then he blamed Mexicans and Muslims and Obama for everything in our country that was wrong.

And he kept right on winning.

Once it was clear that he would be the Republican nominee, I started going after him on Twitter. (Good grief, that sounds lame—going after a race-baiting monster in 140 characters on social media.)

His Republican opponents had made a few attempts to take him down, but they got smashed like little bugs. After calling the early leader in the Republican race "Low-Energy Jeb" and nicknaming one of the island's last survivors "Little Marco," Trump had proved that he could be wickedly effective at destroying anyone who dared to cross him.

So I fired up my Twitter account and crossed him:

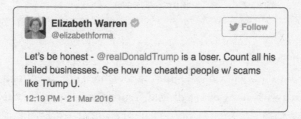

We were off and running. I tweeted about how he cheated hard-working people who had built his hotels and golf courses. I mentioned his bullying, his attacks on women, his racism, his obvious narcissism. And in that first tweetstorm, I did my best to sound the alarm: this guy is dangerous, and he could end up as president of the United States.

I stayed after him, always on the same themes: he is a racist bully and he can't be trusted on economic or foreign policy issues.

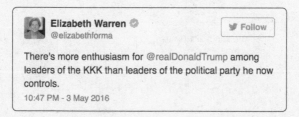

Trump noticed.

One day I was working a Lightning McQueen puzzle with my grandson, Atticus, when my phone dinged. Trump had responded. He'd come up with a name for me—"Goofy." Later he added "Pocahontas." Really? He thought he could bully me into silence by attacking what our family had told my brothers and me about our Native American ancestry? Nice try, but no. He could bluster, but he had nothing—no responses on Trump U, his bankruptcies, Putin, or the KKK.

At this point, a more sensible person might have decided to move out of the line of fire. I thought it was time to double down.

I tried it all—Facebook posts, a Stephen Colbert interview, a *Boston Globe* op-ed, videos. When Trump tried to shame a former Miss Universe, I jumped in with a more substantive point about what he really cares about and what that says about the kind of president he would be:

Elizabeth Warren ✓
@elizabethforma

Follow

Is this what keeps you up at night, @realDonaldTrump? Thinking of new & interesting ways to call women fat or ugly or sluts?

5:04 PM - 30 Sep 2016

Elizabeth Warren ✓
@elizabethforma

Follow

You never tweet at 3am with ways to help students getting crushed by debt or seniors struggling on Social Security, @realDonaldTrump.

5:05 PM - 30 Sep 2016

Elizabeth Warren ✓
@elizabethforma

Follow

You never tweet at 3am with ways to create new jobs for workers or hold Wall Street accountable, @realDonaldTrump.

5:07 PM - 30 Sep 2016

Elizabeth Warren ✓
@elizabethforma

Follow

Nope, @realDonaldTrump: the only things that keep your mind racing at night are your next racist, sexist tweets & disgusting lies.

5:09 PM - 30 Sep 2016

Elizabeth Warren ✓
@elizabethforma

Follow

A thin-skinned bully who thinks humiliating women at 3am qualifies him to be President does not understand America & is not fit to lead.

5:10 PM - 30 Sep 2016

Trump slammed back at me repeatedly, hitting me over and over with his lame nicknames. But he couldn't seem to come up with much more than that. (Sad!)

The tweetstorms began attracting media attention. Some people loved them; others winced. A friend forwarded an e-mail from a friend of hers: "What is our senator doing rolling around in the mud with Donald Trump?"

No kidding. I knew just how she felt. But Trump could be closing in on the presidency, and those tweetstorms and Facebook posts caused millions of people to tune in—at one point, about forty-six million people were following these exchanges. I figured that if tweeting and posting and poking and prodding gave me a chance to reach millions of people, then that's what I should do. Some of those people might not have heard that Donald Trump cheated his workers or defrauded students. Some of them might decide that Donald Trump was not going to fight for them.

Maybe, just maybe, I could help change the perception of Trump as invincible in any war of words. Trump had figured out early on that every over-the-top tweet became a news story. Now there was a fresh story line: someone had found a way to get under Donald Trump's skin and fight back.

And if the cost of taking a shot at the hot-air balloon known as @realDonaldTrump was that I had to take a few hits of my own, then so be it. I planned to keep right on firing.

BLAME THEM

Once she had the votes for the Democratic nomination, Hillary asked if I would speak at the convention in July. I said sure, and I started writing my speech almost immediately. I wanted a chance to talk about how working people were getting slammed, but this time I wanted to tie that message to the dark underside of racism in the Trump campaign.

One of my friends in the Senate told me about stopping to eat at a diner just as the election season hit its peak. Once the plates had been cleared and more coffee had been poured, the waitress told my friend that someone had recognized him, knew he was a Democratic senator, and wanted to come over to talk politics for a few minutes. Would that be okay?

Sure, said the senator.

A man walked up, shook hands, and introduced himself. He smiled, then explained that he was a Trump supporter. The two of them talked a bit, and then the man cut to the heart of the matter: he was supporting Trump because if Hillary wins, "I'd have to go to one of those tanning salons and tell them to spray me as dark as they could. Those are the only people that can get ahead today."

There it was: casual racism, right out in the open. The man didn't yell or spit, but his words were loaded with resentment and hatefulness. They were offered up not over beers with close buddies but as part of an oh-so-polite conversation with a United States senator. And every word was based on the bedrock assurance that the reason this man couldn't get ahead was because *they* were getting all the good opportunities.

Racism isn't new in America.

It isn't new—and no one needs a lecture from me about it. Most people have figured out right from wrong on this issue, and most have made their choices. I sure have.

America's political and economic history is littered with prejudice—prejudice against the Irish, blacks, Asians, Jews, Slovaks, Native Americans, Latinos, Germans, Puerto Ricans, women, gays, lesbians, transgender people. It's a long list. Pick a time, pick a place, pick a prejudice: it's an old, old story.

Over the generations, some prejudices have died out, but others have not. And there have always been politicians ready to exploit the hatred. In 1958, George Wallace ran for governor of Alabama as a moderate, speaking out against the KKK and endorsed by the NAACP. He lost.

Later he told an aide that he had been "out-n****red" by his opponent—and he didn't plan for that to happen again. When he was elected governor a few years later, he used his inaugural address to declare, "Segregation now, segregation tomorrow, segregation forever." His statement was a direct appeal to his most important voting bloc—his *white* voting bloc.

Richard Nixon followed up a few years later with a "southern strategy" that overtly played on racism to lock in Republican votes in the South. In time, Republicans softened their language and began using code words like "states' rights" and launching attacks on "the welfare state."

By 2005, the Republican Party had built so much of its electoral strategy on openly exploiting racism that the chair of the Republican National Committee embarked on an apology tour aimed at repairing relationships with black Americans. And after the drubbing Republicans received in 2012, party leaders undertook an autopsy that concluded that if they did not change their message to include immigrants, Latinos, African Americans, and the LGBTQ community, and if they didn't do a better job of including women, they were doomed.

The report was quite specific: "We must embrace and champion comprehensive immigration reform. If we do not, our Party's appeal will continue to shrink to its core constituencies only." And its warning was unambiguous: "We must be a party that is welcoming and inclusive for all voters."

But Donald Trump saw it differently. On the day back in March 2013 when the Republican report was released, he tweeted, "Does @RNC have a death wish?"

Pundits dismissed his remarks as the ranting of a celebrity billionaire. But by 2015, Trump was attracting attention in a crowded Republican primary by openly stirring bigotry of all kinds. He set himself apart by characterizing Mexican Americans as rapists and criminals, calling African Americans thugs, sweeping all Muslims together as terrorists, treating women with contempt, and so on. When he called me Pocahontas, it was definitely not intended as a sign of respect to the Native Americans he had insulted and attacked for years and who actively opposed him during his campaign.

Trump attracted followers by stoking economic anxiety, and he continued offering bigotry of all kinds. He turned the intensity of their support into an intimidating force at rallies, online, and even on public streets. Many of those who championed him laughed off his racism, claiming that Trump said aloud what everyone was thinking privately.

In February 2016, David Duke, the nationally known former grand wizard of the Ku Klux Klan, endorsed Trump. Before the campaign was over, Trump had been championed on the front page of the Klan's main newspaper.

I wanted to shout, *This is the KKK! White supremacy, lynchings, burning crosses—remember?* The KKK was endorsing their man, and Trump was giving a coy smile in return. I wanted to find the IN CASE OF EMERGENCY BREAK GLASS box, because I believed America was in real danger.

And here was the real heart-stopper: the "us versus them" narrative of the campaign was already so deeply established that the KKK's support caused barely a ripple in the country's swiftly moving political river.

Even members of Trump's own party thought he had crossed the line. A former head of the Republican Party, Michael Steele, said that Trump "captured that racist underbelly, that frustration, that angry underbelly of American life and gave voice to that."

John McCain said that Trump's behavior and "demeaning comments about women and his boasts about sexual assaults, make it impossible to continue to offer even conditional support for his candidacy."

Republican operative Karl Rove called Trump "a complete idiot" and "graceless and divisive." (Gosh, I thought, who would have guessed I would ever want to say, *Go, Karl!*) Even mild-mannered Mitt Romney called Trump "a con man, a fake." Wow.

And those were just the Republicans.

As the chorus of those denouncing Trump swelled, his core supporters grew even more feverish in his defense. This campaign was becoming truly scary.

In the past, the belief that some less powerful group in America was to blame for everything that had gone wrong had gained force at times exactly like this one, times when Americans were angry and worried about our future. Racial hatred, religious bigotry, attacks on immigrants or women or gays: stoking the fears of the "other" is the oldest trick in the book. Whatever worries you, the solution is to scapegoat that other group—which means you'll never demand the changes that would actually fix our problems.

That's the divide-and-conquer strategy I talked about at the Democratic National Convention:

> When white workers in Ohio are pitted against black workers in North Carolina or Latino workers in Florida—who really benefits?
>
> Who benefits? I'll tell you exactly who benefits:
>
> When we turn on each other, bankers can run our economy for Wall Street. When we spend our energy attacking immigrants, oil companies can fight off clean energy. When we argue over who got more crumbs of food stamps, giant corporations can ship the last good jobs overseas.
>
> When we turn on each other, rich guys can push through more tax breaks for themselves, and then we'll never have enough money to support our schools or rebuild our highways or invest in our kids' future.

Who really benefits? The same people who have rigged the system from the start. When Americans are divided, Wall Street, multinational corporations, and race-baiting con artists face a whole lot less opposition in Washington.

ACCOUNTABILITY, THE WELLS FARGO WAY

The presidential campaign rolled on, but in early fall the country learned about a scandal so big and so brazen that everyone seemed to stop for a minute and draw in a sharp breath. I know I did.

It was September 8, during the pause after the political conventions had concluded and before the presidential debates would start. But now Congress was back in session, and I was in D.C. again. The temperature that day was in the nineties, and in the Washington swamp, it felt like all the air had been replaced with something thicker and more primal. I was sitting at my desk and had just cranked up my air conditioner when I saw the news flash: the Consumer Financial Protection Bureau and other regulators had just announced that America's biggest bank, Wells Fargo, had agreed to pay $185 million in fines for cheating its customers. The investigation showed that bank employees had been opening fake accounts in their customers' names and charging fees on those accounts for years.

As I knew well, after the 2008 crash, the bank had settled big claims for illegal foreclosures. And now it had gotten caught once again juicing its profits by cheating its customers.

All I could think was: "These guys sure haven't changed."

The scam looked like a page out of *The Big Book of Frauds*. Wells Fargo employees hadn't been tacking on an extra fee here or there; they'd been opening *brand-new accounts* that no one had ever asked for. Wells Fargo credit card customers had ended up with multiple checking accounts (and checking account fees) they'd never even known they had. In order to produce higher revenues and profits, bank employees had faked documents, charged fees, and moved customers' money between accounts. This hadn't happened once or twice; it had happened thousands and thousands of times for years.

Oh boy, I thought. Heads are really gonna roll this time. Right? *Right?*

Well, yes, heads did roll, but not the heads of the guys in charge. Instead, Wells Fargo fired more than five thousand rank-and-file employees, mostly people making $12 an hour.

But they didn't fire a single senior executive. Not one.

Hold on, I thought, let me get this straight. The bank's view was that thousands of employees had spontaneously started cheating customers, goosing profits, and violating lots of laws along the way—and no one from management knew anything about it or had any responsibility whatsoever. None? Not even a little bit?

What makes the story even more difficult to believe is that the CEO actually knew a lot about those fake accounts.

One of Wells Fargo's big marketing points to investors and stock analysts was that it was a genius at "cross-selling." This meant that every Wells customer loved Wells soooooo much that they opened a checking account, a savings account, a credit card account, another savings account, and so on. Investors liked this story because it meant: (1) Wells must be doing a great job with their customers; and (2) the bank's future profitability was assured. Woo-hoo!

Every three months, just like clockwork, John Stumpf, the CEO of Wells Fargo, got on the phone with the Wall Street players and talked about the amazing number of new accounts they had opened and modestly proclaimed his bank's genius at cross-selling. And when he did this, the bank's stock price went up and up and up, right along with his own bonuses and stock options.

Wells Fargo was a Great American Success Story—only it was a lie.

This lying and swindling had been going on for *years*. And by this point, this slimy cheat-your-customer mentality, this disgusting profits-at-any-price approach, had been woven deep into the corporation's fabric.

After the 2008 crash and bailout, Wells Fargo recovered. By 2016 it was worth $250 billion. The bank wasn't just swimming in money. It was doing the backstroke, the sidestroke, and the crawl through oceans of money.

And evidently the whole idea of following the law—pretty basic stuff like don't forge your customer's name on documents and don't create fake accounts to boost your profits—was merely optional at America's largest bank. Everything was going great, right up until the CFPB and the federal bank regulators started investigating.

So what would happen next? By the time the consumer agency made its announcement, the management team at Wells had known for months that this day was coming. Wells executives had already spent nearly half a year negotiating with the regulators over exactly how much the bank would pay and what steps they would be required to take to reimburse customers. When the news finally broke, they had their PR teams in place and their press releases set to go.

The CEO, John Stumpf, might have assumed that this was a relatively small storm that would blow over in the space of a few days, or a few weeks at most. After all, the country was in the middle of a hard-fought presidential campaign that was sucking up huge amounts of attention, and bank scandals were no longer the stuff of screaming headlines. Stumpf was undoubtedly reassured to see that after the story broke, Wells Fargo stock took a drop, but not a stomach-churning one.

The bank's CEO also had a couple of other reasons not to feel too worried. First was history: the big banks had caused the crash of 2008, then gotten bailed out by taxpayers—no strings attached. So why shouldn't the kid-glove treatment continue? And Wells Fargo, which had been Too Big to Fail before the crash, was now even bigger. Hey, maybe this time around the kid gloves would be even softer.

Besides, Wells Fargo's chief executive was the corporation's ace in the hole. John Stumpf looked like he had been sent over straight from central casting. He had an appealing smile, silver hair, and expensively tailored suits. At the time the scandal broke, he also had a bandaged arm that invited questions about what terrible fate had befallen him. (His company said he hurt his hand playing with his grandchildren.) And now he was in prime battle-ready mode. Thoroughly coached and lightly powdered, he made himself available for interviews on all the news programs and business outlets.

Calm and unruffled when speaking to the media, Stumpf repeated the same talking points again and again. All the money had been refunded, those responsible for the fake accounts had been fired, and, most of all, he was very sorry that Wells had not lived up to its own high standards. His signature move was to look the interviewer directly in the eye and say in somber tones, "I am accountable."

Stumpf's performance was almost heartwarming. Almost.

And maybe the whole story would have quickly slipped into oblivion, except that the Senate Banking Committee scheduled a hearing about the scandal shortly after the story broke.

I hadn't been in the Senate during the financial crisis, but watching the Wells Fargo scam felt like a real tear-out-your-hair moment: the Wells CEO was part of the same group of guys who'd helped the same giant banks sink the economy in 2008 with their greed and recklessness. And now they were back at it, defrauding the American people *again*, this time with plain old lying and cheating. Same song, different dance. Worst of all, it looked like we were about to take another ride on the "Free Pass for CEOs" train. Wait, did I say free? I meant the "Reward the CEOs with Millions and Demand No Accountability" train.

That was the part that still stuck in my craw. In the lead-up to the 2008 crash, these guys had gambled with their investors' money, with their customers' trust, and with the taxpayers' guarantees. They gambled, and every time it came up roses, they stuffed their pockets with cash. Then, when it all turned ugly and investors lost millions and customers got cheated, the CEOs and top brass kept right on stuffing their pockets, smiling all the while. And now we were about to do the same thing again—let Stumpf keep his job, keep his bonus, keep his salary, and keep right on smiling.

So long as that was the case, nothing would ever really change. Every CEO would have a powerful incentive to do whatever it took to inflate their bank's share price, even if it meant cheating people.

I served on the Senate Banking Committee, and there were a ton of questions I wanted to ask Stumpf at our hearing. But senators are typically limited to five minutes each at such hearings—at least, that's the formal rule, so it would be important to jump right in and get to the main points quickly.

At the hearing, I started my questioning by repeating Stumpf's statements about accountability. I pressed him on what he had done to show that he really was taking responsibility. A little more than two minutes in I said:

> You haven't resigned. You haven't returned a single nickel of your personal earnings. You haven't fired a single senior executive. Instead, your definition of "accountable" is to push the blame to your low-level employees who don't have money for a fancy PR firm to defend themselves. That's gutless leadership.

I got in a few more whacks, and so did several other senators on the committee. Suddenly a story that had been going nowhere went viral. Before it was all over, the cross-examination of the Wells Fargo CEO got more than sixty million views online, and Wells Fargo's "gutless leadership" was discussed in countless news stories. Even some conservative outlets picked up on the confrontation. The headlines all declared more or less the same thing: "SHOCK: Elizabeth Warren Said Something We Can All Agree On."

As it turns out, that hearing mattered—at least a little. Stumpf ended up resigning. He gave up his bonus. And there were calls for the regu-

Wells Fargo CEO John Stumpf testifying
before Congress, explaining that he took responsibility
but would keep his job and his bonus

latory agencies and the Department of Justice to launch investigations into what he knew and when he knew it.

The hearing also mattered at least a little for his bank. The Labor Department started an investigation of how Wells Fargo treated its employees, particularly the ones who had gotten fired for doing precisely what the company had pushed them to do. FINRA, the private organization that regulates brokers, also launched an investigation. So did the Department of Justice, the SEC, and multiple states' attorneys general. It was a start.

The lesson I took from all of this? Government matters.

On days in the Senate when I feel like I'm running into a brick wall over and over and my head hurts from getting smashed so many times,

I sometimes sit at my desk, take a deep breath, and ask myself, "Girl, does it make any difference at all that you are here?"

On days like the one when I asked the CEO of Wells Fargo some hard questions, the answer is clear: Yes, it makes a difference.

TURN THE BANKS LOOSE AGAIN

During the Wells Fargo scandal, plenty of Republicans lined up to take their shots at the bank. They were shocked to discover a bank cheating its customers, and they would have none of it! Yeah, right.

At the very same time that they were fulminating for the cameras, the Republicans were also drawing up plans to roll back financial regulations and take the legs out from under the Consumer Financial Protection Bureau. And Donald Trump, now in the home stretch of his campaign, picked up the same playbook as the Wall Street Republicans and called for an end to these terrible, terrible financial regulations.

Was this really happening? Back in 2008, the bank regulators had been asleep at the wheel (or, worse, greasing the skids for the banks so they could get everything they wanted). But in 2016, the CFPB was the cop on the beat. They were investigating, charging fines, holding hearings. The baby agency I had helped start in 2010 wasn't a baby anymore. The consumer agency had led the way alongside the big daddy bank regulator, the Office of the Comptroller of the Currency, to bring charges and major fines against Wells Fargo.

In other words, the regulators were doing their jobs. Not perfectly, not easily, but they were doing their jobs. And now, with Wells Fargo caught in the public spotlight with its burglary tools in one hand and the stolen goods in the other, the Republicans were trying to fire the cops. Months earlier, Jeb Hensarling, the chairman of the powerful House Financial Services Committee, had started calling for the CFPB to be gutted, and when the Wells scandal broke, he never missed a beat: he criticized the CFPB and refused to let its director, Rich Cordray, testify at his committee's hearing about the scam. The message was clear: the bad guys are the government regulators, not the giant banks.

What makes this story especially discouraging is that catching these crooks is very hard work. It doesn't happen every day, and it certainly doesn't happen by magic. Banks and corporations have a lot more money to spend, and they can pay people more, give them nicer offices, and always have state-of-the-art technology. When these giant corporations do something dishonest, they cover their tracks, and they have gotten really, really good at that. They can hire armies of lawyers and accountants to help them keep their books complex and almost impossible to penetrate. True, the Wells Fargo scheme was a pretty simple structure, but executing it was a massive undertaking.

When the Republicans argue that we should fire the cops, it's classic trickle-down ideology, but it's also the loudest, clearest statement possible that they believe that government should work for the giant banks, not for the people the giant banks may be trying to cheat. And there's more. Although regulation is important, so is basic accountability, and the Republicans want no accountability for the CEOs or any other executives when the corporations they lead break the law.

Here's just one example: By 2016, Congress had been working for years on a bipartisan bill to reform criminal justice laws. The bill wouldn't fix everything wrong with these laws, but it would do some good things, such as give judges just a little more discretion to reduce sentences for minor drug offenses. The work on the bill was nearly complete when the Republicans slipped in an amendment that would have made it extremely difficult for any corporate executive ever to be charged with a crime committed by his company. That was the deal: in exchange for helping some of those locked up for years for nonviolent drug offenses, Republicans insisted on a provision granting broad immunity for corporate executives. The Democrats balked and said no, which ultimately caused the whole bill to fall apart.

Really? The problem with accountability for executives who cheat their customers is that there's *too much of it*? Some days I think I work in the craziest place on earth.

Personal accountability for bank CEOs isn't about revenge, although I suspect some of the people who lost their homes because of lies or phony documents would like to inflict just a little pain on the executives who were responsible. No, the reason to demand some accountability is to make sure it won't happen again. If the guys in charge make more money for themselves and their companies when they cheat, then some of them will cheat. If they never have to pay a personal penalty and all the fines get paid by the investors or written off as tax breaks, then more of them will cheat. And if everyone else cheats and gets away with it, then more and more and more of them will cheat. Bankers—just like everyone else—follow incentives, and we need some rules and some cops on the beat to enforce those rules.

And make no mistake: this isn't just about giant banks. It's about every corporation whose leaders think they can skirt the rules and every CEO who thinks he can skate free while someone else takes the hit. It's not just about fairness, either, because cheating is a cancer on any economy. Sometimes it can crash an entire economic system, which is what happened in 2008. And sometimes it just keeps draining away the strength and vitality of the millions of families who are trying to make a living and build some economic security. If we allow cheating to continue, then a rigged system will stay rigged.

Before our Wells Fargo hearing, "accountability" at the bank meant firing more than five thousand hourly workers who were trying to meet the quotas set by their managers. After the hearing—after the CEO of Wells resigned and gave up his bonus—we got another toehold on accountability. The next CEO might not think about how Jamie Dimon managed to get his company, JPMorgan Chase, to foot the bill for billions of dollars of fines while he took home a multimillion-dollar bonus. Instead, that CEO might remember John Stumpf, who lost his job and became a YouTube sensation as a gutless leader.

After the fallout from our Wells Fargo hearing, I figured we were in a good place to fight back against firing the cops. Not bad, I thought. Score one for the forces of light and truth.

But that was September. In October I still felt pretty good, especially on that beautiful afternoon when Hillary Clinton, Maggie Hassan, and I stirred up a big crowd on a college campus in New Hampshire. The worry I felt that day had never left me, but I was cautiously optimistic that come November we would elect a new president, one who would fight hard for fairness and accountability and America's working families.

And then Donald Trump won the race for the White House.

THE DAY AFTER

On the morning after the election, I woke up early. Well, I guess I woke up—I'm not really sure I had slept much. It had been a miserable night.

I blinked and rubbed my eyes as I checked my e-mail. Lots of traffic, and also a note from one of my staffers. The *New York Times* had called. Over the past couple of days, I'd written an op-ed for the paper, and its editors were still holding a spot for it in Thursday's edition. Now, however, they thought the draft I had sent them yesterday might need a few revisions.

Revisions? As terrible as I felt, I laughed out loud. The draft I'd written worked off the assumption that Hillary Clinton had won. It was a summary of what I thought the election was about: a rejection of bigotry and the end of Reagan-style fire-the-cops and cut-taxes-for-the-rich policies. I also pushed hard on President-elect Clinton, urging her to make our government work for the American people—not just for those at the top, but for everyone.

Revisions? Yeah, this draft needed some revisions. I thought maybe I would just make it a two-word op-ed: Oh s**t.

Obviously, not enough voters had believed that Clinton was the candidate most committed to fighting for their families. Millions more people voted for her than for Trump, but not enough to swing the Electoral College. Where it mattered in the vote tally, where America had been hit extra hard by lost jobs and declining opportunities, our side hadn't closed the deal.

Shame on us.

While I was making breakfast, I began to think about some of the people I'd met in the past few months. And it was like I opened a gate. Memories crowded in faster and faster. Faces flashed in my brain. Students who were dealing with staggering loads of debt. Laid-off workers. The mother of two black teenagers who worried about her kids' safety as they walked home from school. A family man who managed a gas station, working six days a week, twelve-hour shifts, no overtime—and still he could barely keep his family out of poverty. A woman from South America who'd been a nurse in her home country but now cleaned office buildings for cash because she had no immigration papers. Teachers who bought classroom supplies out of their own pockets because their schools were out of money. Nurses who worked off the clock because a disability payment didn't cover enough care. I held on to the kitchen counter.

And then one face locked in: an old guy in New Hampshire. It had been the last weekend before Election Day. No Hillary Clinton, no candidates for the U.S. Senate. It was gray and raw outside, spitting rain. My job was to rally the volunteers, to get them out knocking on doors and making phone calls. I did my best.

I saw him near the end, after the speeches and cheers were over, when most people had picked up their clipboards and were breaking up into groups to hit the streets. He was thin to the point of gaunt. His hands were gnarled, and he was missing most of his teeth. But his grip on my arm was strong. He leaned toward my ear and said in a low voice, "It's really hard to get by on $1,122 dollars in Social Security. Really hard."

The weather was dreary, but the turnout was good for a rally in New Hampshire on the last weekend before Election Day.

He paused, never loosening his grip.

"I'm counting on you."

The day after the election, I tried to tell this story to a friend, but I never made it to the end. I couldn't finish. And on the morning after the election, holding on to my kitchen counter, I couldn't stop thinking about how that old guy must be feeling right now.

I had failed him. We had all failed him.

READY TO FIGHT

The next day, I was scheduled to give a speech to the leaders of the many unions that make up the AFL-CIO. Okay, that speech was now in the trash, too. The world had shifted on its axis, but I still planned to show up.

The meeting was being held at the national headquarters of the AFL-CIO—the house that labor built. The organization's building is sleek and modern, with clean edges, high ceilings, and lots of light. The two giant murals on the ground floor celebrate labor in grand terms. In the north lobby, I passed a mosaic with bits of colored marble and gold tiles above the phrase LABOR OMNIA VINCIT. No, I didn't remember enough high school Latin to translate, but after my previous visit, I had looked it up: "Hard work conquers all." Oh Lord, I prayed, please let that be right.

I paused to think about this building. When FDR was straining to pull the economy out of the Great Depression, the American Federation of Labor and the Congress of Industrial Organizations were rival organizations made up of many individual unions. The combined union and this building with its grand murals lay decades into the future. As FDR was sworn in, many predicted that the economic collapse would be the end of unions. But unions regained their footing, increased their memberships, and boosted wages for all working people. Unions had helped build America's middle class, but now they were under attack on multiple fronts, and union membership was declining.

As I walked into the room, I heard raised voices. Union leaders from around the country were seated around a huge conference table, and no one there was happy. Some of the unions had started the campaign season as Bernie supporters and some had been with Hillary from the beginning, but the leadership of all the unions represented in the room had gone with Hillary over Trump. Their members had not been quite so solid.

I wasn't there to talk about how much this hurt. Not with this crowd: they already knew. Many of them—along with thousands of their members—had given up nights and weekends, lived on coffee and pizza, and made speeches and knocked on doors in the rain and wind and snow to try to help Hillary Clinton across the finish line. Every one of them knew what this loss would mean. With the Supreme Court in the balance and Republicans in control of both Congress and the White House, long-established rights to organize and bargain for better working conditions were now on the chopping block. Unions, already weakened, would be hit harder. People in the room were whispering about just how bad it could be.

I was in the House of Labor, and I was thinking about all workers, union and non-union. I was going over the numbers in my head, all of which showed that when union membership goes up, all workers do better, whereas when membership drops, they all do worse. I was thinking about how unions expand benefits for all workers, how unions show up in Washington and in state capitols to fight for the bread-and-butter issues that make a difference for all working families.

For decades, Republicans had been fighting unions on virtually every issue that touched working people—the minimum wage, paid family leave, fair scheduling laws, access to affordable health care, Medicaid, Medicare, and on and on. Republicans had also assaulted unions head-on by trying to shut down the National Labor Relations Board, which deals with companies that violate labor laws, and by attacking the Department of Labor's efforts to protect unions.

Fearful of what a Republican president might do, unions had spent months putting it on the line for Hillary Clinton, and now they had lost. And in the months and years ahead, working people everywhere—Trump voters and Clinton voters alike—would pay a terrible price.

I looked around this room. I thought about people who had gotten their starts down in coal mines or welding iron. Women who had worked double shifts, then gone knocking on doors to help organize workers. Teachers and firefighters and electricians. Nurses, bricklayers, and pilots.

I saw people who had invested in training facilities so the next generation of laborers would have a chance at good jobs, too. And I saw people who had borrowed money to support union families during hard times because brothers and sisters help each other out.

I thought about how much America needs the men and women in these unions, about how much we need them to be on the front lines for workers everywhere. I thought about how that would be especially true now, when the party that had invented trickle-down economics and had used it to boost those at the top while they stepped on everyone else would be running the show.

When I stood up to speak to the union leaders that afternoon, I said:

As the loyal opposition, we will fight harder, we will fight longer, and we will fight more passionately than ever for the rights of every human being in this country to be treated with respect and dignity. We will fight for economic opportunity, not just for some of our children, but for all of our children. We do not control the tools of government, but make no mistake, we know what we stand for. The sun will keep rising, and we will keep fighting—each day, every day, we will fight for the people of this country.

I said it that day and I'll say it again: Whether we do or don't belong to a union, this fight touches all of us. And all of us need to be in this fight.

TEAM TRUMP

In those first days after the election, some people took to the streets chanting, "Not my President." Others said that maybe Trump didn't really mean it when he used all those ugly racial slurs. Besides, he had promised to "drain the swamp" and get rid of all the lobbyists and influence peddlers and Make America Great Again. Give the guy a chance, okay?

Donald Trump had the chance, and he bet on bigotry. Five days after the election, he announced his chief strategist—and the choice was a doozy. Before joining Team Trump, Steve Bannon had been the head of Breitbart News, a far-right website that, during Bannon's tenure, celebrated white supremacists and ran headlines asking questions like "Would

You Rather Your Child Had Feminism or Cancer?" Bannon was shocking enough, but a few days later Trump doubled down on bigotry by nominating Jeff Sessions to be the attorney general of the United States, despite a string of allegations of racism, Sessions's record of consistently opposing voting rights, and his long, rambling rants about immigrants.

As two of the earliest hires in the new administration, these men sent an unmistakable signal. And people responded. Some of Trump's fringe supporters scrawled hateful graffiti in public spaces. There were swastikas, threats, and ugly remarks. Everywhere I went, in airports and fast-food places and on the street, people came up to me and said the message had been received loud and clear. Blacks, women, Latinos, Muslims—pretty much anyone who looked like they'd be unwelcome at a Trump rally—felt a lot less welcome in Trump's America.

So much for the claim that Trump didn't really mean it when he stirred up hatred and bigotry.

Then Trump started making his moves on the economic side. First he brought in a crowd of lobbyists to help him run the transition; then he got down to serious business and started making cabinet appointments. One after another, they were all members of the same old gang: corporate insiders and trickle-down politicians.

For Treasury secretary, Trump nominated Steven Mnuchin, the Goldman Sachs executive who made a fortune after the financial crash by buying a bank and turning it into a foreclosure machine, aggressively— and sometimes illegally—seizing people's homes. Next came Gary Cohn, the president of Goldman Sachs, who was appointed to head up the National Economic Council. His claim to fame was his strong support for the trade deal Trump opposed.

But adherence to the basic philosophy of trickle-down economics wasn't limited to the economic team. Other corporate insiders included Rex Tillerson, the CEO of ExxonMobil, who was the pick for secretary of state. He was famous for his chummy ties to Russian leader Vladimir Putin, as well as for his willingness to put Exxon's profits ahead of America's foreign policy interests. Under Tillerson's leadership, ExxonMobil funneled money to climate deniers and groups that fought environmental regulations. His consistently aggressive stand against the Environmental Protection Agency suggests that he believes that instead of putting a cop on the beat to protect the public from polluters, we should just trust Exxon.

As for the EPA itself, Trump's pick for the head of that agency was truly breathtaking: he chose a climate denier, Scott Pruitt. When he was the Oklahoma attorney general, Pruitt literally shut down his own environmental enforcement unit. He seemed to believe that no one in Oklahoma would violate any environmental regulations, so why not just take the cops off the beat? When he got involved in environmental lawsuits as state attorney general, he almost always picked the side of the polluters rather than the people. Just one example: when brooks and streams in northeastern Oklahoma were overrun with chicken manure from big commercial poultry operations and the EPA was moving in to force the companies to clean up the mess, Pruitt jumped into the lawsuit on the side of the poultry industry. Yay—more chicken poop in the water!

Trump's choice for the head of the Department of Education took a similar approach to regulatory oversight—with the added bonus that she used her multibillion-dollar fortune to support efforts to undermine public schools in her home state of Michigan. Betsy DeVos has long supported initiatives that allow for-profit schools to soak up tax dollars while fighting off bipartisan efforts to raise standards for public schools. She and her family donated a small chunk of their fortune, $1.47 million, to an organization that seeks to cripple the Detroit Public Schools. Neither billionaire DeVos nor her children ever attended a public school, but that did not shake her confidence that her notions of privatizing public education would work just fine for everyone else's families.

Then there was Tom Price, whom Trump picked to head the Department of Health and Human Services, the agency that oversees Medicare, Medicaid, and the national health-care plan. As a congressman, Price again and again proposed privatizing Medicare and Medicaid and repealing the Affordable Care Act outright. And if that's not enough to make you wonder about his priorities, during his time as a congressman he was actively buying and selling stocks in companies in the very industries he was overseeing. The ethics probes have only just begun.

And just one more: Trump's choice for the secretary of labor, Andrew Puzder. This is the person who is supposed to stand up for workers and unions, but Puzder doesn't have much background protecting workers. No, Puzder made his fortune squeezing minimum-wage fast-food workers at Hardees and Carl's Jr. restaurants, and he opposes overtime pay and any increase in the minimum wage. His first memo after he took over his company was a jocular little note saying that no one should be put at the front counter unless they "have their teeth." Ha, ha: the guy obviously has a great sense of humor. After he was nominated, some of his current and former employees came to Washington to describe what it was like to work for him. Laura McDonald told me that for years she had worked a steady fifty to sixty hours a week at Carl's Jr., while getting paid for only forty hours. She described how the company had once been good to work for but became a nightmare once Puzder took over. Roberto Ramirez explained that when his manager stole his paycheck and he complained, the company higher-ups said it wasn't their problem and he should hire a lawyer to work it out. Another worker, a woman who makes a little more than minimum wage at Carl's Jr., cried while describing her experience working at Puzder's company. For some reason, she didn't seem to think he would be a great champion for workers.

After the election, there was a lot of speculation about who Donald Trump "really is" and what he'll "really do" in office. The answer is right there in the team he assembled to govern our nation. Education, health, the economy, criminal justice, wages, the air we breathe and the water we drink—all of these will be directly and profoundly affected by the people who manage the government agencies that are responsible for these aspects of our national enterprise. They will carry out the policies that will touch the lives of every person in this country.

During the campaign, Trump offered trickle-down on steroids, and now that's exactly what he is delivering. In short order, he put together a group that is champing at the bit to undo many of the last vestiges of the programs that provide essential support to America's middle class, like Medicare and Medicaid and policies that support public education. This is a group of people who seem to believe with all their hearts that government is the enemy, and that poor, beleaguered giant corporations should be turned loose to do whatever they want—break the economy, poison the water, cut cozy private deals with Russia, refuse to pay people for the hours they work.

Trump and his team have the power to destroy much of what is left of America's middle class. They have the power to extinguish the hope that our children—all our children—will have a chance to grow up and do better than their parents.

I hope I'm wrong about the dangers we face. Shoot, I *want* to be wrong. But even before he was sworn into office, Trump and the Republican-led Congress made it clear that they had no interest in rebuilding a country that works for Gina, Michael, or Kai—or for millions of other hard-working Americans. And Trump himself never wavered from his prime objective: he was willing to tear the nation apart and leave it in shambles, so long as he could still preen for the cameras and scoop up even more piles of money. With each action and each pronouncement, he reinforced the notion that everything—everything—was all about Donald Trump and not about the American people.

So that means it's up to us. This fight is our fight. Yes, different battle-fields will emerge over time, and our tactics will evolve. No general maps out every clash in advance and then adheres rigidly to a plan; that's the path straight to failure. Smart fighters improve their strength, train hard, and deepen their resolve. They create new weapons and upgrade old ones. They develop greater discipline. They adapt. They keep a sharp eye out for advantages, even small ones. Then, when they commit, they fight like there is no tomorrow. And that's exactly what we must do because—well, with Donald Trump in the White House, there may *be* no tomorrow.

We've also got to be prepared to lose some battles. Without control of Congress or the White House, we will often come up short. We simply don't have the tools and the weapons to win every time. But that doesn't mean we are powerless. It doesn't mean we should not fight back. We have tens of millions of people on our side and the soul of a great nation hanging in the balance. We are, we must be, in this fight all the way.

And here's how we begin. To rebuild an economy that works for everyone—and a Democratic party that will lead that fight—we need to be clear about our values. We need to be clear about where we stand and, more importantly, what's worth fighting for. We need to be clear about where we will and will not compromise. We need, in other words, to be clear about our core principles.

The way I see it, these principles have three parts.

FIGHT BIGOTRY

The first part of our fight is to battle bigotry—wherever, whenever, whatever. This is a no-compromise principle. It is the kind of core, foundational, who-we-are point that we must stand up and make every time it's necessary.

Donald Trump has stirred up something ugly in America. I know he didn't invent it; a lot of that ugliness was already there, ready to be tapped. But I also know that although about sixty-three million people voted for Donald Trump, about seventy-three million voted for someone else for president. And of Trump's sixty-three million voters, there were many who voted for him despite—not because of—the hatefulness of his campaign. In fact, nearly a quarter of the people who cast their vote for him said he wasn't qualified to be president, and 29 percent said he wasn't honest or trustworthy. No one has provided an entirely persuasive explanation of why so many people voted for a man they don't trust, but I cling to the belief that a majority of Americans do not want to see us torn apart by attacks on one another.

But now that the hatefulness is out in the open, we cannot ignore it. Bigots have been empowered, which means the rest of us have to step up.

We can—and we will—say with one voice that we believe in an America that is committed to dignity for all, a country that fully embraces the idea that our differences make us stronger. There will undoubtedly be some bumps and tough moments along the way, but I believe our country will end up on the right side of history and build an open community that values every single individual. I believe our diversity makes us stronger, and there is no question that this principle is worth fighting for.

Our job is to stand up, speak out, fight back. At community meetings and outreach programs. Online, in parks and at community centers, in churches, temples, and mosques. All of us together, we must fight back.

The enemy is hatefulness and bigotry, and we all need to jump into the fight. Dr. Martin Luther King, Jr., said that "injustice anywhere is a threat to justice everywhere," and that must be our rallying cry. When Muslims are singled out for different treatment based on their religion, Christians, Jews and non-believers need to join the fight because the assault touches all of us. Discrimination based on race is not an injustice that only black people should raise; it is the moral obligation of each of us to take up the challenge of building a just society. Immigration actions that tear families apart are a direct threat to the America we love, and they require all of us to defend our neighbors. Women must not be pushed back to second-class status; less access to needed health care and lower pay can't become an accepted, permanent condition. There's no sitting on the sidelines waiting to see if your group is next.

America has a complex history, but at its root is the idea that different people come together to build one nation. We embrace the notion that diversity is not our weakness; it is our strength. We're aiming for more than tolerance; we aim to celebrate the differences that make us who we are. It was our country's unofficial motto when we were founded, and it's right there on the Great Seal of the United States: *E pluribus unum*. Out of many, one.

Good for all those who have spoken up since the election, who have marched and protested, who have rallied for health care and held forums on immigration and fair wages and other topics. And now I think we should hear from everyone else—including corporate America. We need to hear from all the nonpolitical leaders of this country, from the captains of industry and the Masters of the Universe, from the people who lead giant organizations and influence public opinion. Where exactly do they stand on bigotry, and what do they plan to do about it?

Six days after the election, the *Wall Street Journal* held its annual CEO Council. According to its sponsors, the council "connects the world's most ambitious and influential business leaders to discuss the issues shaping the future." In other words, the council provides an opportunity for the rich and powerful to meet the rich and powerful.

Most of the attendees and speakers were CEOs. A governor of the Federal Reserve System was there, along with one of the chief prosecutors of financial crimes. I had also been asked to come. Was this Daniel invited to the lion's den?

I showed up at the appointed hour, and the gathering was just about what you'd expect: lots of white men and a few other people. All of them were seated in a darkened room while the main dish (me) was placed on a low stage, ready to be carved up.

At this conference, just six days after the election, I had something I wanted to say to the leaders of corporate America. As soon as I spotted an opening, I jumped in. I pointed out that Trump had run a campaign based on bigotry and that the early indications showed that he was embracing that bigotry—hook, line, and sinker. Then I looked directly at the CEOs and made my pitch:

Bigotry is bad for business.

I noted that many of their own companies had been on the front lines in the effort to make workplaces friendlier to a broad spectrum of Americans. Many of these same companies had made it clear that they wanted to serve customers of all races and religions and sexual orientations. Many had also pushed back against laws in Indiana and North Carolina that all but encouraged people to discriminate against those identifying as LGBTQ. And good for them. But some of these companies were also making political contributions to help out Donald Trump and the congressional Republicans. Some had given money directly. Some had hidden behind their trade associations. Some had donated through dark money political groups.

Yes, these companies were legally entitled to make those contributions; they were fully protected under the Supreme Court ruling in *Citizens United*. And yes, many of these companies almost certainly had non-hateful reasons for supporting a candidate and a party that has embraced hate. But no matter what they told themselves about the reasons for their support, they cannot aid and abet bigotry and then claim that their own hands are clean.

People don't have to be bigots themselves to profit from bigotry. Bankers can get in bed with open racists and tell themselves that the only reason they associate with these people is to make a deal to roll back financial regulations. Oil barons can buddy up with friends of the KKK and say they're only interested in securing more drilling rights. CEOs of communications giants can help out people who want to round up all Muslims and claim they're just working to get their latest merger approved.

These executives may tell themselves that they *personally* are open-minded about Muslims or Latinos or blacks or women or LGBTQ people or any other group that is targeted by hate. They may declare that they are fair in their hiring and that they welcome customers of all kinds. They can spin any version of a not-my-problem story they want, but when they help people who are advancing bigotry and when they make it easier for bigoted candidates to get elected and easier for them to stay in power, then they profit from each and every hateful act as surely as if they shoved, chanted, and spit right along with the bigots.

It isn't enough to declare in private that our own hearts are good. We stand up in public for those who are attacked and we call on others to stand up. That's how we tell ourselves who we are. That's how we let the rest of the world know what we stand for.

I told the business leaders at the CEO Council that they had to choose sides. With Trump trying to pull our country back toward more separation and more hate, I said, "I don't think it's possible to stand on the sidelines and be quiet about this."

Leadership on the issue of bigotry will come from the grass roots. It will come from the clergy. It will come from elected officials. It will come from sports figures and movie stars and talk show hosts and newspaper columnists and everyone who has a platform. And on this most fundamental of issues, corporate America shouldn't get a pass.

We all stand up, and we also look around to see who isn't standing. And then we call them out.

BUILD OPPORTUNITY

The second part of our fight is to say loud and clear that we will make this economy work for everyone—not just for the top 10 percent, but for everyone.

This isn't "messaging." It's not about finding the right slogan or slicing off the right demographic. It's about understanding at a deep-down level what most of America lives every day: This government doesn't work for them. This government works for the rich and the powerful, and it is leaving everyone else behind.

Yes, there's some good economic news out here. And every time we talk about the stock market or unemployment statistics or the GDP, we think we're drawing an accurate picture of our economy. But those statistics have huge blind spots. Gina can't put groceries on the table just because the stock market is up. Michael can't whittle down his mortgage with the GDP. Kai can't pay off her student loans even if the Labor Department says she's fully employed. It is the lived experience of Gina, Michael, and Kai—and the tens of millions more who have their own stories—that will determine the future of our country. And with every passing year, the economic indicators that Washington obsesses over ignore the lives of more and more people like Gina and Michael and Kai.

The question is simple: How do we build an America that works for all of us?

The answer is right in front of us: We built it once, and we can build it again.

The America we built was far from perfect, but over time it worked better and better for more and more of us. It was an America where income rose across the board, where the 90 percent got a big piece of all the new income produced in this country, where the arc of our national story was bending in the right direction. It was an America where one generation after another felt confident that their children would do better than they had.

Then the story turned darker, as millionaires and corporate executives decided they wanted a bigger piece of our collective pie. In the 1980s, deregulation and trickle-down economics began to tilt our economy, and before long it worked only for those at the top. The change was radical: since the election of Ronald Reagan, almost 100 percent of the new income produced in this country has gone to the richest 10 percent, leaving essentially nothing for everyone else.

Now we face the biggest threat of all: the levers of our government have been handed over to people who still believe in trickle-down and deregulation, and they will do everything they can to amp up the impact of policies that have already hollowed out America's middle class. During his campaign, Donald Trump claimed to be a man of the people; the day he was sworn in, he declared that his inauguration "will be remembered as the day the people became the rulers of this nation again." But talk is cheap. Actions matter far more. And as soon as his election victory was secure, Trump put together a team of advisers and cabinet members bent on helping corporate America enrich itself while allowing working families to fall further and further behind.

President Trump, Senate Majority Leader Mitch McConnell, Speaker of the House Paul Ryan, their followers in Congress—they all ran for office promising to work hard for we the people. Instead, within hours of taking the oath of office, Trump quietly signed an executive order to make FHA mortgages more expensive—likely cutting about forty thousand families out of a chance to buy a home each year. Within weeks of the election, McConnell delivered big favors to his campaign contributors in a drug-approval bill he shepherded through the Senate. Not to be outdone, Ryan immediately put together a budget that would privatize Medicare and a tax cut that would drop about $3 trillion in the pockets of the richest one percent and provide virtually nothing for anyone else. And here's the part that really burns: if any of them had run for office on a platform of reducing homeownership, naming Wall Street insiders to control our economy, giving giant banks more chances to cheat people, and destroying our environment, they would have lost by double digits. This is plain old bait-and-switch, now dressed up in its new gold-plated Trumpian version.

The most extreme of the trickle-down advocates are now in charge, and they are pulling every lever they can to make this country work better for those at the top. Trump campaigned hard for changes to the tax code—cuts that would leave an average of a cool $1.1 million in the pockets of the wealthiest 0.1 percent of the population. And for every dollar of special tax breaks that the rich guys get, how much does the family right in the middle get? A dollar? A dime? A penny? Nope. It would be about one-tenth of a penny. But wait, there's more: for many single parents and large families, taxes would go up. And finally, there's one last little twist of the knife: it just so happens that Trump's tax plan will save many millions for Trump's family businesses. Some people will gobble up every crumb of food at the table, if they get the chance.

As these tax cuts make Trump and his billionaire buddies even richer, they will leave government with even less money to invest in schools, roads, bridges, and medical research. Less money to cut the cost of student loans. Less money to make the shift to green energy. Less money to make our power grid more resilient to climate change, to deal with an opioid-abuse crisis that is destroying lives all across this country, to repair public housing and rebuild public transportation. Less money to do the things we can and must do together to give each other a helping hand and to build real opportunity for all our children.

But those tax cuts would give us more of one thing: debt. The Trump tax cuts would add more than $7 trillion to our $19.5 trillion national debt over a decade—and would add a staggering $21 trillion or so over twenty years. As usual, President Trump will let someone else pick up the bill for his spending: the American taxpayer.

If Trump has his way, the rich will get even richer, and the powerful even more powerful. He has plenty of ideas about how to make that happen; front and center is his belief that regulations that prevent the big banks from blowing up the economy ought to be eliminated. The Consumer Financial Protection Bureau is also in the crosshairs, and for exactly one reason: it does its job so well that a whole lot fewer people are getting cheated on mortgages, credit cards, and a number of other financial products. Regulations that make it possible for more workers to receive overtime pay are also on the chopping block, along with regulations to protect investors from scams and regulations to keep the air breathable and the water drinkable. There are hundreds of other examples, but the theme is clear: some of the rules that help keep markets a little fairer, the economy a little safer, and our lives a little better also crimp short-term profits, and in the cruel new world of Trump trickle-down, that's reason enough to get rid of them.

Thanks to the resilience of the American people, we have managed to survive thirty-five years of trickle-down economics—sometimes more of it, sometimes less. But our middle class may not be strong enough to withstand another four years of these destructive policies. People are already pressed to the breaking point, and they may be crushed by still more years of rising expenses and flat wages. Giant corporations have gotten so good at making Washington do their bidding, so good at wiggling through tax loopholes and regulatory tangles, and so good at shifting the burdens and the risks to families and small businesses, that there is simply too little left over for everyone else. Another round of trickle-down economics threatens both the foundations of our economy and our basic belief that America is a land of opportunity.

As the recent election made plain, people are angry, and they're so angry that it's sometimes hard to believe that we can ever reach across the political divisions in our country. Yes, we are divided by some big issues, and some of our differences run deep. But on a whole range of economic policies—the policies that determine who gets a chance to move forward and who doesn't—there is actually widespread agreement on what is broken and what it will take to fix it:

- More than 70 percent of the American people believe that students should have a chance at a debt-free education.
- Nearly three-quarters of Americans support expanding Social Security.
- Two-thirds of all Americans support raising the federal minimum wage.
- Three-quarters of Americans want the federal government to increase spending on infrastructure.

This is what big majorities of Americans—Democrats, Republicans, independents, Libertarians, and vegetarians—believe. When we tune out the noise and the nonsense, the real story comes through loud and clear: people actually have pretty clear ideas about how to make America work for all of us.

And how do we pay for all those things? Again, a pretty solid majority of America agrees: start by raising taxes for those at the top. Currently, 61 percent of us believe that the wealthiest Americans don't pay their fair share in taxes, and 63 percent favor eliminating tax deductions and loopholes for the very rich. That's not quite a two-to-one majority, but it sure as heck gives us a good starting point.

And what about the other half of trickle-down economics? What about rolling back the tide of deregulation? By a three-to-one margin, Americans want more—not less—regulation over Wall Street. And here's my personal favorite: twice as many Trump voters want to protect or strengthen the CFPB than want to cut back its reach.

Most of America is ready for change, and most of us share a vision of an America that builds opportunity. Restoring that vision is one of the most important things we can do. Why? Because this is the core of what it means to *be* America—the security, the optimism, and the spark that makes us productive and innovative. That core is what makes us who we are.

DEMAND DEMOCRACY

In an America led by Donald Trump and a band of billionaires, bankers, and bigots, how can we go about making this change real?

We stand up and we fight back—and we do so on a very personal level. We start with clarity about the principle we are fighting for: everybody counts and everybody gets a chance to build something. Or to say it another way: America must be a country that respects every human being and that builds opportunity not just for some of us, but for all of us. We fight for a country we can believe in.

Collective action begins with individual action, and each of us must find our own way to speak up. I think of a man named Mateo, who helps manage billing and insurance forms in a busy office for three surgeons. He's shy and soft-spoken. He wears his dark, curly hair long, partly hiding the scars from burns he suffered as a child. He has never talked politics at work. "All kinds of people come in here," he told me, "and besides, the doctors? This is their place."

Trump's election to the presidency hit him hard. "I'm gay, and it's like America wants to go back," he said. "I can't go back. I feel like my country doesn't want me." After President Trump was elected, Mateo thought deeply about what he personally could do. "I'm not brave, but I had to do something." So he decided to wear his "Love Trumps Hate" button every day. At work, he keeps it in his pocket, but when he goes to lunch and to the store and out in the evening, he believes the button says to everyone, "This is where I stand."

Now people who walk by Mateo say things like "Yeah, me too." He got a high five from a young black man at the gas station, and a group of schoolkids cheered him at the food court at the mall. He smiled when he told that story: "It's like we're all connected."

Mateo said the button was a reminder that he could do something. Over Thanksgiving, he volunteered at a shelter for homeless youths, and he plans on going back.

Okay, it's just a button. And it may not even be the best button. But it was Mateo's way to get connected and to make his own statement. It was also his reminder to do more. I say, "Good for you, Mateo!"

And to everyone reading this book, I make the same point: Start with something personal. Pick your own act of defiance, something that says to you—and to others—that you won't go along with the hate. Find a way to connect with other people and strengthen communities that are built on the idea that everyone in America deserves respect and dignity. Commit yourself to joining the fight to give every kid a chance. Contribute time and your best energy to the battle to ensure that this government will serve not just the richest and most powerful, but all of us. Because these personal acts of devotion will connect you to the collective action that makes democracy work.

Individual action leads to the second tool of resistance: we must use our numbers. Most Americans want change, and in a democracy, majorities matter.

I now start every day by reminding myself that Hillary Clinton beat Donald Trump by nearly three million votes. In any other democracy on earth, she would be president, but our outdated Electoral College system gave the win to Donald Trump. Okay, those are the rules, but it doesn't mean that he gets to govern as if he has a mandate. He does not have the wind of democracy at his back. On the contrary, Donald Trump is the President Most People Didn't Want, and the majority has the right—the obligation, in fact—to make the wind blow right back in Trump's face, *hard*.

How do we do that? We use our collective power. Trump clearly loves having a big audience—so let's give him one. He also loves watching television, so let's give him a great show. If we pay attention to what he and his team do, if we respond with a coordinated push in opposition, it will make a big difference. Marches and rallies? You bet. Online protests and viral videos? Yes. Funny stuff, hard-hitting stuff, passionate stuff? Absolutely. We must use our collective voice—use it to challenge what is bad and use it to demand what is good. This is what it means to live our values in real time. This is what democracy looks like and sounds like.

The Women's March on January 21, 2017, was an awakening. Springing up in cities and towns across the country, it was the single biggest demonstration in the history of the United States. It was an organic, spontaneous decision by millions of women to organize a rally that would roar. On the day after Donald Trump was sworn in as president of the United States, we showed all the world that we would not be cowed, we would not be silenced, and we would not let this man speak for who we are as a people. Every marcher added their own flavor and color, but more than anything, we celebrated the power of us, the power of the people. We demonstrated that we can be the loud, determined, unrelenting force that reminds all of America about our values—and our willingness to fight for those values.

The Women's March, however, was only the beginning. For everyone who remains unhappy about Donald Trump's election, don't forget how we got here: we must begin working right now on the 2018 midterm election. If you didn't like how 2016 came out, volunteer for a voter registration drive and help pull in some new people—not in a year, but now. And if there is no place to volunteer, build it yourself. Yes, it's hard—but this is what it takes to make change. Or if that just doesn't work for you, then lobby the state legislatures that still don't have same-day registration and early voting. Helping people get access to voting is one of the most patriotic things you can do. If everyone votes, I guarantee that Donald Trump and his kind will lose.

And there's more: think about running for office yourself. I didn't have any experience when I launched my first campaign in 2012; you, too, can seize the moment and decide to make a difference. You can run or you can help someone else run. The kind of people we need in public office aren't the ones who can collect a few million from the Koch brothers or write a check out of their own accounts. The people we need are the people who need help—who need lots of volunteers to get a campaign up and going. Democracy needs *us*.

Whatever you do, however you step up, do everything possible to make 2018 the year that defies all the statistics about lack of interest in midterm elections and, instead, delivers a higher turnout of voters than in 2016. We can show that democracy works.

Do we need more proof that votes and elections matter? What happened in November 2016 will have an impact on every person, every worker, every family in America. Take my own state, Massachusetts: it's not a big state, but more than a million people here count on Medicare and Medicare Advantage to help cover their medical bills and prescription drugs. Two out of every three students graduating from a college in Massachusetts carry a load of student loan debt. One in seven people in Massachusetts was born outside the United States. Tens of thousands of people in nursing homes depend on Medicaid to help pay the bills. We have 16,000 children in Head Start, and 233,000 families bought health insurance on the Connector marketplace. More than 400,000 members of labor unions rely on the right to bargain collectively for better wages and safer working conditions. More than 32,000 people went to Planned Parenthood of Massachusetts in 2016 for critically important care. Every one of them—and everyone else in Massachusetts—will be touched by the policies that Trump and the Republican leadership are pushing. Touched? No, many of them will be bruised, battered, slammed, beaten, thumped—and some will be broken. Does it matter what Donald Trump and his administration do? You bet it does.

There will be no shortage of horrifying initiatives over the next few years—threats of mass deportations, dangerous Supreme Court nominees, and efforts to rewrite the rules to give even more advantages to the rich and powerful. Shoot, those will be just the beginning. What's worse is that what I describe as horrifying initiatives, Trump and his allies see as glittering opportunities. We can't know which battles Trump and his team will try to mount with the full force of the government and the Republican establishment at their backs, but I know we have to be ready. We have to believe in ourselves, in our cause, and in our absolute, unwavering willingness to get in there and fight.

For inspiration, think back to Franklin Roosevelt. When FDR said he would take on corporations and Wall Street, he didn't mince words. He called out the "privileged princes" and "economic royalty" running corporate America. And when the titans of commerce went after him with vicious attacks, he didn't back down. Instead he declared, "I welcome their hatred."

Today's leaders must show similar courage and do their part to resist Trump. Everyone in this fight has the right to call out their elected representatives and demand that they join the battle, too. Breaking the grip that powerful corporations hold over our government will require members of Congress and many other government officials to stand up— stand up to Big Oil, Big Pharma, Big Tobacco, and Big Lots of Things. Turning the tide will mean taming the money monster that makes it possible for the privileged to hold democracy by the throat. It will mean casting a skeptical eye at the experts for hire and banning federal judges from taking "gifts" from those who would curry favor. It will mean a lot of changes, but most of all, it will mean cultivating a willingness to fight.

Success against a threat of this magnitude will take enormous effort. It will take discipline: we can't treat every single skirmish as a do-or-die battle. Each fight over one of Trump's silly, distracting tweets is a fight we're not having over who really benefits when the Consumer Financial Protection Bureau is hobbled or the EPA is silenced. Sure, some of those tweets matter—but not all of them, and, often, not even the most outrageous ones.

Sometimes we will disagree about when to charge ahead and when to pause. We will need to be smart, to hold steady, to be persistent in our attention to our core issues, and to hold Trump accountable—not for everything, but for the things that will make the biggest differences in people's lives.

We need to be disciplined, but we also need the courage to head straight into the most consequential battles. There will be many different paths to the battlefield, but the first step is the commitment to get in the fight. It is a commitment that should not be lightly taken. Fights are hard, and fights against well-funded groups that have already wrapped their tentacles around every part of American life are *really* hard. Those in power will not go quietly. They will not cede a single inch without putting up resistance. Sometimes the fight will get ugly, and sometimes we will lose. But if we don't fight, we will end up in an even uglier place. And if we don't fight, we will *always* lose.

Summon the courage. Make the commitment. Get in the fight.

THE FIGHT AHEAD

The hardest time for me is about three o'clock in the morning. That's when the worries come back to haunt me. That's when I sometimes think about Gina.

Gina, the woman who reminded me of my mother—only a generation later. Gina, with the quick laugh and the den mother instincts, always looking out for her coworkers at Walmart. Gina, who worked long hours but still ended up at the food pantry by the end of every month.

How did 2016 turn out for her? She proudly voted for Donald Trump, hoping he would "shake things up." She was happy when he won. Then, a month after the election, she said that Walmart had revised its staffing approach. The company had decided to hire a lot more temps, people who were willing to work fewer hours and not get any benefits. Shortly before Christmas, Walmart fired Gina.

As for Michael, his hard times had come earlier—the 2008 recession had cost him his job at DHL, his home, his security. By the start of 2016, it looked like his financial nightmare was pretty much over. He and his wife, Janet, were living in a smaller home in a nearby Chicago suburb, and Michael had worked his way up to the day shift at the Nabisco plant.

But in March, when Nabisco started laying off people at the Chicago plant and moving those jobs to Mexico, he was thrown backward again.

Michael proudly voted for Hillary Clinton. During the campaign, she visited his Nabisco plant to talk to the workers who were about to lose their jobs, and he told me that he was sure that "she won't forget us." But now his future looks grim. Recently he applied for a part-time job back at DHL, and he hopes it will come through. No guaranteed hours, no benefits, but something. He really needs that job because he's got the new mortgage now, and he also worries about paying for health insurance. In a few months, he will turn sixty.

And then there's Kai. Kai didn't vote. She just couldn't get excited about either candidate. Three days before Christmas, she packed up her car and started the long drive from her sister's place in Connecticut back to her parents' home in Colorado.

Nine years after she first set out for college, full of plans and sure she would make a mark in this world, Kai will move back into her old room at her parents' house. She has no idea where she will work—maybe at another restaurant, if she can find a job at a place where the tips are decent. She's given up on completing her degree; now her only goal is to keep up with her student loan payments, one month at a time. With a $90,000 debt load and a job at the bottom of the pay scale, she can't even calculate when she will be out of debt. Marriage? A family? A home of her own? Those dreams look very far away to Kai.

This can't be right. Gina worked hard; so did Michael and Kai. As far as I know, they weren't reckless or stupid or careless. They didn't gamble, or laze about, or sink their life savings into snake-oil futures. No, they worked hard and played by the rules and did their best. Swept up by a tide of change, they now find themselves living in an America that has made the climb into the middle class much harder than it once was—and has made the fall out of the middle class much swifter and more deadly.

When my mother put on her high heels and walked to the local Sears store back in the 1960s, she was flat out of options. She was ready to take whatever Sears handed her. And if Sears didn't come through, there was a hamburger joint across the street. And a dry cleaners, a drugstore, and an insurance agency a block farther up. She wasn't going to come home without a paycheck, not if she could help it.

My mother pulled together every scrap of will and determination she could summon, and she saved our lives. Her minimum-wage job meant we could meet the mortgage payments and keep groceries on the table. My daddy got back to work eventually, and he finally ended up as a janitor. Together they paid down the bills. I made it to college, got married, and became a teacher, just as I'd always dreamed. None of it was easy, but my parents hung on to their place in America's middle class right up until they died.

Yes, I worry about Gina. I know she's every bit as smart and tough as my mother—maybe more so. But Gina needs an America where the playing field isn't tilted so hard against her. Michael just needs a chance, and that's what Kai needs, too.

The danger is real, and the time is short. But we understand what we can do. We can build an America that works for all of us. We know how; we just need to do it.

Our country's future is not determined by some law of physics. It's not determined by some preordained path. It's not even determined by Donald Trump. Our country's future is up to us. We can let the great American promise die or we can fight back. Me? I'm fighting back.

This fight is our fight.

Epilogue

"What was that?"

I'd heard a muffled roar outside, the sound of many voices suddenly rising as one.

Bruce and I were in our apartment in Washington, D.C. It was early morning on Friday, January 20, 2017. The day was chilly and cloudy, threatening rain, and Bruce was already dressed and heading out to find newspapers—he's still old school about morning coffee and papers. I was layering up with socks, an undershirt, and a turtleneck, preparing to sit outside in the cold for a couple of hours while Donald Trump was being sworn in as the forty-fifth president of the United States.

When I'd gotten up around seven and looked out the window, I saw that a steady stream of people was already moving down the street toward the National Mall, the green space that runs from Capitol Hill to the Washington Monument and on to the Lincoln Memorial. I spotted a fellow on the corner with a pushcart loaded with Trump T-shirts, caps, and other souvenirs. Lots of people were wearing red hats, and I assumed they were the famous Make America Great Again caps. People carried signs, backpacks, shopping bags, and umbrellas. The inauguration ceremonies would begin at eleven, so early birds would be outside for a while.

For nearly an hour, I'd heard the sounds of people out on the street, but when the roar went up, I ran over to the window. By now the street was crowded, and I saw that a huge banner had been unfurled above the throng, with people on each end holding poles to keep it aloft. Written on the banner was just one word, all in capitals:

FASCIST

As the noise intensified, there was a lot of pushing and shoving around the people holding up the banner. The police moved in quickly to make sure no one got hurt. The sign disappeared. The pushing and shoving stopped. The noise died back down.

I leaned my forehead against the cold window. *Fascist.* Here, in the United States of America, protesters declaring that the incoming president was a fascist. I had heard the word hurled a few times before, mostly back when I was a kid. But this was different.

In all my life, I had never expected to see a day like this. The person about to be sworn in as the nation's president was a man who had launched multiple attacks on people because of their faith. A man who had made barefaced racism part of his appeal. A man who had spoken of women in the most vulgar ways and made fun of a reporter with a disability. A man who had forced a lot of Americans to stop dead in their tracks to consider the possibility that fascism was alive and well, right here in America.

Even his claim to return power to the people made me clench my teeth. Return it to the people? What, the ultrarich people? The Goldman Sachs people? The Wall Street people? He had already named one billionaire after another to run his incoming administration, and he had been quick to set a terrible example by making it clear that serving in government was not inconsistent with lining your own pockets.

And this man was about to be sworn in as president.

THE NEXT DAY broke bright and sunny.

I was back home in Cambridge, back in my own bed. As I woke up I thought, "One day into his presidency and at least Donald Trump hasn't blown up the world yet. Only 1,460 days to go."

My next thought was about the Women's March on Washington. When I had first heard about it, I wondered whether we would have a similar march in Massachusetts. When I'd asked around, I heard that planning for a "small rally" in Boston was coming together. I said I wanted to join our people at home.

I loved the idea of a big rally in Washington. I loved the symbolism of an enormous crowd of people turning out to celebrate our unity a day after the inauguration of a man trying to tear us apart. But I also thought that if people staged rallies across the country their energy and their numbers would create a special magic. Groups large and small could gather to affirm that we the people are stronger than a hate-filled president.

In the days leading up to the march in Boston, volunteers worked feverishly to set up the rally. The planners came from a variety of places, but they didn't hesitate to jump in. No more fanning the flames of hatred. No more government of billionaires. And why not make our stand in America's oldest public park, Boston Common? Why not stand just miles from where the *Mayflower* landed? Why not stand where the abolitionists, the suffragettes, and the Freedom Riders had gathered? After centuries of progress and setbacks, steps forward and steps back, why not stand here to declare again *out of many, we are one*. It was time to start calling our army together, and the group that organized the Boston march had done an amazing job.

So now it was Saturday morning. I tied the laces on my bright pink tennis shoes, put on my purple Planned Parenthood scarf (knotted just right so everyone could see the logo), and hopped in the Blue Bomber. My state director, Roger Lau; his deputy, Jess Torres; and Bruce were already in the car, ready to go. As we made our way toward the rally, we saw cars backed up on Storrow Drive. I could see that the police were out in force, with roads blocked and traffic diverted. I was worried that we'd be late.

By now we were eight or ten blocks from Boston Common, where the march would begin. And that was when I got my first glimpse of our army. The sidewalks were full of people hurrying toward the Common— women in pink pussy hats, men pushing strollers, kids laughing and running. I saw a little girl riding on her father's shoulders while clutching a hand-lettered sign that read, I FIGHT LIKE A GIRL.

So do I, sweetie.

When I waded into the crowd and moved toward the stage a few minutes later, I realized that the Boston Women's March was like a giant family reunion. Lots of hugs and cheers and catching up. Lots of experienced activists, but also lots of new faces. Lots of babies and great-grannies. Lots of students and older marchers. People with disabilities made an especially strong showing—a reminder that they too would be powerful fighters in the coming battles.

From up on the stage, I saw signs from Planned Parenthood and the ACLU. I spotted a big sign that proclaimed BE THE CHURCH and listed the principles that idea represented—protect the environment, care for the poor, reject racism, fight for the powerless, share earthly and spiritual resources, embrace diversity, love God, enjoy this life. The sign covered it all.

I looked out at the massive crowd. There was an ocean of signs— colorful, clever, creative.

I march so my daughter won't have to

Let's read Trump's tax returns, not his tweets

This is my first protest, but not my last

Not usually a sign guy but geez

This is what democracy looks like

Women's rights are not up for grabs

Brown queer proud and here to stay

We are all immigrants

Donald you ain't seen nasty yet

The power of the people is stronger than the people in power

History has its eyes on you

When I had the chance to speak to the crowd before the march began, I talked about having witnessed the moment when Donald Trump was sworn in as president. The sight was now burned into my brain, and I would never forget it. I didn't *want* to forget it: I wanted to use it as a reminder to fight longer, fight harder, and fight more passionately for an America that works for all of us, not just the people favored by Donald Trump.

There were more cheers and more hugs and more pictures, but the best part was wading back into the crowd. The mood was exuberant but purposeful. Everyone I met looked absolutely committed, ready to join the fight. I offered lots of hugs and knelt down to take pictures with very small marchers (even if they were strapped in to strollers, I think it's fair to say that they still qualified as marchers). Bruce visited with some of his students who had come to join the rally.

We lined up and got ready to begin the march. Senator Ed Markey, Mayor Marty Walsh, Attorney General Maura Healey, and I stood together on the front line. We were joined by the state treasurer, Deb Goldberg, and the state auditor, Suzanne Bump.

Bruce stood right behind Senator Markey and me. He reached out and shook hands with police superintendent-in-chief William Gross, the highest ranking police officer in Boston. Then he introduced himself: "I'm the senator's husband." Bruce paused. "Hers, not his."

I love Massachusetts.

Finally, inching forward, we started marching. The "small rally" had turned into 175,000 marchers, with more turned away because Boston

Common ran out of room. The police did their best to clear a path for us to march, but in the end the crowds were so thick that mostly we were just a huge, slowly moving mass of people.

We weren't fully organized yet, but the power was there, the energy everywhere. On a cold, bright Saturday morning, something special was happening. Every step brought us closer together—everyone on Boston Common, everyone in Washington, everyone in little towns and big cities across America and around the world.

We stood up in different places and we spoke out in different ways, but we made it clear that we believe in basic human dignity. We declared that everyone counts. We talked and held signs that pointed to many different paths, but all those paths pointed toward building opportunity, not just for some of our people but for all of them. And our very act of marching delivered the loudest possible proclamation of our deep-down, unshakeable belief that we can make democracy work again by insisting that this government serve the people. We *are* an army—an army filled with optimism and hope and fierce determination.

As I marched in Boston with tens of thousands of others that day, I had no illusions. I knew it would be a hard fight. I knew there would be dark moments. But I knew that we had tens of millions of people with us and that this fight would be our fight.

MASSACHUSETTS STATE SENATOR KAREN E. SPILKA

Afterword to the 2018 Edition

Even before I opened my eyes that morning, I lay in bed wondering, "What fights are on for today?"

It was Tuesday, February 7, 2017. We were barely into the third week of the Trump presidency, and, as one pillar of our democracy after another cracked and tilted sideways, I was starting to wonder if this is what it felt like to be caught in a building during an earthquake. Eleven days earlier, Trump had launched a surprise political attack on Muslims, declaring a travel ban that sent me sprinting to Boston's Logan Airport to join one of the many spontaneous demonstrations that erupted all across the country to protest the ban. The ongoing Republican effort to roll back health care coverage for millions of Americans was gathering steam, and nearly everyone I met at the grocery store or on the sidewalk was caught somewhere between angry and deeply worried. Meanwhile, the nominations for Team Trump—his cabinet and other top appointments—were coming thick and fast, each one seeming more extreme than the last.

I felt like I was fighting in every direction, and today would be no different. I clenched my jaws and opened my eyes.

Bruce was already half awake. "You ok?" he asked me.

"No," I said.

I had a speech to finish. Later that day I would be giving a speech about the nomination of Senator Jeff Sessions to be the attorney general of the United States. Back in the 1980s, Sessions had been considered too racist to be confirmed as a federal judge, and Democrats and Republicans had joined together to reject his nomination. "But that was then," I said, "and now, NOW, Donald Trump nominates him to be AG and not one Republican—not one—will even talk about what he did. This just isn't *right.*"

It wasn't even seven o'clock yet, and my heart was already pounding.

Bruce was quiet for a minute. He shifted under the covers and put his arms around me. "I know it's hard. You'll figure this out. But first you need to eat breakfast. We have blackberries."

I knew it would be a long day. It wasn't just the Sessions debate. We would also be voting on Betsy DeVos for secretary of education, a nomination I had vehemently opposed. That morning, I was scheduled to join other members of the Senate Armed Services Committee for a classified briefing on cyber security. Later, there would be a meeting of the Democratic leadership, a discussion with the general running U.S. operations in Afghanistan, and a meeting with the chief of police for Leicester, Massachusetts.

I closed my eyes for a minute. It wouldn't just be the scheduled work. There would be more unscheduled meetings, more unscheduled calls, and probably more unscheduled bad news coming from the Trump White House.

Time to get going. Shower. Breakfast. Out the door.

AS I HEADED in to my office, I thought about Jeff Sessions, turning over in my mind what I wanted to say when I got my chance to speak on the Senate floor. I thought about an earlier attorney general, Robert F. Kennedy, and a trip Bruce and I had taken in 2015. We had traveled to Alabama with Congressman John Lewis to honor the fiftieth anniversary of the march from Selma to Montgomery, Alabama. Half a century earlier, John had been one of the young men who had been severely beaten as he marched alongside Dr. Martin Luther King Jr. to protest segregation.

During our trip, John pointed out various landmarks and told us stories about the march. He also made sure we met with other people who had been part of that fateful time. In the basement of the First Baptist Church of Montgomery, over doughnuts and coffee, I visited with an elderly man who had spent eleven hours in that same church basement back in May 1961. He had been crowded into the church along with Dr. King and hundreds of other people, while a mob outside threatened to burn down the church—with everyone in it. Why? Because First Baptist had offered refuge to civil rights workers.

The man said that many of his fellow protesters feared for their lives. The basement was sweltering, but they were certain that if they left, some of them would be beaten or possibly lynched. As the hours ticked by, the mob outside grew louder. Frightened and alone, the people inside the church needed help, and the person they called was the attorney general of the United States, Robert Kennedy. Later, Dr. King thanked Kennedy for sending federal marshals to disperse the mob that might have killed so many people that night.

It was one of Bobby Kennedy's finest hours, and the story provided an eloquent reminder of the important role of the attorney general. The AG is the person who promises to enforce the law to protect the rights of every American—even if it means calling out federal marshals to do so.

And now Senator Jeff Sessions was Donald Trump's nominee to be attorney general. In the Senate chamber, Senator Sessions had launched one diatribe after another against *them*. He delivered long speeches about people who didn't look like him and didn't sound like him. As his face got redder and the pitch of his voice rose higher and higher, he would condemn the "complete capitulation to lawlessness" and talk about how *they* put *us* at risk. He would go on and on, getting more and more agitated. By the end, he often was what my grandmother called "spitting mad."

And now President Trump had chosen this man to be the number one law enforcement official in the country. The man responsible for protecting our rights, our liberty, our freedom, and our values. The man to call in a crisis.

What on earth had happened? Had the world turned upside down? Ever since Donald Trump had become president, it sure felt like it.

TUESDAY EVENING ARRIVED, and I still hadn't been assigned a time to speak about the Sessions nomination on floor of the Senate. Finally, a little before seven o'clock, I got my opening. As I headed from my office to the Senate floor with my notes tucked under my arm, I was thinking about the bruising fight over Betsy DeVos, Trump's nominee for secretary of education. Earlier that day, her nomination had made history when the Senate vote split 50–50. For the first time ever, a vice president of the United States had to be hauled up to the Capitol to drag a nominee across the finish line. Now a woman who didn't believe in public education would be in charge of the federal department responsible for public education. What price would our children pay? What price would our country pay?

I stepped into the chamber and walked up to my desk. Actually, I still think of it as Ted Kennedy's desk, because for forty-seven years, that's whose desk it had been. The youngest Kennedy brother had been known as The Lion of the Senate, both for his effectiveness and his unwavering courage. My heart always speeds up a little when I stand up to speak from the desk he used to fight so many battles.

The job of presiding over the Senate chamber rotates among members of the political party in the majority—now, of course, the Republicans. On this evening, the presiding officer was Senator Steve Daines from Montana.

I asked to be recognized, and I started by reviewing Jeff Sessions's record. Everything about his racist views was taken from public documents: his anti-immigrant speeches, his joke about the KKK, his claim that a white attorney back in Alabama who had represented black clients had been "a disgrace to his race." There was plenty of other ground to cover as well: his attacks on equal marriage, including his assertion that employers should be able to fire people because they married someone of the same sex. There was his claim that *Roe v. Wade* is constitutionally unsound, and his votes against equal pay for equal work and against the Violence

Against Women Act. I also discussed his support for longer prison sentences and his push to reduce prisoners' chances to earn early release.

And I was just getting warmed up. As I reviewed his record, I asked, "Where are the senators who will say no to Senator Sessions as attorney general of the United States?"

While I was speaking, the chamber was nearly empty, but I noticed that a few people were scurrying down to the main desk in the front of the Senate chamber where the presiding officer sits; then, just as quickly, they would turn and rush out again. It flicked through the back of my mind that something was going on, but I didn't know what.

I swung into the next part of my speech and started to document Senator Sessions's record as the U.S. attorney for Alabama, back when it had been his job to prosecute cases in Alabama that involved federal laws. In 1986, when President Reagan nominated him to a federal judgeship, that nomination had come before the Senate for a vote.

Back then, Ted Kennedy had served on the Judiciary Committee, which held a hearing on Sessions's nomination. By the time the committee had finished taking evidence about Sessions's work as U.S. attorney, Senator Kennedy was convinced that Sessions was not qualified to be a federal judge and spoke out strongly against him.

Now, more than thirty years later, standing at Ted Kennedy's desk, I began to read his speech opposing the Sessions nomination. Senator Kennedy described Sessions as "a throwback to a shameful era which I know both black and white Americans thought was in our past." Kennedy called Sessions "a disgrace," not only opposing him for the federal judgeship, but also calling on him to resign from his current job as U.S. attorney.

After the Kennedy speech, I turned to a letter from Coretta Scott King, the widow of Dr. Martin Luther King, Jr., and an influential civil rights leader in her own right. Mrs. King hadn't been able to travel to Washington in 1986 to testify at the hearing on the Sessions nomination, but she had written a firsthand account of his record as the U.S. attorney in Alabama.

Mrs. King's letter is sharp and eloquent. She began with a description of how, as Alabama's U.S. attorney, Sessions had "used the awesome power of his office to chill the free exercise of the vote by black citizens."

She described his "hostility to the enforcement of those laws" that protect the right to vote. She gave voice to the fears of elderly black men and women who had been subjected to intimidation and threats. And the events she described hadn't happened a hundred years ago during Reconstruction—they had occurred in the 1980s.

I was still only a little way into Mrs. King's letter when I heard three loud bangs.

Startled, I stopped reading and looked up. Senator Daines had just slammed down the presiding officer's gavel.

Reading from a sheet of paper, Senator Daines said, "The Senator is reminded that it is a violation of Rule XIX of the Standing Rules of the Senate to impute to another Senator or Senators any conduct or motive unworthy or unbecoming a Senator."

Huh? Did I really hear him say "unworthy or unbecoming"? What could that mean? I was standing in the very chamber where just the previous summer Senator Ted Cruz had delivered a speech calling Senate Majority Leader Mitch McConnell a liar and Senator Tom Cotton had stood up to call Senator Harry Reid's leadership "cancerous." But no one had cracked the gavel on them. In fact, I had never heard of any senator called out on Rule XIX.

So I pushed back.

I asked Senator Daines whether, under the rule, I was barred from accurately quoting Senator Kennedy's remarks or Mrs. King's letter because they reflected badly on Senator Sessions.

Daines stared down at me: "The Senator is warned."

I didn't quite know what it meant to be "warned," but I sure wasn't about to stop reading Mrs. King's letter.

So I waited a moment, asked for permission to continue, then went back to my speech.

But it wasn't over. As I continued my speech, Senator McConnell hustled into the chamber. He went straight to his desk and demanded recognition. Then he said:

Mr. President, the Senator has impugned the motives and conduct of our colleague from Alabama, as warned by the Chair. Senator Warren said

Senator Sessions "has used the awesome power of his office to chill the free exercise of the vote by Black citizens." I call the Senator to order under the provisions of rule XIX.

I shot back: "I am surprised that the words of Coretta Scott King are not suitable for debate in the United States Senate. I ask leave of the Senate to continue my remarks."

McConnell objected, and the presiding officer mustered his full authority and commanded, "The Senator will take her seat."

What? Mitch McConnell was going to shut me up for reading a letter to the United States Senate from Coretta Scott King? He was going to bar me from the Senate for reading her indictment of a man who, when he had the power, prosecuted civil rights workers for helping register elderly black citizens to vote? He was going to silence me for reading Mrs. King's moving description of what it meant to blacks in Alabama to face intimidation and harassment from the man who had just been nominated to be attorney general of the United States?

I was beyond mad. I was furious.

But I was also determined that this would NOT happen, so I appealed the ruling of the presiding officer. This meant that every senator would have to come back to the chamber and vote—on the record—about whether to silence me or let me finish reading Mrs. King's letter.

McConnell folded his arms. He wanted to shut me down, and if that meant bringing in every single senator to vote on it, he was ready.

Senators began to gather. Some came in from dinner or a quiet evening at home. Others were pulled out of speeches or other events. As each new person came into the room, someone would rush up and whisper an explanation of what was going on.

While members were gathering for a vote, a Republican senator approached me with a smile. The senator said that maybe things had gotten a bit out of hand and that this could all be resolved amicably. According to this senator, the majority leader was willing to accept my public apology and, if I seemed sincere, he would drop the censure charge and I would be allowed to remain on the floor. I couldn't read Coretta Scott King's letter, of course, but by apologizing I would get out of trouble.

"No," I said.

"What?" the senator asked.

"No," I said again. In fact, hell no.

The senator was obviously shocked. It was clear that Mitch was angry. "This isn't good for you. This isn't who you want to be."

"Sorry," I said, "but this *is* who I am. I will not apologize for reading Mrs. King's letter. And I will not sit down and shut up."

Soon the entire Senate would vote on whether I would be *forced* to sit down and shut up. Just before the vote, Mitch McConnell stood to address the Senate and explained the issue this way:

> Senator Warren was giving a lengthy speech. She had appeared to violate the rule. She was warned. She was given an explanation. Nevertheless, she persisted.

Ultimately, every Republican voted to shut me up. And that was enough to get me kicked out.

I was instructed to leave the floor of the Senate and told that I would not be permitted to speak again until after the vote on the Sessions nomination had been completed.

Now *I* was spitting mad. I walked straight out of the chamber and into one of the side rooms where a small group of my staff had been watching the whole episode on C-SPAN.

"What can we do?" I asked them.

"You could read Mrs. King's letter, and we could live stream it."

"Let's do it," I replied.

And so we did. The lighting wasn't great. The sound was a little hollow. But we made a video right then and there and put it out on social media. Last time I checked, nearly thirteen million people had watched this video, and millions more had viewed Coretta Scott King's words online.

I finally made it home sometime after midnight. When I walked in the door, I started with an apology for being so late. But Bruce interrupted immediately. "I've been watching. You did the right thing."

Dinner was sometime in the early morning hours—scrambled eggs, toast, and more blackberries. Then I brushed my teeth and fell into bed.

THE NEXT DAY, the Senate confirmed Jeff Sessions as attorney general of the United States. Every Republican voted for him.

Once the vote was over, Sessions gave his farewell speech in the Senate while his Republican colleagues surrounded him and applauded.

With Sessions safely sworn in as attorney general, I was free to return to the Senate. There was plenty to do: the next votes were already lined up, and I needed to focus.

Over the next weeks and months we would wrestle with one crisis and another. Afghanistan. North Korea. Russian hacking. Cybersecurity. The firing of FBI Director James Comey. Trump's first budget. Withdrawing from the Paris climate accord. The border wall. A cliff-hanging vote over health care. Charlottesville. Dreamers. Iran. The challenges would keep coming fast and hard.

WHEN I LOOK back, I think of it this way: that night in February wasn't about me. First, it was about Coretta Scott King and her eloquent testimony describing the enduring legacy of racism and hate in America. And as so many events subsequently proved, she was right.

After his confirmation as attorney general, Sessions immediately set to work. He threw his support behind more private prisons to lock up more people. He instructed U.S. attorneys to launch a new war on marijuana and to send more nonviolent drug offenders to prison. He doubled down on President Trump's Muslim ban. He took steps to roll back settlements with police departments designed to reduce violence and protect people's constitutional rights. He gave a thumbs-up to states' attempts to limit voting rights. And, in a crowning moment, Sessions himself delivered the news that President Trump would end the program that allows Dreamers to live, work, and study in the United States. With that announcement, eight hundred thousand young people faced eventual deportation. These young people, who had come to America as children, were about to be ripped away from the only home most of them had ever known.

As the attorney general's actions proved, Trump's nomination of Jeff Sessions was just one more wink-wink, nod-nod signal of support to every white nationalist and Nazi sympathizer who believes that now is the time for the white power movement to help set the course for our nation. Several months later, after deadly violence at a white nationalist rally in Charlottesville, Virginia, President Trump declared there were "very fine people, on both sides," prompting former KKK Grand Wizard David Duke to announce that he was delighted by the presidential statement. Meanwhile, Jeff Sessions staunchly defended the president's appalling remarks. A few months later, when the president stirred up more racial division by telling NFL team owners that they should fire players and throw them out of the game if they protested racial injustice simply by kneeling during the national anthem, Sessions once again jumped to the president's defense.

Yes, that night in February, as the Senate debated the Sessions nomination, was about injustice and racism—and for me, it demonstrated just how much we still need to hear Coretta Scott King's voice. Anyone who thinks the virulent legacy of racism has ended is willfully blind.

But that night in February was about something else as well. It was about every woman who has ever been told to sit down and shut up—and who is damn tired of it.

The words still echo in my head from the presiding officer: *The senator will take her seat.* That's the sort of instruction given to unruly first graders and grown women who have gotten just a little too pushy.

The morning after I was silenced, Senator Tom Udall of New Mexico went to the Senate chamber to speak against the Sessions nomination. Tom is a friend, a very decent man who argues passionately for greater environmental responsibility and pushes hard for the poorest people, Native Americans. With his usual understatement, he asked for recognition from the presiding officer, then began to read Coretta Scott King's letter. No one interrupted him.

Senators Jeff Merkley from Oregon, Sherrod Brown from Ohio, and Bernie Sanders from Vermont all read the letter as well. No one interrupted.

And then the story line began to change.

Nevertheless, she persisted. Women everywhere raised their voices and claimed Mitch McConnell's words as their own. Those words turned up on T-shirts and pink hats. Coffee mugs and tote bags. Decorations for mortar boards at graduation and the title of a new children's book. Women (and friends of women) had found another rallying cry—and they used it to rally.

AND IT DIDN'T stop with rallies. Women are speaking out everywhere. Ever since Donald Trump's election, they have been volunteering, organizing, and running for office in record numbers. 2017 was also the year that women spoke up, one after another after another until their voices were a mighty force and the #metoo movement rocked the world.

Women—and friends of women—have been digging in for a long fight against the Republican effort to tear our democracy apart.

People all across the country have stepped up and said, Count me in. In the space of a few months, organizations that have been working on the front lines for reproductive health, for environmental justice, and for a fighting chance for all of our children have welcomed hundreds of thousands of new members. New organizations have sprung up, meeting in living rooms and church basements from Alaska to Florida. Online organizations have formed, grown, divided, re-formed, and grown some more. People have pitched in $5 here and $20 there and signed up to knock on doors and hold signs, putting momentum behind candidates for public office, both those already in the fight and those ready to jump in and run for the first time. Neighbors and strangers have been welcomed, as people have come together with a common goal to make democracy work again.

In 2017, I held seventeen town halls back home in Massachusetts. People stood in long lines, giving up beautiful afternoons and lovely evenings they might have spent out having fun somewhere else. They crowded into high school and college auditoriums, filling them to capacity and spilling over to cafeterias, classrooms, and sometimes even parking lots outside. At every event, I got the same question: What more can I do?

People understand the urgency of the moment, and they are ready to act.

There are many battles, but none has been more intense than the fight over health care. By the time Donald Trump took office, House Republicans had voted sixty-four times to repeal Obamacare. (Back in 2015, I called a friend in the House and began our conversation with a casual, "What are you all up to?" and he responded, "Repealing Obamacare. That's all we do over here. Just vote over and over to repeal Obamacare.") Senate Republicans had also voted for repeal, and during his campaign Trump had gotten in on the action, promising repeatedly that he would repeal Obamacare "on day one." After Trump's inauguration, with the Republicans firmly in control, it looked like millions of people were on the verge of losing their health care coverage and that the cost of health insurance would go up for millions more.

Put plainly: Democrats didn't have the votes to stop the Republicans. But if we didn't have the votes, we did have one big advantage on our side—all those millions of people who were ready to rewire democracy. People spoke out. Across this country, men and women and even a lot of kids got deeply engaged in the health care fight. They posted stories online. They tweeted, emailed, called, sent letters, and made phone calls. They showed up for rallies and protests and sit-ins. They held signs and held vigils outside senators' home-state offices. They came to Washington by plane, train, bus, car, and even on foot. They brought little babies with complex medical needs, toting oxygen tanks and special feeding equipment. They held up pictures of their grandparents in nursing homes and aunties who were fighting breast cancer. They parked their wheelchairs in the waiting rooms of Republican senators. They got arrested. They made it personal. Most of all, they did not give up.

The Republicans didn't give up either. First in the House and then in the Senate, they kept banging away at Obamacare, trying every trick in the book to destroy one of the most important pieces of legislation in our lifetime. Each plan they offered was worse than the last; each attempt to pass a new version of Trumpcare came closer to succeeding. But the army of resisters held strong, and the final vote to repeal Obamacare failed in the Senate. It looked like health care delivery would survive unscathed.

So the Republicans found another way. They bounced back from their loss over health care repeal to craft a tax bill with one aim: more than $1.4 trillion in giveaways to the richest and most powerful, paid for by pretty much everyone else. The tax bill provided lavish handouts to real estate developers (think Donald Trump), billionaires (think Republican donors like the Koch brothers and the Mercer family), and giant banks (think Wells Fargo, the fake-account bank). And the bonus sweetener used to get those last few Republican votes? Reduce the number of Americans with health care by thirteen million and sharply increase insurance payments for millions more. What Republicans couldn't get done with a straight-up vote on health care, they managed to tuck into their tax bill.

Wow—a tax bill that steals from the poor to give to the rich, and knocks millions of people off health care as an added kicker. It's almost like Republican policymakers had heard something about the gap between the rich and everyone else and said, "We can make it WAY bigger—WAY, WAY bigger!"

So why push this tax bill? It was great for the rich donors—period. The CEOs and billionaires who had given uncounted bushel barrels of money to elect these Republicans wanted their payoff *now*. In fact, as one Republican House member said in a moment of candor, "My donors are basically saying, 'Get it done or don't ever call me again.'" I kid you not.

Republicans justified the tax giveaway by trotting out the stale (and phony) argument that if the rich got richer, they would toss a few crumbs to everyone else. It was plain old trickle-down economics, and they repeated it like a mantra. It didn't matter that the evidence showed it had never worked that way—trickle-down was their story, and they were sticking to it.

But even if this had been the plan, wouldn't a president who had put his name on a book called *The Art of the Deal* strike a bargain to make sure that some of the money actually did trickle down? To give away more than a trillion dollars without extracting a single promise from corporate America—not one single promise to increase a paycheck or build a factory or hire a worker—would be just plain dumb. And it seems even dumber when corporate CEOs were pretty open about their plans for their windfall. One CEO after another went on a quarterly earnings call or answered a pesky reporter's question by patiently explaining that they planned to give any tax bonus to their shareholders and corporate executives. Sheesh. When the tax bill passed, I wondered if a bunch of billionaires had gotten together to break out the French champagne and Russian caviar and toast a Republican majority that helps the wealthy and sticks everyone else with the bill.

But the Republicans aren't through. As long as they control our government, the Republicans could still destroy even more: Social Security, Medicare, Medicaid, the Children's Health Insurance Program, what's left of the private health insurance market, and any other critical piece of America's health care system and our social safety net. They have turned stewardship of our planet over to the oil companies, opening millions of acres for new drilling and mining at the same time that they cut safety regulations. And then there are the cuts to every other way we invest in each other—education, infrastructure, homeownership. Maybe they will have blown it all up by the time you read these pages.

Even so, I'm not giving up—not for a minute. I hang on to the memory of how we beat them back on health care. I hold tight to the vision of the Women's March, the health-care protests, the science rallies, and the outpouring of protests following the Muslim bans. I recall the 2017 elections in Virginia, New Jersey, Washington, and Alabama, and I look forward to the elections coming up in 2018 and again in 2020. And I cling to a critical fact: people matter. When enough people show up and make their voices heard, we *can* make a difference. I know this because I lived it firsthand; I've lived it alongside millions of others who are making their voices heard.

LATE IN THE summer of 2017, I jumped up onstage at a high school in Concord, Massachusetts. The energy in that room was awesome. Fifteen hundred people had shown up, and they were ready to make change.

Before I started speaking, I paused to look out at the crowd, and I felt a deep thrill. I saw it: here, *right here,* was democracy at work.

The questions were smart and thoughtful and sometimes funny. People asked about free speech, transgender people who serve in the military, and how to build an economy that works for everyone. But the question asked more than any other was a variation on "How can I make my voice heard in Washington?"

I gave my best advice, urging everyone to speak out and to keep speaking out again and again. Both onstage and afterwards, I pressed everyone to stay in the game.

Long after the town hall was over, the crowd had thinned out, and the photo line was down to the last dozen or so people, a young couple stepped up. They laughed and talked about how glad they were to be there on that beautiful Friday night. They said they were both committed to the fight. As we put our arms around each other for a picture, the woman paused, glanced down, and said quietly, "Here's what I gave myself for my birthday."

She held up her right arm. On the inside of her wrist in a neat script was a tattoo: *Nevertheless, she persisted.*

And that's what we will do. We will persist. We will persist, resist, insist, and fight every day for the astonishing gift we've inherited from the generations of Americans who came before us: our democracy.

Elizabeth Warren
Cambridge, Massachusetts
February 2018

NOTES

1: THE DISAPPEARING MIDDLE CLASS

7 *The rate was already low:* John Schmitt, "The Minimum Wage Is Too Damn Low," Issue Brief, Center for Economic and Policy Research, March 2012, http://cepr.net /documents/publications/min-wage1-2012-03.pdf.

8 *cannot keep herself and her baby above the poverty line:* In 2016, the federal poverty level was defined as $16,020 in annual income for a family of two. Working forty hours per week, earning the federal minimum wage of $7.25 per hour, a mother would earn only $15,080 each year. Department of Health and Human Services, "Federal Poverty Level (FPL)," https://www.healthcare.gov/glossary/federal-poverty-level-FPL/.

8 *the power to recommend a raise for thirty million Americans:* Raising the minimum wage to $10.10 by July 2015 would have led to higher wages for more than 30 million workers. David Cooper and Doug Hall, "Raising the Federal Minimum Wage to $10.10 Would Give Working Families, and the Overall Economy, a Much-Needed Boost," Briefing Paper, Economic Policy Institute, March 13, 2013, http://www.epi .org/files/2013/IB354-Minimum-wage.pdf.

9 *I'm at the far right end of the horseshoe:* Video posted here: http://www.help.senate.gov /hearings/keeping-up-with-a-changing-economy-indexing-the-minimum-wage.

9 *workers' pay hadn't kept pace with inflation:* If the minimum wage had kept pace with inflation since 1968, it would have been around $9.22–$10.52 per hour in 2012. Schmitt, "The Minimum Wage Is Too Damn Low."

9 *Profits had gone up:* Floyd Norris, "Corporate Profits Grow and Wages Slide," *New York Times*, April 4, 2014, https://www.nytimes.com/2014/04/05/business/economy /corporate-profits-grow-ever-larger-as-slice-of-economy-as-wages-slide.html.

9 *Executives had gotten raises:* Rebecca Hiscott, "CEO Pay Has Increased by 937 Percent Since 1978," *Huffington Post*, June 12, 2014, http://www.huffingtonpost.com/2014 /06/12/ceo-pay-report_n_5484622.html.

9 *and one of the country's leading experts:* Testimony by Professor Arindrajit Dube before the U.S. Senate Committee on Health, Education, Labor and Pensions, March 13, 2013, http://www.help.senate.gov/imo/media/doc/Dube1.pdf.

15   *the country's total wealth is at an all-time high:* Josh Zumbrun, "Americans' Total Wealth Hits Record, According to Federal Reserve Report," *Wall Street Journal*, June 9, 2016, http://www.wsj.com/articles/americans-total-wealth-hits-record-according-to -federal-reserve-report-1465488231.

15   *Adjusted for inflation, the minimum wage today is* lower: In 1965, the minimum wage was $1.25 per hour. That's $9.52 in 2016 dollars. U.S. Department of Labor, "Minimum Wage—U.S. Department of Labor—Chart 1," https://www.dol.gov/featured /minimum-wage/chart1; U.S. Department of Labor, Bureau of Labor Statistics, "CPI Inflation Calculator," https://data.bls.gov/cgi-bin/cpicalc.pl.

15   *two-bedroom apartment anywhere in America:* National Low Income Housing Coalition, "Out of Reach 2016: No Refuge for Low Income Renters," http://nlihc.org/sites /default/files/oor/OOR_2016.pdf.

15   poverty-level income *for her family:* MIT Living Wage Calculator, "Living Wage Calculation for Oklahoma County, Oklahoma," http://livingwage.mit.edu/counties/40109.

16   *opposes a living wage:* Noam Scheiber, "Trump's Labor Pick, Andrew Puzder, Is Critic of Minimum Wage Increases," *New York Times*, December 8, 2016, http:// www.nytimes.com/2016/12/08/us/politics/andrew-puzder-labor-secretary-trump .html; Eric Morath, "Andy Puzder, Donald Trump's Labor Pick, Is a Key Voice Against the 'Fight for $15,'" *Wall Street Journal*, December 9, 2016, http://blogs.wsj .com/economics/2016/12/09/andy-puzder-donald-trumps-labor-pick-is-a-key-voice -against-the-fight-for-15/.

17   *The stock market is up up up:* Adam Shell, "Dow Closes at Record High but Doesn't Top 20,000 Yet," *USA Today*, December 13, 2016, http://www.usatoday.com/story /money/markets/2016/12/13/asian-stocks-mixed-following-wall-street-losses /95365132/; Oliver Renick, "U.S. Stocks Climb to Record Highs as Energy, Tech Shares Rally," *Bloomberg*, December 13, 2016, https://www.bloomberg.com/news /articles/2016-12-13/u-s-index-futures-rise-with-oil-as-market-girds-for-fed-hike; Matt Egan, "Boom: Dow Hits 20,000 for First Time Ever," *CNN Money*, January 25, 2017, http://money.cnn.com/2017/01/25/investing/dow-20000-stocks/.

17   *Corporate profits are breaking new records:* "The Problem with Profits," *Economist*, March 26, 2016, http://www.economist.com/news/leaders/21695392-big-firms-united -states-have-never-had-it-so-good-time-more-competition-problem.

17   *Inflation has remained low for years:* "The Lowdown: Explaining Low Inflation," *Economist*, October 1, 2015, http://www.economist.com/news/united-states/21669952 -persistent-low-inflation-results-more-cheap-oil-and-strong-dollar-lowdown; Federal Reserve Bank of Cleveland, "Recent Inflation Trends," January 14, 2016, https://www.clevelandfed.org/en/newsroom-and-events/publications/economic -trends/2016-economic-trends/et-20160114-recent-inflation-trends.aspx.

17   *double what it was a generation ago:* Federal Reserve Bank of St. Louis, "Real Gross Domestic Product," updated December 22, 2016, https://fred.stlouisfed.org/series /GDPC1.

17   *Unemployment is down:* U.S. Department of Labor, Bureau of Labor Statistics, "Employment Characteristics of Families Summary," April 22, 2016, https://www.bls .gov/news.release/famee.nr0.htm.

17   *Citadel, a prominent hedge fund:* Brian Warner, "How Much Does It Cost to Book Your Favorite Band/Artist for a Private Concert?," Celebrity Net Worth, May 21, 2014, http://www.celebritynetworth.com/articles/celebrity/much-cost-book-favorite-band -private-concert/; "Maroon 5 Performs at Citadel 25th Anniversary Bash," YouTube, November 15, 2015, https://www.youtube.com/watch?v=wZUcGjRcDtQ; "Citadel's 25th Anniversary," YouTube, November 8, 2015, https://www.youtube.com/watch?v =wXur45fnR_Q; Shia Kapos, "Katy Perry Headlines Chicago Bash for Citadel's Anniversary," *Crain's Chicago*, November 9, 2015, http://www.chicagobusiness.com/article /20151109/BLOGS03/151109846/katy-perry-headlines-chicago-bash-for-citadels -anniversary; Lawrence Delevingne, "Katy Perry and Andrea Bocelli; Hedge Funds

Party Despite Losses," Reuters, December 16, 2015, http://www.reuters.com/article/us
-hedgefunds-holidayparties-idUSKBN0TZ33P20151216; Brendan Byrne, "Ken Griffin
Has Katy Perry at Citadel Birthday Party," *ValueWalk*, November 10, 2015, http://www
.valuewalk.com/2015/11/citadel-katy-perry/.

17 *half a century:* U.S. Department of Agriculture, "Official USDA Food Plans: Cost of
Food at Home at Four Levels, U.S. Average, February 2015," https://www.cnpp.usda
.gov/sites/default/files/CostofFoodFeb2015.pdf.

17 *buying a new condo:* E. B. Solomont, "220 CPS Officially Has a $250M Mansion in the
Sky," *Real Deal*, May 5, 2016, http://therealdeal.com/2016/05/05/220-cps-now-officially
-has-a-250m-mansion-in-the-sky-photos/; Robert Frank, "Kenneth Griffin Goes on a
Record-Setting Real Estate Spending Spree," *New York Times*, October 3, 2015, http://
www.nytimes.com/2015/10/04/business/kenneth-griffin-goes-on-a-record-setting
-real-estate-spending-spree.html.

17 *twelve typical American homes:* U.S. Census Bureau, "2013 Housing Profile: United
States, American Housing Survey Factsheets," May 2015, http://www2.census.gov
/programs-surveys/ahs/2013/factsheets/ahs13-1_UnitedStates.pdf.

18 *Chicago and Miami:* "Kenneth Griffin's $300M Residential Spending Spree," *Real
Deal*, October 4, 2015, http://therealdeal.com/2015/10/04/a-look-at-billionaire-kenneth
-griffins-300m-residential-spending-spree/.

20 *smack in the middle:* U.S. Census Bureau, "Historical Income Tables," Table H-11:
Size of Household by Median and Mean Income, September 13, 2016, http://www
.census.gov/data/tables/time-series/demo/income-poverty/historical-income
-households.html.

22 *can't pay their bills on time:* National Foundation for Credit Counseling, "The 2015
Consumer Financial Literacy Survey," April 7, 2015, p. 3, https://www.nfcc.org/wp
-content/uploads/2015/04/NFCC_2015_Financial_Literacy_Survey_FINAL.pdf.

22 *an unexpected expense of $400:* Board of Governors of the Federal Reserve System,
"Report on the Economic Well-Being of U.S. Households in 2015," May 2016, pp. 1,
22, https://www.federalreserve.gov/2015-report-economic-well-being-us-households
-201605.pdf.

22 *in the past half century:* Richard Fry and Anna Brown, "In a Recovering Market, Homeownership Rates Are Down Sharply for Blacks, Young Adults," Pew Research Center,
December 15, 2016, http://www.pewsocialtrends.org/2016/12/15/in-a-recovering
-market-homeownership-rates-are-down-sharply-for-blacks-young-adults.

22 *than his counterpart did in 1972:* U.S. Census Bureau, Table P-2. Race and Hispanic
Origin of People by Median Income and Sex: 1947 to 2015, http://www2.census.gov
/programs-surveys/cps/tables/time-series/historical-income-people/p02.xls.

22 *"struggling to get by" or "just getting by":* Board of Governors of the Federal Reserve
System, "Report on the Economic Well-Being of U.S. Households in 2015," pp. 1, 7.

24 *In 2015, Walmart:* Walmart 2016 Annual Report, pp. 18, 9, http://s2.q4cdn.com
/056532643/files/doc_financials/2016/annual/2016-Annual-Report-PDF.pdf.

24 *the country's four hundred richest people:* "Forbes 400," 2016 ranking, http://www
.forbes.com/forbes-400/list/#version:static; Bernie Sanders, *Our Revolution: A Future
to Believe In* (New York: Thomas Dunne Books, St. Martin's Press, 2016), p. 223;
Thomas Frank, *Listen, Liberal: Or, What Ever Happened to the Party of the People?*
(New York: Metropolitan Books, 2016), p. 3; Sean Gorman, "Bernie Sanders Says
Walmart Heirs Are Wealthier Than Bottom 40 Percent of Americans," PolitiFact,
March 14, 2016, http://www.politifact.com/virginia/statements/2016/mar/14/bernie
-s/bernie-sanders-says-walmart-heirs-are-wealthier-bo/; David De Jong and Tom
Metcalf, "A Wal-Mart Heir Is $27 Billion Poorer Than Everyone Thought," *Bloom-
berg*, November 6, 2015, https://www.bloomberg.com/news/articles/2015-11-06/a-wal
-mart-heir-is-27-billion-poorer-than-everyone-calculated.

24 *Walmart pays such low wages:* Americans for Tax Fairness, "Walmart on Tax Day:
How Taxpayers Subsidize America's Biggest Employer and Richest Family," April

2014, http://americansfortaxfairness.org/files/Walmart-on-Tax-Day-Americans-for-Tax-Fairness-1.pdf.

24   *$1 million in direct subsidies:* Democrats of the House Committee on Education and the Workforce, "Low Wages at a Single Wal-Mart Store Cost Taxpayers About $1 Million Every Year, Says New Committee Staff Report," press release, May 30, 2013, http://democrats-edworkforce.house.gov/media/press-releases/low-wages-at-a-single-wal-mart-store-cost-taxpayers-about-1-million-every-year-says-new-committee-staff-report.

24   *$7 billion in subsidies:* Americans for Tax Fairness, "Walmart on Tax Day."

25   *Walmart the Welfare Queen:* Bernie Sanders rightly argues: "The Walton family has got to get off of welfare." Sanders, *Our Revolution,* p. 223.

25   *$153 billion:* Ken Jacobs, "Americans Are Spending $153 Billion a Year to Subsidize McDonald's and Wal-Mart's Low Wage Workers," *Washington Post,* April 15, 2015, https://www.washingtonpost.com/posteverything/wp/2015/04/15/we-are-spending-153-billion-a-year-to-subsidize-mcdonalds-and-walmarts-low-wage-workers; Ken Jacobs, Ian Perry, and Jenifer MacGillvary, "The High Public Cost of Low Wages: Poverty-Level Wages Cost U.S. Taxpayers $152.8 Billion Each Year in Public Support for Working Families," UC Berkeley Center for Labor Research and Education, April 2015, http://laborcenter.berkeley.edu/pdf/2015/the-high-public-cost-of-low-wages.pdf.

25   *make every public college tuition-free* and *pay for preschool for every child:* Jordan Weissmann, "Here's Exactly How Much the Government Would Have to Spend to Make Public College Tuition-Free," *Atlantic,* January 3, 2014, http://www.theatlantic.com/business/archive/2014/01/heres-exactly-how-much-the-government-would-have-to-spend-to-make-public-college-tuition-free/282803/; Anya Kamenetz, "Clinton's Free-Tuition Promise: What Would It Cost? How Would It Work?," NPR *All Things Considered,* July 28, 2016, http://www.npr.org/sections/ed/2016/07/28/487794394/hillary-s-free-tuition-promise-what-would-it-cost-how-would-it-work; Robert Lynch and Kavya Vaghul, "The Benefits and Costs of Investing in Early Childhood Education," Washington Center for Equitable Growth, December 2, 2015, http://equitablegrowth.org/report/the-benefits-and-costs-of-investing-in-early-childhood-education/.

25   *services for veterans:* U.S. Department of Veterans Affairs, "Care and Benefits for Veterans Strengthened by $169 Billion VA Budget," press release, February 2, 2015, https://www.va.gov/opa/pressrel/pressrelease.cfm?id=2675.

25   *double all federal research and development:* Matt Hourihan and David Parkes, "Federal R&D in the FY 2016 Budget: An Overview," American Association for the Advancement of Science, March 2, 2015, https://www.aaas.org/fy16budget/federal-rd-fy-2016-budget-overview.

25   *double federal spending on transportation and water infrastructure:* Congressional Budget Office, "Public Spending on Transportation and Water Infrastructure, 1956 to 2014," March 2015, https://www.cbo.gov/sites/default/files/114th-congress-2015-2016/reports/49910-Infrastructure.pdf.

25   *"distraction":* J. D. Foster, "A Better Approach Than the Minimum Wage Distraction," U.S. Chamber of Commerce, Above the Fold, January 10, 2014, https://www.uschamber.com/above-the-fold/better-approach-the-minimum-wage-distraction.

25   *"cynical effort":* Sean Hackbarth, "Los Angeles Shows Us the Real Reason Why Unions Are Pushing for Minimum Wage Increases," U.S. Chamber of Commerce, Above the Fold, May 29, 2015, https://www.uschamber.com/above-the-fold/los-angeles-shows-us-the-real-reason-why-unions-are-pushing-minimum-wage-increases.

27   *Walmart deliberately overhires:* Hiroko Tabuchi, "Next Goal for Walmart Workers: More Hours," *New York Times,* February 25, 2015, http://www.nytimes.com/2015/02/26/business/next-goal-for-walmart-workers-more-hours.html.

28   *Today millions of hardworking people:* Ibid.; Lonnie Golden, "Irregular Work Scheduling and Its Consequences," Economic Policy Institute, April 9, 2015, http://www.epi.org/publication/irregular-work-scheduling-and-its-consequences/.

29   *earned back in 1970:* In 2015 constant dollars, the median fully employed male in 1970 was earning $36,346. By 2015, that same median, fully employed male was earning $37,138—a raise of 2 percent over a forty-five-year period. U.S. Census Bureau, "Historical Income Tables; People," Table P-2, September 13, 2016, http://www2.census.gov/programs-surveys/cps/tables/time-series/historical-income-people/p02.xls.

30   *a comparable family did back in 1971:* U.S. Department of Labor, Bureau of Labor Statistics, "Consumer Expenditure Survey, 2015," Table 1400: Size of Consumer Unit: Annual Expenditure Means, Shares, Standard Errors, and Coefficients of Variation, https://www.bls.gov/cex/2015/combined/cusize.pdf; U.S. Department of Labor, Bureau of Labor Statistics, "Consumer Expenditure Survey, 1972–73," Table 2: Selected Family Characteristics, Annual Expenditures, and Sources of Income Classified by Family Size, United States, https://www.bls.gov/cex/1973/Standard/cusize.pdf. Data inflation-adjusted (CPI).

Some people have difficulty believing this. They see out-of-control consumerism being discussed everywhere. Amelia Warren Tyagi and I addressed this "Over-Consumption Myth" in our book, *The Two-Income Trap*, in 2003. As we wrote there, "What the finger-waggers have forgotten are the things families *don't* spend money on anymore" (p. 17).

30   *The problem is that the other expenses:* U.S. Department of Labor, Bureau of Labor Statistics, "Consumer Expenditure Survey, 2015," Table 1400: Size of Consumer Unit; U.S. Department of Labor, Bureau of Labor Statistics, "Consumer Expenditure Survey, 1972–73," Table 2: Selected Family Characteristics. Data on childcare are from Sabino Kornich, assistant professor of sociology, Emory University. Data inflation-adjusted (CPI).

30   *Figure 1:* Data for transportation, shelter, and health insurance compare 1972–73 to 2013. The men's earnings statistic compares 1970 to 2015. U.S. Census Bureau, Table P-2. College data are for in-state tuition and fees at a four-year public university 1971–72 and 2015–16. College Board, "Tuition and Fees and Room and Board over Time," Table 2: Average Tuition and Fees and Room and Board (Enrollment-Weighted) in Current Dollars and in 2016 Dollars, 1971–72 to 2016–17, https://trends.collegeboard.org/college-pricing/figures-tables/tuition-fees-room-and-board-over-time.

31   *sending everyone to work:* Pew Research Center, "The Rise in Dual Income Households," June 18, 2015, http://www.pewresearch.org/ft_dual-income-households-1960-2012-2/.

31   *There were new costs:* Elizabeth Warren and Amelia Warren Tyagi, *The Two-Income Trap: Why Middle-Class Mothers and Fathers Are Going Broke* (New York: Basic Books, 2003). The book was reissued in 2016 with an updated subtitle: *Why Middle-Class Parents Are (Still) Going Broke.*

31   *full-time care for kids under four:* Brigid Schulte and Alieza Durana, "The New America Care Report," *New America Better Life Lab,* September 2016, p. 5, https://na-production.s3.amazonaws.com/documents/FINAL_Care_Report.pdf.

32   *11 percent of their take-home pay in savings:* Federal Reserve Bank of St. Louis, "Personal Saving Rate," https://research.stlouisfed.org/fred2/series/PSAVERT#.

32   *They also had only a sliver:* Board of Governors of the Federal Reserve System, "Consumer Credit—G.19," http://www.federalreserve.gov/releases/g19/HIST/cc_hist_mt_levels.html; U.S. Department of Commerce, Bureau of Economic Analysis, "Disposable Personal Income," http://www.bea.gov/iTable/index_nipa.cfm.

34   *DHL eliminated 14,900 jobs:* Aaron Smith, "DHL to Cut 9,500 U.S. Jobs," *CNN Money,* November 10, 2008, http://money.cnn.com/2008/11/10/news/companies/dhl/?postversion=2008111010.

38   *it discriminated against two hundred thousand black and Latino families:* U.S. Department of Justice, "Justice Department Reaches $335 Million Settlement to Resolve Allegations of Lending Discrimination by Countrywide Financial Corporation," press

release, December 21, 2011, https://www.justice.gov/opa/pr/justice-department-reaches-335-million-settlement-resolve-allegations-lending-discrimination.

39 *People analyzing loan data:* James Rufus Koren, "OneWest Bank Shut Out Nonwhite Borrowers While Owned by Steve Mnuchin-led Group, Advocates Say," *Los Angeles Times*, November 17, 2016, http://www.latimes.com/business/la-fi-onewest-redlining-20161115-story.html.

39 *And in city after city:* Brentin Mock, "Redlining Is Alive and Well—and Evolving," *Citylab*, September 28, 2015, http://www.citylab.com/housing/2015/09/redlining-is-alive-and-well-and-evolving/407497/; Jessica Silver-Greenberg and Michael Corkery, "Evans Bank Settles New York 'Redlining' Lawsuit," *New York Times*, September 10, 2015, https://www.nytimes.com/2015/09/11/business/dealbook/evans-bank-settles-new-york-redlining-lawsuit.html; Emily Badger, "What It Looks Like When a Bank Goes out of Its Way to Avoid Minorities," *Washington Post*, September 25, 2015, https://www.washingtonpost.com/news/wonk/wp/2015/09/25/what-it-looks-like-when-a-bank-structures-its-business-to-avoid-minorities/.

39 *"That told me who was targeted":* Chase, Michael's lender, was sued multiple times for racial discrimination in its mortgage lending program, but none of the lawsuits stuck. "Miami Sues JPMorgan for Racial Discrimination in Mortgage Lending," *Reuters*, June 16, 2014, http://www.nbcnews.com/business/business-news/miami-sues-jpmorgan-racial-discrimination-mortgage-lending-n132291; Andrew Khouri, "L.A. Sues JPMorgan Chase, Alleges Predatory Home Loans to Minorities," *Los Angeles Times*, May 30, 2014, http://www.latimes.com/business/realestate/la-fi-re-jpmorgan-mortgage-lawsuit-20140530-story.html; Aaron Smith, "NAACP Drops Lawsuit Against Wells Fargo," *CNN Money*, April 8, 2010, http://money.cnn.com/2010/04/08/news/companies/wells_fargo_naacp/; Robert Barnes, "High Court to Hear Case on Banks, Lending Practices," *Washington Post*, January 17, 2009, http://www.washingtonpost.com/wp-dyn/content/article/2009/01/16/AR2009011604463.html.

39 *In the wake of the Great Recession:* Rakesh Kochhar, Richard Fry, and Paul Taylor, "Wealth Gaps Rise to Record Highs Between Whites, Blacks, Hispanics," Pew Research Center, July 26, 2011, http://www.pewsocialtrends.org/2011/07/26/wealth-gaps-rise-to-record-highs-between-whites-blacks-hispanics/.

40 *"70 percent more likely to lose their homes":* Renae Merle, "Minorities Hit Harder by Foreclosure Crisis," *Washington Post*, June 19, 2010, http://www.washingtonpost.com/wp-dyn/content/article/2010/06/18/AR2010061802885.html.

40 *more than twice as likely to be turned down for a mortgage:* Brena Swanson, "Zillow: Black and Hispanic Homeowners Denied Mortgages More Often," *HousingWire*, February 9, 2015, http://www.housingwire.com/articles/32882-zillow-black-and-hispanic-homeowners-denied-mortgages-more-often.

40 *hurdles for homeownership are higher for both blacks and Latinos:* Center for Responsible Lending, "The Nation's Housing Finance System Remains Closed to African-American, Hispanic, and Low-Income Consumers Despite Stronger National Economic Recovery in 2015," policy brief, September 2016, http://responsiblelending.org/sites/default/files/nodes/files/research-publication/2015_hmda_policy_brief_2.pdf.

40 *Connecticut real estate firm:* Nora Naughton, "Stamford's Harbor Point Pays $40K in Racial Discrimination Settlement," *Stamford Advocate*, June 24, 2016, http://www.stamfordadvocate.com/local/article/Harbor-Point-agrees-to-40-000-settlement-over-8319198.php.

40 *California apartment complex:* U.S. Department of Housing and Urban Development, "HUD Reaches Agreement with California Landlords Resolving Claims of Discrimination Against Mexican Applicants," press release, March 23, 2016, https://portal.hud.gov/hudportal/HUD?src=/press/press_releases_media_advisories/2016/HUDNo_16-035.

40 *in some of President Trump's apartment buildings:* Jonathan Mahler and Steve Eder, "'No Vacancies' for Blacks: How Donald Trump Got His Start, and Was First Accused of Bias," *New York Times*, August 27, 2016, http://www.nytimes.com/2016/08/28/us /politics/donald-trump-housing-race.html.

40 *destroyed trillions of dollars in family wealth:* Chris Isidore, "America's Lost Trillions," *CNN Money*, June 9, 2011, http://money.cnn.com/2011/06/09/news/economy /household_wealth; National Low Income Housing Coalition, "Report Shows African Americans Lost Half Their Wealth Due to Housing Crisis and Unemployment," August 20, 2013, http://nlihc.org/article/report-shows-african-americans-lost-half -their-wealth-due-housing-crisis-and-unemployment.

40 *American history is littered:* Alexis C. Madrigal, "The Racist Housing Policy That Made Your Neighborhood," *Atlantic*, May 22, 2014, http://www.theatlantic.com /business/archive/2014/05/the-racist-housing-policy-that-made-your-neighborhood /371439/; Fair Housing Center of Greater Boston, "1934–1968: FHA Mortgage Insurance Requirements Utilize Redlining," http://www.bostonfairhousing.org/timeline /1934-1968-FHA-Redlining.html.

41 *criminal justice:* Randall Kennedy, *Race, Crime, and the Law* (New York: Pantheon Books, 1997); Michelle Alexander, *The New Jim Crow: Mass Incarceration in the Age of Colorblindness* (New York: New Press, 2010); Andrew Kahn and Chris Kirk, "What It's Like to Be Black in the Criminal Justice System," *Slate*, August 9, 2015, http://www.slate .com/articles/news_and_politics/crime/2015/08/racial_disparities_in_the_criminal _justice_system_eight_charts_illustrating.html.

41 *employment:* Devah Pager, "The Use of Field Experiments for Studies of Employment Discrimination: Contributions, Critiques, and Directions for the Future," *Annals of the American Academy of Political and Social Sciences* 609, no. 1 (2007): 104–33, http://scholar.harvard.edu/files/pager/files/annals_pager.pdf.

41 *education:* Gillian B. White, "The Data Are Damning: How Race Influences School Funding," *Atlantic*, September 30, 2015, http://www.theatlantic.com/business/archive /2015/09/public-school-funding-and-the-role-of-race/408085/; Jason A. Grissom and Christopher Redding, "Discretion and Disproportionality: Explaining the Underrepresentation of High-Achieving Students of Color in Gifted Programs," *AERA Open* 2, no. 1 (January–March 2016): 1–25, http://news.vanderbilt.edu/files /Grissom_AERAOpen_GiftedStudents1.pdf.

41 *auto lending:* Consumer Financial Protection Bureau, "CFPB and DOJ Reach Resolution with Toyota Motor Credit to Address Loan Pricing Policies with Discriminatory Effects," press release, February 2, 2016, http://www.consumerfinance.gov/about-us /newsroom/cfpb-and-doj-reach-resolution-with-toyota-motor-credit-to-address -loan-pricing-policies-with-discriminatory-effects/.

41 *bankruptcy relief:* Dov Cohen and Robert M. Lawless, "Less Forgiven: Race and Chapter 13 Bankruptcy," chap. 10 in *Broke: How Debt Bankrupts the Middle Class*, ed. Katherine Porter (Stanford, CA: Stanford University Press, 2012).

41 *health care:* Vijay Das and Adam Gaffney, "Racial Injustice Still Rife in Health Care," *CNN*, July 28, 2015, http://www.cnn.com/2015/07/28/opinions/das-gaffney -racial-injustice-health-care/.

41 *stores that sell fresh produce:* Kelly M. Bower, Roland J. Thorpe Jr., Charles Rohde, and Darrell J. Gaskin, "The Intersection of Neighborhood Racial Segregation, Poverty, and Urbanicity and Its Impact on Food Store Availability in the United States," *Preventive Medicine* 58 (January 2014): 33–39, https://www.ncbi.nlm.nih.gov/pmc /articles/PMC3970577/pdf/nihms540300.pdf.

41 *for every dollar earned by whites:* Kenneth J. Cooper, "The Costs of Inequality: Faster Lives, Quicker Deaths," *Harvard Gazette*, March 14, 2016, http://news .harvard.edu/gazette/story/2016/03/the-costs-of-inequality-faster-lives-and -quicker-deaths/.

41 *roughly $11 to $13 for white grads:* Laura Sullivan, Tatjana Meschede, Lars Dietrich, Thomas Shapiro, Amy Traub, Catherine Ruetschlin, and Tamara Draut, "The Racial Wealth Gap: Why Policy Matters," Demos and Brandeis University's Institute for Assets & Social Policy, March 10, 2015, p. 2, http://www.demos.org/sites/default /files/publications/RacialWealthGap_1.pdf.

41 *more likely to be unemployed:* U.S. Department of Labor, Bureau of Labor Statistics, "Employment Situation Summary," January 6, 2017, https://www.bls.gov/news.release /empsit.nr0.htm.

41 *in retirement savings:* Monique Morrissey, "The State of American Retirement," Economic Policy Institute, chart 10, March 3, 2016, http://www.epi.org/publication /retirement-in-america/.

47 *the credential it conferred was useless:* Casey Quinlan, "Why Students Say Their Degrees from The Art Institute Are 'Worthless,' " *ThinkProgress*, May 22, 2015, https:// thinkprogress.org/why-students-say-their-degrees-from-the-art-institute-are -worthless-c346be20d899#.btp5sgtdm.

49 *no diploma to show for it:* Ben Casselman, "The Cost of Dropping Out," *Wall Street Journal*, November 22, 2012, http://www.wsj.com/articles/SB10001424127887324595 90457811740094347206; FINRA, "Financial Capability in the United States 2016," p. 24, http://www.usfinancialcapability.org/downloads/NFCS_2015_Report_Natl _Findings.pdf; Caroline Ratcliffe and Signe-Mary McKernan, "Forever in Your Debt: Who Has Student Loan Debt, and Who's Worried?," Urban Institute, June 2013, Figure 2, http://www.urban.org/sites/default/files/alfresco/publication-pdfs/412849 -Forever-in-Your-Debt-Who-Has-Student-Loan-Debt-and-Who-s-Worried-.PDF; Mary Nguyen, "Degreeless in Debt: What Happens to Borrowers Who Drop Out," *Education Sector*, February 2012, Chart 2, http://educationpolicy.air.org/sites/default /files/publications/DegreelessDebt_CYCT_RELEASE.pdf; Board of Governors of the Federal Reserve System, "Report on the Economic Well-Being of U.S. Households in 2014: Education and Student Loans," Figure 16, http://www.federalreserve.gov /econresdata/2015-economic-well-being-of-us-households-in-2014-education -student-loans.htm#f13r; Christina Chang Wei and Laura Horn, "Federal Student Loan Debt Burden of Noncompleters," U.S. Department of Education, Stats in Brief, April 2013, http://nces.ed.gov/pubs2013/2013155.pdf.

49 *have college diplomas but no jobs:* U.S. Department of Labor, Bureau of Labor Statistics, "The Employment Situation—July 2016," Table A-4, news release, August 5, 2016, http://www.bls.gov/news.release/pdf/empsit.pdf.

50 *one out of every ten people:* College Board, "Trends in College Pricing 2016," Figure 20: Enrollment by Level of Enrollment and Attendance Status over Time, https:// trends.collegeboard.org/college-pricing/figures-tables/enrollment-level-enrollment -and-attendance-status-over-time.

50 *has quadrupled:* College Board, "Trends in College Pricing 2015," p. 17, Table 2A, http://trends.collegeboard.org/sites/default/files/2015-trends-college-pricing-final -508.pdf.

50 *must borrow money to make it to graduation:* Institute for College Access & Success, "Quick Facts About Student Debt," March 2014, http://ticas.org/sites/default/files /pub_files/Debt_Facts_and_Sources.pdf.

50 *$1.4 trillion in student loan debt:* Board of Governors of the Federal Reserve System, "Consumer Credit—G.19," October 2016, https://www.federalreserve.gov/releases/g19 /current/.

51 *The unemployment rate for people sixteen to twenty-four:* U.S. Department of Labor, Bureau of Labor Statistics, "Employment and Unemployment Among Youth Summary," news release, August 18, 2015, http://www.bls.gov/news.release/youth.nr0.htm.

51 *about $100 billion a year:* Board of Governors of the Federal Reserve System, "Student Loans Owned and Securitized, Outstanding," January 9, 2017, https://research .stlouisfed.org/fred2/series/SLOAS.

51   *eighteen and thirty-five live with their parents:* Richard Fry, "For First Time in Modern Era, Living with Parents Edges Out Other Living Arrangements for 18- to 34-Year-Olds," Pew Research Center, Social & Demographic Trends, May 24, 2016, http://www.pewsocialtrends.org/2016/05/24/for-first-time-in-modern-era-living-with-parents-edges-out-other-living-arrangements-for-18-to-34-year-olds/.

51   *will earn more than their parents:* Raj Chetty, David Grusky, Maximilian Hell, Nathaniel Hendren, Robert Manduca, and Jimmy Narang, "The Fading American Dream: Trends in Absolute Income Mobility Since 1940," National Bureau of Economic Research, December 2016, http://www.equality-of-opportunity.org/papers/abs_mobility_paper.pdf.

51   *Despite their better educations:* Josh Boak and Carrie Antlfinger, "Millennials Are Falling Behind Their Boomer Parents," Associated Press, January 13, 2017, http://bigstory.ap.org/article/8b688578bf764d3998cca899a448aa33.

52   *Millions of college graduates:* Jaison R. Abel and Richard Deitz, "Working as a Barista After College Is Not as Common as You Might Think," *Liberty Street Economics* (blog), Federal Reserve Bank of New York, January 11, 2016, http://libertystreeteconomics.newyorkfed.org/2016/01/working-as-a-barista-after-college-is-not-as-common-as-you-might-think.html#.V8ohovkrLIX.

52   *an economy where the most sustained job growth:* Annie Lowrey, "Recovery Has Created Far More Low-Wage Jobs Than Better-Paid Ones," *New York Times*, April 27, 2014, http://www.nytimes.com/2014/04/28/business/economy/recovery-has-created-far-more-low-wage-jobs-than-better-paid-ones.html.

53   *Bankruptcy filings for people sixty-five and over:* Pamela Foohey, Robert M. Lawless, Katherine Porter, and Deborah Thorne, "Graying of U.S. Bankruptcy: Fallout from Life in a Risk Society" (unpublished manuscript); Deborah Thorne, Elizabeth Warren, and Teresa A. Sullivan, "The Increasing Vulnerability of Older Americans: Evidence from the Bankruptcy Court," *Harvard Law & Policy Review* 3, no. 1 (Winter 2009): 87, 95 table 2.

53   *For fifteen million seniors, Social Security:* Center on Budget and Policy Priorities, "Policy Basics: Top Ten Facts About Social Security," August 12, 2016, http://www.cbpp.org/research/social-security/policy-basics-top-ten-facts-about-social-security.

53   *Among seniors who live in nursing homes:* National Center for Health Statistics, "Nursing Home Care," July 6, 2016, https://www.cdc.gov/nchs/fastats/nursing-home-care.htm.

53   *don't have a single dollar put away:* Morrissey, "The State of American Retirement," Retirement Inequality Chartbook, March 3, 2016, http://www.epi.org/publication/retirement-in-america/#chart5.

53   *people are living longer:* U.S. Census Bureau, "2010 Census Shows 65 and Older Population Growing Faster Than Total U.S. Population," November 30, 2011, https://www.census.gov/newsroom/releases/archives/2010_census/cb11-cn192.html.

53   *twenty more years:* Social Security Administration, "Calculators: Life Expectancy," accessed December 31, 2016, https://www.ssa.gov/planners/lifeexpectancy.html.

53   *four years longer than in 1970:* This figure is an average of the growth in life expectancy for men (5.5 years) and women (3.0 years) from 1970 to 2016. Social Security Administration, "Social Security History—Life Expectancy for Social Security," https://www.ssa.gov/history/lifeexpect.html.

53   *more than $82,000 a year:* Genworth, "Compare Long Term Care Costs Across the United States," Annual Costs: National Median (2016), https://www.genworth.com/about-us/industry-expertise/cost-of-care.html.

53   *the costs just keep going up:* Amy Kisling, David P. Paul III, and Alberto Coustasse, "Assisted Living: Trends in Cost and Staffing," paper presented at 2015 Business and Health Administration Association Annual Conference, p. 2, http://mds.marshall.edu/cgi/viewcontent.cgi?article=1137&context=mgmt_faculty.

53   *$25 trillion for retirement:* Investment Company Institute, "Retirement Assets Total $25.0 Trillion in Third Quarter 2016," December 22, 2016, https://www.ici.org/research/stats/retirement/ret_16_q3?WT.mc_id=ret_16_q3.

54   *A handful of CEOs and superstars:* For example, people in the top 20 percent of income are seventeen times more likely to have a 401(k) than people in the bottom 20 percent, and the really big retirement accounts are owned by the top one-tenth of one percent. Morrissey, "The State of American Retirement."

54   *only $18,433 tucked away:* Jack VanDerhei, Sarah Holden, Luis Alonso, Steven Bass, and AnnMarie Pino, "401(k) Plan Asset Allocation, Account Balances, and Loan Activity in 2013," Employee Benefit Research Institute Issue Brief, December 2014, Figure 9, p. 13, https://www.ebri.org/pdf/briefspdf/EBRI_IB_408_Dec14.401(k)-update.pdf.

54   *Zero. Zip:* Morrissey, "The State of American Retirement."

54   *retirement plans that guaranteed benefits for life:* Patrick W. Seburn, "Evolution of Employer-Provided Defined Benefit Pensions," *Monthly Labor Review* 14 (December 1991): 20–21, http://www.bls.gov/mlr/1991/12/art3full.pdf.

54   *down to about 13 percent:* Employee Benefit Research Institute, "FAQs About Benefits—Retirement Issues. What Are the Trends in U.S. Retirement Plans?," https://www.ebri.org/publications/benfaq/index.cfm?fa=retfaq14.

54   *the oldest living American:* After a very full life, she died in July 2016. Reis Thebault, "Goldie Michelson, the Oldest Person in America, Dies at 113," *Boston Globe*, July 9, 2016, https://www.bostonglobe.com/metro/2016/07/09/goldie-michelson-oldest-person-america-dies/BlHCjyS0xCooBFRPnLKudI/story.html.

54   *less than $16,200 a year:* Ke Bin Wu, "Source of Income for Older Americans, 2012," AARP Public Policy Institute Fact Sheet, December 2013, p. 1, http://www.aarp.org/content/dam/aarp/research/public_policy_institute/econ_sec/2013/sources-of-income-for-older-americans-2012-fs-AARP-ppi-econ-sec.pdf.

54   *CEOs got a 3.9 percent raise:* Lawrence Mishel and Alyssa Davis, "Top CEOs Make 300 Times More Than Typical Workers," Economic Policy Institute, June 21, 2015, http://www.epi.org/publication/top-ceos-make-300-times-more-than-workers-pay-growth-surpasses-market-gains-and-the-rest-of-the-0-1-percent.

54   *Hoping to correct that obvious mistake:* Chris Isidore, "Tie Social Security benefits to CEO pay, says Elizabeth Warren," *CNN Money*, November 6, 2015, http://money.cnn.com/2015/11/06/news/economy/social-security-ceo-pay-elizabeth-warren/.

55   *still working after age sixty-five:* Ben Steverman, "'I'll Never Retire': Americans Break Record for Working Past 65," *Bloomberg*, May 13, 2016, https://www.bloomberg.com/news/articles/2016-05-13/-i-ll-never-retire-americans-break-record-for-working-past-65.

55   *the amount of mortgage debt has jumped 82 percent:* Consumer Financial Protection Bureau, Office for Older Americans, "Snapshot of Older Consumers and Mortgage Debt," May 2014, p. 8, http://files.consumerfinance.gov/f/201405_cfpb_snapshot_older-consumers-mortgage-debt.pdf.

55   *Rent is getting higher too:* "Housing America's Older Adults: Meeting the Needs of an Aging Population," Harvard University, Joint Center for Housing Studies, 2014, p. 1, http://www.jchs.harvard.edu/sites/jchs.harvard.edu/files/jchs-housing_americas_older_adults_2014.pdf.

56   *owe more than their homes are worth:* Lori A. Trawinski, "Nightmare on Main Street: Older Americans and the Mortgage Market Crisis," AARP Public Policy Institute Research Report, July 2012, p. 15, http://www.aarp.org/content/dam/aarp/research/public_policy_institute/cons_prot/2012/nightmare-on-main-street-AARP-ppi-cons-prot.pdf.

56   *cover basic expenses by using credit cards:* Amy Traub, "In the Red: Older Americans and Credit Card Debt," AARP and Demos, Middle Class Security Project, 2013, Tables 2–3, pp. 9–10, http://www.demos.org/sites/default/files/publications/older-americans-and-credit-card-debt-AARP-ppi-sec.pdf.

56   *bankruptcy is the only answer:* Foohey, Lawless, Porter, and Thorne, "Graying of U.S. Bankruptcy"; Thorne, Warren, and Sullivan, "The Increasing Vulnerability of Older Americans."

59   *worse off than their parents:* Heather Long, "56% of Americans Think Their Kids Will Be Worse Off," *CNN Money,* January 28, 2016, http://money.cnn.com/2016/01 /28/news/economy/donald-trump-bernie-sanders-us-economy/.

59   *Social Security will completely disappear:* Frank Newport, "Many Americans Doubt They Will Get Social Security Benefits," Gallup, August 13, 2015, http://www.gallup .com/poll/184580/americans-doubt-social-security-benefits.aspx.

59   *"the American economy is rigged to advantage the rich and powerful":* "U.S. Voters Want Leader to End Advantage of Rich and Powerful: Reuters/Ipsos Poll," Reuters, November 8, 2016, http://www.reuters.com/article/us-usa-election-poll-mood-id USKBN1332NC.

59   *"But the system isn't as rigged as you think":* The White House, "Remarks by the President at Commencement Address at Rutgers, the State University of New Jersey," May 15, 2016, https://www.whitehouse.gov/the-press-office/2016/05/15/remarks -president-commencement-address-rutgers-state-university-new.

60   *After vowing to "drain the swamp":* Charlotte Alter and RyanTeague Beckwith, "Draining the Swamp?," *Time,* January 17, 2017, http://time.com/donald-trump -drain-swamp/.

60   *Canada or most of Europe:* Miles Corak, "Economic Mobility," *Pathways* (Special Issue 2016): 51–57, Stanford Center on Poverty and Inequality, http://inequality .stanford.edu/sites/default/files/Pathways-SOTU-2016.pdf.

60   *cut nearly in half over the last generation:* Chetty, Grusky, Hell, et al., "The Fading American Dream."

2: A SAFER ECONOMY

62   *America's boom-and-bust economy:* Choices of dates are a composite of major financial panics, drawn from Charles W. Calomiris and Gary Gorton, "The Origins of Banking Panics: Models, Facts, and Bank Regulation," in *Financial Markets and Financial Crises,* ed. R. Glenn Hubbard, pp. 109–73 (Chicago: University of Chicago Press, 1991), http://aida.econ.yale.edu/~nordhaus/homepage/documents/calomiris _gorton_panic.pdf; and Andrew J. Jalil, "A New History of Banking Panics in the United States, 1825–1929: Construction and Implications," *American Economic Journal: Macroeconomics* 7, no. 3 (July 2015): 295–330, https://www.aeaweb.org/articles ?id=10.1257/mac.20130265.

63   *Thousands of banks failed:* Federal Deposit Insurance Corporation, *The First Fifty Years: A History of the FDIC, 1933–1983* (Washington, DC: FDIC, 1984), p. 36, Table 3-1, https://www.fdic.gov/bank/analytical/firstfifty/chapter3.pdf.

63   *economic downturn tore through people's lives:* William E. Leuchtenburg, *Franklin D. Roosevelt and the New Deal* (New York: Harper & Row, 1963), pp. 1, 3; Adam Cohen, *Nothing to Fear: FDR's Inner Circle and the Hundred Days That Created Modern America* (New York: Penguin Press, 2009), p. 272; Alexander Keyssar, "Unemployment," in *The Reader's Companion to American History,* ed. Eric Foner and John A. Garraty, p. 1095 (Boston: Houghton Mifflin, 1991); T. H. Watkins, *The Hungry Years: A Narrative History of the Great Depression in America* (New York: Henry Holt, 1999); David M. Kennedy, *Freedom from Fear: The American People in Depression and War, 1929–1945* (New York: Oxford University Press, 1999); John Kenneth Galbraith, *The Great Crash, 1929* (New York: Houghton Mifflin Harcourt, 2009).

68   *Federal Deposit Insurance Corporation:* The American Bankers Association vehemently opposed FDIC insurance. Initially Roosevelt also resisted FDIC insurance, but he eventually decided it was inevitable and signed it into law. Leuchtenburg, *Franklin D. Roosevelt and the New Deal,* p. 60; Jean Edward Smith, *FDR* (New York: Random House, 2007), p. 332; Federal Deposit Insurance Corporation, *The First Fifty Years,* pp. 41, 43.

69   *good deal for the U.S. economy:* Federal Deposit Insurance Corporation, *The First Fifty Years*, pp. 3–4, 52, https://www.fdic.gov/bank/analytical/firstfifty/chapter1.pdf and https://www.fdic.gov/bank/analytical/firstfifty/chapter3.pdf.

69   *Glass-Steagall:* "The Glass-Steagall Banking Act of 1933," *Harvard Law Review* 47, no. 2 (December 1933): 325.

70   *the Securities and Exchange Commission:* Franklin D. Roosevelt, "Statement on Signing the Securities Bill," May 27, 1933, http://www.presidency.ucsb.edu/ws/?pid=14654.

71   *Fiercely independent, Arnold was widely respected:* Spencer Weber Waller, *Thurman Arnold: A Biography* (New York: New York University Press, 2005), p. 128.

71   *The turnaround was immediate:* Gary Reback, *Free the Market* (New York: Portfolio, 2009), p. 23; Wilson D. Miscamble, "Thurman Arnold Goes to Washington: A Look at Antitrust Policy in the Later New Deal," *Business History Review* 56, no. 1 (Spring 1982): 5; Richard A. Posner, "A Statistical Study of Antitrust Enforcement," *Journal of Law and Economics* 13, no. 2 (October 1970): 365–66.

71   *"hit them all at once":* Ellis W. Hawley, *The New Deal and the Problem of Monopoly: A Study in Economic Ambivalence* (New York: Fordham University Press, 1995), p. 430.

71   *breaking up these huge corporations:* Gene M. Gressley, "Thurman Arnold, Antitrust, and the New Deal," *Business History Review* 38, no. 2 (Summer 1964), p. 225; Spencer Weber Waller, "The Antitrust Legacy of Thurman Arnold," *St. John's Law Review* 78, no. 3 (2004), pp. 589–90, http://scholarship.law.stjohns.edu/cgi/viewcontent.cgi?article=1297&context=lawreview.

71   *all the way to the Supreme Court:* One of the most famous of these cases involved Alcoa, a firm that had captured the vast majority of the aluminum market. The trial turned out to be the longest in history (up to that time) and Alcoa spent millions of dollars on the case, but the government ultimately won. Alva Johnston, "Thurman Arnold's Biggest Case—I," *New Yorker*, January 24, 1942; Spencer Weber Waller, "The Antitrust Legacy of Thurman Arnold," pp. 591–92.

72   *"Stalin Delano Roosevelt":* Arthur M. Schlesinger, *The Politics of Upheaval, 1935–1936* (Boston: Houghton Mifflin, 2003), 3:329.

72   *substitute "Raw Deal" for "New Deal":* Ralph Young, *Dissent: The History of an American Idea* (New York: New York University Press, 2015), p. 377.

72   *"socialist government":* Robert F. Burk, *The Corporate State and the Broker State: The Du Ponts and American National Politics, 1925–1940* (Cambridge, MA: Harvard University Press, 1990), p. 188.

72   Time *magazine:* "Death of Howe," *Time*, April 27, 1936.

72   *"a thirty-eight-caliber revolver":* Sally Denton, *The Plots Against the President: FDR, a Nation in Crisis, and the Rise of the American Right* (New York: Bloomsbury Press, 2012), p. 158.

72   *In June 1936, Roosevelt went to Philadelphia:* Smith, *FDR*, pp. 366–69; Jefferson Cowie, *The Great Exception: The New Deal and the Limits of American Politics* (Princeton, NJ: Princeton University Press, 2016), pp. 1–4; Franklin D. Roosevelt, "Acceptance Speech for the Renomination for the Presidency, Philadelphia, Pa.," June 27, 1936, http://www.presidency.ucsb.edu/ws/?pid=15314; Jack Beatty, "Conventions in History: The Most Frightful Five Minutes of FDR's Life," WBUR *On Point*, July 8, 2016, http://www.wbur.org/onpoint/2016/07/08/1936-democratic-convention-fdr.

73   *"and I welcome their hatred":* Franklin D. Roosevelt, "Address at Madison Square Garden, New York City," October 31, 1936, http://www.presidency.ucsb.edu/ws/index.php?pid=15219&st=&st1=.

75   *Gross Domestic Product (GDP):* U.S. Department of Commerce, Bureau of Economic Analysis, "GDP & Personal Income," Table 1.1.1. Percent Change from Preceding Period in Real Gross Domestic Product, December 22, 2016, https://www.bea.gov/iTable/index_nipa.cfm.

75   *our families got richer*: Russell Sage Foundation, "Real Mean and Median Income, Families and Individuals, 1947–2012, and Households, 1967–2012," Chartbook of Social Inequality, http://www.russellsage.org/sites/all/files/chartbook/Income%20 and%20Earnings.pdf.

75   *would see his income grow 65 percent*: U.S. Census Bureau, Table P-2. Race and Hispanic Origin of People by Median Income and Sex: 1947 to 2015, www2.census .gov/programs-surveys/cps/tables/time-series/historical-income-people/p02.xls.

76   *Lewis Powell to write a secret memo*: Lewis Powell, "Confidential Memorandum: Attack on the Free Enterprise System," August 23, 1971, http://law2.wlu.edu/powellarchives /page.asp?pageid=1251.

76   *Powell was an unlikely firebrand*: Joan Biskupic and Fred Barbash, "Retired Justice Lewis Powell Dies at 90," *Washington Post*, August 26, 1998, http://www.washingtonpost .com/wp-srv/national/longterm/supcourt/stories/powell082698.htm; Linda Green-house, "Lewis Powell, Crucial Centrist Justice, Dies at 90," *New York Times*, August 26, 1998, http://www.nytimes.com/1998/08/26/us/lewis-powell-crucial-centrist-justice -dies-at-90.html?pagewanted=all; Lewis F. Powell III, "Justice Powell and General Lee's College," *Washington and Lee Law Review* 56, no. 1 (1999): 9–10, http:// scholarlycommons.law.wlu.edu/cgi/viewcontent.cgi?article=1532&context=wlulr.

76   *Powell served on the board of directors*: Jane Mayer, *Dark Money: The Hidden History of the Billionaires Behind the Rise of the Radical Right* (New York: Doubleday, 2016), pp. 72–75.

76   *galvanized his CEO readership*: Moyers and Company, Excerpt from Jacob Hacker and Paul Pierson, *Winner-Take-All Politics: How Washington Made the Rich Richer— and Turned Its Back on the Middle Class* (New York: Simon and Schuster, 2010), September 14, 2012, http://billmoyers.com/content/the-powell-memo-a-call-to-arms-for -corporations/.

78   *"the bottom of the economic pyramid"*: Franklin Delano Roosevelt, "Radio Address from Albany, New York: 'The "Forgotten Man" Speech,'" April 7, 1932, http://www .presidency.ucsb.edu/ws/?pid=88408.

78   *a "Business Advisory Panel" of corporate CEOs*: Kim Phillips-Fein, *Invisible Hands: The Businessmen's Crusade Against the New Deal* (New York: W. W. Norton, 2010), pp. 243–47.

78   *An increasingly subservient Congress*: The Depository Institutions Deregulation and Monetary Control Act, signed into law by President Jimmy Carter in 1980, was a major step in the softening of bank regulation. Elijah Brewer III, "The Depository Institutions Deregulation and Monetary Control Act of 1980," *Economic Perspectives* 4, no. 15 (September 1980), https://www.chicagofed.org/publications/economic-perspectives /1980/sep-oct-brewer-1.

79   *now slowed way down*: Albert A. Foer, "The Federal Antitrust Commitment: Providing Resources to Meet the Challenge," American Antitrust Institute, Table 8, March 23, 1999, http://www.antitrustinstitute.org/files/whitepaper_021120071704 .pdf.

80   *"magic of the marketplace"*: Ronald Reagan, "Remarks at the Annual Meeting of the Boards of Governors of the World Bank Group and International Monetary Fund," September 29, 1981, http://www.presidency.ucsb.edu/ws/?pid=44311.

80   *"unleash" corporations*: Donald J. Trump, "Unleashing America's Prosperity to Create Jobs and Increase Wages," August 8, 2016, https://www.donaldjtrump.com /press-releases/unleashing-americamericas-prosperity-to-create-jobs-and-increase -wages.

80   *picked an Environmental Protection Agency director*: Eric Lipton and Coral Davenport, "Scott Pruitt, Trump's E.P.A. Pick, Backed Industry Donors Over Regulators," *New York Times*, January 14, 2017, https://www.nytimes.com/2017/01/14/us/scott -pruitt-trump-epa-pick.html.

80 *a Secretary of Labor opposed to rules:* Melanie Trottman, Julie Jargon, and Michael C. Bender, "Trump Picks Fast-Food Executive Andy Puzder as Nominee for Labor Secretary," *Wall Street Journal*, December 8, 2016, https://www.wsj.com/articles/trump -expected-to-name-fast-food-executive-andy-puzder-as-labor-secretary -1481210445.

80 *"the lowering of the taxes":* Aaron Blake, "Everything That Was Said at the Second Donald Trump vs. Hillary Clinton Debate, Highlighted," *Washington Post*, October 9, 2016, https://www.washingtonpost.com/news/the-fix/wp/2016/10/09/everything-that-was -said-at-the-second-donald-trump-vs-hillary-clinton-debate-highlighted/.

81 *risky new financial instruments:* Nelson D. Schwartz and Julie Creswell, "What Created This Monster?," *New York Times*, March 23, 2008, http://www.nytimes.com /2008/03/23/business/23how.html.

82 *the S&Ls jumped 50 percent:* Kenneth J. Robinson, "Savings and Loan Crisis," November 22, 2013, Federal Reserve Bank of Richmond, Federal Reserve History, http://www.federalreservehistory.org/Events/DetailView/42; FDIC, "History of the 80s," vol. 1, "An Examination of the Banking Crises of the 1980s and Early 1990s," ch. 4, "The Savings and Loan Crisis and Its Relationship to Banking," 1997, https:// www.fdic.gov/bank/historical/history/vol1.html.

82 *prosecuted more than a thousand bank executives:* Timothy Curry and Lynn Shibut, "The Cost of the Savings and Loan Crisis: Truth and Consequences," *FDIC Banking Review* 13, no. 2 (2000): 26–35, https://www.fdic.gov/bank/analytical/banking/2000dec /brv13n2_2.pdf; Kitty Calavita, *Big Money Crime: Fraud and Politics in the Savings and Loan Crisis* (Berkeley: University of California Press, 1997), p. 131.

82 *when the last S&L was shuttered:* U.S. General Accounting Office, "Financial Audit: Resolution Trust Corporation's 1995 and 1994 Financial Statements," July 1996, www.gao.gov/archive/1996/ai96123.pdf.

82 *education, job training, veterans' benefits, social services, and transportation:* Karl Galbraith, "Federal Budget Estimates, Fiscal Year 1995," Bureau of Economic Analysis, February 1994, https://bea.gov/scb/pdf/national/niparel/1994/0294gd.pdf.

83 *the few remaining provisions of Glass-Steagall were repealed:* James Lardner, "A Brief History of the Glass-Steagall Act," Demos, November 10, 2009, http://www.demos .org/publication/brief-history-glass-steagall-act.

83 *The results were immediate:* Hubert P. Janicki and Edward Simpson Prescott, "Changes in the Size Distribution of U.S. Banks: 1960–2005," *Economic Quarterly* 92, no. 4 (Fall 2006): 291–316, https://www.richmondfed.org/~/media/richmondfedorg/publications /research/economic_quarterly/2006/fall/pdf/janicki_prescott.pdf. For a chart showing the consolidation, see Jeff Desjardins, "The Making of the 'Big Four' Banking Oligopoly in One Chart," *Visual Capitalist*, January 25, 2016, http://www.visualcapitalist.com/the -banking-oligopoly-in-one-chart/.

83 *By 2008, just five uber-banks:* Steve Schaefer, "Five Biggest U.S. Banks Control Nearly Half Industry's $15 Trillion in Assets," *Forbes*, December 3, 2014, http://www.forbes. com/sites/steveschaefer/2014/12/03/five-biggest-banks-trillion-jpmorgan-citi- bankamerica/#2694071a1d43.

83 *change the law after the fact:* Lardner, "A Brief History of the Glass-Steagall Act."

84 *even more profitable:* FDIC, "Annual Financial Data—Commercial Bank Reports— CB04: Net Income, 1934–2015," https://www5.fdic.gov/hsob/SelectRpt.asp?EntryTyp =10&Header=1.

84 *As he signed the repeal of Glass-Steagall:* U.S. Department of the Treasury, "Statement by President Bill Clinton at the Signing of the Financial Modernization Bill," November 12, 1999, https://www.treasury.gov/press-center/press-releases/Pages/ls241.aspx.

84 *Credit card agreements:* Mitchell Pacelle, "Growing Profit Source for Banks: Fees from Riskiest Card Holders," *Wall Street Journal*, July 6, 2004, http://www.wsj.com /articles/SB108907380815455722.

84   *incomprehensible terms:* Joseph S. Enoch, "Senate Panel Slams Abusive Credit Card Practices," *Consumer Affairs*, March 7, 2007, https://www.consumeraffairs.com/news04/2007/03/senate_credit_cards02.html.

84   *tens of billions of dollars in profits:* Tamara Draut and Javier Silva, "Borrowing to Make Ends Meet: The Growth of Credit Card Debt in the '90s," Demos, September 2003, www.demos.org/sites/default/files/publications/borrowing_to_make_ends_meet.pdf.

87   *the SEC chair said:* Time after time, the SEC looked the other way as all kinds of financial firms loaded up on risks. Stephen Labaton, "S.E.C. Concedes Oversight Flaws Fueled Collapse," *New York Times*, September 26, 2008, http://www.nytimes.com/2008/09/27/business/27sec.html.

87   *"handcuffed":* Amit R. Paley and David S. Hilzenrath, "SEC Chair Defends His Restraint During Financial Crisis," *Washington Post*, December 24, 2008, http://www.washingtonpost.com/wp-dyn/content/article/2008/12/23/AR2008122302765.html.

87   *lasted years, maybe even decades:* Charles Riley, "Prosecutors: Madoff Fraud Started in 1970s," *CNN Money*, October 2, 2012, http://money.cnn.com/2012/10/01/investing/madoff-fraud/.

87   *lost more than $17 billion:* Jacqueline Palank, "Bernard Madoff Investors to Receive Another Payout," *Wall Street Journal*, June 16, 2016, http://blogs.wsj.com/bankruptcy/2016/06/16/bernard-madoff-investors-to-receive-another-payout/.

87   *willfully blind:* Zachary A. Goldfarb, "The Madoff Files: A Chronicle of SEC Failure," *Washington Post*, September 3, 2009, http://www.washingtonpost.com/wp-dyn/content/article/2009/09/02/AR2009090203851.html.

87   *as journalist Matt Taibbi put it:* Matt Taibbi, "Why Didn't the SEC Catch Madoff? It Might Have Been Policy Not To," *Rolling Stone*, May 31, 2013, http://www.rollingstone.com/politics/news/why-didnt-the-sec-catch-madoff-it-might-have-been-policy-not-to-20130531.

88   *major U.S. airlines:* Associated Press, "Airline Consolidation Has Created Airport Monopolies, Increased Fares," *Denver Post*, July 17, 2015, http://www.denverpost.com/business/ci_28501683/airline-consolidation-has-created-airport-monopolies-increased-fares.

88   *80 percent of all domestic airline seats:* Jack Nicas, "Airline Consolidation Hits Smaller Cities Hardest," *Wall Street Journal*, September 10, 2015, http://www.wsj.com/articles/airline-consolidation-hits-smaller-cities-hardest-1441912457#:M1ZMKtAVWk5eBA.

88   *Two beer companies:* Haley Sweetland Edwards, "The Bubbling Concern Over Two Beer Giants' Blockbuster Merger," *Time*, July 26, 2016, http://time.com/4422937/beer-merger-budweiser-miller-coors/; Anjali Athavaley and Lauren Hirsch, "Mega Beer Deal Offers Molson Coors a Bigger Swig of U.S. Market," *Reuters*, October 13, 2015, http://www.reuters.com/article/us-sabmiller-m-a-abi-molson-idUSKCN0S72XQ20151013.

88   *83 percent of the country's health insurance market:* David McLaughlin, "Health Insurer Deals Face Market Review That Felled Past Tie-Ups," *Bloomberg*, May 23, 2016, http://www.bloomberg.com/news/articles/2016-05-23/health-insurer-deals-face-market-review-that-felled-past-tie-ups.

88   *CVS, Walgreens, and Rite Aid:* Nathan Bomey, "Walgreens in $17.2B Deal to Acquire Rite Aid," *USA Today*, October 28, 2015, http://www.usatoday.com/story/money/2015/10/27/walgreens-rite-aid/74684642/.

88   *Monsanto:* Peter Whoriskey, "Monsanto's Dominance Draws Antitrust Inquiry," *Washington Post*, November 29, 2009, http://www.washingtonpost.com/wp-dyn/content/article/2009/11/28/AR2009112802471.html; Dan Mitchell, "Why Monsanto Always Wins," *Fortune*, June 27, 2014, http://fortune.com/2014/06/26/monsanto-gmo-crops/; Antonio Regalado, "As Patents Expire, Farmers Plant Generic GMOs," *MIT*

Technology Review, July 30, 2015, https://www.technologyreview.com/s/539746/as
-patents-expire-farmers-plant-generic-gmos/.

88   *85 percent of the U.S. beef market:* Christopher Leonard, *The Meat Racket: The Secret Takeover of America's Food Business* (New York: Simon & Schuster, 2014), p. 208.

88   *half of all chickens:* Christopher Leonard, "How the Meat Industry Keeps Chicken Prices High," *Slate*, March 3, 2014, http://www.slate.com/articles/life/food/2014/03 /meat_racket_excerpt_how_tyson_keeps_chicken_prices_high.html.

89   *Tyson Foods:* Ibid.

89   *In Massachusetts, nearly two out of three towns:* Massachusetts Office of Consumer Affairs & Business Regulation, "Communities That Have Granted a License to More Than One Cable Operator," http://www.mass.gov/ocabr/government/oca-agencies /dtc-lp/competition-division/cable-tv-division/statistics-and-general-info/license -to-more-than-one-cable-operator.html; Massachusetts Office of Consumer Affairs & Business Regulation, "Competition in the Cable Television Market," http://www .mass.gov/ocabr/government/oca-agencies/dtc-lp/competition-division/cable-tv -division/consumer-rights-fact-sheets/consumer-rights-fact-sheets/competition-in -cable-tv.html.

89   *That's why I fought the merger:* Todd Shields, "Warren Among Six Senators Seeking to Stop Comcast-TWC Deal," *Bloomberg*, April 21, 2015, https://www.bloomberg .com/news/articles/2015-04-21/senators-ask-regulators-to-block-comcast-time -warner-cable-deal.

90   *big banks began building:* Board of Governors of the Federal Reserve System, "Consumer Credit—G.19—Consumer Credit Historical Data," January 9, 2017, https:// www.federalreserve.gov/releases/g19/hist/.

90   *They boosted profits:* Edmund Sanders, "Advertising & Marketing; Charges Are Flying over Card Pitches; As Banks Offer Increasingly Attractive Credit Deals, Their Tactics Are Being Challenged in a Rash of Lawsuits and Government Warnings," *Los Angeles Times*, June 15, 1999; "Credit-Card Companies Can't Tinker with the Rules," *Atlanta Journal-Constitution*, editorial, March 5, 1999; "Secret History of the Credit Card: Interview: Elizabeth Warren," PBS *Frontline*, November 23, 2004, http://www.pbs.org /wgbh/pages/frontline/shows/credit/interviews/warren.html.

90   *Family bankruptcies shot up:* Thomas A. Garrett, "100 Years of Bankruptcy: Why More Americans Than Ever Are Filing," Federal Reserve Bank of St. Louis, Spring 2006, https://www.stlouisfed.org/publications/bridges/spring-2006/100-years-of -bankruptcy-why-more-americans-than-ever-are-filing; Robin Greenwood and David Scharfstein, "The Growth of Finance," *Journal of Economic Perspectives* 27, no. 2 (Spring 2013): 3–28, www.people.hbs.edu/dscharfstein/Growth_of_Finance _JEP.pdf.

90   *and go after home mortgages?:* Financial Crisis Inquiry Commission, "The Financial Crisis Inquiry Report: Final Report of the National Commission on the Causes of the Financial and Economic Crisis in the United States," January 2011, https://www .gpo.gov/fdsys/pkg/GPO-FCIC/pdf/GPO-FCIC.pdf.

90   *This time financial firms packaged:* Ibid.

90   *The bank regulators knew:* Zachary A. Goldfarb and Brady Dennis, "Government Report Blames Regulators and Financial Institutions for Economic Crisis," *Washington Post*, January 27, 2011, http://www.washingtonpost.com/wp-dyn/content /article/2011/01/27/AR2011012702940.html.

91   *twenty-six million people couldn't find a full-time job:* Financial Crisis Inquiry Commission, "The Financial Crisis Inquiry Report," p. xv.

91   *nine million people lost their homes:* Laura Kusisto, "Many Who Lost Homes to Foreclosure in Last Decade Won't Return—NAR," *Wall Street Journal*, April 20, 2015, http://www.wsj.com/articles/many-who-lost-homes-to-foreclosure-in-last-decade -wont-return-nar-1429548640.

91   *businesses were shuttered:* U.S. Department of Labor, Bureau of Labor Statistics, "The Recession of 2007–2009," February 2012, https://www.bls.gov/spotlight/2012/recession/; Small Business Association, Office of Advocacy, "Frequently Asked Questions About Small Business," September 2012, https://www.sba.gov/sites/default/files/FAQ_Sept_2012.pdf.

91   *Entrepreneurship plummeted:* Jim Clifton, "American Entrepreneurship: Dead or Alive?," Gallup, January 13, 2015, http://www.gallup.com/businessjournal/180431/american-entrepreneurship-dead-alive.aspx; U.S. Department of Labor, Bureau of Labor Statistics, "Entrepreneurship and the U.S. Economy," April 28, 2016, https://www.bls.gov/bdm/entrepreneurship/entrepreneurship.htm.

91   *College students hit graduation:* Thomas Luke Spreen, "Recent College Graduates in the U.S. Labor Force: Data from the Current Population Survey," *Monthly Labor Review* 136, no. 2 (February 2013): 8–9, https://www.bls.gov/opub/mlr/2013/02/art1full.pdf.

91   *an even bleaker future:* Shaila Dewan, "Frayed Prospects, Despite a Degree," *New York Times*, July 19, 2013, http://www.nytimes.com/2013/07/20/business/recent-graduates-lose-out-to-those-with-even-fresher-degrees.html.

91   *Retirement savings took a nosedive:* Theresa Ghilarducci, "The Recession Hurt Americans' Retirement Accounts More Than Anybody Knew," *Atlantic*, October 16, 2015, http://www.theatlantic.com/business/archive/2015/10/the-recession-hurt-americans-retirement-accounts-more-than-everyone-thought/410791/.

91   *Thousands of suicides:* Aaron Reeves, Martin McKee, and David Stuckler, "Economic Suicides in the Great Recession in Europe and North America," *British Journal of Psychiatry* 210, no. 1 (June 2014), http://bjp.rcpsych.org/content/bjprcpsych/early/2014/05/23/bjp.bp.114.144766.full.pdf.

91   *$22 trillion:* This is the sum of $13 trillion in lost economic output, and $9.1 trillion in home equity losses. U.S. Government Accountability Office, "Financial Regulatory Reform: Financial Crisis Losses and Potential Impacts of the Dodd-Frank Act," January 16, 2013, pp. 17, 21, http://www.gao.gov/assets/660/651322.pdf; Eleazar David Melendez, "Financial Crisis Cost Tops $22 Trillion, GAO Says," *Huffington Post*, February 14, 2013, http://www.huffingtonpost.com/2013/02/14/financial-crisis-cost-gao_n_2687553.html.

91   *"Washington and the regulators are there to serve the banks":* Mary Orndorff Troyan, "Spencer Bachus Finally Gets His Chairmanship," *Birmingham News*, December 9, 2010, http://blog.al.com/sweethome/2010/12/spencer_bachus_finally_gets_hi.html.

93   *"made it impossible for bankers to function":* Emily Flitter and Steve Holland, "Trump preparing plan to dismantle Obama's Wall Street reform law," *Reuters*, May 18, 2016, http://www.reuters.com/article/us-usa-election-trump-banks-idUSKCN0Y900J.

93   *Republicans like Newt Gingrich say:* Newt Gingrich, talk at the Heritage Foundation, December 13, 2016, video available at http://www.heritage.org/events/2016/12/gingrich.

93   *My first cosponsor:* Dan Merica, "Warren Pushes for Return of Glass-Steagall After Clinton Adviser Says She Won't Back Measure," CNN, July 15, 2015, http://www.cnn.com/2015/07/15/politics/elizabeth-warren-hillary-clinton-glass-steagall/.

93   *added to the Republican platform:* Peter Schroeder, "GOP Platform to Call for Return to Glass-Steagall," *Hill*, July 18, 2016, http://thehill.com/policy/finance/288148-gop-platform-to-call-for-return-to-glass-steagall.

94   *"malfeasance, incompetence, complacency":* Rana Foroohar, "The Financial World's Rotten Culture Is Still a Threat—to All of Us," *Time*, October 13, 2016, http://time.com/4529456/the-financial-worlds-rotten-culture-is-still-a-threat-to-all-of-us/.

95   *Deutsche Bank:* Landon Thomas Jr., "Deutsche Bank Singled Out in I.M.F. Stability Warning," *New York Times*, October 5, 2016, http://www.nytimes.com/2016/10/06/business/dealbook/deutsche-bank-singled-out-in-imf-stability-warning.html.

95   *Wells Fargo was caught:* Consumer Financial Protection Bureau, "Consumer Financial Protection Bureau Fines Wells Fargo $100 Million for Widespread Illegal Practice of Secretly Opening Unauthorized Accounts," press release, September 8, 2016, http://www.consumerfinance.gov/about-us/newsroom/consumer-financial -protection-bureau-fines-wells-fargo-100-million-widespread-illegal-practice -secretly-opening-unauthorized-accounts/.

95   *And Citigroup:* Aruna Viswanatha, "Citibank to Pay $425 Million to Settle Benchmark Probes," *Wall Street Journal,* May 25, 2016, http://www.wsj.com/articles /citibank-to-pay-425-million-to-settle-cases-over-alleged-benchmark-manipulation -1464182888.

95   *The Federal Reserve Bank and the FDIC:* Michael Corkery, "Wells Fargo's 'Living Will' Plan Is Rejected Again by Regulators," *New York Times,* December 13, 2016, http://www .nytimes.com/2016/12/13/business/dealbook/wells-fargo-regulators.html.

95   *in 2016, the big banks are not significantly safer:* Natasha Sarin and Lawrence H. Summers, "Have Big Banks Gotten Safer?" Brookings Papers on Economic Activity, September 2016, https://www.brookings.edu/wp-content/uploads/2016/09/2 _sarinsummers.pdf.

3: MAKING—AND BREAKING—THE MIDDLE CLASS

99   *what we owed to each other:* The Social Security Act of 1935, H.R. 7260, 74th Congress (1935), https://www.ssa.gov/history/35act.html.

100   *a new social contract:* William E. Leuchtenburg, *Franklin D. Roosevelt and the New Deal* (New York: Harper & Row, 1963), pp. 132–33.

100   *In the 1950s and 1960s:* Patricia J. Gumport, Maria Iannozzi, Susan Shaman, and Robert Zemsky, "Trends in United States Higher Education from Massification to Post-Massification," National Center for Postsecondary Improvement, 1997, http:// web.stanford.edu/group/ncpi/documents/pdfs/1-04_massification.pdf.

100   *new elementary and high schools:* States' Impact on Federal Education Policy Project, "Federal Education Policy and the States, 1945–2009: A Brief Synopsis," November 2009, p. 45, http://www.archives.nysed.gov/common/archives /files/ed_background_overview_essay.pdf.

100   *The impact was immediate:* Thomas D. Snyder, ed., "120 Years of American Education: A Statistical Portrait," U.S. Department of Education, Office of Educational Research and Improvement, National Center for Education Statistics, January 1993, pp. 26, 65, 67–68, https://nces.ed.gov/pubs93/93442.pdf.

101   *funding basic research:* Farhad Manjoo, "Obama Was Right: The Government Invented the Internet," *Slate,* July 24, 2012, http://www.slate.com/articles/technology /technology/2012/07/who_invented_the_internet_the_outrageous_conservative _claim_that_every_tech_innovation_came_from_private_enterprise_.html; Thomas Levenson, "Let's Waste More Money on Science," *Boston Globe,* December 11, 2016, https://www.bostonglobe.com/ideas/2016/12/11/let-waste-more-money-science /afvbusk8G5T5IcrgldkmJJ/story.html; National Institutes of Health, National Cancer Institute, "NCI's Role in Cancer Research," March 19, 2015, https://www.cancer .gov/research/nci-role.

101   *to do truly remarkable things:* Research of every kind—medical, scientific, engineering, psychology, social science—was honored and supported. In the 1930s, medical research became a federal priority through the National Institutes of Health. In the 1940s, the National Science Foundation expanded research funding in all directions. In 1958, a new research initiative—commonly known today by its acronym, DARPA— was located in the Department of Defense to expand the frontiers of technology beyond immediate military needs. The same year, Congress set up NASA to explore space. National Institutes of Health, "A Short History of the National Institutes of Health, WWI and the Ransdell Act of 1930," https://history.nih.gov/exhibits/history

/docs/page_04.html; National Science Foundation, "A Timeline of NSF History," https://www.nsf.gov/about/history/overview-50.jsp; Defense Advanced Research Projects Agency, "History and Timeline," http://www.darpa.mil/about-us/timeline/where-the-future-becomes-now.

102   *union membership had been cut almost in half:* Irving Bernstein, *The Lean Years: A History of the American Worker, 1920–1933* (Chicago: Haymarket Books, 2010), pp. 84, 335.

102   *During his first term, he pushed through laws:* The National Industrial Recovery Act. See Craig Phelan, *William Green: Biography of a Labor Leader* (Albany: State University of New York Press, 1989), pp. 64–66.

102   *"If I were a factory worker":* Nelson Lichtenstein, *The Most Dangerous Man in Detroit: Walter Reuther and the Fate of American Labor* (New York: Basic Books, 1995), p. 61.

102   *unions joined other groups:* The Fair Labor Standards Act of 1938.

103   *Union membership rose dramatically:* Will Kimball and Lawrence Mishel, "Unions' Decline and the Rise of the Top 10 Percent's Share of Income," Economic Policy Institute, Economic Snapshot, February 3, 2015, http://www.epi.org/publication/unions-decline-and-the-rise-of-the-top-10-percents-share-of-income/; Claude S. Fischer and Michael Hout, *Century of Difference: How America Changed in the Last One Hundred Years* (New York: Russell Sage Foundation, 2006), Figure 5.8, https://www.russellsage.org/sites/all/files/Fischer_Hout_Tables%20Figures.pdf.

103   *a greater share of the wealth:* Kimball and Mishel, "Unions' Decline and the Rise of the Top 10 Percent's Share of Income."

104   all *workers did better:* Matthew Walters and Lawrence Mishel, "How Unions Help All Workers," Economic Policy Institute, August 26, 2003, http://www.epi.org/publication/briefingpapers_bp143/.

104   *IBM:* Years later, IBM was still successfully avoiding unionization. Patrick Thibodeau, "IBM Union Calls It Quits," Computerworld, January 5, 2016, http://www.computerworld.com/article/3019552/it-industry/ibm-union-calls-it-quits.html.

105   *increased his earnings by about 65 percent:* U.S. Census Bureau, Table P-2. Race and Hispanic Origin of People by Median Income and Sex: 1947 to 2015, www2.census.gov/programs-surveys/cps/tables/time-series/historical-income-people/p02.xls.

105   *From 1935 to 1980:* Thomas Piketty and Emmanuel Saez, "Income Inequality in the United States, 1931–2002," later updated with Anthony B. Atkinson (November 2004), http://eml.berkeley.edu/~saez/pikettysaezOUP04US.pdf, updated tables at http://eml.berkeley.edu/~saez/TabFig2015prel.xls; Economic Policy Institute, "When Income Grows, Who Gains?," http://stateofworkingamerica.org/who-gains/.

106   *people at* every *income level:* Ibid.

106   *In fact, incomes were growing:* Pew Research Center, "The Lost Decade of the Middle Class," August 22, 2012, p. 9, http://www.pewsocialtrends.org/files/2012/08/pew-social-trends-lost-decade-of-the-middle-class.pdf.

107   *excluded from Social Security:* Ira Katznelson, *When Affirmative Action Was White: An Untold History of Racial Inequality in Twentieth-Century America* (New York: W. W. Norton, 2005), p. 22.

107   *black-white wealth gap:* Urban Institute, "Nine Charts About Wealth Inequality in America," February 2015, http://apps.urban.org/features/wealth-inequality-charts/; Henry S. Terrell, "Wealth Accumulation of Black and White Families: The Empirical Evidence," *Journal of Finance* 26, no. 2 (May 1971): 363–77; Francine D. Blau and John W. Graham, "Black-White Differences in Wealth and Asset Composition," *Quarterly Journal of Economics* 105, no. 2 (May 1990): 321–39.

111   *Rutgers, a public law school that cost $460:* Tami Luhby, "Could Elizabeth Warren Have Made It in Today's America?," *CNN Money*, June 9, 2014, http://money.cnn.com/2014/06/09/news/economy/elizabeth-warren/.

112   *a new section of the interstate highway:* West Orange Photo Galleries, "I-280 Construction Train: 1970s," http://www.westorangehistory.com/i-280_construction_train.html; AARoads, "Interstate 280," http://www.aaroads.com/guide.php?page=i0280nj.

114   *"voodoo economics"*: George H. W. Bush, Speech at Carnegie Mellon University, April 10, 1980, http://archives.nbclearn.com/portal/site/k-12/flatview?cuecard=33292.

114   *study after careful study*: Jane G. Gravelle and Donald J. Marples, "Tax Rates and Economic Growth," Congressional Research Service, January 2, 2014, https://fas.org/sgp /crs/misc/R42111.pdf; Jerry Tempalski, "Revenue Effects of Major Tax Bills: Updated Tables for All 2012 Bills," U.S. Department of the Treasury, Office of Tax Analysis, Table 2, February 2013, https://www.treasury.gov/resource-center/tax-policy/tax -analysis/Documents/WP81-Table2013.pdf; Michael Ettlinger and Michael Linden, "The Failure of Supply-Side Economics," Center for American Progress, August 1, 2012, https://www.americanprogress.org/issues/economy/news/2012/08/01/11998/the -failure-of-supply-side-economics/; Nouriel Roubini, "Supply Side Economics: Do Tax Rate Cuts Increase Growth and Revenues and Reduce Budget Deficits? Or Is It Voodoo Economics All Over Again?," 1997, http://people.stern.nyu.edu/nroubini/SUPPLY .HTM; Paul Krugman, *Peddling Prosperity: Economic Sense and Nonsense in an Age of Diminished Expectations* (New York: W. W. Norton, 1994).

114   *Reagan slashed rates across the board:* Economic Recovery Tax Act of 1981, H.R. 4242, 97th Congress, 1981, https://www.congress.gov/bill/97th-congress/house-bill /4242.

114   *Donald Trump, for one:* Richard Rubin, "Donald Trump Got a Big Break on 2005 Taxes," *Wall Street Journal*, March 17, 2016, http://www.wsj.com/articles/donald -trump-got-a-big-break-on-2005-taxes-1458249902.

115   *investing overseas:* James Kvaal, "Removing Tax Subsidies for Foreign Investment," *Tax Notes*, June 12, 2006, https://cdn.americanprogress.org/wp-content/uploads/kf /TAXNOTESKVAAL.PDF.

115   *In 2015, the* New York Times *reported:* Patricia Cohen, "When Company Is Fined, Taxpayers Often Share Bill," *New York Times*, February 3, 2015, https://www.nytimes .com/2015/02/04/business/when-a-company-is-fined-taxpayers-often-share-the -punishment.html.

116   *a collective $2.3 trillion overseas:* Credit Suisse, "Parking A-Lot Overseas," March 17, 2015, Exhibit 5, p. 8, http://bit.ly/1dzsUSj.

116   *average federal income taxes run about 3 percent:* Gabriel Zucman, "Taxing Across Borders: Tracking Personal Wealth and Corporate Profits," *Journal of Economic Perspectives* 28, no. 4 (Fall 2014), Figure 2, p. 128, http://gabriel-zucman.eu/files /Zucman2014JEP.pdf. And even if the income from non–tax haven foreign subsidiaries is added in, Fortune 500 companies are still only paying a 6–10 percent average effective tax rate on the $2.1 trillion in profits that are offshore. Credit Suisse, "Parking A-Lot Overseas," p. 4; Kimberly A. Clausing, "The Nature and Practice of Capital Tax Competition," in Peter Dietsch and Thomas Rixen, eds., *Global Tax Governance: What Is Wrong with It and How to Fix It* (Colchester, UK: ECPR Press, 2016); Citizens for Tax Justice, "Fortune 500 Corporations Are Likely Avoiding $600 Billion in Corporate Tax Using Offshore Tax Havens," *Tax Justice* (blog), September 3, 2015, http://www.taxjusticeblog.org/archive/2015/09/fortune_500_corporations_are_l .php#.V7kjEvkrLIU.

116   *one of the highest in the world:* Just to take two examples: Fox News commentator Eric Bolling said, "We have the highest corporate tax rate in the free world." Derek Tsang, "Does the U.S. Have the Highest Corporate Tax Rate in the Free World?," PolitiFact, PunditFact, September 9, 2014, http://www.politifact.com/punditfact /statements/2014/sep/09/eric-bolling/does-us-have-highest-corporate-tax-rate-free -world/. And Disney's president and CEO, Bob Iger, said in a Fox Business Network interview, "We know that America is very high—among the highest in the world, if not the highest—in terms of corporate tax rates. That's something that I believe has to change. We've got to become more competitive." Jason Garcia, "*Orlando Sentinel*: After Record Profits, Disney CEO Calls for Corporate Tax Changes," Citizens for

Tax Justice, August 8, 2012, http://ctj.org/ctjinthenews/2012/08/orlando_sentinel
_after_record_profits_disney_ceo_calls_for_corporate_tax_changes_1.php
#.WGsuQFPafIU.

116 *higher corporate tax rates than the United States:* Citizens for Tax Justice, "The U.S.
Collects Lower Level of Corporate Taxes Than Most Developed Countries," April 9,
2015, http://ctj.org/ctjreports/2015/04/the_us_collects_lower_level_of_corporate
_taxes_than_most_developed_countries.php.

117 *"The problem is that our tax rate is so much higher":* Megan Murphy, "Jamie Dimon
on Trump, Taxes, and a U.S. Renaissance," *Bloomberg Businessweek,* December 22,
2016, https://www.bloomberg.com/news/features/2016-12-22/jamie-dimon-on-trump
-taxes-and-a-u-s-renaissance.

117 *tax evasion:* Zucman, "Taxing Across Borders," p. 121. See also Kevin S. Markle and
Douglas A. Shackelford, "Cross-Country Comparisons of Corporate Income Taxes,"
National Tax Journal 65, no. 3 (September 2012): 493–527, https://www.ntanet.org
/NTJ/65/3/ntj-v65n03p493-527-cross-country-comparisons-corporate.pdf.

117 *For five years:* Robert S. McIntyre, Matthew Gardner, and Richard Phillips, "The
Sorry State of Corporate Taxes," Citizens for Tax Justice, February 2014, http://www
.ctj.org/corporatetaxdodgers/sorrystateofcorptaxes.pdf. Even when companies
challenge this claim, their arguments don't hold up. Bob McIntyre, "GE and Verizon's Claims About Their Taxes Don't Stand Up," *Tax Justice* (blog), April 14, 2016,
http://www.taxjusticeblog.org/archive/2016/04/just_plain_wrong_ge_and_verizo
.php#.V77-SKLyQY0.

117 *corporations pay about one out of every ten dollars:* Office of Management and Budget, "Historical Tables," Table 2.2—Percentage Composition of Receipts by Source:
1934–2021, https://www.obamawhitehouse.archives.gov/omb/budget/Historicals.

118 *Starting in 1986:* Chris Good, "Norquist's Tax Pledge: What It Is and How It Started,"
ABC News, November 26, 2012, http://abcnews.go.com/blogs/politics/2012/11/nor
quists-tax-pledge-what-it-is-and-how-it-started/.

118 *"drown it in the bathtub":* National Public Radio, "Conservative Advocate," *Morning
Edition,* May 25, 2001, http://www.npr.org/templates/story/story.php?storyId=1123439;
Paul Krugman, "The Tax-Cut Con," *New York Times,* September 14, 2003, http://www
.nytimes.com/2003/09/14/magazine/the-tax-cut-con.html?pagewanted=all.

118 *defense spending rose:* Office of Management and Budget, "Historical Tables,"
Table 3.1—Outlays by Superfunction and Function: 1940–2021, https://www.obama
whitehouse.archives.gov/omb/budget/Historicals. All data adjusted for inflation (CPI).

118 *now on the chopping block:* Veronique de Rugy, "President Reagan, Champion Budget-
Cutter," American Enterprise Institute, June 9, 2004, https://www.aei.org/publication
/president-reagan-champion-budget-cutter/.

118 *school funding was slashed:* States' Impact on Federal Education Policy Project, "Federal Education Policy and the States, 1945–2009: A Brief Synopsis."

118 *Republicans bargained for another 15 percent cut:* First Focus, "Children's Budget 2015,"
June 24, 2015, p. 45, https://firstfocus.org/resources/report/childrens-budget-2015/.

119 *thirty-one states had cut their K–12 funding:* Michael Leachman, Nick Albares, Kathleen Masterson, and Marlana Wallace, "Most States Have Cut School Funding, and
Some Continue Cutting," Center on Budget and Policy Priorities, January 25, 2016,
http://www.cbpp.org/sites/default/files/atoms/files/12-10-15sfp.pdf.

119 *a shot at the middle class:* Pew Research Center, "The American Middle Class Is Losing Ground," December 9, 2015, pp. 25–26, http://www.pewsocialtrends.org/files/2015
/12/2015-12-09_middle-class_FINAL-report.pdf.

119 *States cut their support for public colleges:* State Higher Education Executive Officers
Association, "State Higher Education Finance: FY 2013," 2014, p. 22, Figure 4,
http://www.sheeo.org/sites/default/files/publications/SHEF_FY13_04252014.pdf;
U.S. Department of the Treasury with the U.S. Department of Education, "The

Economics of Higher Education," December 2012, pp. 21–22, https://www.treasury.gov/connect/blog/Documents/20121212_Economics%20of%20Higher%20Ed_vFINAL.pdf.

119   *Instead of reducing the burden on student borrowers:* Doug Lederman and Libby A. Nelson, "Loans and the Deficit," *Inside Higher Ed*, July 18, 2011, https://www.insidehighered.com/news/2011/07/18/loans-and-deficit.

119   *$10,312 a year for an in-state student:* University of Houston, "Tuition and Fees," http://www.uh.edu/financial/undergraduate/tuition-fees/.

119   *University of Massachusetts Lowell:* UMass Lowell, "Tuition and Fees," https://www.uml.edu/thesolutioncenter/bill/tuition-fees/default.aspx.

119   *70 percent of college graduates had to borrow money:* Jeffrey Sparshott, "Congratulations, Class of 2015. You're the Most Indebted Ever (For Now)," *Wall Street Journal*, May 8, 2015, http://blogs.wsj.com/economics/2015/05/08/congratulations-class-of-2015-youre-the-most-indebted-ever-for-now/.

119   *a load burden of $1.4 trillion:* Board of Governors of the Federal Reserve System, "Consumer Credit," June 2016, http://www.federalreserve.gov/releases/g19/current/.

119   *there are an estimated six hundred thousand unfilled jobs:* Katherine S. Newman and Hella Winston, "Straight from High School to a Career," *New York Times*, April 15, 2016, http://www.nytimes.com/2016/04/15/opinion/straight-from-high-school-to-a-career.html.

119   *But federal funding for career, technical, and adult education:* Katherine S. Newman and Hella Winston, *Reskilling America: Learning to Labor in the Twenty-First Century* (New York: Metropolitan Books, Henry Holt, 2016), pp. 115, 118–19, 189, 198.

120   *Today, about 10 percent of all students:* College Board, "Trends in College Pricing 2016," Figure 20: Enrollment by Level of Enrollment and Attendance Status over Time, https://trends.collegeboard.org/college-pricing/figures-tables/enrollment-level-enrollment-and-attendance-status-over-time.

120   *20 percent of all student loan debt:* College Board, "Trends in College Pricing 2016," Enrollment by Level of Enrollment and Attendance Status over Time, Figure 20, p. 30, https://trends.collegeboard.org/sites/default/files/2016-trends-college-pricing-web_0.pdf.

120   *40 percent of all the student loan defaults:* Department of Education, Federal Student Aid, "Official Cohort Default Rates for Schools," FY 2013 official cohort default rates by institution type, September 28, 2016, https://www2.ed.gov/offices/OSFAP/defaultmanagement/cdr.html.

122   *about $174 billion in profits:* For many years now, Republicans have lobbied to change how the government accounts for the cost of federal lending programs. While the current accounting method already factors in expectations on default rates and how much money the government expects to get back in repayment, Republicans want to treat government lending as though the government were a private business, where capital is more expensive. Of course, the government is not a private business. It's able to borrow more cheaply since our government has a record of making good on its debts, and the purpose of our lending programs is not to maximize profits for the federal government. They exist to help hardworking Americans. But changing the accounting would make government lending programs seem more expensive and less desirable—which is the point. Changing the accounting would also open up the opportunity for some government officials to "estimate" whatever they think is the right amount of risk adjustment and, as a result, give those estimators the power to finagle all of the federal accounting numbers. The question of profits on student loans gets tangled up in this debate, with Republicans arguing that the government wouldn't really be making $174 billion in profits—if we would just change the accounting system. Yeah, right. Last year, the nonpartisan Government Accountability Office took a comprehensive look at the data and—surprise!—roundly rejected this ideological push to make

federal credit programs look more expensive than they actually are. Congressional Budget Office, "CBO February 2013 Baseline Projections for the Student Loan Program," February 2013, available at https://www.cbo.gov/sites/default/files/recurringdata /51310-2013-02-studentloan.pdf; U.S. Government Accountability Office, "Credit Reform: Current Method to Estimate Credit Subsidy Costs Is More Appropriate for Budget Estimates than a Fair Value Approach," January 2016, http://www.gao.gov /assets/680/674905.pdf.

123 *the government had lent a generous helping hand:* Pro Publica, Bailout Tracker, January 3, 2017, http://projects.propublica.org/bailout/.

123 *a truly astronomical sum—$1.1 trillion:* U.S. Government Accountability Office, "Federal Reserve System: Opportunities Exist to Strengthen Policies and Processes for Managing Emergency Assistance," Table 8, July 2011, p. 131, http://www.sanders .senate.gov/imo/media/doc/GAO%20Fed%20Investigation.pdf.

123 *the entire U.S. GDP:* Federal Reserve Bank of St. Louis, "Gross Domestic Product," December 22, 2016, https://fred.stlouisfed.org/series/GDP.

123 *pulling the plug on small business loans:* Karen G. Mills and Brayden McCarthy, "The State of Small Business Lending: Credit Access During the Recovery and How Technology May Change the Game," Harvard Business School Working Paper, No. 15-004, July 2014, http://www.hbs.edu/faculty/Pages/item.aspx?num=47695.

123 *pay less than 1 percent interest:* Federal Reserve Discount Window, "Current Discount Rates," https://www.frbdiscountwindow.org/en/Pages/Discount-Rates/Current-Dis count-Rates.aspx.

124 *a heartfelt but not very exciting speech:* Senator Warren Introduces the Bank on Students Loan Fairness Act, May 8, 2013, https://www.youtube.com/watch?v=P-4FhsyvJdM.

124 *online editorials:* Van Jones, "A Trillion Dollar Anvil Dragging Us Down," *CNN Opinion*, June 6, 2013, http://www.cnn.com/2013/06/06/opinion/jones-student-loans /index.html; Howard Dean, "What's Really at Stake in the Fight over Student Loan Reform?," *Roll Call*, June 12, 2013, http://www.rollcall.com/news/whats_really_at _stake_in_the_fight_over_student_loan_reform_commentary-225571-1.html.

124 *Twenty-five colleges in Massachusetts:* Office of U.S. Senator Elizabeth Warren, "Higher Education Institutions, Organizations Endorse Sen. Elizabeth Warren's Bank on Students Act," press release, May 23, 2013, http://www.warren.senate.gov /?p=press_release&id=106.

126 *According to the scorekeepers:* Congressional Budget Office, Letter to Senator Elizabeth Warren regarding S. 2292, the Bank on Students Emergency Loan Refinancing Act, June 4, 2014, https://www.cbo.gov/sites/default/files/113th-congress-2013-2014 /costestimate/s22921_0.pdf.

126 *the bill died:* U.S. Senate Roll Call Vote 113th Congress, 2nd Session, #185, June 11, 2014, http://www.senate.gov/legislative/LIS/roll_call_lists/roll_call_vote_cfm.cfm ?congress=113&session=2&vote=00185.

127 *he settled one of the lawsuits:* Rosalind S. Helderman, "Trump Agrees to $25 Million Settlement in Trump University Fraud Cases," *Washington Post*, November 18, 2016, https://www.washingtonpost.com/politics/source-trump-nearing-settlement-in -trump-university-fraud-cases/2016/11/18/8dc047c0-ada0-11e6-a31b-4b6397e625d0 _story.html.

128 *new construction and plain old maintenance:* As a proportion of GDP, we spend less in total on infrastructure today than we did in the 1960s—or the 1980s. Elizabeth C. McNichol, "It's Time for States to Invest in Infrastructure," Center on Budget and Policy Priorities, Plicy Futures, February 23, 2016, Figure 4, p. 9, http://www.cbpp .org/sites/default/files/atoms/files/2-23-16sfp.pdf.

128 *America currently spends nothing:* Lawrence H. Summers, "Reflections on Secular Stagnation," speech at Julius-Rabinowitz Center, Princeton University, February 19, 2015, http://larrysummers.com/2015/02/25/reflections-on-secular-stagnation/.

128   *grade of D+:* American Society of Civil Engineers, "Infrastructure Grades for 2013," http://www.infrastructurereportcard.org/.

128   *for more than a year:* CBS Minnesota (WCCO), "Friday Marks 7 Years Since I-35W Bridge Collapse," August 1, 2014, http://minnesota.cbslocal.com/2014/08/01/friday -marks-7-years-since-i-35w-bridge-collapse/.

128   *Small businesses:* Carissa Wyant, "Bridge Collapse Forces Layoffs," *Minneapolis/ St. Paul Business Journal*, August 10, 2007, http://www.bizjournals.com/twincities /stories/2007/08/06/daily42.html; Diane L. Cormany, "Small Retailers Struggle to Survive Bridge Collapse," MinnPost, January 4, 2008, https://www.minnpost.com /politics-policy/2008/01/small-retailers-struggle-survive-bridge-collapse.

129   *an aging power grid:* NPR *Fresh Air*, "Aging and Unstable, the Nation's Electrical Grid Is 'the Weakest Link,'" August 22, 2016, http://www.npr.org/2016/08/22 /490932307/aging-and-unstable-the-nations-electrical-grid-is-the-weakest-link.

129   *many small towns and rural areas have been delayed:* Darrell M. West and Jack Karsten, "Rural and Urban America Divided by Broadband Access," Brookings Institution, July 18, 2016, https://www.brookings.edu/blog/techtank/2016/07/18 /rural-and-urban-america-divided-by-broadband-access/.

129   *the upkeep of our eighty-four thousand dams and levees:* Keith Miller, Kristina Costa, and Donna Cooper, "Ensuring Public Safety by Investing in Our Nation's Critical Dams and Levees," Center for American Progress, September 20, 2012, https://www .americanprogress.org/issues/economy/report/2012/09/20/38299/ensuring-public -safety-by-investing-in-our-nations-critical-dams-and-levees/.

129   *catastrophic floods:* Alex Prud'homme, "California's Next Nightmare," *New York Times Magazine*, July 1, 2011, http://www.nytimes.com/2011/07/03/magazine /sacramento-levees-pose-risk-to-california-and-the-country.html; "Prepare for a Flood of New Levee Work," *Sacramento Bee*, editorial, April 17, 2016, http://www .sacbee.com/opinion/editorials/article72191562.html.

129   *South Florida beaches:* Les Neuhaus, "Reeking, Oozing Algae Closes South Florida Beaches," *New York Times*, July 1, 2016, http://www.nytimes.com/2016/07/02/us /reeking-oozing-algae-closes-south-florida-beaches.html.

129   *Baton Rouge in 2016:* Steve Hardy and David J. Mitchell, "Planned, Forgotten: Unfin- ished Projects Could've Spared Thousands from Louisiana Flood," *Advocate* (Baton Rouge), August 22, 2016, http://www.theadvocate.com/baton_rouge/news/article _fc9f928c-6592-11e6-bad5-d3944fe82f0e.html; Craig E. Colten, "Suburban Sprawl and Poor Preparation Worsened Flood Damage in Louisiana," *Conversation*, August 22, 2016, https://theconversation.com/suburban-sprawl-and-poor-preparation -worsened-flood-damage-in-louisiana-64087.

129   *Internet speeds in U.S. cities:* Claire Cain Miller, "Why the U.S. Has Fallen Behind in Internet Speed and Affordability," *New York Times*, October 30, 2014, http://www .nytimes.com/2014/10/31/upshot/why-the-us-has-fallen-behind-in-internet-speed -and-affordability.html.

130   *China is spending 8.6 percent of its GDP on infrastructure:* Jonathan Woetzel, Nick- las Garemo, Jan Mischke, Martin Hjerpe, and Robert Palter, "Bridging Global Infra- structure Gaps," McKinsey Global Institute, June 2016, http://www.mckinsey.com /industries/capital-projects-and-infrastructure/our-insights/Bridging-global -infrastructure-gaps.

130   *about 2.4 percent of GDP:* Ibid.

130   *The overall quality of infrastructure in the United States:* World Economic Forum, Global Competitiveness Index Report 2015–2016, "Competitiveness Rankings— Infrastructure," http://reports.weforum.org/global-competitiveness-report-2015 -2016/competitiveness-rankings/.

132   *federal investment in research:* Federal investments in research have fallen from about 10 percent of the federal budget in the 1960s to less than 4 percent today. "New

MIT Report Details Benefits of Investment in Basic Research," MIT Energy Initiative, April 27, 2015, http://energy.mit.edu/news/new-mit-report-details-benefits-of-investment-in-basic-research/. See also American Association of the Advancement of Science, "Historical Trends in Federal R&D," June 2016, http://www.aaas.org/page/historical-trends-federal-rd, and the table "R&D as Percent of the Federal Budget: FY 1962–2017, in outlays," http://www.aaas.org/sites/default/files/Budget%3B.jpg.

132 *rare sea turtles:* Jane J. Lee, "Exclusive Video: First 'Glowing' Sea Turtle Found," *National Geographic,* September 28, 2015, http://news.nationalgeographic.com/2015/09/150928-sea-turtles-hawksbill-glowing-biofluorescence-coral-reef-ocean-animals-science150928-sea-turtles-hawksbill-glowing-biofluorescence-coral-reef-ocean-animals-science/.

132 *the American economy gets back $2.20:* Global Health Initiative, "In Your Own Backyard: How NIH Funding Helps Your State's Economy," Family USA, June 2008, http://familiesusa.org/sites/default/files/product_documents/in-your-own-backyard.pdf.

133 *NIH is leaving good science on the table:* National Institutes of Health, "Research Project Success Rates by NIH Institute for 2015," Research Portfolio Online Reporting Tools, https://report.nih.gov/success_rates/Success_ByIC.cfm.

133 *biochemistry research scientists:* Gavin Stern, "NIH Director Loses Sleep as Researchers Grovel for Cash," Scripps Howard Foundation Wire, July 30, 2014, http://www.shfwire.com/nih-strangled/.

133 *"on the cusp of a revolution":* Hearing before the U.S. Senate Committee on Health, Education, Labor, and Pensions, "Examining the State of America's Mental Health System," January 24, 2013, transcript at https://www.gpo.gov/fdsys/pkg/CHRG-113shrg78506/html/CHRG-113shrg78506.htm.

134 *$236 billion caring for people with Alzheimer's:* Alzheimer's Association, "2016 Alzheimer's Disease Facts and Figures," fact sheet, March 2016, https://www.alz.org/documents_custom/2016-Facts-and-Figures-Fact-Sheet.pdf.

135 *Alzheimer's could bankrupt Medicare:* Alzheimer's Association, "Changing the Trajectory of Alzheimer's Disease: How a Treatment by 2025 Saves Lives and Dollars," p. 6, https://www.alz.org/documents_custom/trajectory.pdf; Alzheimer's Association, "2016 Alzheimer's Disease Facts and Figures"; Harry Johns, "Change the Trajectory of Alzheimer's or Bankrupt Medicare," *Roll Call,* February 4, 2015, http://www.rollcall.com/news/change_the_trajectory_of_alzheimers_or_bankrupt_medicare_commentary-239851-1.html.

135 *NIH allocate to Alzheimer's research:* Richard J. Hodes, Testimony before the Senate Special Committee on Aging, March 25, 2015, pp. 1–2, http://www.aging.senate.gov/imo/media/doc/Hodes_3_25_15.pdf.

135 *20 percent less funding:* Eduardo Porter, "Government R&D, Private Profits and the American Taxpayer," *New York Times,* May 26, 2015, http://www.nytimes.com/2015/05/27/business/giving-taxpayers-a-cut-when-government-rd-pays-off-for-industry.html.

136 *$162 billion to basic research:* American Association for the Advancement of Science, "Historical Trends in Federal R&D." Calculated using nondefense R&D totals.

136 *majority of Americans agree:* Cary Funk and Lee Rainie, "Chapter 3: Support for Government Funding," Americans, Politics and Science Issues, Pew Research Center, July 1, 2015, http://www.pewinternet.org/2015/07/01/chapter-3-support-for-government-funding/.

138 *His best line:* David Nather, "Elizabeth Warren, Newt Gingrich Team Up for NIH," *Boston Globe,* July 27, 2015, https://www.bostonglobe.com/news/politics/2015/07/27/elizabeth-warren-and-newt-gingrich-agree-call-for-more-nih-funding/CPpaRgBL2w2hZej2n1rgPL/story.html.

139   *The walls were adorned:* Michael Collins, "Senators' Offices Showcase Tennessee Art, Artifacts," *Commercial Appeal* (Memphis, TN), January 2, 2016, http://archive .commercialappeal.com/news/national/senators-offices-showcase-tennessee-art -artifacts-273257f1-2c81-23dd-e053-0100007f0273-363827971.html.

139   *$5 billion a year to NIH's budget:* Mary Ellen McIntire, "HELP Panel Democrats Offer Bill for Annual NIH, FDA Funding," *Morning Consult*, March 3, 2016, https://morningconsult.com/alert/elizabeth-warren-help-committee-nih-fda -funding/.

140   *In the final markup:* In a press release from Senator Alexander's office after the final markup, he said of NIH funding: "We continue to work to find an amount that the House will agree to, the Senate will pass and the president will sign." U.S. Senate Committee on Health, Education, Labor & Pensions Press Release, "Senate Health Committee Approves Last of 19 Bipartisan Bills, Completing Work on Companion to House-Passed 21st Century Cures Act," April 6, 2016, http://www.help.senate .gov/chair/newsroom/press/senate-health-committee-approves-last-of-19 -bipartisan-bills-completing-work-on-companion-to-house-passed-21st-century -cures-act.

140   *"Republicans Blame Warren for 'Cures' Delay":* Joe Williams, "Republicans Blame Warren for 'Cures' Delay," *CQ*, June 22, 2016, http://www.cq.com/doc/news-4914102?0.

140   *loaded it up with giveaways:* For more information on our concerns with this bill, see my speech here (video): Office of U.S. Senator Elizabeth Warren, "Senator Warren Delivers Remarks on the Proposed 21st Century Cures Bill," press release, November 28, 2016, https://www.warren.senate.gov/?p=press_release&id =1307.

141   *2 percent of what the NIH already spends:* National Institutes of Health, "Estimates of Funding for Various Research, Condition, and Disease Categories (RCDC)," February 10, 2016, https://report.nih.gov/categorical_spending.aspx.

143   *nothing was ever the same:* Joseph A. McCartin, *Collision Course: Ronald Reagan, the Air Traffic Controllers, and the Strike That Changed America* (New York: Oxford University Press, 2011), pp. 289–319.

143   *11 percent of workers:* U.S. Department of Labor, Bureau of Labor Statistics, "Union Members Summary," January 28, 2016, https://www.bls.gov/news.release/union2 .nr0.htm.

144   *known for union busting:* Hella Winston, "How Charter Schools Bust Unions," *Slate*, September 29, 2016, http://www.slate.com/articles/business/the_grind/2016/09/the _lengths_that_charter_schools_go_to_when_their_teachers_try_to_form_unions .html.

146   *gobbled up by the top 10 percent:* Piketty and Saez, "Income Inequality in the United States, 1931–2002," later updated with Atkinson (November 2004).

147   *the wealth gap between black and white families tripled:* Data are from Panel Study of Income Dynamics, computed by the Institute on Assets and Social Policy at Brandeis University.

147   *gap had grown to $245,000:* Data are from Panel Study of Income Dynamics, computed by the Institute on Assets and Social Policy at Brandeis University. Data from the Survey of Consumer Finance also show a growing gap, but with smaller magnitude. Urban Institute, "Nine Charts About Wealth Inequality in America," Chart 3 with data, http://apps.urban.org/features/wealth-inequality-charts/.

147   *tax cuts did not boost the economy:* Era Dabla-Norris, Kalpana Kochhar, Nujin Suphaphiphat, Frantisek Ricka, and Evridiki Tsounta, "Causes and Consequences of Income Inequality: A Global Perspective," International Monetary Fund, June 2015, http://www.imf.org/external/pubs/ft/sdn/2015/sdn1513.pdf; Gravelle and Marples, "Tax Rates and Economic Growth."

147   *Tax Policy Center:* Lily L. Batchelder, "Families Facing Tax Increase Under Trump's Tax Plan."

147 *"since Ronald Reagan"*: Aaron Blake, "The First Trump-Clinton Presidential Debate Transcript, Annotated," *Washington Post*, September 26, 2016, https://www.washingtonpost.com/news/the-fix/wp/2016/09/26/the-first-trump-clinton-presidential-debate-transcript-annotated/.

147 *Mitch McConnell*: Brian Beutler, "It's Unanimous! GOP Says No to Unemployment Benefits, Yes to Tax Cuts for the Rich," *Talking Points Memo*, July 13, 2010, http://talkingpointsmemo.com/dc/it-s-unanimous-gop-says-no-to-unemployment-benefits-yes-to-tax-cuts-for-the-rich.

147 *Paul Ryan*: John McCormack, "Paul Ryan: More Important to Cut Top Tax Rate Than Expand Child Tax Credit," *Weekly Standard*, August 20, 2014, http://www.weeklystandard.com/paul-ryan-more-important-to-cut-top-tax-rate-than-expand-child-tax-credit/article/803461.

4: THE RICH AND POWERFUL TIGHTEN THEIR GRIP

152 *our side thought*: Reid Wilson, "Reid In: Cromnibus Decoded Edition," *Washington Post*, December 10, 2014, https://www.washingtonpost.com/news/post-politics/wp/2014/12/10/read-in-cromnibus-decoded-edition/.

152 *the other side wanted*: Siobhan Hughes, " 'Cromnibus' Highlights: IRS Cuts; No Raise for Biden; Break on School Lunches," *Wall Street Journal*, Washington Wire, December 10, 2014, http://blogs.wsj.com/washwire/2014/12/10/cromnibus-highlights-irs-cuts-no-raise-for-biden-break-on-school-lunches/; Robert Pear, "From Contribution Limits to the Sage Grouse: What Is in the Spending Bill?," *New York Times*, December 12, 2014, http://www.nytimes.com/2014/12/13/us/key-points-from-the-spending-bill.html.

152 *President's administrative orders on immigration*: Susan Crabtree, "Conservatives Push Short-Term Spending Bill as Way to Defund 'Amnesty,' " *Washington Examiner*, November 13, 2014, http://www.washingtonexaminer.com/conservatives-push-short-term-spending-bill-as-way-to-defund-amnesty/article/2556148.

152 *Washington D.C.'s move to legalize marijuana*: "Congress's Double-Edged Marijuana Stance," *New York Times*, editorial, December 10, 2014, http://www.nytimes.com/2014/12/11/opinion/congresss-double-edged-marijuana-stance.html.

152 *such as the ongoing work*: Jake Sherman and John Bresnahan, "The President, the Panic and the Cromnibus," *Politico*, December 12, 2014, http://www.politico.com/story/2014/12/barack-obama-cromnibus-113543; Wilson, "Reid In: Cromnibus Decoded Edition."

155 *"a main culprit"*: Eric Lipton and Ben Protess, "House, Set to Vote on 2 Bills, Is Seen as an Ally of Wall St.," *New York Times*, October 28, 2013, http://dealbook.nytimes.com/2013/10/28/house-set-to-vote-on-2-bills-is-seen-as-an-ally-of-wall-st.

155 *A whopping $22 trillion:* This is the sum of $13 trillion in lost economic output, and $9.1 trillion in home equity losses. U.S. Government Accountability Office, "Financial Regulatory Reform: Financial Crisis Losses and Potential Impacts of the Dodd-Frank Act," January 16, 2013, pp. 17, 21 http://www.gao.gov/assets/660/651322.pdf; Eleazar David Melendez, "Financial Crisis Cost Tops $22 Trillion, GAO Says," *Huffington Post*, February 14, 2013, http://www.huffingtonpost.com/2013/02/14/financial-crisis-cost-gao_n_2687553.html.

155 *$10* trillion *of risky swaps:* Office of U.S. Senator Elizabeth Warren, "Warren and Cummings Investigation Finds That Repeal of Dodd-Frank Provision Now Allows Banks to Keep Nearly $10 Trillion in Risky Trades on Books," press release, November 10, 2015, http://www.warren.senate.gov/?p=press_release&id=1000.

156 *I went to the floor of the Senate:* "Sen. Warren Calls on House to Strike Repeal of Dodd-Frank Provision in Funding Bill," speech on the Senate floor, December 10, 2014, https://www.youtube.com/watch?v=H20Dhc85OhM; and Office of U.S. Senator Elizabeth Warren, "Senator Warren Calls on House to Strike Repeal of Dodd-Frank

Provision from Government Spending Bill," press release, December 10, 2014, https://www.warren.senate.gov/?p=press_release&id=667.

157 *interviews:* For example: Noah Bierman and Jessica Meyers, "As Clock Ticks, Warren Balks at Spending Bill," *Boston Globe*, December 10, 2014, https://www.bostonglobe .com/news/nation/2014/12/10/senator-elizabeth-warren-house-speaker-nancy -pelosi-oppose-provision-adding-uncertainty-bill-keeping-government-open /CyfUitKFXNt9WaD1sZlXUJ/story.html; "Elizabeth Warren: Bank Giveaway a Budget Deal Breaker," *The Rachel Maddow Show*, December 10, 2014, http://www .msnbc.com/rachel-maddow/watch/warren—bank-giveaway-a-budget-deal-breaker -370243651919.

157 *e-mailed supporters:* E-mail, "Urgent Action: Stop the Republicans' Wall Street Give- away," December 10, 2014.

157 *Facebook and Twitter:* Facebook and Twitter posts: https://www.facebook.com /senatorelizabethwarren/posts/390285221133977; https://twitter.com/SenWarren /status/542762280010932225; https://twitter.com/SenWarren/status/543162743302 660097.

157 *I went back to the Senate on Thursday:* "Sen. Warren Urges Republicans to Oppose Bailout Provision in Government Funding Bill," speech on the Senate floor, Decem- ber 11, 2014, https://www.youtube.com/watch?v=tRDJDq6PkWQ.

157 *Jamie Dimon:* Steven Mufson and Tom Hamburger, "Jamie Dimon Himself Called to Urge Support for the Derivatives Rule in the Spending Bill," *Washington Post*, Decem- ber 11, 2014, https://www.washingtonpost.com/news/wonk/wp/2014/12/11/the -item-that-is-blowing-up-the-budget-deal/.

157 *zealously defending the provision:* "ABA Statement on Swaps Push-Out Provision in Omnibus Bill," statement by James Balentine, American Bankers Association, December 10, 2014, http://web.archive.org/web/20160204144323/http://www.aba .com/Press/Pages/121014SwapsProvisionOmnibusBill.aspx; Lori Montgomery and Sean Sullivan, "Warren Leads Liberal Democrats' Rebellion over Provisions in $1 Trillion Spending Bill," *Washington Post*, December 10, 2014, https://www.washing tonpost.com/business/economy/warren-leads-liberal-democrats-rebellion-over -provisions-in-1-trillion-spending-bill/2014/12/10/c5c915e4-80b5-11e4-9f38 -95a187e4c1f7_story.html ("Banking lobbyists defended the provision as a relatively minor change that, according to Francis Creighton, chief lobbyist for the Financial Services Roundtable, 'will make it easier for financial institutions to use derivatives as a hedge against risk, which is an important part of making the economy work'").

158 *final cost of the shutdown:* Toluse Olorunnipa, Kathleen Miller, and Brian Wing- field, "Shutdown Hit Boehner's Favorite Diner as $24 Billion Lost," *Bloomberg*, October 17, 2013, http://www.bloomberg.com/news/articles/2013-10-17/shutdown -hit-boehner-s-favorite-diner-as-24-billion-lost; Tim Mullaney and Paul David- son, "Shutdown Cost Billions in Wages, Shopping and More," *USA Today*, Octo- ber 18, 2013, http://www.usatoday.com/story/money/business/2013/10/17/costs-of -shutdown/3002745/.

158 *They posed so much risk:* In a surprise to many observers, the one giant bank that did not get tagged in 2016 as Too Big to Fail was Citigroup. The bank had already started shedding divisions, shrinking itself and making itself less complex. Jesse Hamilton and Elizabeth Dexheimer, "Five Big Banks' Living Wills Are Rejected by U.S. Regu- lators," *Bloomberg*, April 13, 2016, http://www.bloomberg.com/news/articles/2016 -04-13/five-big-banks-living-wills-rejected-by-u-s-banking-agencies.

159 *"We can have democracy in this country":* The Morrow Book of Quotations in Ameri- can History, compiled by Joseph R. Conlin (New York: William Morrow, 1984), p. 48.

160 *the average winning Senate campaign:* Center for Responsive Politics, "Winning vs. Spending," OpenSecrets.org, November 2, 2016, https://www.opensecrets.org/overview /bigspenders.php?cycle=2016&display=A&sort=D&Memb=S; Center for Respon-

sive Politics, "2016 Outside Spending, by Super PAC," OpenSecrets.org, January 17, 2017, https://www.opensecrets.org/outsidespending/summ.php?cycle=2016&disp=R&pty=A&type=S. Calculations based on data available as of January 4, 2017.

160   *the 2016 presidential election:* Anu Narayanswamy, Darla Cameron, and Matea Gold, "Money Raised as of Nov. 28," *Washington Post*, December 9, 2016, https://www.washingtonpost.com/graphics/politics/2016-election/campaign-finance/.

160   *he raked in huge donations:* Rebecca Ballhaus, "$100 Million? How Trump's Self-Funding Pledges Panned Out," *Wall Street Journal*, November 7, 2016, http://blogs.wsj.com/washwire/2016/11/07/pretty-much-self-funding-an-election-eve-look-at-trumps-campaign-financing/.

160   *"a consensus nominee":* Thomas Ferraro, "Republican Would Back Garland for Supreme Court," Reuters, May 6, 2010, http://www.reuters.com/article/us-usa-court-hatch-idUSTRE6456QY20100506.

161   *filling a Supreme Court vacancy:* Linda Qui, "Do Presidents Stop Nominating Judges in Their Final Year?" PolitiFact, February 14, 2016, http://www.politifact.com/truth-o-meter/statements/2016/feb/14/marco-rubio/do-presidents-stop-nominating-judges-final-year/. Then-senator Joe Biden in the last five months of President Bush's term in 1992 speculated that if a Supreme Court vacancy came up, Congress should wait until after the election to hold hearings. C. Eugene Emery Jr., "In Context: The 'Biden Rule' on Supreme Court Nominations in an Election Year," PolitiFact, March 17, 2016, http://www.politifact.com/truth-o-meter/article/2016/mar/1/context-biden-rule-supreme-court-nominations/.

161   *"I will always put Kansans ahead":* "About Jerry Moran," Jerry Moran for U.S. Senate, https://www.moranforkansas.com/about-jerry/.

161   *"Never backing down":* Jerry Moran for U.S. Senate, https://www.moranforkansas.com/.

161   *"I have my job to do":* Emmarie Huetteman, "Backlash as Senator Breaks Ranks on Supreme Court Hearings," *New York Times*, March 25, 2016, http://www.nytimes.com/2016/03/26/us/politics/jerry-moran-garland-nomination-republican-backlash.html.

162   *$100 billion every year:* "America's Largest Private Companies: #2 Koch Industries," *Forbes*, 2016 Rankings, http://www.forbes.com/companies/koch-industries/.

162   *offensive from the right:* Justin Wingerter, "Conservative Groups Threaten to Fund Ads, Primary Opponent Against Sen. Jerry Moran," *Topeka Capital-Journal*, March 25, 2016, http://cjonline.com/news/2016-03-25/conservative-groups-threaten-fund-ads-primary-opponent-against-sen-jerry-moran.

162   *Koch-funded groups:* Philip Wegmann, "Reinforced by Grassroots, Senate Republicans Hold Line on Supreme Court Nomination," *Daily Signal*, April 4, 2016, http://dailysignal.com/2016/04/04/reinforced-by-grassroots-senate-republicans-hold-line-on-supreme-court-nomination/.

162   *he reversed his position:* Kristen East, "Kansas Senator Reverses Position on Garland Hearings," *Politico*, April 2, 2016, http://www.politico.com/story/2016/04/jerry-moran-merrick-garland-senate-court-hearings-221493.

164   *make America greater for billionaires:* Jane Mayer, *Dark Money: The Hidden History of the Billionaires Behind the Rise of the Radical Right* (New York: Doubleday, 2016); Tim Dickinson, "Inside the Koch Brothers' Toxic Empire," *Rolling Stone*, September 24, 2014, http://www.rollingstone.com/politics/news/inside-the-koch-brothers-toxic-empire-20140924.

164   *30 percent to 70 percent of their time raising money:* Lawrence Lessig, *Republic, Lost: The Corruption of Equality and the Steps to End It*, rev. ed. (New York: Twelve, 2015), p. 13.

165   *Congressman Steve Israel:* Carl Hulse, "Steve Israel of New York, a Top House Democrat, Won't Seek Re-election," *New York Times*, January 5, 2016, http://www.nytimes.com/2016/01/06/us/politics/steve-israel-house-democrat-new-york.html.

165   *"Not what our founders had in mind":* "Congressional Fundraising," *Last Week Tonight with John Oliver*, April 3, 2016, https://www.youtube.com/watch?v=Ylomy1Aw9Hk.

165 *$100,000 cure for hepatitis:* Madeline R. Vann, "How to Pay for Costly Hepatitis C Drugs," *Everyday Health,* December 14, 2015, http://www.everydayhealth.com /news/how-pay-costly-hepatitis-c-drugs/.

165 *Bernie Sanders raised hundreds of millions:* Bernie Sanders, *Our Revolution: A Future to Believe In* (New York: Thomas Dunne Books, St. Martin's Press, 2016), 114.

165 *Donald Trump raised about $280 million:* Bill Allison, Mira Rojanasakul, Brittany Harris, and Cedric Sam, "Tracking the 2016 Presidential Money Race," *Bloomberg,* December 9, 2016, https://www.bloomberg.com/politics/graphics/2016-presidential -campaign-fundraising/.

166 *I raised millions:* Federal Election Committee, "Financial Summary," 8/16/2011– 12/31/2012, http://www.fec.gov/fecviewer/CandidateCommitteeDetail.do?&tabIndex =1&candidateCommitteeId=S2MA00170.

166 *$50 or less:* Mindy Myers, "One Year Ago Today, We Made History," *Huffington Post,* January 23, 2014, http://www.huffingtonpost.com/mindy-myers/elizabeth-warren -senate_b_4228603.html.

166 *"Hey, what gives?":* Office of U.S. Senator Elizabeth Warren, "Warren to President- Elect Trump: You Are Already Breaking Promises by Appointing Slew of Special Interests, Wall Street Elites, and Insiders to Transition Team," press release, Novem- ber 15, 2016, https://www.warren.senate.gov/?p=press_release&id=1298.

167 *replaced them with former lobbyists:* Lee Fang, "Donald Trump's Big Ethics Move Is to Replace Lobbyists with Former Lobbyists," *Intercept,* November 22, 2016, https://theintercept.com/2016/11/22/trump-transition-lobbyists-2/; Aaron Blake, "4 Ways in Which 'the Swamp' Is Doing Just Fine in the Trump Era," *Washington Post,* January 3, 2017, https://www.washingtonpost.com/news/the-fix/wp/2017/01 /03/4-ways-in-which-the-swamp-is-doing-just-fine-in-the-trump-era/?utm_term =.225dc25f85a8.

167 *Right after the election, Trump's former campaign manager:* Shane Goldmacher, Isaac Arnsdorf, Josh Dawsey, and Kenneth P. Vogel, "Trump's Ex-Campaign Manager Starts Lobbying Firm," *Politico,* December 21, 2016, http://www.politico.com/story /2016/12/corey-lewandowski-consulting-firm-232888.

167 *lobbyists make about $2.6 billion:* Lee Drutman, "How Corporate Lobbyists Con- quered American Democracy," *Atlantic,* April 20, 2015, http://www.theatlantic .com/business/archive/2015/04/how-corporate-lobbyists-conquered-american -democracy/390822/.

167 *Corporations now spend more money lobbying:* Ibid.; Ida A. Brudnick, "Legislative Branch: FY2016 Appropriations," Congressional Research Service, February 1, 2016, https://fas.org/sgp/crs/misc/R44029.pdf.

167 *Chamber of Commerce is a well-funded giant:* "Of $164 million in contributions to the Chamber, more than half of the money came from just 64 donors.... And the top 1,500 donors provided 94 percent of the total donations." David Brodwin, "The Chamber's Secrets," *U.S. News & World Report,* October 22, 2015, http://www .usnews.com/opinion/economic-intelligence/2015/10/22/who-does-the-us-chamber -of-commerce-really-represent.

168 *"if not in the entire country":* U.S. Chamber of Commerce, "Building History," https:// www.uschamber.com/about/history/building-history.

168 *Daniel Webster:* Webster was my predecessor as senator from Massachusetts— widely regarded as one of the greatest senators in U.S. history—and a two-time secretary of state in the early nineteenth century.

168 *"to reflect the organization's prestigious mission":* U.S. Chamber of Commerce, "Building History."

169 *raised $260 million:* Danny Hakim, "Big Tobacco's Staunch Friend in Washington: U.S. Chamber of Commerce," *New York Times,* October 9, 2015, http://www.nytimes

.com/2015/10/10/business/us-chamber-of-commerces-focus-on-advocacy-a-boon
-to-tobacco.html.

169   *"We have to raise $5 million a week to run this place":* Sheryl Gay Stolberg, "Pugna-
cious Builder of the Business Lobby," *New York Times,* June 1, 2013, http://www
.nytimes.com/2013/06/02/business/how-tom-donohue-transformed-the-us
-chamber-of-commerce.html.

169   *"He zips around town":* Ibid.

169   *highest-paid trade association head:* This total includes base and bonus. "Inside
Compensation: CEO Salaries at Large Associations 2016 (Top Paid)," CEO Update,
https://www.ceoupdate.com/articles/compensation/inside-compensation-ceo
-salaries-large-associations-2016-top-paid.

169   *If the price is high enough:* Jim VandeHei, "Business Lobby Recovers Its Clout by Dis-
pensing Favors for Members," *Wall Street Journal,* September 11, 2001, http://www.wsj
.com/articles/SB100015411979219346.

170   *pass anti-smoking initiatives:* Senators Sheldon Whitehouse, Elizabeth Warren,
Barbara Boxer, Bernard Sanders, Sherrod Brown, Jeff Merkley, Richard Blumen-
thal, and Edward Markey, "The U.S. Chamber of Commerce: Out of Step with the
American People and Its Members," June 14, 2016, https://www.whitehouse.senate
.gov/imo/media/doc/Chamber%20of%20Commerce%20Report.pdf; Office of U.S.
Senator Sheldon Whitehouse, "Senators Issue Report on U.S. Chamber of Commerce
Lobbying," press release, June 14, 2016, https://www.whitehouse.senate.gov/news
/release/senators-issue-report-on-us-chamber-of-commerce-lobbying.

170   *the chamber fought against those restrictions:* "U.S. Chamber of Commerce Files
Friend of Court Brief," *CSP Daily News,* January 31, 2012, http://www.cspdailynews
.com/category-news/tobacco/articles/us-chamber-commerce-files-friend-court
-brief.

170   *"stays in the background":* Hakim, "Big Tobacco's Staunch Friend in Washington."

170   *"all the deniability they need":* James Verini, "Show Him the Money," *Washington
Monthly,* July/August 2010, http://jamesverini.com/show-him-the-money/.

170   *a return of 22,000 percent:* Raquel Meyer Alexander, Stephen W. Mazza, and Susan
Scholz, "Measuring Rates of Return for Lobbying Expenditures: An Empirical Case
Study of Tax Breaks for Multinational Corporations," *Journal of Law and Politics*
25, no. 401 (2009), http://papers.ssrn.com/sol3/papers.cfm?abstract_id=1375082.

171   *outperformed the S&P 500 by 11 percent a year:* "Money and Politics," *Economist,*
October 1, 2011, http://www.economist.com/node/21531014.

171   *Jack Abramoff:* "Convictions in the Abramoff Corruption Probe," Associated Press,
October 26, 2011, http://www.huffingtonpost.com/huff-wires/20111026/us-abramoff
-convictions/.

171   *"Surprised it's so little":* Alex Blumberg and David Kestenbaum, "Jack Abramoff on
Lobbying," NPR *Planet Money,* December 20, 2011, http://www.npr.org/sections
/money/2011/12/20/144028899/the-tuesday-podcast-jack-abramoff-on-lobbying.

172   *An award-winning 1963 study:* Raymond A. Bauer, Ithiel De Sola Pool, and Lewis
Anthony Dexter, *American Business and Public Policy: The Politics of Foreign Trade,*
2nd ed. (New Brunswick, NJ: AldineTransaction, 2007), p. 324.

172   *Many businesses resisted the idea:* Drutman, "How Corporate Lobbyists Conquered
American Democracy."

172   *pay for prescriptions without any price negotiations:* Ibid.

172   *$25 billion a year:* "The Washington Wishing-Well," *Economist,* June 13, 2015, http://
www.economist.com/news/business/21654067-unstoppable-rise-lobbying
-american-business-bad-business-itself-washington.

172   *In the 1950s and 1960s:* Lee Drutman, "How Corporate Lobbyists Conquered American
Democracy."

173   *"For every dollar spent on lobbying":* Ibid.

174 *A few years ago the* Onion *published a satirical story:* "American People Hire High-Powered Lobbyist to Push Interests in Congress," *Onion,* October 6, 2010, http://www.theonion.com/article/american-people-hire-high-powered-lobbyist-to-push-18204.

174 *Association of Government Relations Professionals:* Paul C. Barton, "Congressional Staffers Capitalize on the Experience," *Tennessean,* May 26, 2014, http://www.tennessean.com/story/news/politics/2014/05/26/congressional-staffers-capitalize-experience/9611045/.

175 *it officially moved to Bermuda:* James Politi, "Lazard Aims for New York Listing in March," *Financial Times,* December 20, 2004, http://www.ft.com/cms/s/0/2adcc78c-522c-11d9-961a-00000e2511c8.html.

175 *behind job-cutting deals:* David Dayen, "Elizabeth Warren's Real Beef with Antonio Weiss: What Her Fight Against Him Is *Actually* About," *Salon,* December 23, 2014, http://www.salon.com/2014/12/23/elizabeth_warrens_huge_battle_why_shes_really_fighting_so_hard_against_antonio_weiss/.

175 *domestic economic policy:* Victoria McGrane and Dana Cimilluca, "Obama to Nominate Lazard Banker for a Top Treasury Post," *Wall Street Journal,* November 12, 2014, http://www.wsj.com/articles/obama-considering-investment-banker-for-top-treasury-post-1415822173.

176 *After Weiss was nominated:* Jeanna Smialek, "Lazard's Weiss Due $21.2 Million to Leave for Treasury," *Bloomberg,* November 21, 2014, http://www.bloomberg.com/news/articles/2014-11-21/weiss-due-as-much-as-21-2-million-to-leave-lazard-for-treasury.

177 *David Schmidt, a specialist in executive compensation:* Ibid.

177 *almost $140 billion more than the next bank:* Eamon Javers, "Citigroup Tops List of Banks Who Receive Federal Aid," CNBC, March 16, 2011, http://www.cnbc.com/id/42099554.

178 *Government Sachs:* Julie Creswell and Ben White, "The Guys from 'Government Sachs,'" *New York Times,* October 17, 2008, http://www.nytimes.com/2008/10/19/business/19gold.html.

178 *pay totaling $3.4 million:* "Pay for Eric Cantor's Wall Street Post: $3.4 Million," *Wall Street Journal,* Washington Wire, September 2, 2014, http://blogs.wsj.com/washwire/2014/09/02/pay-for-eric-cantors-wall-street-post-3-4-million/.

178 *"advise clients on strategic matters":* "Moelis & Company Announces the Appointment of Eric Cantor as Vice Chairman and Member of the Board of Directors," press release, September 2, 2014, http://www.moelis.com/News/SitePages/news-feed-details.aspx?feedId=248.

179 *"go-to guy":* Eric Lipton and Ben Protess, "Law Doesn't End Revolving Door on Capitol Hill," *New York Times,* February 1, 2014, http://dealbook.nytimes.com/2014/02/01/law-doesnt-end-revolving-door-on-capitol-hill/.

179 *125 former members of Congress:* Eric Lichtblau, "Lawmakers Regulate Banks, Then Flock to Them," *New York Times,* April 13, 2010, http://www.nytimes.com/2010/04/14/business/14lobby.html?pagewanted=all.

179 *Navient, the spin-off from student loan giant Sallie Mae:* Center for Responsive Politics, "Lobbyists Representing SLM Corp, 2015," OpenSecrets.org, https://www.opensecrets.org/lobby/clientlbs.php?id=D000022253&year=2015.

179 *The oil and gas industry's stable of lobbyists:* "Political Footprint of the Oil and Gas Industry—June 2015," Taxpayers for Common Sense, fact sheet, June 1, 2015, http://www.taxpayer.net/library/article/political-footprint-of-the-oil-and-gas-industry-2015.

180 *"poised to preside over a rollback of financial regulations":* Dakin Campbell, "Goldman Is Back on Top in the Trump Administration," *Bloomberg Businessweek,* December 22, 2016, https://www.bloomberg.com/news/articles/2016-12-22/goldman-is-back-on-top-in-the-trump-administration.

180 *"The Happiest Place on Earth":* Ibid. This appeared in the headline of the print version of this article: "Goldman Sachs Happiest Place on Earth," *Bloomberg Business-*

week, December 26, 2016, https://www.scribd.com/article/334884947/Goldman
-Sachs-Happiest-Place-On-Earth.

180 *"It is a widely held view within the bank"*: Creswell and White, "The Guys from 'Government Sachs.'"

180 *the* New York Times *crisply described Secretary Paulson's pick*: Ibid.

181 *nominated Steve Mnuchin*: Sam Levin, "Inside Trump Treasury Nominee's Past Life
as 'Foreclosure King' of California," *Guardian*, December 2, 2016, https://www
.theguardian.com/us-news/2016/dec/02/steve-mnuchin-profile-donald-trump
-treasury; Martin Crutsinger, Julie Bykowicz, and Julie Pace, "Treasury Nominee
Mnuchin Was Trump's Top Fundraiser," Associated Press, November 29, 2016,
http://bigstory.ap.org/article/6a89fd6b303441b5b8df5779350d4c44/treasury
-nominee-mnuchin-was-trumps-top-fundraiser.

181 *Mnuchin was not only a Wall Street insider*: Ibid.; Gideon Resnick, "Trump Picks
Foreclosure King Mnuchin for Treasury Secretary," *Daily Beast*, November 29, 2016,
http://www.thedailybeast.com/articles/2016/11/29/trump-picks-foreclosure-king
-mnuchin-for-treasury-secretary.html.

183 *Froman was personally helping pick*: David Dayen, "The Most Important WikiLeaks
Revelation Isn't About Hillary Clinton," *New Republic*, October 14, 2016, https://
newrepublic.com/article/137798/important-wikileaks-revelation-isnt-hillary-clinton.

184 *according to an analysis published by the* Washington Post: Christopher Ingraham
and Howard Schneider, "Industry Voices Dominate the Trade Advisory System,"
Washington Post, February 27, 2014, http://www.washingtonpost.com/wp-srv
/special/business/trade-advisory-committees/.

184 *posted revenues of $30 billion*: Aamer Madhani, "Oreo Maker Ignores Trump, Clin-
ton Criticism, Begins Layoffs in Chicago," *USA Today*, March 23, 2016, http://www
.usatoday.com/story/news/2016/03/23/nabisco-begins-layoffs-at-chicago-plant
-despite-criticism-from-trump-clinton/82159194/.

185 *$90 million in incentives*: Ibid.

185 *7.5 percent of their earnings*: Matt Krantz, "Oreo Maker Pays Crumbs in Taxes,"
USA Today, March 11, 2016, http://www.usatoday.com/story/money/markets/2016
/03/11/oreo-maker-pays-crumbs-taxes/81663574/.

185 *building a plant in Mexico*: Madhani, "Oreo Maker Ignores Trump, Clinton Criticism, Begins Layoffs in Chicago."

187 *as Steelworkers president Leo Gerard testified*: Testimony of Leo W. Gerard, International President, United Steelworkers, before the Senate Finance Committee,
June 25, 2014, https://www.finance.senate.gov/imo/media/doc/14%2006%2025%20
Testimony%20-%20Trade%20Enforcement%20Challenges%20and%20Opportuni-
ties2.pdf. Gerard's testimony shows how the process can hurt U.S. workers (p. 14):

> A perfect example of this is the coated free sheet paper trade problem. The USW
> filed a case and, while dumping was found, the injury was determined not to be
> significant enough for relief. Several years later, we filed essentially the same
> case but, by that time, more than 7,000 workers had lost their jobs, capacity was
> shut down and companies were on the brink. Relief was provided and many of
> the remaining workers have their jobs as a result. But, a substantial portion
> of the industry will never come back.

188 *Nabisco closed plants*: The Bakery, Confectionery, Tobacco Workers and Grain
Millers International Union, "The Facts," http://www.fightforamericanjobs.org
/the-facts/.

188 *boycott Mexican-made Nabisco products*: To learn more, visit http://www.fight
foramericanjobs.org/.

188 *focus on cutting costs*: Annie Gasparro, "Mondelez CEO Stands by Efforts to Cut
Costs," *Wall Street Journal*, August 23, 2015, http://www.wsj.com/articles/mondelez

-ceo-stands-by-efforts-to-cut-costs-1440372517; Craig Giammona, "Mondelez Combats Slump with Cost Cutting, Lifting Profit," *Bloomberg*, July 27, 2016, https://www .bloomberg.com/news/articles/2016-07-27/mondelez-combats-sales-slump-with -cost-cutting-lifting-profit.

188   *raking in about $20 million a year:* Greg Trotter, "Mondelez CEO's Total Compensation Down in 2015, Falls to $19.7 million," *Chicago Tribune*, March 28, 2016, http://www.chicagotribune.com/business/ct-mondelez-rosenfeld-compensation -0329-biz-20160328-story.html; BCTGM Local 300, "Nabisco 600 Series, Part Two," July 14, 2016, https://www.facebook.com/fightforamericanjobs/videos/112687 0114044462/.

189   *forced big banks to return nearly $12 billion:* Consumer Financial Protection Bureau, "CFPB Monthly Complaint Snapshot Spotlights Debt Collection Complaints," December 27, 2016, http://www.consumerfinance.gov/about-us/newsroom/cfpb -monthly-complaint-snapshot-spotlights-debt-collection-complaints/.

189   *a $185 million fine:* Jesse Hamilton, "Wells Fargo Is Fined $185 Million over Unapproved Accounts," *Bloomberg*, September 8, 2016, https://www.bloomberg.com/news /articles/2016-09-08/wells-fargo-fined-185-million-over-unwanted-customer -accounts.

189   *give Viagra to sex offenders:* James Oliphant and Kim Geiger, "More House Democrats Targeted by Third-Party Groups," *Los Angeles Times*, October 19, 2010, http:// articles.latimes.com/2010/oct/19/nation/la-na-outside-money-20101020.

189   *a television commercial:* Alan Pyke, "Republican Debate Will Feature Goofy Attack Ad on the Agency That Protects You from Scams," *ThinkProgress*, November 10, 2015 http://thinkprogress.org/economy/2015/11/10/3721257/attack-ad-soviet-cfpb/.

190   *AAN's board includes:* Ibid.

191   *"social welfare":* Mike McIntire and Nicholas Confessore, "Tax-Exempt Groups Shield Political Gifts of Businesses," *New York Times*, July 7, 2012, http://www.nytimes.com /2012/07/08/us/politics/groups-shield-political-gifts-of-businesses.html.

191   *secret money:* For example, AAN does not disclose its donors. Some donors can be determined from their own disclosures, but not AAN's. Zachary Roth, "The Newest Dark Money Power Player: American Action Network," MSNBC, March 18, 2014, http://www.msnbc.com/msnbc/the-newest-dark-money-power-player-american -action-network. (AAN's super PAC does disclose its donors.)

191   *the corporation's point of view:* Liz Whyte, "Corporations, Advocacy Groups Spend Big on Ballot Measures," *Time*, October 23, 2014, http://time.com/3532419/ballot -measures-corporations/.

192   *As one reporter noted:* Ibid.

192   *weapons manufacturers were spending tens of millions:* Paul Farhi, "Influx of Ads for Military Weapons Throwing Commuters for Loop," *Washington Post*, June 25, 2010, http://www.washingtonpost.com/wp-dyn/content/article/2010/06/24 /AR2010062406207.html.

192   *Or consider the American Petroleum Institute:* Erin Quinn, "Who Needs Lobbyists? See What Big Business Spends to Win American Minds," Center for Public Integrity, January 15, 2015, https://www.publicintegrity.org/2015/01/15/16596/who-needs -lobbyists-see-what-big-business-spends-win-american-minds.

192   *A recent academic paper:* Florens Focke, Alexandra Niessen-Ruenzi, and Stefan Ruenzi, "A Friendly Turn: Advertising Bias in the News Media," working paper, March 3, 2016, http://papers.ssrn.com/sol3/papers.cfm?abstract_id=2741613.

193   Farm News *fired their cartoonist:* Christine Hauser, "Cartoonist Fired from Farm News for Pro-Farmer Cartoon," *New York Times*, May 5, 2016, http://www.nytimes .com/2016/05/06/business/media/cartoonist-fired-from-farm-news.html.

194   *had been receiving "prizes":* Elizabeth Warren, Letter to Peter Hancock, CEO of AIG Companies, April 28, 2015, http://www.warren.senate.gov/files/documents /AnnuitiesLetters.pdf.

194    $17 billion *a year:* Thomas Perez and Jeff Zients, "The Retirement Problem That Costs Americans $17 Billion a Year," *CNN Money,* September 15, 2015, http://money .cnn.com/2015/09/15/retirement/retirement-advisers-fiduciary-duty/.

195   *$80 billion:* Testimony of Robert Litan before the Senate Subcommittee on Employment and Workplace Safety, Senate Committee on Health, Education, Labor, and Pensions, July 21, 2015, http://www.help.senate.gov/imo/media/doc/Litan.pdf.

195   *Litan's claim ran exactly counter:* Council of Economic Advisers, "The Effects of Conflicted Investment Advice on Retirement Savings," February 2015, https:// www.whitehouse.gov/sites/default/files/docs/cea_coi_report_final.pdf; Sendhil Mullainathan, Markus Noeth, and Antoinette Schoar, "The Market for Financial Advice: An Audit Study," National Bureau of Economic Research Working Paper 17929, March 2012, http://www.nber.org/papers/w17929; Department of Labor, "Regulating Advice Markets: Definition of the Term 'Fiduciary,' Conflicts of Interest—Retirement Investment Advice, Regulatory Impact Analysis for Final Rule and Exemptions," April 2016, https://www.dol.gov/agencies/ebsa/laws-and -regulations/rules-and-regulations/completed-rulemaking/1210-AB32-2/ria .pdf.

196   *a letter to the president of Brookings:* Letter from Elizabeth Warren to Strobe Talbott, president of the Brookings Institution, September 28, 2015, http://www.warren .senate.gov/files/documents/2015-9-28_Warren_Brookings_ltr.pdf.

196   *The* Washington Post *picked up on my complaint:* Tom Hamburger, "How Elizabeth Warren Picked a Fight with Brookings—and Won," *Washington Post,* September 29, 2015, https://www.washingtonpost.com/politics/how-elizabeth-warren-picked-a-fight -with-brookings—and-won/2015/09/29/bfe45276-66c7-11e5-9ef3-fde182507eac_story .html.

196   *"a spectacularly unpersuasive hack-job":* Dylan Matthews, "Elizabeth Warren Exposed a Shocking Instance of How Money Corrupts DC Think Tanks," Vox, September 30, 2015 (updated April 6, 2016), http://www.vox.com/2015/9/30/9427461 /elizabeth-warren-brookings-institution.

196   *had not undergone peer review:* Luigi Zingales, "Is Money Corrupting Research?," *New York Times,* October 9, 2015, http://www.nytimes.com/2015/10/10/opinion/is-money -corrupting-research.html.

196   *"paid for research to try to discredit the proposed rule":* Jane Dokko, "Caveat Emptor: Watch Where Research on the Fiduciary Rule Comes From," Brookings, Up Front, July 29, 2015, http://www.brookings.edu/blogs/up-front/posts/2015/07/29-research -fiduciary-rule-comes-from.

196   *"McCarthyism":* Patrick Temple-West, "Backlash to Warren's Think-Tank Attack: 'McCarthyism' from the Left," *Politico,* September 30, 2015, http://www.politico.com /story/2015/09/backlash-to-elizabeth-warren-think-tank-attack-214302.

196   *"silencing any viewpoints different from" my own:* Ann Wagner, "Elizabeth Warren's Heavy Hand," *Hill,* October 13, 2015, http://thehill.com/opinion/op-ed/256834 -elizabeth-warrens-heavy-hand.

197   *rules about conflict of interest:* Eric Lipton, Nicholas Confessore, and Brooke Williams, "Think Tank Scholar or Corporate Consultant? It Depends on the Day," *New York Times,* August 8, 2016, http://www.nytimes.com/2016/08/09/us/politics/think-tank -scholars-corporate-consultants.html.

198   *eighty-three thousand heart attacks and deaths:* Peter Whoriskey, "As Drug Industry's Influence over Research Grows, So Does the Potential for Bias," *Washington Post,* November 24, 2012, https://www.washingtonpost.com/business/economy/as-drug -industrys-influence-over-research-grows-so-does-the-potential-for-bias/2012/11 /24/bb64d596-1264-11e2-be82-c3411b7680a9_story.html.

199   *But Whitehouse later discovered:* Senator Whitehouse also tells this story in his new book. Sheldon Whitehouse with Melanie Wachtell Stinnett, *Captured: The Corporate Infiltration of American Democracy* (New York: New Press, 2017), pp. 75–76.

199   *97 percent of climate scientists agree that climate change is here:* NASA, "Scientific Consensus: Earth's Climate Is Warming," January 18, 2017, http://climate.nasa.gov /scientific-consensus/.

199   *global warming endangers the health of our children:* "American Academy of Pediatrics Links Global Warming to the Health of Children," October 26, 2015, https://www .aap.org/en-us/about-the-aap/aap-press-room/pages/Global-Warming-Childrens -Health.aspx.

199   *"millions of people face greater risk to their health":* "A Health Professionals' Declaration on Climate Change," American Lung Association, September 21, 2016, http:// www.lung.org/get-involved/become-an-advocate/advocacy-alerts/health -professionals-climate-change.html.

199   *humans are affecting the change in climate:* Lee Rainie and Cary Funk, "An Elaboration of AAAS Scientists' Views," Pew Research Center, July 23, 2015, http://www .pewinternet.org/2015/07/23/an-elaboration-of-aaas-scientists-views/.

200   *option the billionaire Koch brothers took:* University of Massachusetts Amherst, Political Economy Research Institute, "Top 100 Polluter Indexes," https://www.peri .umass.edu/top-100-polluter-indexes.

200   *They funded phony op-eds:* Denise Robbins, Kevin Kalhoefer, and Andrew Seifter, "Study: Newspaper Opinion Pages Feature Science Denial and Other Climate Change Misinformation," Media Matters for America, September 1, 2016, http:// mediamatters.org/research/2016/09/01/study-newspaper-opinion-pages-feature- science-denial-and-other-climate-change-misinformation/212700.

200   *fake experts:* Mayer, *Dark Money*, pp. 208–10.

200   *$88 million that anyone could count:* "Koch Industries: Secretly Funding the Climate Denial Machine," Greenpeace, http://www.greenpeace.org/usa/global -warming/climate-deniers/koch-industries/; Kate Sheppard, "Inside Koch's Climate Denial Machine," *Mother Jones*, April 1, 2010, http://www.motherjones.com /blue-marble/2010/04/inside-kochs-climate-denial-machine.

200   *One study turned up $558 million in secret donations:* Robert J. Brulle, "Institutionalizing Delay: Foundation Funding and the Creation of U.S. Climate Change Counter- Movement Organizations," *Climatic Change* 122, no. 4 (February 2014), http://drexel .edu/~/media/Files/now/pdfs/Institutionalizing%20Delay%20-%20Climatic%20 Change.ashx?la=en.

200   *99.9 percent of the signers:* John Cook, "The 5 Telltale Techniques of Climate Change Denial," CNN Opinion, July 22, 2015, http://www.cnn.com/2015/07/22/opinions /cook-techniques-climate-change-denial/.

200   *only 33 percent of Americans:* Pew Research Center, "Public and Scientists' Views on Science and Society," January 29, 2015, p. 47, http://www.pewinternet.org/files/2015 /01/PI_ScienceandSociety_Report_012915.pdf.

201   *remember the accident that spewed more than 200 million gallons:* "Why BP Is Paying $18.7 Billion," *New York Times*, July 2, 2015, https://www.nytimes.com/interactive /2015/07/02/us/bp-oil-spill-settlement-background.html.

202   *Calling climate change a "hoax":* Louis Jacobson, "Yes, Donald Trump did call climate change a Chinese hoax," *PolitiFact*, June 3, 2016, http://www.politifact.com /truth-o-meter/statements/2016/jun/03/hillary-clinton/yes-donald-trump-did-call -climate-change-chinese-h/.

203   *Figure 8:* Doug Kendall, "Not So Risky Business: The Chamber of Commerce's Quiet Success Before the Roberts Court—An Early Report for 2012–2013," Constitutional Accountability Center, May 1, 2013, http://theusconstitution.org/text-history /1966/not-so-risky-business-chamber-commerces-quiet-success-roberts-court -early-report.

204   *They discovered that the five conservative justices:* Lee Epstein, William M. Landes, and Richard A. Posner, "How Business Fares in the Supreme Court," *Minnesota Law Review*

97 (2013): 1450–51, http://www.minnesotalawreview.org/wp-content/uploads/2013/04/EpsteinLanderPosner_MLR.pdf.

204 *unlimited campaign spending by corporations:* Citizens United v. FEC, 558 U.S. 310 (2010).

204 *prevented workers from suing their employers:* Ledbetter v. Goodyear Tire & Rubber Co., 550 U.S. 618 (2007).

204 *easier for sophisticated, deep-pocketed corporations:* Bell Atlantic Corp. v. Twombly, 550 U.S. 544 (2007); Ashcroft v. Iqbal, 556 U.S. 662 (2009).

204 *that helped out big corporations:* Adam Liptak, "Corporations Find a Friend in the Supreme Court," New York Times, May 4, 2013, http://www.nytimes.com/2013/05/05/business/pro-business-decisions-are-defining-this-supreme-court.html.

204 *Several outfits specialize:* Senator Sheldon Whitehouse tangled with these groups back when he was an attorney general in Rhode Island. "Corporate America has these kinds of front groups on duty every day, actively looking for litigation that will advance their causes." Whitehouse, *Captured*, pp. 68–69.

204 *invitations judges to attend fancy retreats:* Chris Young, Reity O'Brien, and Andrea Fuller, "Corporations, Pro-Business Nonprofits Foot Bill for Judicial Seminars," Center for Public Integrity, March 28, 2013, https://www.publicintegrity.org/2013/03/28/12368/corporations-pro-business-nonprofits-foot-bill-judicial-seminars.

205 *a political retreat in Palm Springs:* Eric Lipton, "Scalia Took Dozens of Trips Funded by Private Sponsors," New York Times, February 26, 2016, http://www.nytimes.com/2016/02/27/us/politics/scalia-led-court-in-taking-trips-funded-by-private-sponsors.html.

205 *Through the years Scalia took:* Ibid.

205 *In 2014 alone, Scalia took:* Ibid.

205 *"You get one shot":* Joan Biskupic, *American Original: The Life and Constitution of Supreme Court Justice Antonin Scalia* (New York: Sarah Crichton Books/Farrar, Straus and Giroux, 2009), p. 346.

205 *The night he died:* Amy Brittain and Sari Horwitz, "Justice Scalia Spent His Last Hours with Members of This Secretive Society of Elite Hunters," Washington Post, February 24, 2016, https://www.washingtonpost.com/world/national-security/justice-scalia-spent-his-last-hours-with-members-of-this-secretive-society-of-elite-hunters/2016/02/24/1d77af38-db20-11e5-891a-4ed04f4213e8_story.html.

205 *Earlier in the day:* Molly Hennessy-Fiske, "Scalia's Last Moments on a Texas Ranch—Quail Hunting to Being Found in 'Perfect Repose,'" Los Angeles Times, February 14, 2016, http://www.latimes.com/local/lanow/la-na-scalia-ranch-20160214-story.html.

206 *an organization claiming to represent small businesses:* Chris Frates, "Koch Bros.–Backed Group Gave Millions to Small Business Lobby," CNN, November 21, 2013, http://www.cnn.com/2013/11/21/politics/small-business-big-donor/index.html.

206 *aggressively attacking President Obama's nominee:* Carl Hulse, "Small-Business Lobbying Group Steps into Supreme Court Fight," New York Times, FirstDraft, March 25, 2016, http://www.nytimes.com/politics/first-draft/2016/03/25/small-business-lobbying-group-steps-into-supreme-court-fight/.

206 *Another outfit backed by the Koch brothers:* Anna Palmer, "GOP Group Launches Supreme Court Ads vs. Dems," Politico, February 29, 2016, http://www.politico.com/story/2016/02/supreme-court-republicans-ads-219993.

206 *promising to appoint a justice "like Justice Scalia":* Donald J. Trump, "Donald J. Trump Finalizes List of Potential Supreme Court Justice Picks," September 23, 2016, https://www.donaldjtrump.com/press-releases/donald-j.-trump-adds-to-list-of-potential-supreme-court-justice-picks.

207 *The examples he went on to cite:* Michael R. Bloomberg, "Go Out and Defeat the Demagogues," Boston Globe, May 3, 2016, https://www.bostonglobe.com/opinion/2016/05/03/out-and-defeat-demagogues/S8J2UQ1dllbdSBjRGpxl8I/story.html.

209   *a $25,000 contribution:* Richard Luscombe, "Trump's Donation to Florida's Attorney General: The Controversy Explained," *Guardian*, September 7, 2016, https://www .theguardian.com/us-news/2016/sep/07/donald-trump-donation-pam-bondi-florida -attorney-general.

210   *chronically unsafe mines:* Alexander C. Kaufman, "Donald Trump Taps Billionaire Who Owned Deadly Coal Mine for Commerce Secretary," *Huffington Post*, November 17, 2016, http://www.huffingtonpost.com/entry/trump-wilbur-ross_us_582b4c04e4b 01d8a014abacb.

210   *squeezing minimum wage workers:* Christine L. Owens, "NELP Raises Serious Concerns over Fast-Food CEO's Nomination for Labor Secretary," National Employment Law Project, December 8, 2016, http://www.nelp.org/news-releases/nelp-raises-serious -concerns-over-fast-food-ceos-likely-nomination-for-labor-secretary/; Jodi Kantor and Jennifer Medina, "Workers Say Andrew Puzder Is 'Not the One to Protect' Them, but He's Been Chosen To," *New York Times*, January 15, 2017, https://www.nytimes.com /2017/01/15/us/politics/andrew-puzder-labor-secretary.html.

210   *"We expect a return on our investment":* Jane Mayer, "Betsy DeVos, Trump's Big-Donor Education Secretary," *New Yorker*, November 23, 2016, http://www.newyorker.com /news/news-desk/betsy-devos-trumps-big-donor-education-secretary; Kate Zernike, "Betsy DeVos, Trump's Education Pick, Has Steered Money from Public Schools," *New York Times*, November 23, 2016, https://www.nytimes.com/2016/11/23/us /politics/betsy-devos-trumps-education-pick-has-steered-money-from-public -schools.html.

210   *cozying up to Vladimir Putin:* Zeeshan Aleem, "Donald Trump's Pick for Secretary of State Is a Putin-Friendly Exxon CEO," Vox, December 13, 2016, http://www.vox .com/2016/12/10/13908108/rex-tillerson-secretary-state-vladimir-putin-exxon -donald-trump.

210   *"the president can't have a conflict of interest":* "Donald Trump's New York Times Interview: Full Transcript," *New York Times*, November 23, 2016, http://www.nytimes.com /2016/11/23/us/politics/trump-new-york-times-interview-transcript.html.

210   *after he was elected he refused:* Andy Sullivan, Emily Stephenson, and Steve Holland, "Trump Says Won't Divest from His Business While President," Reuters, January 11, 2017, http://www.reuters.com/article/us-usa-trump-finance-idUSKBN14V21I.

5: THE MOMENT OF UPHEAVAL

213   *With only fifteen days to go:* The polling average on October 24, 2016, showed Clinton with a 6.5-point lead. "2016 General Election: Trump vs. Clinton," *Huffington Post*, November 8, 2016, http://elections.huffingtonpost.com/pollster/2016-general-election -trump-vs-clinton.

214   *Obama flirted with:* Matt Bai, "Obama vs. Boehner: Who Killed the Debt Deal?" *New York Times Magazine*, March 28, 2012, http://www.nytimes.com/2012/04/01/magazine /obama-vs-boehner-who-killed-the-debt-deal.html.

214   *weaken the Environmental Protection Agency:* Sara Jerde, "Trump Says He Will Cut the EPA as Prez: 'We'll Be Fine with The Environment,'" *Talking Points Memo*, October 18, 2015, http://talkingpointsmemo.com/livewire/donald-trump-epa-dept-of-education.

214   *roll back key bank regulations:* Michael Corkery, "Trump Expected to Seek Deep Cuts in Business Regulations," *New York Times*, November 9, 2016, http://www.nytimes .com/2016/11/10/business/dealbook/trump-expected-to-seek-deep-cuts-in -business-regulations.html.

214   *cut back on workplace safety inspections:* Tom Musick, "OSHA Under Trump: A Closer Look," *Safety+Health*, January 20, 2017, http://www.safetyandhealthmagazine .com/articles/15180-osha-under-trump-a-closer-look.

214   *repeal the Affordable Care Act:* Donald J. Trump, "Healthcare Reform to Make America Great Again," https://www.donaldjtrump.com/positions/healthcare-reform.

214   *even more big tax cuts:* Donald J. Trump, "Tax Plan," https://www.donaldjtrump.com/policies/tax-plan.

215   *But there were no details:* Jesse Hamilton and Elizabeth Dexheimer, "Victorious Donald Trump Is Devil Wall Street Doesn't Know," *Bloomberg*, November 9, 2016, https://www.bloomberg.com/news/articles/2016-11-09/victorious-donald-trump-is-the-devil-wall-street-doesn-t-know.

218   *For me, 2016 started back in early 2013:* The very day I was sworn in to the Senate, one polling firm included my name in their calls asking about potential 2016 presidential candidates. Public Policy Polling, "Clinton Could Be Hard to Beat if She Runs in 2016," National Survey Results, January 10, 2013, http://www.publicpolicypolling.com/pdf/2011/PPP_Release_National_011013.pdf.

218   *anyone who wanted to put themselves forward for president:* Three years later, with Hillary Clinton on the verge of picking her running mate, Rachel Maddow asked me if I thought I was capable of serving in that role and being number two in line for the presidency. I'd learned a lot over those three years, and I said yes. Ian Schwartz, "Rachel Maddow to Elizabeth Warren: Are You Ready to Be Commander in Chief?; Warren: 'Yes,'" *Real Clear Politics*, June 10, 2016, http://www.realclearpolitics.com/video/2016/06/10/rachel_maddow_to_elizabeth_warren_are_you_ready_to_be_commander_in_chief_warren_yes.html.

224   *our Native American ancestry:* This was similar to a line of attack used against me in the 2012 senate race. As I wrote in 2014, "My brothers and I knew who we were. We knew our family stories." Ultimately, the Republican attacks did not succeed. Elizabeth Warren, *A Fighting Chance* (New York: Metropolitan, 2014), pp. 239–42.

226   *I planned to keep right on firing:* My partner in these wars was Lauren Miller, who is as fearless as any human being I know when it comes to taking on bullies.

227   *he had been "out-n****red":* Jeff Stein, "Trump and the Racist Ghost of George Wallace," *Newsweek*, March 1, 2016, http://www.newsweek.com/donald-trump-george-wallace-racist-ghost-432164.

227   *"Segregation now, segregation tomorrow, segregation forever!":* Alabama Department of Archives & History, "The Inaugural Address of Governor George Wallace," January 14, 1963, p. 2, http://digital.archives.alabama.gov/cdm/singleitem/collection/voices/id/2952/rec/5.

228   *The report was quite specific:* Republican National Committee, "Growth and Opportunity Project," 2013, pp. 8, 22, http://goproject.gop.com/rnc_growth_opportunity_book_2013.pdf.

228   *when the Republican report was released:* Shushannah Walshe, "RNC Completes 'Autopsy' on 2012 Loss, Calls for Inclusion Not Policy Change," ABC News, March 18, 2013, http://abcnews.go.com/Politics/OTUS/rnc-completes-autopsy-2012-loss-calls-inclusion-policy/story?id=18755809.

228   *"Does @RNC have a death wish?":* Kyle Cheney, "Trump Kills GOP Autopsy," *Politico*, March 4, 2016, http://www.politico.com/story/2016/03/donald-trump-gop-party-reform-220222.

228   *openly stirring bigotry of all kinds:* Lydia O'Connor and Daniel Marans, "Here Are 13 Examples of Donald Trump Being Racist," *Huffington Post*, February 29, 2016, http://www.huffingtonpost.com/entry/donald-trump-racist-examples_us_56d47177e4b03260bf777e83; Steve Benen, "Trump Mistakes a Black Supporter as a 'Thug,'" MSNBC, *The Rachel Maddow Show, The Maddow Blog*, October 31, 2016, http://www.msnbc.com/rachel-maddow-show/trump-mistakes-black-supporter-thug.

228   *the Native Americans he had insulted and attacked:* Shawn Boburg, "Donald Trump's Long History of Clashes with Native Americans," *Washington Post*, July 25, 2016, https://www.washingtonpost.com/national/donald-trumps-long-history-of-clashes

-with-native-americans/2016/07/25/80ea91ca-3d77-11e6-80bc-d06711fd2125_story
.html.

229   *former Grand Wizard of the Ku Klux Klan, endorsed Trump:* Eric Bradner, "Donald Trump Stumbles on David Duke, KKK," CNN, February 29, 2016, http://www.cnn .com/2016/02/28/politics/donald-trump-white-supremacists/.

229   *the front page of the Klan's main newspaper:* Peter Holley, "KKK's Official Newspaper Supports Donald Trump for President," *Washington Post*, November 2, 2016, https:// www.washingtonpost.com/news/post-politics/wp/2016/11/01/the-kkks-official -newspaper-has-endorsed-donald-trump-for-president/.

229   *Michael Steele, said:* Ben Smith and Sheera Frenkel, "Former Republican Party Chairman Says He Won't Vote for Trump," BuzzFeed, October 24, 2016, https:// www.buzzfeed.com/bensmith/former-republican-party-chairman-says-he-wont -vote-for-trump.

229   *John McCain said:* Office of U.S. Senator John McCain, "Statement by Senator John McCain Withdrawing Support of Donald Trump," press release, October 8, 2016, http://www.mccain.senate.gov/public/index.cfm/press-releases?ID=774F9EE9-B0F1 -4CC6-8659-945EB6E09A5F.

229   *Karl Rove called Trump:* Karl Rove, "Unity Won't Come Easy for Either Party," *Wall Street Journal*, April 27, 2016, http://www.wsj.com/articles/unity-wont-come-easy -for-either-party-1461799058; Maggie Haberman, "At Odds Publicly, Donald Trump and Karl Rove Hold a Private Meeting," *New York Times*, June 2, 2016, https://www .nytimes.com/2016/06/03/us/politics/karl-rove-donald-trump.html.

229   *Mitt Romney called Trump:* "Full Transcript: Mitt Romney's Remarks on Donald Trump and the 2016 Race," *Politico*, March 3, 2016, http://www.politico.com/story /2016/03/full-transcript-mitt-romneys-remarks-on-donald-trump-and-the-2016 -race-220176.

230   *$185 million in fines:* Jesse Hamilton, "Wells Fargo Is Fined $185 Million over Unap-proved Accounts," *Bloomberg*, September 8, 2016, https://www.bloomberg.com /news/articles/2016-09-08/wells-fargo-fined-185-million-over-unwanted-customer -accounts.

231   *big claims for illegal foreclosures:* U.S. Department of Justice, "Wells Fargo Bank Agrees to Pay $1.2 Billion for Improper Mortgage Lending Practices," press release, April 8, 2016, https://www.justice.gov/opa/pr/wells-fargo-bank-agrees-pay-12-billion -improper-mortgage-lending-practices.

231   *Wells Fargo fired:* Matt Egan, "5,300 Wells Fargo Employees Fired over 2 Million Phony Accounts," *CNN Money*, September 9, 2016, http://money.cnn.com/2016/09 /08/investing/wells-fargo-created-phony-accounts-bank-fees/; Reuters, "Wells Fargo Employees Who Lost Their Jobs Are Suing the Bank," *Fortune*, September 26, 2016, http://fortune.com/2016/09/26/wells-fargo-sales-lawsuit/.

232   *it was worth $250 billion:* Matt Egan, "Who Owns Wells Fargo Anyway? You, Me and Warren Buffett," *CNN Money*, September 8, 2016, http://money.cnn.com/2016/09/08 /investing/wells-fargo-fake-accounts-warren-buffett/.

232   *had known for months:* Deon Roberts, "Emails Show Wells Fargo Kept Sales Probe to Itself for at Least 6 Months," *Charlotte Observer*, January 11, 2017, http://www .charlotteobserver.com/news/business/banking/bank-watch-blog/article125973184 .html.

232   *Wells Fargo stock took a drop:* Share prices had dropped about 9 percent from $49.77 on September 7 (the day before the announcement) to $45.31 on September 28, the day before the hearing.

233   *playing with his grandchildren:* Rick Rothacker, "What Happened to Wells Fargo CEO's Hand?," *Charlotte Observer*, September 20, 2016, http://www.charlotteobserver .com/news/business/banking/article102899917.html.

233   *"I am accountable":* Abigail Stevenson, "Wells Fargo CEO John Stumpf on Alleged Abuses: 'I Am Accountable,'" *CNBC Mad Money*, September 13, 2016, http://www

.cnbc.com/2016/09/13/wells-fargo-ceo-john-stumpf-on-alleged-abuses-i-am
-accountable.html.

234   *The headlines all declared more or less the same thing:* C. E. Dyer, "SHOCK: Elizabeth
Warren Just Said Something We Can All Agree On," Federalist Papers Project, September 21, 2016, http://thefederalistpapers.org/us/shock-elizabeth-warren-just-said
-something-we-can-all-agree-on.

235   *John Stumpf testifying before Congress:* Brett Molina and Matt Krantz, "Wells Fargo
CEO Grilled by House Panel," *USA Today,* September 29, 2016, http://www.usatoday
.com/story/money/business/2016/09/29/live-wells-fargo-ceo-hearing/91260900/.

235   *to launch investigations:* Nomi Prins, "Ex-Wells Fargo CEO John Stumpf Deserves
Jail—Not a Plush Retirement," *Guardian,* October 14, 2016, https://www.theguardian
.com/commentisfree/2016/oct/14/john-stumpf-retirement-wells-fargo-ceo-jail-time;
James B. Stewart, "Wells Fargo Tests Justice Department's Get-Tough Approach," *New
York Times,* September 22, 2016, https://www.nytimes.com/2016/09/23/business/wells
-fargo-tests-justice-departments-get-tough-approach.html; Paul Blake, "Senators Call
on Justice Department to Investigate Wells Fargo's Top Brass," ABC News, October 5,
2016, http://abcnews.go.com/Business/senators-call-justice-department-investigate
-wells-fargos-top/story?id=42570235.

235   *mattered at least a little for his bank:* Rick Rothacker and Deon Roberts, "Running
Tally: Who's Investigating Wells Fargo?" *Charlotte Observer,* October 20, 2016,
http://www.charlotteobserver.com/news/business/banking/article109441837.html.

236   *the Republicans were also drawing up plans:* Jonathan Tamari, "Toomey, McGinty
Spar over Who Looks Out for Business and Who Favors Consumers," *Philadelphia Inquirer,* September 12, 2016, http://www.philly.com/philly/blogs/capitolinq
/Toomey-McGinty-spar-over-who-looks-out-for-business-and-who-favors
-consumers.html; U.S. Senate Committee on Banking, Housing, & Urban Affairs,
"Shelby Statement on the CFPB's Unconstitutional Structure," statement by Senator Richard Shelby, press release, October 11, 2016, http://www.banking.senate.gov
/public/index.cfm/republican-press-releases?ID=FF23615E-CFF0-4AA6-9F9F
-A743A7815F38.

236   *The consumer agency had led the way:* A 2013 article in the *Los Angeles Times,* which
prompted an investigation by the office of Los Angeles city attorney Mike Feuer,
sparked the investigation by federal regulators. E. Scott Reckard, "Wells Fargo's
Pressure-Cooker Sales Culture Comes at a Cost," *Los Angeles Times,* December 21,
2013, http://www.latimes.com/business/la-fi-wells-fargo-sale-pressure-20131222
-story.html; James Rufus Koren, "Wells Fargo to Pay $185 Million Settlement for
'Outrageous' Sales Culture," *Los Angeles Times,* September 8, 2016, http://www
.latimes.com/business/la-fi-wells-fargo-settlement-20160907-snap-story.html.

236   *calling for the CFPB to be gutted:* Victoria Finkle, "Jeb Hensarling Plan Rekindles
Debate as Republicans Aim to Dismantle Dodd-Frank," *New York Times,* June 7,
2016, https://www.nytimes.com/2016/06/08/business/dealbook/republicans-plan-to
-dismantle-dodd-frank-rekindles-a-debate.html.

236   *he criticized the CFPB:* Jim Puzzanghera, "Republicans Say There's Another Villain
in the Wells Fargo Scandal," *Los Angeles Times,* September 28, 2016, http://www
.latimes.com/business/la-fi-wells-fargo-regulators-20160927-snap-story.html;
Yuka Hayashi, "5 Things to Watch at Wells Fargo's House Hearing," *Wall Street
Journal,* September 28, 2016, http://blogs.wsj.com/briefly/2016/09/28/5-things-to
-watch-at-wells-fargos-house-hearing/.

237   *the Republicans slipped in an amendment:* James Arkin, "Hopes Fade for Criminal Justice Reform This Year," *Real Clear Politics,* June 30, 2016, http://www.realclearpolitics
.com/articles/2016/06/30/hopes_fade_for_criminal_justice_reform_this_year
_131064.html; Greg Dotson and Alison Cassady, "Three Ways Congressional Mens
Rea Proposals Could Allow White Collar Criminals to Escape Prosecution," Center
for American Progress, March 11, 2016, https://www.americanprogress.org/issues

/criminal-justice/reports/2016/03/11/133113/three-ways-congressional-mens-rea
-proposals-could-allow-white-collar-criminals-to-escape-prosecution/.

242   *Republicans had been fighting unions:* Jordain Carney, "GOP Blocks Minimum Wage, Sick Leave Proposals," *Hill*, August 5, 2015, http://thehill.com/blogs/floor-action /senate/250382-gop-blocks-minimum-wage-sick-leave-proposals; Jonathan Cohn and Jeffrey Young, "Not Just Obamacare: Medicaid, Medicare Also on GOP's Chopping Block," November 15, 2016, http://www.huffingtonpost.com/entry/obamacare -medicaid-medicare-gop-chopping-block_us_582a19b8e4b060adb56fbae7; Alec MacGillis, "Nuclear War," *New Republic*, July 15, 2013, https://newrepublic.com /article/113850/senate-republicans-filibuster-nlrb-nominees; Tim Devaney, "Republicans Attack Persuader Rule," *Hill*, April 27, 2016, http://thehill.com/regulation/labor /277860-republicans-attack-persuader-rule.

244   *appointing Jeff Sessions to be the attorney general:* Suzanne Gamboa, "Latinos Blast Trump's AG Pick Jeff Sessions over Race, Immigration," NBC News, November 18, 2016, http://www.nbcnews.com/news/latino/latinos-blast-trump-s-ag-pick-jeff -sessions-over-race-n685951; Brian Tashman, "Two Peas in a Racist Pod: Jeff Sessions' Alarming History of Opposing Civil Rights," *Salon*, November 19, 2016, http://www.salon.com/2016/11/19/two-peas-in-a-racist-pod-jeff-sessions-alarming -history-of-opposing-civil-rights_partner/; Scott Zamost, "Sessions Dogged by Old Allegations of Racism," CNN, November 18, 2016, http://www.cnn.com/2016/11/17 /politics/jeff-sessions-racism-allegations/.

244   *people responded:* Southern Poverty Law Center, "Update: Incidents of Hateful Harassment Since Election Day Now Number 701," November 18, 2016, https://www .splcenter.org/hatewatch/2016/11/18/update-incidents-hateful-harassment-election -day-now-number-701.

244   *chummy ties to Russian leader Vladimir Putin:* Zeeshan Aleem, "Donald Trump's Pick for Secretary of State Is a Putin-Friendly Exxon CEO," *Vox*, December 13, 2016, http://www.vox.com/2016/12/10/13908108/rex-tillerson-secretary-state-vladimir-putin -exxon-donald-trump.

244   *climate deniers and groups that fought environmental regulations:* Alexander C. Kaufman, "Exxon Continued Paying Millions to Climate-Change Deniers Under Rex Tillerson," *Huffington Post*, January 9, 2017, http://www.huffingtonpost.com/entry /tillerson-exxon-climate-donations_us_5873a3f4e4b043ad97e48f52.

245   *When he got involved in environmental lawsuits:* Chris Mooney, Brady Dennis, and Steven Mufson, "Trump Names Scott Pruitt, Oklahoma Attorney General Suing EPA on Climate Change, to Head the EPA," *Washington Post*, December 8, 2016, https://www.washingtonpost.com/news/energy-environment/wp/2016/12/07/trump -names-scott-pruitt-oklahoma-attorney-general-suing-epa-on-climate-change-to -head-the-epa.

245   *Pruitt jumped into the lawsuit:* Eric Lipton and Coral Davenport, "Scott Pruitt, Trump's E.P.A. Pick, Backed Industry Donors over Regulators," *New York Times*, January 14, 2017, https://www.nytimes.com/2017/01/14/us/scott-pruitt-trump-epa-pick.html.

245   *She and her family donated a small chunk:* Allie Gross, "Lawmakers deciding the future of Detroit schools accepted thousands from pro-charter DeVos family," *Detroit Metro Times*, May 17, 2016, http://www.metrotimes.com/news-hits/archives /2016/05/17/lawmakers-deciding-the-future-of-detroit-schools-accepted-thousands -from-pro-charter-devos-family.

245   *ever attended a public school:* Alyson Klein, "DeVos Would Be First Ed. Sec. Who Hasn't Been a Public School Parent or Student," *Education Week*, December 6, 2016, http://blogs.edweek.org/edweek/campaign-k-12/2016/12/betsy_devos_would_be _first_ed_.html.

245   *actively buying and selling stocks:* Manu Raju, "Trump's Cabinet Pick Invested in Company, Then Introduced a Bill to Help It," *CNN Politics*, January 16, 2017, http:// www.cnn.com/2017/01/16/politics/tom-price-bill-aiding-company.

246   *getting paid for only forty hours:* Lisa Baertlein and Sarah N. Lynch, "Fast-Food Workers Protest Trump's Labor Secretary Nominee," Reuters, January 12, 2017, http://www.reuters.com/article/usa-congress-puzder-idUSL1N1F11W7.

246   *hire a lawyer to work it out:* Tal Kopan, "Democrats to Attack Labor Nominee's Employee Treatment," *CNN Politics,* January 10, 2017, http://www.cnn.com/2017/01 /10/politics/andrew-puzder-restaurants-employee-mistreatment-report/; Restaurant Opportunities Centers United, "Secretary of Labor Violations?," January 10, 2016, pp. 17–18, http://rocunited.org/wp-content/uploads/2017/01/PuzdersLabor ProblemFinal-2.pdf.

248   *seventy-three million voted for someone else:* David Wasserman, "2016 Popular Vote Tracker," Cook Political Report, January 3, 2017, http://cookpolitical.com/story/10174

248   *said he wasn't honest or trustworthy:* Gary Langer, Gregory Holyk, Chad Kiewiet de Jonge, Julie Phelan, Geoff Feinberg, and Sofi Sinozich, "Huge Margin Among Working-Class Whites Lifts Trump to a Stunning Election Upset," ABC News, November 9, 2016, http://abcnews.go.com/Politics/huge-margin-working-class -whites-lifts-trump-stunning/story?id=43411948.

249   *"injustice anywhere is a threat to justice everywhere":* Martin Luther King, Jr., "Letter from a Birmingham Jail", 2, http://okra.stanford.edu/transcription/document_images /undecided/630416-019.pdf.

249   *rallied for health care:* Jeremy C. Fox, "Thousands Protest Health Care Repeal at Faneuil Hall," *Boston Globe,* January 15, 2017, https://www.bostonglobe.com/metro/2017/01/15 /thousands-protest-health-care-repeal-faneuil-hall/CMBwr3f8vGpp7gTsyi7lCM/story .html; Corey Williams, "Thousands Rally to Resist Republican Health Law Repeal Drive," Associated Press, January 15, 2017, http://bigstory.ap.org/article/4912cac35 997415f9ce737dbba332aac/thousands-show-sanders-health-care-rally-michigan.

249   *forums on immigration:* "Community Forum on Trump-Era Immigration," *Martha's Vineyard Times,* December 28, 2016, http://www.mvtimes.com/2016/12/28/community -forum-trump-era-immigration/; Steven H. Foskett Jr., "Worcester Forum Seeks to Ease Post-Election Anxiety," *Worcester Telegram & Gazette,* December 1, 2016, http:// www.telegram.com/news/20161130/worcester-forum-seeks-to-ease-post-election -anxiety.

249   *fair wages:* Shira Schoenberg, "Workers rally in Boston for $15 minimum wage," MassLive.com, November 29, 2016, http://www.masslive.com/politics/index.ssf /2016/11/workers_rally_in_boston_for_15.html.

250   Bigotry is bad for business: "Video of Sen. Elizabeth Warren: Bigotry Is Bad for Business," *Wall Street Journal,* November 15, 2016, http://www.wsj.com/video/sen -elizabeth-warren-bigotry-is-bad-for-business/81EA7639-8221-4488-8E52 -BE16179BAFFA.html.

252   *almost 100 percent of the new income produced:* Thomas Piketty and Emmanuel Saez, "Income Inequality in the United States, 1931–2002," later updated with Anthony B. Atkinson (November 2004) (online at http://eml.berkeley.edu/~saez /pikettysaezOUP04US.pdf, updated tables at http://eml.berkeley.edu/~saez/Tab Fig2015prel.xls).

253   *make FHA mortgages more expensive:* Andrew Khouri, "HUD Suspends FHA Mortgage Insurance Rate Cut an Hour After Trump Takes Office," *Los Angeles Times,* January 20, 2017, http://www.latimes.com/business/la-fi-trump-fha-cut-20170120 -story.html.

253   *drug-approval bill:* Office of U.S. Senator Elizabeth Warren, "Senator Warren Delivers Remarks on the Proposed 21st Century Cures Bill," press release, November 28, 2016, https://www.warren.senate.gov/?p=press_release&id=1307.

253   *Not to be outdone, Ryan immediately put together:* Michael Hiltzik, "Paul Ryan Is Determined to Kill Medicare. This Time He Might Succeed," *Los Angeles Times,* November 23, 2016, http://www.latimes.com/business/hiltzik/la-fi-hiltzik-medicare -ryan-20161114-story.html; Kelsey Snell, "Tax Reform Shaping Up To Be One of

Washington's First Fights Under Trump," *Washington Post*, November 17, 2016, https://www.washingtonpost.com/news/powerpost/wp/2016/11/17/tax-reform -shaping-up-to-be-one-of-washingtons-first-fights-under-trump/; Jim Nunns, Len Burman, Ben Page, Jeff Rohaly, and Joe Rosenberg, "An Analysis of the House GOP Tax Plan," Tax Policy Center, September 16, 2016, pp. 2, 8, Table 5, p. 13, http://www .taxpolicycenter.org/sites/default/files/alfresco/publication-pdfs/2000923-An -Analysis-of-the-House-GOP-Tax-Plan.pdf.

253   *cuts that would leave an average of a cool $1.1 million*: Jim Nunns, Len Burman, Ben Page, Jeff Rohaly, and Joe Rosenberg, "An Analysis of Donald Trump's Revised Tax Plan," Tax Policy Center, October 18, 2016, http://www.taxpolicycenter.org/sites/default /files/alfresco/publication-pdfs/2000924-an-analysis-of-donald-trumps-revised -tax-plan.pdf; Dylan Matthews, "Analysts: Donald Trump Changed His Tax Plan and Made It Even More Tilted Toward the Rich," *Vox*, November 8, 2016, http://www .vox.com/policy-and-politics/2016/10/11/13241764/donald-trump-new-tax-plan-tpc -clinton.

254   *save many millions for Trump's family businesses*: Jean Eaglesham and Lisa Schwartz, "Trump's Tax Plan Could Preserve Millions in Savings for His Businesses," *Wall Street Journal*, January 29, 2017, https://www.wsj.com/articles/trumps-tax-plan-could -preserve-millions-in-savings-for-his-businesses-1485691210.

254   *would add more than $7 trillion*: Nunns, Burman, Page, et al., "An Analysis of Donald Trump's Revised Tax Plan"; Matthews, "Analysts: Donald Trump Changed His Tax Plan"; Federal Reserve Bank of St. Louis, "Federal Debt: Total Public Debt," updated December 14, 2016, https://fred.stlouisfed.org/series/GFDEBTN.

255   *a chance at a debt-free education*: "New National Poll Shows 80% of Americans Support Addressing College Affordability Crisis," Demos, October 7, 2016, http://www .demos.org/press-release/new-national-poll-shows-80-americans-support -addressing-college-affordability-crisis.

255   *support expanding Social Security*: Public Policy Polling, "National Survey Results," October 21, 2016, http://www.socialsecurityworks.org/wp-content/uploads/2016/10 /NationalResults.pdf.

255   *raising the federal minimum wage*: "Poll Results: Minimum Wage," YouGov, April 13, 2016, https://today.yougov.com/news/2016/04/13/poll-results-minimum -wage/.

255   *increase spending on infrastructure*: Frank Newport, "Americans Say 'Yes' to Spending More on VA, Infrastructure," Gallup, March 21, 2016, http://www.gallup.com/poll /190136/americans-say-yes-spending-infrastructure.aspx.

256   *don't pay their fair share in taxes*: Frank Newport, "Americans Still Say Upper-Income Pay Too Little in Taxes," Gallup, April 15, 2016, http://www.gallup.com /poll/190775/americans-say-upper-income-pay-little-taxes.aspx.

256   *eliminating tax deductions and loopholes*: Frank Newport, "Americans React to Presidential Candidates' Tax Proposals," Gallup, March 17, 2016, http://www.gallup .com /poll/190067/americans-react-presidential-candidates-tax-proposals.aspx.

256   *By a three-to-one margin*: Celinda Lake, Bob Carpenter, David Mermin, and Zoe Grotophorst, "Strong Bipartisan Support More Financial Reform," Lake Research Partners and Chesapeake Beach Consulting, memo to interested parties, July 12, 2016, http://ourfinancialsecurity.org/wp-content/uploads/2016/07/LRPpublicmemo.AFR _.CRL_.WSReform.f.071216.pdf.

256   *want to protect or strengthen the CFPB*: Nik DeCosta-Klipa, "Trump Voters Don't Want Trump to Get Rid of Elizabeth Warren's Consumer Agency," Boston.com, December 21, 2016, http://www.boston.com/news/politics/2016/12/21/trump-voters -dont-want-trump-to-get-rid-of-elizabeth-warrens-consumer-agency.

258   *It was the single biggest demonstration in the history of the United States*: Matt Broomfield, "Women's March Against Donald Trump Is the Largest Day of Protests

in U.S. History, Say Political Scientists," *Independent*, January 23, 2017, http://www.independent.co.uk/news/world/americas/womens-march-anti-donald-trump-womens-rights-largest-protest-demonstration-us-history-political-a7541081.html.

259   *more than a million people here count on Medicare*: Centers for Medicare and Medicaid Services, "On Its 50th Anniversary, More Than 55 Million Americans Covered by Medicare," press release, July 28, 2015, https://www.cms.gov/Newsroom/MediaReleaseDatabase/Press-releases/2015-Press-releases-items/2015-07-28.html.

259   *Two out of every three students graduating from a college*: This covers four-year institutions. Institute for College Access and Success, "Massachusetts—4-Year or Above," College InSight, 2013–14, http://college-insight.org/#spotlight/go&h=99a93483bf37f385a9369e23ecb51377.

259   *One in seven people in Massachusetts*: U.S. Census Bureau, "QuickFacts: Massachusetts," http://www.census.gov/quickfacts/table/PST045215/25.

259   *people in nursing homes depend on Medicaid*: Massachusetts Executive Office of Health and Human Services and Executive Office of Elder Affairs, "Long-Term Care in Massachusetts: Facts at a Glance," January 26, 2009, pp. 4–5, http://www.mass.gov/eohhs/docs/eohhs/ltc-factsheet.pdf.

259   *We have 16,000 children in Head Start*: Kids Count Data Center, "Head Start Enrollment by Age Group," updated March 2014, http://datacenter.kidscount.org/data/tables/5938-head-start-enrollment-by-age-group#detailed/2/23/false/36,868,867,133,38/1830,558,559,1831,122/12570.

259   *233,000 families bought health insurance*: Louise Norris, "Massachusetts Marketplace History and News: 23K Enrolled by November 17; ConnectorCare Subsidies Less Robust in 2017," HealthInsurance.org, November 20, 2016, https://www.healthinsurance.org/massachusetts-state-health-insurance-exchange/.

259   *More than 400,000 members of labor unions*: U.S. Department of Labor, Bureau of Labor Statistics, "Union Membership in Massachusetts and Connecticut—2012," Table A: Union Affiliation of Employed Wage and Salary Workers in Massachusetts and Connecticut, Annual Averages, 2003–2012, https://www.bls.gov/regions/new-england/news-release/unionmembership_massachusettsandconnecticut.htm.

259   *More than 32,000 people went to Planned Parenthood of Massachusetts*: Planned Parenthood League of Massachusetts, "Annual Report: FY16," p. 2, https://www.plannedparenthood.org/planned-parenthood-massachusetts/who-we-are/our-publications.

260   *he didn't mince words*: Sally Denton, *The Plots Against the President: FDR, a Nation in Crisis, and the Rise of the American Right* (New York: Bloomsbury Press, 2012), p. 158; Franklin D. Roosevelt, "Address at Madison Square Garden, New York City," October 31, 1936, http://www.presidency.ucsb.edu/ws/index.php?pid=15219&st=&st1.

EPILOGUE

268   *"Be the Church"*: Ian Holland, January 21, 2017, https://twitter.com/PastorIanH/status/822980024663994369.

268   *There was an ocean of signs*: Globe staff, "People Were Really Creative with Their Signs at Women's Marches," *Boston Globe*, January 21, 2017, https://www.bostonglobe.com/news/nation/2017/01/21/signs-from-women-march-protests/KgTxZ54KJZLoN7YOAmr4EL/story.html; Joan Wickersham, "You Said It All in Those Women's March Signs," *Boston Globe*, January 25, 2017, https://www.bostonglobe.com/opinion/2017/01/25/you-said-all-those-women-march-signs/8LkyVPCzwtfoa17s9fea9O/story.html.

AFTERWORD TO THE 2018 EDITION

273   *He delivered long speeches:* For example, see Senator Jeff Sessions's floor speeches on June 12, 2013, and August 5, 2014.

273   *"complete capitulation to lawlessness":* Senator Jeff Sessions, floor speech, August 5, 2014.

274   *"a disgrace to his race":* Michelle Ye Hee Lee, "Jeff Sessions's Comments on Race: For the Record," *Washington Post*, December 2, 2016, https://www.washingtonpost.com /news/fact-checker/wp/2016/12/02/jeff-sessionss-comments-on-race-for-the-record/.

276   *I had never heard of any senator:* I would gladly cite the last time a senator was called out on a Rule XIX violation, but the Senate archivists were unable to find any example.

278   *Ultimately, every Republican voted to shut me up:* Senator Cruz didn't show up that evening, so he never cast a vote on whether to censure me, and Senator Sessions stayed out of the debate, so he did not vote either.

279   *Every Republican voted for him:* Senator Sessions voted "present" on his own confirmation.

279   *more private prisons:* Jon Schuppe, "Private Prisons: Here's Why Sessions' Memo Matters," NBC News, February 26, 2017, https://www.nbcnews.com/news/us-news /private-prisons-here-s-why-sessions-memo-matters-n725316.

279   *instructed U.S. Attorneys to launch:* Evan Halper, "29 States Have Legal Pot. Jeff Sessions Wants to Stamp It Out, and He's Closer Than You Think," *Los Angeles Times*, October 9, 2017, http://www.latimes.com/politics/la-na-pol-congress-pot-20171007-story.html.

279   *President Trump's Muslim ban:* Madeline Conway, "Sessions Dismisses Hawaii Judge in Travel Ban Case as 'Sitting on an Island in the Pacific,'" *Politico*, April 20, 2017, http:// www.politico.com/story/2017/04/20/jeff-sessions-judge-hawaii-island-in-the-pacific -237412.

279   *took steps to roll back settlements:* Andrew Kaczynski, "Attorney General Jeff Sessions: Consent Decrees 'Can Reduce Morale of the Police Officers,'" CNN Politics, April 14, 2017, http://www.cnn.com/2017/04/14/politics/kfile-sessions-consent-decrees/index .html.

279   *gave a thumbs-up to states' attempts:* Mark Joseph Stern, "The Purges Are Coming," *Slate*, August 8, 2017, http://www.slate.com/articles/news_and_politics/jurisprudence /2017/08/jeff_sessions_doj_just_gave_states_the_green_light_to_purge_voter_rolls .html.

279   *Sessions himself delivered the news:* Tal Kopan, "Sessions as Face of DACA Decision Reveals Internal Struggle," CNN Politics, September 5, 2017, http://www.cnn.com /2017/09/05/politics/jeff-sessions-trump-daca-decision/index.html.

280   *"very fine people, on both sides":* White House, remarks by President Trump on infrastructure, August 15, 2017, https://www.whitehouse.gov/briefings-statements/remarks -president-trump-infrastructure/.

280   *prompting former KKK Grand Wizard David Duke:* Z. Byron Wolf, "Trump's Defense of the 'Very Fine People' at Charlottesville White Nationalist March has David Duke Gushing," CNN Politics, August 15, 2017, http://www.cnn.com/2017/08/15/politics /donald-trump-david-duke-charlottesville/index.html.

280   *Jeff Sessions staunchly defended:* Sari Horwitz, "Sessions Defends Trump's Response to Charlottesville Violence," *Washington Post*, August 14, 2017, https://www .washingtonpost.com/world/national-security/sessions-defends-trumps-response -to-charlottesville-violence/2017/08/14/56e148e0-80e4-11e7-b359-15a3617c767b _story.html.

280   *Sessions once again jumped:* Dan Gartland, "One Day After Touting Free Speech, Jeff Sessions Says NFL Should Restrict Players' Speech," *Sports Illustrated*, September 27, 2017, https://www.si.com/nfl/2017/09/27/jeff-sessions-nfl-national-anthem-protests.

282   *promising repeatedly that he would repeal Obamacare:* Josh Voorhees, "Trump Says He Never Promised to Quickly Repeal Obamacare. Here's a Bunch of Times He Prom-

ised Exactly That," *Slate*, March 24, 2017, http://www.slate.com/blogs/the_slatest/2017/03/24/trump_says_he_never_promised_to_repeal_obamacare_quickly_a_list_of_times.html.

283   *More than $1.4 trillion in giveaways:* Lynnley Browning and Benjamin Bain, "Trump, Real Estate Investors Get Late-Added Perk in Tax Bill," *Bloomberg*, December 17, 2017, https://www.bloomberg.com/news/articles/2017-12-18/trump-real-estate-investors-get-last-minute-perk-in-tax-bill; Peter Rudegeair and Emily Glazer, "Wells Fargo Profit Rises, Helped by Tax Law," *Wall Street Journal*, January 12, 2018, https://www.wsj.com/articles/wells-fargo-profit-rises-helped-by-tax-law-1515762757; Tara Golshan, "4 Winners and 4 Losers from the Republican Tax Bill," *Vox*, December 22, 2017, https://www.vox.com/2017/12/20/16790040/gop-tax-bill-winners.

283   *"Get it done or don't ever call me again":* Dylan Scott, "House Republican: My Donors Told Me to Pass the Tax Bill 'Or Don't Ever Call Me Again,'" *Vox*, November 7, 2017, https://www.vox.com/policy-and-politics/2017/11/7/16618038/house-republicans-tax-bill-donors-chris-collins.

284   *planned to give any tax bonus:* Toluse Olorunnipa, "Trump's Tax Promises Undercut by CEO Plans to Help Investors," *Bloomberg*, November 29, 2017, https://www.bloomberg.com/news/articles/2017-11-29/trump-s-tax-promises-undercut-by-ceo-plans-to-reward-investors.

ACKNOWLEDGMENTS

I've had a lot of plain old good luck in my life, but one of my most recent pieces of good fortune occurred the day Alexander Blenkinsopp said he would help me with this book. I had worked with Alex at the Consumer Financial Protection Bureau, and then on my Senate campaign, so I already knew he was smart, disciplined, and hard-working. But it was while working on *This Fight Is Our Fight* that I saw his deep passion to make America a better country. I discovered that he could maintain his cheerfulness and good humor even while he worked under nearly impossible demands and very tight deadlines. And as he tried to keep me on schedule, I also learned that he has the steeliness of a drill sergeant. I am in his debt for helping me tell the story of what has gone wrong with America's middle class and what we can do to rebuild it.

I also owe an enormous debt to my daughter and sometimes coauthor, Amelia Warren Tyagi. Despite her busy schedule running a growing company and trying to keep up with my three perfect grandchildren, she once again played a pivotal role in this book—helping to keep trains running, keeping me focused on the core issues, shaping the thinking that went into the manuscript, and adding her own unique advice, which often began with "Mom, you're getting boring again." If I somehow managed to stay on the narrow path of saying something important and keeping it interesting, Amelia deserves a lot of the credit.

I have been blessed by good friends who were also willing to read early drafts and point out parts that were unclear or should be expanded. They suggested adding new headings, improving paragraphs, and dropping whole stories. There are too many of you to name, and I don't want to forget anyone, but you know who you are—and I hope you know that I am deeply grateful. I also appreciate fact-checking help from Daniel Morrocco and Irina Şubulică, both of whom worked long hours under severe time pressure.

The graphs in the book presented their own challenges, since it was my hope that we could make the presentation of material both clear and interesting. Michelle LeClerc pulled that off with great skill and patiently took on countless versions and tweaks as we worked together to try to get it right. James O'Mara assisted Michelle and added his own careful details to the work.

I am deeply grateful to the people who were willing to share their stories with me, and I have done my best to be faithful in the retelling, with the understanding that, when asked, I obscured specific details that could reveal their identities. Mike Belleville is a very special guy, and his fierce determination to press Congress to support more research for Alzheimer's was an inspiration for me and, I hope, for others. My thanks go to both Mike and his wife, Cheryl, for their help. Michael J. Smith was also generous with his time and his heart, willing to go over details of very painful periods in his life because he thought it might help others. Thank you to Michael, his wife, Janet, and their daughter, Ashley.

I also owe an enormous debt to Gina and Kai. I can't say much more about them than we've already agreed to include in the book, but their courage in the face of a world that is tilted against them makes me proud to know them. They will be a part of my life forever.

My editor, John Sterling, was extraordinary in helping me with my previous book, *A Fighting Chance*. I am deeply grateful that he was willing to bring his considerable talents and thoughtful insights to this book as well. Without him, I doubt I would have undertaken this effort. Stephen

Rubin, president and publisher of Henry Holt, Sara Bershtel, publisher of Metropolitan Books, Maggie Richards, Holt's deputy publisher and director of sales and marketing, and Pat Eisemann, Holt's director of publicity, made up the best possible team to work with. Rick Pracher designed the superb jacket, and Kelly Too did an excellent job of designing the book's interior; both reminded me that some people are visually creative, and, although I'm not one of them, I appreciate the results. Kenn Russell, Holt's managing editor, somehow kept the book on track despite a very tight schedule, and Bonnie Thompson, the book's copy editor, did a first-rate job of ensuring that the text was crisp and clear. John's able assistant, Fiona Lowenstein, was always helpful. Everyone at Holt is a true professional, but they are also people passionately committed to books—and to the stories we can tell only through those books. I am grateful to them all.

Once again, Bob Barnett served as a thoughtful adviser, always ready with wise counsel or a deliciously funny barb.

The basic ideas in this book originated during my life as an academic, but much of the fight that I've been able to wage so far has been made possible by all the talented advisers I've been lucky enough to collect over the years and all the people who work long hours in my Boston, Springfield, and Washington offices. We share a vision of an America built on respect and opportunity for everyone, and they throw themselves into their work with incredible dedication and astonishing skill. Whether it is helping a veteran get the benefits he is owed, organizing a health care roundtable, or investigating what's going on at the SEC, they keep fighting for what is right. I love them—each and every one—and I am filled with gratitude for all that they make possible.

I am also deeply grateful to the people of Massachusetts. I'm grateful that you took a chance on someone who had never run for office and that you sent me into the ring in Washington to fight for you. Every single day, I try my hardest to be your voice in Washington, and every single day, you remind me how much is at stake for millions of amazing, hardworking, generous people. You provide me with the strength and motivation to stay in this fight, no matter what. Representing this great commonwealth has been the honor of a lifetime.

And finally, a heartfelt thank you to my family. I've already given a shout-out to Amelia, but all the others bring their own special touches. There is no one more fun—and more interesting—to discuss an issue with than my son, Alex Warren, and, as he will discover, many ideas that originally sprouted during one of our phone conversations eventually made it into to the pages of this book. Elise Warren and Sushil Tyagi are more than patient in-laws; they are beloved family members who help make us a stronger, happier clan. My grandchildren, Octavia, Lavinia, and Atticus, make life seem infinitely more precious and far more fun. My final thank you is for Bruce. He is last because when I think about trying to thank him, my heart fills up and I run out of words.

INDEX

Page numbers in *italics* refer to figures, tables, and illustrations.